RESTORATION DRAMA AND THE IDEA OF LITERATURE

RESTORATION DRAMA AND THE IDEA OF LITERATURE

KATHERINE MANNHEIMER

UNIVERSITY OF VIRGINIA PRESS
Charlottesville and London

University of Virginia Press
© 2023 by the Rector and Visitors of the University of Virginia
All rights reserved
Printed in the United States of America on acid-free paper

First published 2023

9 8 7 6 5 4 3 2 1

Library of Congress Cataloging-in-Publication Data

Names: Mannheimer, Katherine, author.
Title: Restoration drama and the idea of literature / Katherine Mannheimer.
Description: Charlottesville : University of Virginia Press, 2023. | Includes bibliographical references and index.
Identifiers: LCCN 2023031754 (print) | LCCN 2023031755 (ebook) | ISBN 9780813950426 (hardcover ; acid-free paper) | ISBN 9780813950433 (paperback ; acid-free paper) | ISBN 9780813950440 (ebook)
Subjects: LCSH: English drama—Restoration, 1660-1700—History and criticism. | Authors and readers—England—History—17th century. | Theater—Great Britain—History—17th century. | Theatrical publishing—England—History—17th century. | Books and reading—England—History—17th century. | Literature—Philosophy. | Canon (Literature) | LCGFT: Literary criticism.
Classification: LCC PR691 .M36 2023 (print) | LCC PR691 (ebook) | DDC 822/.409—dc23/eng/20230824
LC record available at https://lccn.loc.gov/2023031754
LC ebook record available at https://lccn.loc.gov/2023031755

Cover art: An actress (possibly Hannah Norsa) in the role of Polly Peachum in John Gay's *The Beggar's Opera*. (Harry Beard Collection; © Victoria and Albert Museum, London)

CONTENTS

Acknowledgments | vii

Introduction   1

1   Of Heirs and Bold Purloiners: Thomas Shadwell's Alternative Models of Literary Inheritance in *The Lancashire Witches* and *The Squire of Alsatia*   27

2   "Can My Imagination Feel?": Reading, Theatricality, and the Mind-Body Problem in Aphra Behn's *The Luckey Chance* and *The Emperor of the Moon*   76

3   Textual Timelessness, Performative Time: Posterity in William Congreve's *Love for Love* and *The Way of the World*   131

4   "Take This Sad Ballad, Which I Bought at Fair": Pastoral Performance and Print Capitalism in John Gay's *The What D'Ye Call It* and *The Beggar's Opera*   172

Conclusion   219

Notes | 239
Bibliography | 279
Index | 295

ACKNOWLEDGMENTS

I am so grateful to the many people who have helped me to shape, deepen, and complicate this book. One couldn't ask for a group of colleagues more generous, funny, wise, and brilliant than mine; in particular, I'd like to thank Morris Eaves, Kenneth Gross, Rosemary Kegl, Bette London, John Michael, and the late James Longenbach and Russell Peck—both profoundly missed—for advice, encouragement, and guidance. Thank you to my whole department for their camaraderie and sense of shared purpose. Thank you to our staff—Sherri Gunter, Sarah Jones, Kathy Kingsley, Carrie Morriss, and Cara Smith—for facilitating everything we do while always maintaining their capacity for irony.

Thank you to Matthew McDonald and Emily Kohlhase for help in checking and correcting my citations.

Over the years I have been fortunate to share my emerging ideas in a number of different forums, and I have benefitted from the questions and conversation that resulted. Thanks especially to Al Coppola, Anna Battigelli, Deborah Payne Fisk, and Robert Markley for providing me with the opportunity to present my work on their conference panels, and to my fellow panel members. Thank you to Misty Anderson and Devoney Looser for helping to shepherd early versions of my work into print, and to the editors at the *Yale Review* for giving me the chance to connect Aphra Behn's meditations on the mind-body problem to the experience of the COVID-19 pandemic. Thank you especially to Marcie Frank for illuminating conversations, incisive feedback, and extraordinarily kind mentorship.

Thank you to Dean Gloria Culver, and to the School of Arts and Sciences at the University of Rochester, for their generous subvention, as well as a semester's leave from teaching.

Many thanks to the staff at the University of Virginia Press, and especially to Angie Hogan for her support and excellent judgment.

Thank you to my family for their faith in the importance of my work despite their bafflement as to its specifics.

Finally, I would like to thank all of my teachers, throughout my life, whose influence on me seems to grow only greater with time.

RESTORATION DRAMA AND
THE IDEA OF LITERATURE

INTRODUCTION

DRAMA IN THE RESTORATION OCCUPIED an unprecedented position in relation to the printed page. Between the years 1642 and 1660, the theaters had been closed, yet this same period had witnessed the emergence of a veritable canon of imaginative writing in print, as the pioneering publisher Humphrey Moseley—followed by Henry Herringman and Jacob Tonson—assembled a list of the best poets and playwrights of the past and present, packaged their collected works, and marketed the results as a coherent series, purporting to rival the classics in prestige and merit.[1] In the field of drama, notably, this incipient print canon served as the only real bridge to an older theatrical legacy: the eighteen-year lapse in public performance meant that memories of actual productions had grown increasingly dim. Moreover, once the theaters did reopen, a new set of remuneration structures for playwrights reinforced this growing sense of plays' value as reading matter; in particular, the ability to sell playscripts to booksellers comprised a newly important component of playwrights' income, while also contributing to their identity as proprietary artists. All of these conditions helped to create a context in which printed books—and, prominently among these, printed plays—were becoming central to what scholars such as David Scott Kastan have identified as a nascent concept of "literature" as a distinct cultural field.[2]

Drama, however, as a medium inherently split between page and stage, was perfectly poised at this juncture to look skeptically at the dependency of this cultural field upon print and print culture.

As Benjamin Bennett has argued, drama—to an extent unparalleled by any other literary mode—has always had a conflicted relationship to textuality. On the one hand, when reading a play, we become aware of the "ontological . . . defective[ness]" of the text—its "fail[ure] to represent the whole 'work.'"[3] Yet, on the other hand, a staged production leaves us with the inevitable sense that what we are experiencing is a *"mere* interpretation," so that "the text . . . now paradoxically does represent the object of interpretation (the work) after all."[4]

Part of what I am contending in this book is that Restoration playwrights were uniquely able to activate this neither-nor quality of drama in ways that raised key questions about the centrality of the print medium to an emergent sense of an English literary heritage. Specifically, by playing print off of performance, each of the writers I discuss—though each in a different way—challenged the values of abstraction, permanence, and property implied by a literary tradition in print. Restoration playwrights thus demonstrated drama's singular potential as an experimental site for testing (and contesting) print's expanding cultural authority—and, with it, the ways in which the print market defined (and limited) imaginative writing.

Restoration Drama and the Idea of Literature focuses primarily on four authors: Thomas Shadwell, Aphra Behn, William Congreve, and John Gay. However, I hope to suggest the ways in which these writers' practices were representative of larger trends. Again and again, we find these dramatists (and, I would argue, their contemporaries) systematically exploiting the gap between text and performativity in ways that signal the shortcomings of a literary tradition increasingly identified with printed books. Whether by printing their plays with unusual textual elements, by featuring characters who must weigh competing insights derived from intellectual and bodily information, by hinging their plays' plots on legal or other documents, or by engaging with "popular" cultural products that defy easy generalizations about print and orality, these authors point to the hermeneutic and ethical limits of communicating through—and entrusting our cultural legacy to—texts alone.

The latter half of this introduction lays out the specific historical backdrop against which my argument unfolds: the work of the publishers whose output helped to define an emerging literary canon in print and the growing sense of the playwright's role as a proprietary author contributing to that canon. First, however, I examine a 1664 essay on Shakespeare by the poet, playwright, and philosopher Margaret Cavendish (1623?–1673)—a remarkable document that allows me to home in on the unique manner in which Restoration writers were able to grasp, and plumb the implications of, the incipient canon's reliance on print values.[5]

In certain ways, Margaret Cavendish's experience with theater parallels that of Restoration England as a whole. She recounts in her autobiographical memoir that, prior to the Civil War, her family lived in London half the year, where, in winter, they would "go sometimes to Plays."[6] During the Interregnum, it seems doubtful that she would have had the opportunity to see the work of Shakespeare performed—almost certainly not professionally. As an attendant to the exiled Queen Henrietta Maria, she likely saw court masques, of which the queen was quite fond, as well as productions by French or Italian acting troupes.[7] Once married (in 1645), Cavendish and her husband seem to have engaged frequently in reading aloud—specifically, in reading aloud from Shakespeare. These readings may even have been performed "before sizeable," if "private," groups.[8] Thus, while Cavendish's exposure to live performance did not cease entirely in the 1640s, it seems safe to say that her primary experience of Shakespeare (and of English drama more generally) would, like that of most of her generation, have been centered on the page.[9] (Indeed, Jeffrey Masten has traced the ways in which Cavendish's own collection of plays, which she published in 1662, reflects her close attention not only to the thematic content of Shakespeare's work but also to the bibliographic and paratextual details of his folios.[10])

Once the monarchy was restored, in 1660, and the Cavendishes returned to London, there is no definitive evidence that Margaret Cavendish attended the theater, but, as Fiona Ritchie explains, a number of factors suggest strongly that she would have done so: her husband, William Cavendish, had a "keen interest in the theatre"—he wrote his own plays as well, and may have acted in court masques[11]—and, given his close association with the King (by whose personal request the theaters reopened), "it is conceivable that the couple attended the playhouse with him." Furthermore, the Cavendishes' residence, off of Fleet Street, was "not far from the King's Theatre in Vere Street or the Duke of York's playhouse in Lincoln's Inn Fields."[12]

Like many of her contemporaries, then, Cavendish's access to English drama could be said to have been divided, more or less, into separate historical phases. Indeed, as Ann Baynes Coiro succinctly puts it, "perhaps the single most important effect of the closing of the theatres" was the fact that "most people grew accustomed to experiencing 'theatricality' through reading."[13] How did this experience change Britons' understanding of what drama could do and mean? How did it change their sense of what a text can be—and of the relationship between a printed page and a live, performing body? It is no coincidence, I argue, that a member of the generation whose access to drama underwent these two major shifts is also the author of what scholars consider to be "the first . . . general prose assessment of Shakespeare as a dramatist"— and, indeed, of what many consider to be one of "the earliest pieces of formal literary criticism" in English.[14] The traumatic upheavals of the Civil War and its aftermath forced Restoration readers, writers, and audiences to reckon in unprecedented ways with the power (and shortcomings) of print in safeguarding and transmitting an artistic tradition that appeared newly vulnerable. At the same time—and Cavendish's essay speaks to this directly—drama, whether as printed literature or as staged performance, seems well positioned to help reconcile differences, to demonstrate the ability of a shared cultural heritage to remind us of what we hold in common.

In keeping with Cavendish's changing modes of encountering Shakespeare over the course of her life, one of the most striking elements of her essay on Shakespeare is its similarly oscillating focus on his plays as textual entities, on the one hand, and, on the other, as inescapably embodied phenomena. For example, every single one of Cavendish's multiple references to Shakespeare's audience is to his "Readers,"[15] yet (in a passage I examine at more length below) she also describes the experience of reading the plays as a feeling of being "Present" at the events that constitute their plots. However, even as Cavendish's dual emphasis reflects her (and the Restoration's) historically divided experience of drama, I would argue that it also reflects something inherent to the medium itself—its strange fusion of text and occasion, imagination and spectacle. With my discussion of Cavendish's essay I hope to illustrate the ways in which Restoration-era writers' historical circumstances might have helped them to perceive the value of plays both as scripts for performance and as texts for reading—as part of an emerging field of printed literature that was increasingly considered central to England's identity. But I also hope to show how drama itself, precisely in its ontological doubleness, allowed Restoration writers to delve into what a print canon is and means—what the written word can (or cannot) express of who we are, both as a linguistic community and as human beings.

Margaret Cavendish's "Letter 123" from her collection *Sociable Letters* treats Shakespeare as though he is already part of a literary canon in print.[16] She refers to his "Playes,"[17] but also specifically to "his Book,"[18] implying that his work is best understood not as a series of individual works for the stage (experienced one performance at a time) but as a monumental accomplishment—a kind of library or canon unto itself—in which characters from one play rub shoulders with the characters from another. Encompassing "the Divers, and Different Humours, or Natures, or Several Passions in Mankind," this one great book brings together both comedy and tragedy, the "Fool" and the "Wise man," the "Mean Country Wench" and the "Great Lady": more than could any three-hour production, Shakespeare's collected works in print not only contain the "Phrases, Garbs, Manners, Actions, [and] Words" of "Clowns" and "Kings" alike, but indeed represent their whole "Course[s] of Life."[19] Shakespeare's vast spectrum of characters, Cavendish suggests, are best appreciated not within any one play but in the larger—almost encyclopedic—achievement that is his "Book."[20]

In collecting his plays into a single, timeless space, Shakespeare's "Book" also ensures his legacy for the future. Shakespeare is not simply "Express[ing] . . . the Extravagancies of Madness [and] the Subtilty of Knaves," Cavendish asserts, but "Deliver[ing] [them] to Posterity."[21] This posterity will consist, to be sure, of some latter-day iteration of the "Readers" Cavendish repeatedly refers to—but also, notably, of writers: Shakespeare had "so much [wit] . . . above others," Cavendish explains, "that those, who Writ after him, were Forced to Borrow of him, or rather to Steal from him."[22] Clearly, Cavendish sees Shakespeare as part of a printed lineage: his work will be read and rewritten by those who follow him, and is, in turn, a reworking of earlier texts (she excuses Shakespeare's own "Borrow[ings]" when she notes that he did "take Some of his Plots out of History," but only because he lacked sufficient "Subjects" for his prodigious "Wit and Eloquence to Work on"[23]).

Even as Cavendish celebrates the universality and transcendence of Shakespeare's legacy in print, however, she also points to a seemingly contradictory element his work—namely, its ability to plunge us into a live sensory experience in which writer and reader, actor and audience, past and present, blur together. She writes, "In his Tragick Vein, he Presents Passions so Naturally, and Misfortunes so Probably, as he Peirces the Souls of his Readers with such a True Sense and Feeling thereof, that it Forces Tears through their Eyes, and almost Perswades them, they are Really Actors, or at least Present at those Tragedies."[24] The ordeal described here is as physical as it is mental: in addition to having their souls "Peirce[d]," Shakespeare's readers find tears being "Force[d] through their Eyes."[25] Indeed, emotional and bodily feeling become so intertwined that the line between imagination and material fact breaks down: the readers come to believe that they "are Really Actors, or at least Present at those Tragedies." Cavendish's phrasing here is conspicuously equivocal: do Shakespeare's readers feel they are "Actors" in the sense of participants—or of players? Are they being made to feel "Present" at actual events (say, Julius Caesar's assassination), or at those events' theatrical recreation (a staging of act 3 of *Julius Caesar*)? But perhaps this ambiguity is itself the point: The "Passions" and "Misfortunes" of Shakespeare's characters are depicted with such immediacy that reading Shakespeare ceases to offer us an opportunity to observe humanity from a birds-eye view—as suggested by Cavendish's earlier catalogues of fools and knaves, wenches and ladies. Rather, reading thrusts us, imaginatively, into a dynamic space that erodes our sense of the line separating reality from representation.

Just as Shakespeare's readers cannot maintain a birds-eye view of his plays, Shakespeare himself—despite Cavendish's praise of his "Clear Judgment, . . . Subtil Observation, . . . [and] Deep Apprehension"—seems ultimately to enjoy much less of a godly remove than we might suppose. Cavendish asserts,

> So Well he hath Express'd in his Playes all Sorts of Persons, as one would think he had been Transformed into every one of those persons he hath Described; and as sometimes one would think he was Really himself the Clown or Jester he Feigns, so one would think, he was also the King, and Privy Counsellor; also as one would think he were Really the Coward he Feigns, so one would think he were the most Valiant, and Experienced Souldier; Who would not think he had been such a man as his Sir John Falstaff? And who would not think he had been Harry the Fifth? & certainly Julius Caesar, Augustus Caesar, and Antonius, did never Really Act their parts Better, if so Well, as he hath Described them . . . ; nay, one would think that he had been Metamorphosed from a Man to a Woman, for who could Describe Cleopatra Better than he hath done, and many other Females of his own Creating, as Nan Page, Mrs. Page, Mrs. Ford, the Doctors Maid, Bettrice, Mrs. Quickly, Doll Tearsheet, and others, too many to Relate?[26]

On the one hand, Shakespeare comes across here as, in some sense, a better author than God: in what appears to be a competition to epitomize some ideal essence of "Julius Caesar, Augustus Caesar, [or] Antonius," Shakespeare's characters win higher marks than the men who actually lived and died here on earth. Indeed, in a kind of reversal of Cavendish's acknowledgement that Shakespeare was "Forced to take Some of his Plots out of History," it now seems that History took its plots out of Shakespeare—that the real-life Caesar was, all along, merely (and inadequately) "Act[ing]" out the part that Shakespeare wrought definitively in his play.

On the other hand, Cavendish's account also represents a significant demotion in creative agency. She implies Shakespeare is not so much the author of his own plays as an actor in them (Shakespeare was in fact both): when she writes that he "Feigns ... the Clown or Jester," just as he "Feigns ... the Coward [or] ... Souldier," Cavendish suggests not only that he "invents" these personages but also that he "pretends to be" them (*OED*, s.v. "feign").[27] What is more, this actorly status is not associated with any real mastery or control: it wouldn't surprise Cavendish to learn that Shakespeare hadn't so much played as "been ... sir John Falstaff," or "been Harry the Fifth."[28] She envisions this shape-shifting as a curiously passive process: "One would think he had *been* Transformed," she writes, or "*been* Metamorphosed" into the persons he writes about.[29] Far from a Peter Quince–like writer/performer, Shakespeare becomes a kind of feckless Bottom, ensorcelled by powers beyond his ken, less a player than a plaything, a character in someone else's—perhaps Cavendish's own—drama.

Here, we arrive again at the doubleness to which I alluded earlier. Cavendish credits Shakespeare with authoring a great Book that comprehends all of humanity within its covers, and that improves upon or even replaces history itself as a kind of master narrative of civilization. However, Shakespeare's characters exhibit such an aching vividness that Shakespeare's own contribution seems to consist less in verbal invention than in the kind of empathy gained by an actor called upon to play multiple types of roles.

To what extent does Cavendish's dual sense of Shakespeare stem from her temporally layered experience of his plays—as theater, as text, and as theater again? More basically, to what extent does this notion of the great Renaissance playwright result from the way in which drama itself straddles page and stage—a dividedness that Cavendish and her contemporaries would have been uniquely primed to apprehend? Cavendish never mentions playgoing in her essay: as noted above, all encounters with Shakespeare's work are referred to as acts of "Read[ing]."[30] Yet Cavendish's language is full of the theater: of feigning, acting, metamorphosing, transforming. Even as

Cavendish purports to discuss Shakespeare's plays as reading texts, her thinking about them seems insistently shaped by the theater.

To phrase the question slightly differently: when Cavendish praises Shakespeare for the way that he "Express[es] [his characters] ... to the Life," does her sense of their lifelikeness reflect the fact that her readerly imagination has been enhanced by the memory of seeing Shakespeare's work onstage (whether in her youth or more recently, after the theaters had been reopened)? Or, more broadly, might Cavendish posit that there is something about plays in general that demands that we, as readers, be perpetually staging them, somehow or other, in our minds, bringing the characters to life?

In the third preface to her own collection of plays, in 1662, Cavendish wrote that she

> ... did take
> Much pleasure and delight these Playes to make;
> For all the time my Playes a making were,
> My brain the Stage, my thoughts were acting there.[31]

It seems that Cavendish did not expect her plays ever to be acted publicly: she wrote them during the Interregnum, in the 1640s and 1650s, and even once the theaters had reopened, no original plays by women were yet appearing onstage.[32] Nonetheless, she suggests that her plays, *as plays,* invite a certain type of imaginative work—different, perhaps, than that which another mode might elicit: Cavendish's plays have provided a means by which her thoughts can act themselves out, even take on a life of their own, while she looks on. Indeed, playwriting grants her thoughts such autonomy that it is as if the plays are "a making" themselves.[33]

The work of David Brewer suggests that there may, in fact, be something unique to drama that allows its characters—if not also the playwright's very "thoughts"—to accrue a special kind of independence and power.[34] He disagrees with historians of the novel who have asserted that it is "precisely ... [the] disembodiment" of novelistic characters that allows these figures to gain a particular kind of imaginative purchase over readers.[35] Rather, Brewer contends that readers' ongoing fascination with certain characters can be attributed to "neither their materiality nor their immateriality per se, but rather the ways in which one enable[s] the other in a perpetual feedback loop."[36] Brewer is most interested in those characters for whom, starting in the eighteenth century, readers seemed to feel compelled to project "further adventures"—whether in unauthorized sequels, backstories, or other forms of imaginative extension. More often than not, he avers, "the characters for whom further adventures were invented tended to be those whose immateriality was paradoxically guaranteed by the sheer material proliferation of different and differing editions, formats, and performances."[37] Such figures didn't necessarily need to start out as dramatis personae, Brewer explains: Don Quixote, for example, was one of the most popular subjects for "further adventures," and, though he did end up accruing many eighteenth-century theatrical appearances, he did not originate in that context. Yet we can easily see how those characters whose most visible instantiations were as figures in plays—Falstaff or Captain Macheath—came ready-made for the "feedback loop" Brewer describes: at birth, so to speak, they were already creatures of both page and stage.

The ability of characters to cross over into new media and new modes—often, as Brewer notes, in "unauthorized" ways—creates a situation in which the author recedes. As Brewer points out, in the theater, every new production (perhaps every new performance) generates a new iteration of a character; and while a role's potential for endless reinterpretation would logically seem to testify to the talents of the playwright, audiences and readers often attribute the richness of a role to the character him- or herself. As the number of actors cast in a certain part grows (Brewer cites the example of Falstaff), so, too, does a sense among theatergoers—but also among the readers inhabiting the wider cultural milieu in which these performances circulate—that "no single actor's interpretation can adequately contain" the character.[38] Thus, Falstaff himself begins to seem endlessly manifold, what eighteenth-century bookseller Thomas Davies called an "exhaustless fund of wit and humour."[39] Yet this "exhaustless[ness]" seems to come at the expense of the author's own capacities—that is, in Davies's formulation it is Falstaff, and not Shakespeare, who is the font of imagination, fancy, and comic genius.

Indeed, we seem now to be back amid the uncanny confusions of agency traced by Cavendish, in which the playwright—whether Shakespeare or, in her 1662 preface, Cavendish herself—seems to fade beside the "live" thoughts and figures taking shape on their plays' implied stages. Drama, it would appear, unlike other literary forms, strangely destabilizes the positions of author and audience, creator and creation, in ways that call into question our most basic understandings of what it means to write and to read.

I return to the history of Shakespeare criticism—and, specifically, its focus on Shakespeare's characters—in my conclusion. For now, though, I want to summarize how Cavendish's discussion of Shakespeare helps to pinpoint some of the key concepts that emerge in the central four chapters of this study. As we have seen, Cavendish celebrates Shakespeare's value as a print author: "his Book" allows him to "Deliver to Posterity" a universal corpus of writing that transcends—as no theatrical production could do—the specifics of time and space ("Express[ing] the Divers, and Different Humours, or Natures, or Several Passions in Mankind" and representing a variety of characters in their full "Course[s] of Life"). This great Book likewise participates in a textual lineage, so that "those, who Writ after him, [are] Forced to Borrow of him, or rather to Steal from him"—just as he himself has taken many of his "Plots out of History." Meanwhile, Shakespeare as author stands preeminent over this oeuvre as creator and owner, as only a print author can (his literary property is in danger of being "St[o]l[en]" by other writers), and, indeed, ascends even to a god-like status at certain moments (so that his own Caesar out-Caesars the actual man).[40] However, Cavendish's essay also reveals these values of transcendence, permanence, and proprietary authorship—values fundamental to an incipient print canon—to be oddly precarious. Recall that, far from an abstract or exalted experience, reading Shakespeare's texts, according to Cavendish, is a violently physical ("Peirc[ing]," "Force[ful]") tribulation, one that demands our full "Presen[ce]." So, too, Shakespeare himself, even if to some degree part of an emergent authorial pantheon, becomes a lump of clay in the hands of other, Ovidian gods, "Transformed" and "Metamorphosed" into "every one of those persons he hath Described"—allowing those "persons," in turn, to become all the more lifelike, all the more authoritative.

In short, Cavendish's "Letter 123," written only four years into the Restoration, offers a glimpse of the unique ways in which Restoration writers were poised to understand, and leverage, drama's disruptive force within an expanding world of print. Although the writers I examine in this book did not witness firsthand the cultural upheavals of the Civil War, as Cavendish did (Shadwell and Behn were born at the very onset of the Interregnum, and Congreve and Gay lived their entire lives under the restored monarchy), I argue that the split conception of drama that Cavendish illustrates—a split conception induced by the sustained closure (and subsequent reopening) of the theaters, at the same time that a steadily solidifying canon in print began to make its cultural mark—did not quickly dissipate. Indeed, as I demonstrate in my conclusion, this cleaved awareness of the dramatic mode continued into the early nineteenth century and beyond, and even ramifies backward (as we see in Cavendish's essay) to inform critical understandings of Shakespeare that remain operative to this day.

In the four chapters of this book, I examine the ways in which Restoration dramatists focalize many of the same issues touched on in Cavendish's "Letter 123." Cavendish, we recall, implies that print—specifically, Shakespeare's capacious and comprehensive "Book"—is the key to "Posterity." Yet she also suggests that posterity itself may (or even should) be constantly revised, and that this process is a theatrical one: so, for example, the real Julius Caesar's subpar performance can be superseded by the superior oratory of *Julius Caesar*, forging a new and improved historical legacy. Similarly, Thomas Shadwell and William Congreve question, from different angles, the nature of artistic heritage, and the extent to which print's supposed permanence—as opposed to the theater's constant reincarnations—might (or might not) succeed in shepherding these bequests into the future. Whereas Shadwell is particularly concerned with how to bridge the theatrical void of the Interregnum, Congreve grapples with how best to ensure his own plays' legacy going forward.

Aphra Behn, by contrast, is less interested in the different forms in which we might pass down our beliefs and identities than in the varying means by which we access those forms (specifically, by reading versus spectating), and in how our utilization of one means versus another can affect our understanding of—or, indeed, the very nature of—who we are. Like Cavendish, Behn suggests that reading implicates our bodies in ways we might not expect; at the same time, she insists that the reverse is also true—that our physical perceptions often depend very much on the kinds of imaginative and inferential capacities we associate with reading.

Finally, John Gay assesses the competing claims to moral authority of print and embodied communion. For if Cavendish implies that Shakespeare's printed oeuvre offers a degree of human insight that an individual performance could not—a panoply of humankind too bustling and diverse to fit into a single night at the theater—at the same time she suggests that true moral understanding can only be attained, as it were, in the flesh; that the richness of Shakespeare's characterizations could result only from his having "been Transformed into every one of those persons he hath Described." Similarly, Gay flirts with the notion that a more natural, performative mode of expression—ballad singing, rural pastimes, folk rituals—might save us from an increasingly market-mediated, commodified literary sphere. However, as we will see, he ultimately concludes that such performances remain inextricable from the larger mechanisms of print capitalism.

At this point, I have alluded several times to the mid-seventeenth century's emerging canon of imaginative writing in print, a growing cultural presence that I see Restoration dramatists as increasingly positioning themselves in relation to—but one that they also probe, question, and seek to expand. It is to this emerging print corpus—this body of texts that authors and readers alike were coming to view as part of an artistic tradition bearing a particular kind of prestige as well as economic value—to which I refer in my title, *Restoration Drama and the Idea of Literature*.

Of course, many different historical junctures have been identified by scholars as the moment when key elements of what we now call "literature" were first hammered out in Britain.[41] These include Chaucer's development of a vernacular poetics; the Renaissance's new cultural emphasis on imaginative writing; the rise, in the eighteenth century, of an educated middle class who could support a robust literary industry; and Romanticism's celebration of individual genius.[42] Clearly, to privilege any one of these moments over the others is also to privilege a very particular definition of the term "literature" itself.[43] Does literature consist of the work of what Richard Helgerson termed "self-crowned laureates"—individual writers who laid claim to a kind of unique poetic authority?[44] Is literature any piece of writing that (adapting Lukas Erne's classifications) insists on its "generic respectability" while anticipating a specific kind of "readerly reception"?[45] Can a notion of literature be said to arise only after an institutionalized discipline of literary studies develops, and succeeds in distinguishing itself against other fields of knowledge, such as the sciences?[46] Before a concept of literature exists, must a society first agree upon the standards for judging and ranking its constituent texts?[47] Or does an idea of literature first enter the public consciousness only after it has entered the public domain?[48]

For the purposes of this study, I use the definition of literature posited by David Kastan in his work on the revolutionary bookseller Humphrey Moseley (fl. 1627–61). Along with John Barnard, Ann Baynes Coiro, Paul Hammond, Paulina Kewes, and others, Kastan finds evidence of what we would now call a distinct "market niche" for poetry and drama arising within the seventeenth-century book trade.⁴⁹ While my focus is not on the operations of the era's book publishing, the work of these scholars has established the basic historical contexts that I use as my starting point. In particular, their work helps to define "literature" in the Restoration as a widely acknowledged set of printed texts that—via an expanding cultural marketplace—also helped to establish the figure of the proprietary author.

Kastan has argued that the work of one publisher above all others—Humphrey Moseley—was fundamental to the creation of a widespread understanding, in the mid-seventeenth century, of what "English literature might be," of what might comprise its "organizing principles," and of "what texts might constitute it."⁵⁰ Moseley systematically went about selecting and curating "the best writing of his generation," bringing out, between 1646 and 1656, editions of Milton, Waller, Crashaw, Suckling, Cowley, Denham, and Vaughan. Just as importantly, by printing all of these editions in a uniform style, he created a "recognizable series" of books, all with nearly identical layouts and typefaces.⁵¹ "Unquestionably what is most remarkable about Moseley's career," Kastan thus concludes, "is the degree to which," for the first time in English history, "he recognized and developed a market for literary works."⁵²

But the impact was not just economic: this "market" for literary works was also "mak[ing] . . . visible," for the first time, "a coherent literary field."⁵³ By implicitly asserting that the works in his series represented "an organized body of texts with common characteristics," Kastan argues, Moseley enabled "disparate and idiosyncratic exemplars of imaginative writing" to be seen as "a unified and coherent cultural project."⁵⁴ (As Peter Lindenbaum puts it, each of Moseley's books was "by various means made to look like part of a series: Moseley's English Poets."⁵⁵) Moreover, by according the volumes a degree of bibliographic dignity unusual for English authors—utilizing, for example, engraved frontispieces and prefaces to the reader—Moseley signaled the works' prestige, and suggested their status as modern "classics." So significant does Kastan view Moseley's achievement, indeed, that he declares the winter of 1645—when Moseley began printing his series—as marking the "invent[ion] [of] English literature."⁵⁶

Drama in particular constituted an important part of Moseley's publishing program.⁵⁷ Moseley established his reputation with the first Beaumont and Fletcher folio, in 1647, but this was just the beginning. In 1653, Moseley entered over forty plays in the stationers' register, suggesting his ambitious plans for the coming years; and he did, in fact, entirely dominate the publication of drama throughout the Interregnum.[58] By the mid-1650s he was bringing out a series of collected plays in octavo: *Five New Playes,* by Richard Brome, and *Six New Playes,* by James Shirley (both 1653), followed by Philip Massinger's *Three New Playes* (1655), Lodowick Carlell's *Two New Playes* (1657), and Thomas Middleton's *Two New Playes* (1657). As Paulina Kewes notes, the "level of standardization and uniformity of Moseley's play collections" exceeded even that of his poetry series: the identical phrasing for the titles, the consistent typographical layout, the engraved portrait of the author on each volume's frontispiece, and the single-minded focus on plays only (to the exclusion of non-dramatic poetry) all contributed to a clear sense of these books as part of a larger whole.[59] Meanwhile, the volumes' deliberate paratextual content—including commendatory verses, dedications, separate title pages for each play, and formal lists of dramatis personae—insisted, even more specifically, on this series' "status as literature."[60]

Until Moseley began his landmark undertaking, plays had occasionally been published in collections, but these collections had themselves never been collected together. Readers could purchase monumental folios—whether Jonson's works in 1616, the Shakespeare edition of 1623, or Moseley's own Beaumont and Fletcher volume in 1647; and Kewes adds that there were a few isolated instances of octavo collections being published as well (Marston in 1633, Chapman in 1652[61]). However, booksellers and book buyers did not necessarily perceive these publications as part of a broader cultural category. Humphrey Moseley changed all this.[62]

There may have been a direct connection between this new sense of plays as literary reading matter, on the one hand, and the 1642 closure of the theaters, on the other.[63] Indeed, many scholars have argued that it was only with the shuttering of the playhouses that the play-text could come to be regarded as something more than a mere record of performance.[64] Especially considering that, early on, no one could foresee an end to the ban on live theater, the plays printed during this time were not viewed even as hypothetical scripts for future productions: as Michael Gavin points out, these circumstances allowed for plays that "had gone unpublished for decades [to be] sent to the press for the first time," given that "they no longer faced the threat of infringing productions at rival theatres."[65] The readership for these works could thus no longer be considered a mere extension of theatrical audiences; nor could the reading of plays be deemed a mere supplement to playgoing.[66] Rather, reading a printed play became a worthwhile activity in its own right. As Coiro puts it, Moseley's achievement was to create a situation in which, once the theaters reopened, "the stage faced a world where theatrical texts had become dramatic literature."[67]

In addition to Moseley, two other booksellers were similarly instrumental in shaping a canon both of pre-Interregnum and contemporary writing (including both poetry and plays): Henry Herringman and Jacob Tonson. Indeed, Paul Hammond asserts that the lists of these two publishers "are in themselves almost a late seventeenth-century canon."[68] Moseley, often working from manuscript sources, had undertaken much of the initial labor of assembling a group of authors, but Herringman then acquired the rights to many of these in the 1660s (after Moseley's death), adding Dryden, Etherege, and Sedley to the roster. (It is possible that he also employed Dryden as an editorial assistant.[69]) Stephen Bernard thus credits Herringman with helping to usher in the conditions under which "the modern literary publisher [also became] an agent responsible for [an author's] literary reputation."[70]

Jacob Tonson eventually acquired most of Herringman's authors, beginning with Dryden, in 1679.[71] His 1688 folio edition of *Paradise Lost* was a particular milestone: complete with 300 pages of annotations "expound[ing] the poem's vocabulary and theology," the volume contributed profoundly "to the emerging canonical status of Milton," giving his masterpiece "a classical scholarly treatment which at that date had been accorded to no other English poem."[72] Not coincidentally, Tonson specialized in translations of the classics, including most notably, perhaps, Dryden's monumental Virgil of 1697 (the first work of a living writer to be marketed and sold by subscription). Translation was also fundamental to the Dryden-Tonson *Miscellanies* (1684–94), a poetry series that—with its larger aim of forming a "canon of contemporary [English] writers" who could "measure up to the challenge of the classics"—is believed by John Barnard to have played an especially crucial role in defining the literary tastes of a "polite" or "leisured middle class."[73] Barnard sees this series as capping off the earlier efforts of Moseley and Herringman, resulting in the solidification of a stand-alone category of imaginative literature in print, epitomized by a group of authors who were consistently published, purchased, and read together.[74]

As suggested by the discussion above, I see the book trade as particularly crucial to budding concepts of literariness and canonicity in the Restoration. However, my primary focus is not the central role of the print marketplace in defining a nascent literary field but, rather, the way in which Restoration drama seized upon this centrality, questioning the relationship between this new field and the print medium. As I have already noted, Restoration playwrights were uniquely prepared to think about this relationship, for two reasons: first, while a playwright's work is usually intended to transcend the confines of the written word—to be read, perhaps, but also (most typically) to be spoken aloud, performed, and embodied—Restoration dramatists were working at the tail end of a period in which plays had been experienced primarily on the page, and during which (as we have now seen in some detail) plays had become a conspicuous component of a new print canon. Second, Restoration dramatists—unlike their predecessors in the first half of the century—were able to earn money directly from the sale of their play-texts.

This latter fact bears dwelling on at length: whereas Renaissance playwrights had sold their scripts to the actors' companies, Restoration dramatists retained the rights to their scripts.[75] The money they could make from selling their work in print, along with the income they were receiving from third-night benefits at the theater (also a post-1660 innovation), allowed playwrights to become proprietary authors in ways that their early century counterparts had not. Whereas pre-Interregnum dramatists were able to dedicate themselves fully to writing only if they were gentleman-amateurs, employees of an acting company, or dependents of the patronage system, this new state of affairs meant that, as Kewes puts it, playwrights after 1660 had to become "entrepreneur[s]."[76]

So completely revolutionary was the Restoration's shift in how playwrights were remunerated that Judith Milhous and Robert D. Hume call the development nothing less than "stunning," ascribing to it an almost incalculable impact "on the whole history of playwriting and publication."[77] They add that, given the incentive Restoration playwrights now had to extend the length of their plays' theatrical runs—a sixth-night benefit, and later a ninth-night benefit, were introduced by the end of the century—it soon became "customar[y]" for them to "supervise . . . rehearsals," and even to "exercise . . . a degree of control over casting and scenery" in ways that early century playwrights had had no reason to do.[78] Just as crucially, because playwrights' other source of income derived from the sale of their plays to publishers, they also necessarily began to view their plays not only as the bases of popular productions that would fill seats for several days running but also as reading matter that would be offered alongside other books, and listed as such in booksellers' catalogues. Milhous and Hume assert that it was the Restoration dramatists' ownership of their plays, and the fact that their earnings could derive both from theatrical success and from their plays' perceived appeal to readers, that ultimately caused drama to "become vastly more 'literary'" than ever before.[79]

In this regard, Milhous and Hume join scholars such as Brean Hammond, Kewes, and Mark Rose in viewing literature's origins as dependent less on the book trade per se—that is, on the kinds of books for sale and how they were packaged and promoted—than on the author figure whom that trade helped to construct. It is only once the author attains a particular "social and economic visibility," Kewes argues, that his or her work can also be invested with a particular kind of value and prestige.[80] Moreover, because "the financial rewards of the dramatist" in the late seventeenth century so "vastly exceeded those of writers working in other genres,"[81] one could argue that Restoration dramatists were the first professional authors.[82] Writing may even have provided a handful of dramatists, including Dryden, Shadwell, and Behn, with the majority of their income.[83] These circumstances led to a new emphasis on originality and, accordingly, to a growing perception of a written work's value as rooted in an individual author's distinctive artistic choices: Milhous and Hume echo Kewes in affirming that, whereas "demand for and pride in originality in composition is occasionally found in the first half of the seventeenth century, it is very much on the rise after 1660 and more so by the 1690s."[84] Thus, whereas "at the start of the seventeenth century plays were *not* generally regarded as literary," this perception very "soon began to change."[85]

Shakespeare's and Jonson's largely successful bids for artistic prestige notwithstanding, then, Kewes sees the Restoration's new remuneration structures as constituting the decisive transformation of "writer[s] of . . . play[s]" into "dramatic poet[s],"[86] and thus contributing to a larger understanding of literary authorship more broadly. Indeed, Milhous and Hume provide a number of statistics that reinforce this conclusion: between 1590 and 1642, they note, nearly half of all plays were written either anonymously or collaboratively (or both).[87] By contrast, 85.5% of plays published in the 1660–1720 period are identified on their title pages as having been written by a single, named author, suggesting a context in which playwrights were beginning to forge "literary reputation[s]" and in which authors' names carried a very specific kind of meaning and cultural capital.[88] Similarly, Milhous and Hume point out that in booksellers' advertisements appearing between 1660 and 1665, "twenty-five of the thirty-one advertised plays have the author's name in the advertisement," seemingly indicating that, as of 1660, "plays were starting to be seen as literary productions by individuals."[89] Interestingly, Kewes views the Restoration's transformation of playwright into poet as applying both forward and backward in time: Kewes suggests that Shakespeare's cultural apotheosis—arguably achieved only in the late eighteenth century—can be attributed to the changes that occurred during the Restoration era.[90] (I expand on this suggestion in my conclusion.)

The idea of the playwright as proprietary author owed as much to larger intellectual developments, of course, as to changing economic arrangements: as Kevin Pask observes, the notion of "literary property in the form of the individual labor later known as originality and creativity" was ultimately rooted in "Locke's theory of individual producer as property owner."[91] (And although Locke's *Two Treatises of Government* was published in 1690, it had been written seven years earlier.) Like Brean Hammond, Pask concedes that a full-fledged poetics of originality would not be articulated until the Romantic period, but deems the Restoration to be "probably the first moment in which originality secures sufficient cultural authority to provoke anxiety."[92] Thus, whereas classical imitation had still been a core value for Jonson, for example, in the Restoration we find countless defenses by playwrights of their use of prior sources, and an increasing number of charges of plagiarism and illegitimacy—including Cavendish's references in "Letter 123" to the writers forced to "Borrow" or "Steal" from Shakespeare.[93]

Interestingly, Pask sees the period's new anxiety around originality as bound up specifically with drama: he locates in Gerard Langbaine's dramatic bibliographies "the first sustained attempts to trace the sources of English literary texts," a project he sees as guided by Langbaine's "highly developed—indeed, overdeveloped—sense of plagiarism."[94] Although Langbaine's bibliographies were published some thirty years after the reopening of the theaters—in 1687 and 1691—they drew upon catalogues that had accompanied the earliest days of the Restoration: in 1661 Francis Kirkman, a London bookseller, had put out *A True, Perfect, and Exact Catalogue of All the Comedies, Tragedies, Tragi-Comedies, Pastorals, Masques, and Interludes, that Were Ever Yet Printed and Published, till this Present Year*; Langbaine's first bibliography, in 1680, was a revision of Kirkman's 1671 catalogue.[95] Thus, the importance of identifying accurate versions of artistically distinct plays by individuated authors appears to have been insisted upon by booksellers (and, it seems, by book buyers) from the very first moments of the patent theaters' opening.

Why does this concern over literary theft center first on drama, as opposed to other genres? The dynamics of the print marketplace may once again be salient here. On the one hand, because of its unique historical context, Restoration drama needed to reach back across an eighteen-year gap in order to establish its own position; its legitimacy depended, in large part, on its ability to conjure up an earlier moment in time, to emulate the past. On the other hand, however, Pask sees Kirkman's and Langbaine's catalogues as bearing witness to a growing tendency to equate value with novelty—an equation he attributes to an emergent print capitalism and its attendant ideologies.[96] Restoration drama, in participating in this new market for print, was also forced to respond to this new set of priorities—even as it sought to serve as a kind of emblem for a "restored" cultural tradition.

As we have now seen, the foundation of *Restoration Drama and the Idea of Literature* is historical in nature; its central task, however, is hermeneutic.[97] In other words, though I take as my premise the notion that late seventeenth-century booksellers had begun to curate and market a nascent poetic tradition we would now call "English literature," my purpose here is not to document this tradition's emergence or development over time. Rather, I aim to show how individual plays critiqued the growing authority of print and reading within this inchoate cultural category. I do this via a set of close, extended analyses of the plays themselves—specifically, by looking at how the plays leverage drama's innate tensions between page and stage.

In a sense, then, I approach the works I examine here as theoretical texts—as spaces of questioning, speculation, and exploration—rather than as historical evidence "proving" the existence of a larger cultural or societal change. Accordingly, this study does not contain detailed considerations of print runs, contemporary reading practices, or purchaser demographics. Nor do I scrutinize firsthand accounts of playgoers' reactions, or seek to determine each play's profit margins. I do not consider in any great depth the biographies of the actors who would have first performed these plays, except where I think they bear directly on my work of interpretation.[98] Rather than trying to recapture how Restoration drama was originally read and/or staged, I aim to examine how the era's plays can be seen to articulate, complicate, and revise the central concepts underlying an incipient literary field in print. To that end, where possible, I anchor the plays' intellectual undertakings in relevant philosophical, cultural, aesthetic, ideological, and other discourses of the period. But my focus remains on textual analysis, and on what the plays themselves have to tell us. To borrow a phrase from Jonathan Kramnick, one might say my intention in this book is to practice literary history "from the inside out."[99]

Scholars of Restoration drama vary in how they define the period temporally: while all studies agree on its beginning in 1660 (with the restoration of the monarchy), end dates can range from 1688 (the Glorious Revolution) to 1714 (the death of Queen Anne and the corresponding annulment of the patent holders' contracts) to 1737 (the introduction of the Licensing Act). The span of years I have chosen to examine is (more or less) 1660–1714, for a few reasons.

The reopening of the theaters after their eighteen-year closure lies at the core of the Restoration dramatists' historical identity, and gives them their peculiar sense of urgency in theorizing their own contributions. Accordingly, I discuss some of the critical debates taking place during the mid- to late-1660s regarding the nature of drama, and what the relationship ought to be between the new plays being composed and those written in the first half of the century. However, as many historians agree, questions central to the emergence of the new literary field—of how to define the field, and of how to identify what belongs to it and why—were not being widely debated until the influence wielded by the circle of court patrons had begun to weaken.[100] Throughout the 1660s, as Gavin notes, "many aspects of literary production, especially those connected to drama," were still "tightly regulated . . . [by] patronage," and "critical reception centered around the aristocracy."[101] It is only a decade later that we see the aristocratic patronage system, and the related phenomenon of the "gentleman-amateur" writer, starting to wane.[102] Indeed, Harold Love views Rochester's *Allusion to Horace* (ca. 1675) and Dryden's *MacFlecknoe* (ca. 1678) as emblematizing this moment of change.[103] As Love explains, "amateurism" constituted both "an aesthetic" and "a system of literary production"; like patronage, it was premised on the notion of the inherent superiority of judgment and wit among the high-born, and it still "exercised a considerable influence on the work of professionals" even "as late as the generation of Rochester."[104] By the late

1670s, however, the authority attached to both amateurism and the traditions of patronage showed "signs of erosion."[105] The standards of courtly taste gave way (in part) to other measures of artistic success, and to other methods of assessing a work's wider, long-term cultural impact.[106] Thus, although Shadwell was writing as early as 1668, and although he had been using his critical prefaces throughout the 1670s to debate Dryden publicly on questions of literary succession, the earliest of his plays that I analyze in this study (*The Lancashire Witches*) dates from 1681: it is here that I see Shadwell first taking up the problem of literary legitimacy directly within his plays.[107]

Given the crucial role played by remunerative, proprietary authorship in the creation of these playwrights' ideas of literary value, my study tapers off in the early years of the eighteenth century. Under the new structure of theater management inaugurated in 1714, new plays more or less ceased to be profitable, and it was no longer possible to support oneself primarily as a playwright. As Hume sums up the situation, if "the theatre ... had [once] been ... [t]he young writer's best hope, ... [by] the mid-1720s ... no one was making a living by writing plays."[108] As theaters focused overwhelmingly on older plays in repertoire, living playwrights were no longer at the center of aesthetic and cultural debates.[109] The plays being written, accordingly, demonstrated less of a drive to define drama's position vis-à-vis the larger literary landscape.

I step outside of the 1660–1714 time frame in my final chapter in order to consider John Gay, whose career began at the very end of this range (his 1712 burlesque *The Mohocks* was never performed, and *The Wife of Bath* ran for two nights in 1713, the same year that Gay published his first major poem, *Rural Sports*). Gay serves as a useful conclusory figure, I contend, because he was working at the time when playwriting, once the only viable form of professional authorship, was being economically eclipsed by the kind of writing demanded by a growing readership: essays, reviews, and prose fiction were changing what it meant to be a proprietary author—shifting, in turn, the terms of the debate around whom literature was by and for.[110] Significantly, *The Beggar's Opera* premiered the same year that Alexander Pope published the first version of his *Dunciad*, in 1728, and I argue that this play can be seen as registering similar anxieties around the impact of print capitalism on culture. Yet I also find it notable that, unlike Pope (but like the other authors I examine here), Gay uses drama—with its unique ability to position print against performance—as his tool of choice when it comes to analyzing this impact.

As mentioned previously, the broader argument of *Restoration Drama and the Idea of Literature* is largely made possible by histories of theater and the book trade. However, my main interest is in how the close examination of individual plays can focalize particular theoretical debates and the ways in which dramatists were engaged with them. In viewing the plays in this study as meditations on the role of print in an emergent literary canon, I emphasize their status as objects to be read—as texts that self-consciously present themselves to us as texts, complete with prefatory essays, annotations, even glossaries—as well as the way they confront reading thematically (as seen in their dialogue, plots, and recurring motifs). But, just as importantly, I also consider how each of the plays I discuss actively works to theorize the inherent gap—and slippage—between its readerly orientation and its theatrical bearings. In this way, the plays also theorize the tension in all literature—dramatic or not—between the innovative and the iterative, the abstract and the tangible, the permanent and the ephemeral, the written and the oral.

Perhaps counterintuitively, all of the plays I examine in this book are comedies. The lofty ambitions of heroic tragedy (and especially heroic tragedy in verse) might seem the more natural subject for a study of Restoration drama's engagement with "literature." My focus on comedy, however, is very deliberate: as plays that take place in a social setting that (broadly) mirrors their audiences' own, Restoration comedies comment on contemporary culture in a more direct way than Restoration tragedies. While I certainly don't read these plays as historically accurate renderings of late seventeenth-century life, I believe they depict attitudes toward reading and writing that are more grounded in the day-to-day reality of the period than those we might see depicted in heroic drama. Moreover, for many playwrights, the very disconnect between the comic register and concepts of print canonicity becomes a fruitful resource: comedy's appeal to the somatic, the topical, and the popular troubles the definition of "the literary" in the same way that theater does more generally, but writ large. And it is for this reason that I have kept the word *drama* in my title as opposed to the more specific *comedy:* although I concentrate on comic drama, it is my contention that the plays under discussion here are ultimately serving to illuminate—more starkly, I think, than tragedy could—the more general problem of literariness posed by drama as a whole.

The four chapters of my book together trace a critical and chronological arc. As I alluded to briefly above, I focus first on plays that seek to establish Restoration drama's position vis-à-vis a larger cultural heritage—and that attempt to determine to what degree this heritage hinges on print as opposed to theatricality. I then turn to plays that wrestle even more directly with what we might call drama's existential status as a literary subcategory, given its unique ability to encompass both textuality (with its overtones of scholarly insight, abstract reasoning, and imagination) as well as performance (and, hence, the body, sexuality, and sense perception). From there I move on to consider plays that contemplate what Restoration drama's own literary legacy will be, and that experiment with how some of drama's theatrical elements might be recreated virtually—as language on the page—for the readers of the future. Finally, I look at plays that ask whether, in the context of an increasingly commercially driven literary landscape, reading and writing have begun to lose their authority and prestige, and whether embodied performance might (or might not) provide us with a sense of moral grounding and authenticity felt to be missing from a world ever more defined by global trade and communication networks.

In chapter 1, "Of Heirs and Bold Purloiners: Thomas Shadwell's Alternative Models of Literary Inheritance in *The Lancashire Witches* and *The Squire of Alsatia*," I read Shadwell's two most popular plays of the 1680s as explorations of the diverging structures of literary succession implicit in print as opposed to in performance. I have selected these plays in part for their seemingly non-theatrical, or even antitheatrical, uses of print: *The Lancashire Witches* boasts an elaborate annotative apparatus, tracing its eponymous witches' spectacular antics to various textual sources; at the same time, it employs a system of contrasting typefaces that allows readers to access (or even privilege, if they so choose) those portions of the play that had been censored in performance. *The Squire of Alsatia,* meanwhile, features a printed key to its colorful "cant" words—whose curious semantic inversions provided, by all accounts, one of the highlights of the play's theatrical run. These plays are also notable for their incorporation of previous playwrights' texts: *The Lancashire Witches* borrows heavily, often verbatim, from Jonson's *Masque of Queenes,* while *The Squire of Alsatia* revisits Terence's *Adelphi,* frequently in direct translation. Finally, both plays link poetic inheritance to property inheritance, which Shadwell also aligns with textual authority (in the form of legal writings). I contend, however, that Shadwell ultimately seeks to undermine such exclusively word-based models of succession, and instead promotes a model that draws upon the theater's improvisatory timing, its alternative forms of reproduction, and its tradition of allusive (but uncited) reappropriation. Thus, whereas his primary rival, Dryden, consistently maintained that Restoration drama's more textual elements would guarantee its place among the great works of the past—that the Restoration playwrights would prove themselves only through the kinds of verbal and stylistic nuance that reward careful reading and rereading—Shadwell can be seen to make a case for a model of literary succession that embraces drama's doubleness: its status both as text and as theater.

My second chapter, "'Can My Imagination Feel?': Reading, Theatricality, and the Mind-Body Problem in Aphra Behn's *The Luckey Chance* and *The Emperor of the Moon*," construes Behn's final two plays as systematically questioning the boundaries separating reading from spectating. In both *The Luckey Chance* and *The Emperor of the Moon*, Behn suggests—along with Thomas Hobbes and Margaret Cavendish—that fantasy can shape our experience of reality as strongly as sense perception can. At the same time, she questions the traditional division between the written word and theatricality, insisting that our engagement with the printed page can involve our bodies as much as our minds, and that the stage may affect us as much through what it invites us to think and envision as through what it invites us to witness directly. Behn thus scuttles long-held distinctions championed by Ben Jonson, among others, according to which drama's claims to cultural authority—and those of "literature" more broadly—were based on its appeal to our spirits or souls, rather than on its sensorial manifestations.

Chapter 3, "Textual Timelessness, Performative Time: Posterity in William Congreve's *Love for Love* and *The Way of the World*," considers Congreve's final two comedies (1698 and 1700) as explorations of how drama's intertwined components of text and performance might make us rethink not only our relationship to the traditions of the past (as in Shadwell), or the interplay of mind and body in how we interpret each other's acts of expression (as in Behn), but also what our social and cultural bequest might look like. In both *Love for Love* and *The Way of the World*, texts (contracts, deeds, wills, and bonds, as well as, by analogy, neoclassicism's dramaturgical "rulebook") initially appear to function as bulwarks against contingency and accident, ensuring a particular kind of future—whether the continued prosperity of the families within the plays or the reception of Congreve's work by later generations. In the end, however, Congreve critiques this notion of a future pinned in place by the written word, showing how more flexible, open-ended forms of representation might offer, paradoxically, a more reliable legacy. Congreve thus gestures toward a form of drama in which "literary" posterity is secured by a "live" sense of adaptability and continuous transformation.

Chapter 4, "'Take this Sad Ballad, which I bought at Fair': Pastoral Performance and Print Capitalism in John Gay's *The What D'Ye Call It* and *The Beggar's Opera*," examines two plays that essentially bookend Gay's career (1715 and 1728, respectively). I argue that in both Gay questions the validity of a literary field mediated by an increasingly market-centered print economy. In many ways, this chapter brings us full circle—from the plays of the 1680s, in which concepts of literary legitimacy are bound up, in part, with emerging concepts of commercial success and entrepreneurial innovation, to a moment in which an expanding cohort of Grub Street writers (as satirized in Pope's 1728 *Dunciad*) are perceived to be threatening the very notions of literary value that proprietary authorship had once been so crucial in launching. At first, Gay seems to imply that a more natural, embodied mode of expression might provide the cure for a society ever more alienated by the buying and selling of words. Ultimately, however, I suggest that Gay is exposing this premodern, performative idyll as already inextricable from a global print capitalism. Gay's collapse of these two apparent opposites can be seen most clearly in his use of the ballad form (almost casually in *The What D'Ye Call It*, but then much more systematically in *The Beggar's Opera*). To a large extent, ballads—indeed, like drama itself—seem to epitomize the contradictions that Gay's scenarios and plotlines explore: commingling written and oral, urban and rural, commerce and collectivity, the ballad is an art form that (again, like drama itself) is always somehow suggesting that a more authentic version lies just beyond (or behind) the one we are currently experiencing. Thus, with his emphasis on how we understand the relationship between past and future, performative bodies and printed books, cultural value and the print marketplace, Gay can be seen to tie together many of the concerns articulated in the first three chapters of this book.

Finally, a brief conclusion looks back over each of my four chapters, suggesting that, in scrutinizing print's role in the conceptualization of an English tradition of imaginative writing, Restoration drama ultimately cleared a path for the eighteenth-century ascendancy of Shakespeare. Tracing some of the central tenets of Georgian-era Shakespeare reception back to the theoretical debates aired by the Restoration playwrights covered in this book, I argue that such historical continuities help us to see not only that the Restoration pioneered a number of important literary-critical concepts, but that the period helped to establish drama itself as a unique kind of crucible. That is, because drama is a mode that, in straddling page and stage, has always only uncomfortably belonged to the category of "literature" (the category, literally, of letters and literacy), Restoration dramatists used it to test some of the core values—cultural preservation, posterity, imaginative abstraction, and proprietary authorship—by which the print canon is often defined. Correspondingly, I contend, it is no coincidence that, paradoxical as it may seem, it is Shakespeare (a man who was, primarily, a writer of plays) who is still largely thought of, even today, as "the glory of English letters"—whose work is still seen as a prime site in which what it means to read, and what it means to write, is continuously reexamined and reaffirmed.

1

OF HEIRS AND BOLD PURLOINERS

Thomas Shadwell's Alternative Models of Literary Inheritance in The Lancashire Witches *and* The Squire of Alsatia

JOHN DRYDEN HAS BEEN CALLED "the first English critic to ... posit the existence of literary ages or periods[,] and the first to seek to arrange poets in an order from those originating a literary culture to his own day."[1] It makes perfect sense, I would argue, that the first critic to consider questions of a literary heritage was also one of the foremost Restoration dramatists: as John O'Brien notes, the closure of the London playhouses during the English Civil War and Interregnum meant that Restoration theater itself came to serve "as a potent symbol of the difference between the present and a past that was conceived *as* past, as a time existing on the other side of an historical breach that gave birth to a more modern culture."[2] In important ways, all Restoration playwrights were fixated on the question of literary succession, on the problem of how to authorize and legitimize their work in the shadow of the dramatists Dryden would famously refer to as the "Gyant Race, before the Flood"—a group whose internal coherence had been asserted, in the intervening years, by the canon-forming publishing projects of Humphrey Moseley and Henry Herringman.[3] Accordingly, as Marcie Frank notes, "much of Restoration writing," especially for the stage, was, to a unique extent, "rewriting."[4] Yet (or therefore) the notion of literary originality—and its inverse, plagiarism—was also first emerging during this period.[5]

As discussed in my introduction, booksellers operating during the Commonwealth and Restoration eras had helped to form an inchoate concept of "literature" and the literary canon. Dryden was now at the forefront of the Restoration's attempt to reconcile itself with this slowly solidifying field, and to define its place within it. Yet if Dryden ultimately became the more distinguished figure in this movement, John C. Ross makes the case for Thomas Shadwell as its (rivalrous) co-leader: "Of all of the playwrights of this era, only Shadwell and . . . Dryden continued active through four decades," he points out. He therefore argues that their oeuvres, more than those of any other dramatists, enable us to trace the full arc of critical disputes and controversies from the reopening of the theaters to the turn of the eighteenth century.[6] Indeed, much of the famous preface war between Dryden and Shadwell—beginning, in 1668, with Shadwell's preface to *The Sullen Lovers,* and culminating in Dryden's *MacFlecknoe* (circulating in manuscript circa 1678/79)—focused on the question of how best to maintain, and continue to renovate, drama's earlier seventeenth-century legacy, specifically vis-à-vis Ben Jonson.[7]

This chapter, via an extended examination of *The Lancashire Witches* (1681) and *The Squire of Alsatia* (1688), articulates Shadwell's view of artistic heritage beyond his quarrel with Dryden over Jonson's contribution, and beyond their (related) dispute over the merits of wit comedy versus humors comedy. More specifically (and more sweepingly), I show how Shadwell's vision of the Restoration's poetic inheritance—in a departure from Dryden's emphasis on textuality—adopts a more performative model of procreation and appropriation. As the following discussion shows, Shadwell's divergent conception of England's literary legacy can be discerned formally, or structurally, in these plays' uses of print and theater. But it can also be found in Shadwell's thematic treatment of patrimony: indeed, each of the plots I examine here is premised on a kind of breakdown among male heirs. Additionally, both plays adapt the work of earlier playwrights (Heywood and Brome; Shakespeare; possibly Beaumont and Fletcher; Jonson; Terence) in ways that embody these problems of inheritance. In *The Lancashire Witches,* Shadwell reveals the limits of textual authority and elevates a kind of theatrical, sacramental reconstitution over linear—or patrilinear—models of continuance. In *The Squire of Alsatia,* he extends this project, while also further defining what a theatrical genealogical paradigm might look like—implying that the most successful model of inheritance may be one that eschews timeless, property-based forms of masculine authority in favor of a shrewd sense of improvisatory timing and an agility of movement through space.

For John Dryden, the primary means of connection to the dramaturgical past was a verbal one: language—prosody, meter, and the use of rhyme—became Dryden's link to his dramatist forebears, as well as the medium through which he would improve upon his inheritance. (See my introduction for more detail on Renaissance writers' Restoration-era presence in print.) As David Bruce Kramer has elucidated, a tension marked Dryden's approach to his playwriting predecessors: on the one hand, Dryden "often took care to situate himself precisely at the end of a chain of forefathers who would account for the way he writes."[8] On the other hand, "Shakespeare, Jonson, Beaumont and Fletcher, honored as they remained on the English stage, were no longer a suitable pattern for imitation by English playwrights[;] for so far as Dryden and many others were concerned, a new kind of history and culture had commenced with Charles II's return in 1660."[9] As we will see, Dryden regarded these earlier playwrights' use of language as his fundamental bequest from them, yet it was also his own improvements upon this language—not unlike the improvements one might make to a magnificent but weather-beaten family estate—that, he believed, would ultimately prove him their rightful heir.

This tension is already visible in many of the assertions Dryden makes about the English playwrights who came before him: as Kramer documents, he often retroactively attributes to them the newer stylistic practices that he himself favors. For example, as is well known, Dryden staked much of his dramatic reputation on the use of rhyme, and, accordingly, although rhymed drama had in fact originated in France, Dryden legitimates his own artistic choices by falsely claiming a native precedent: "our old Comedies before *Shakespeare*... were all writ in verse of six feet, or *Alexandrin's*," he declares in his *Essay of Dramatick Poesie* (1668), "such as the *French* now use."[10] Likewise, he insists in a dedicatory epistle to *The Rival Ladies* that the 1561 tragedy *Gorboduc* was written in "*English* Verse" (i.e., rhymed couplets) when in fact it is written in blank verse.[11] Similarly, he holds, incorrectly, that Jonson's *Catiline* contains "many Scenes of rhyme together."[12] In rewriting dramaturgical history in this way, as Kramer contends, Dryden "begot his own fathers."[13] More specifically, though, he was begetting his own stylistic fathers—attempting to reconcile the past with his own, more contemporary-flavored uses of meter and rhyme.

At the same time that he alleges verbal or stylistic precedent for his work, however, Dryden makes the case that it is also through language that the dramaturgy of his own time may rise above the achievements of the past: "the Language . . . of our Age [is] improv'd and refin'd above the last," he writes in his 1672 "Defense of the Epilogue [of the second part of *The Conquest of Granada*]," and "our Playes" have benefited as a result.[14] These improvements include "rejecting such old words or phrases which are ill sounding, or improper": "any man who understands *English*," Dryden insists, "[has only to] read diligently the works of *Shakespear* and *Fletcher;* and I dare undertake that he will find, in every page either some Solecism of Speech, or some notorious flaw in Sence."[15] (Note the particularly textual—as opposed to theatrical—emphasis here: Dryden writes not of hearing the words spoken onstage but of "read[ing]" them "diligently.") Dryden then proceeds to delineate grammatical and syntactical infelicities on the part of Jonson (such as prepositions at the end of sentences, redundancies in phrasing, and so on),[16] adding (dubiously) that Jonson can hardly be blamed for not being familiar with the "Well placing of Words for the sweetness of pronunciation," which, after all, "was not known till Mr. *Waller* introduc'd it."[17]

Finally, Dryden attributes his own era's improvements in language to the superior "Conversation" of the Restoration—which he ascribes to the "easy and plyant . . . discourse" cultivated in Charles II's court.[18] "Conversation" and "discourse" would seem to imply an oral foundation for the Restoration's literary advantages. Indeed, as Harold Love has shown, for the aristocratic circle still exerting a considerable influence during the 1660s and 1670s, "writing was [thought to be] at its best when it mimicked the fluency and polish of the best upper-class conversation."[19] Specifically, Love adds, the "elegance and colloquial ease" of the court wits remained essential to Dryden's style.[20] For Dryden, however, writing was ultimately not a leisure activity but a career—requiring serious training and professionalism.[21] Accordingly, Dryden held up classicism—literature composed in languages that were, quite specifically, no longer spoken—as a new source of authority.[22] Love sees the "classicizing program" of Dryden's written prefaces in particular as working increasingly to challenge the literary-critical authority of the court, promoting textual expertise over informal conversation.[23] The improved "discourse" of Dryden's age, then, would seem to be informed by aristocratic elegance, but also strengthened by scholarly rigor. It is through these improvements in sound and sense—undertaken by those who "read diligently"—that Dryden proposes to build upon the verbal foundations of his playwright forefathers.

By contrast, Shadwell prioritizes the lived, social world—rather than textuality—as a conveyor of cultural knowledge. This focus can be seen in the famous controversy between the two playwrights over humors- versus wit-based comedy. Michael Alssid sums up the long-running quarrel by explaining that, whereas Dryden emphasized the mannered "wit" that he deemed the Restoration's primary verbal advantage, Shadwell "believed that comedy should represent, above all, a variety of characters" displaying different "humors," through which "the grotesqueness and silliness of the human spirit" might be revealed, and "such variety of characters could hardly be possible if the stage were given over primarily to fine ladies and gentlemen who were little more than mouthpieces for the playwright's clever style."[24] Not content merely to privilege humors over wit, however—or "spirit" over "style"—Shadwell actually makes the case, using Jonson as his touchstone, for a more expansive understanding of *wit* in the first place, one not limited to words alone: "I have known some of late so Insolent to say, that *Ben Johnson* wrote his best *Playes* without Wit; imagining, that all the Wit in *Playes* consisted in bringing two persons upon the Stage to break Jests, and to bob one another, which they call Repartie, not considering that there is more wit and invention requir'd in the finding out good Humor, and Matter proper for it, then [*sic*] in all their smart reparties."[25] Although Shadwell's stress here falls on the faculties of the playwright (the "wit . . . requir'd" to write good plays), another criterion hovers in the background—namely, that of a play's stageability: in the "Repartie"-centered plays that he describes, a sense of static artificiality prevails, so that "two persons" are "br[ought] . . . upon the Stage" like pawns or puppets. The witticisms that issue from their mouths may appear to require more sophistication than does the creation of colorful personae, but they actually betray a kind of superficiality that requires no spark of "invention" and that generates a lifeless theatrical experience. "Wit," then, is amplified, in Shadwell's account, from a mere facility with language into a specifically theatrical skill.

Shadwell proposes a similar redefinition of terms after Dryden complains of Jonson's "incorrect" language (recall Dryden's condemnation, in the "Defence of the Epilogue," of Jonson's grammatical idiosyncrasies): "I think flat and dull things are as incorrect, and shew as little Judgment in the Author, nay less[,] than sprightly and mettled Nonsense does," he declares in his Preface to the *Humorists* (1671).²⁶ "Correctness," here, has less to do with standards of language or logic than with vivacity or vigor ("sprightl[iness]," "mettle"). That which is "correct," it seems, is true to life, rather than true to the rules of grammar.

We have begun to see, then, how Shadwell, in opposition to Dryden, pursues a less explicitly verbal or linguistic approach to the Restoration's dramaturgical heritage, emphasizing theatricality and liveliness—or lifelikeness—over the textual lineage to which Dryden lays claim. To be sure, Shadwell seems as deeply invested as Dryden in bridging the gap of the Commonwealth period by invoking early century predecessors; however, continuity between the two eras will be provided not by written attributes alone but by an agile, lifelike representation of human foibles.

This is not to say that Dryden understood verbal skill to be the be-all and end-all of playwriting, either. Indeed, as Blair Hoxby has shown, much of Dryden's dramaturgy is premised on the recognition that words' power is limited.²⁷ Certainly, Dryden's famous defense of the use of rhymed verse in heroic tragedy suggests that he continued to see language—specifically, "literary" language—as central to these plays' effects. Yet, as Hoxby notes, if Dryden's heroic dramas leaned heavily on a "rhetoric of the passions," his "pathetic tragedies," including *Aureng-Zebe, All for Love,* and *Troilus and Cressida,* rely "on scenic tableaux of grief that employ gesture and posture to make their point": this more "baroque" theatrical mode, Hoxby contends, "presupposes that the body is a more reliable indicator of the soul's passions than are mere words."²⁸ Dianne Dugaw similarly finds that, especially starting in the 1680s, "Dryden's ... poetry and drama ... increasingly take on a pansensory, multimedia aspect, in which words are not enough."²⁹ As both Hoxby and Dugaw demonstrate, then, Dryden's work as a playwright draws heavily not just on rhetoric but on the power of visually striking scenes, dramatic spectacle, and emotionally laden body language.³⁰

As I set up my analysis of Shadwell's use of theatricality vis-à-vis textuality, however, I would note that Dryden's dramaturgical focus, as the aforementioned scholars affirm, remains centered on the singular, suspended, almost timeless moment. As Hoxby observes in regard to *Aureng-Zebe,* Dryden works to "freeze the passions momentarily in tableaux that, like many of Ovid's metamorphoses, seem to concentrate the meaning of the story in a gesture or pose that resembles a work of visual art."³¹ The play places little emphasis on "dramatic action" per se, prioritizing instead scenic effects that serve as a kind of punctuation for, or crystallization of, the work's larger themes.³² Theatricality in Dryden's plays may thus seek to exceed the reach of the word, but, as I will show in my reading of *The Lancashire Witches* and *The Squire of Alsatia,* Shadwell's use of theatricality—encompassing improvised sleights of hand, quick changes, and the adoption of multiple roles or masks—seems much more aimed at actively subverting any verbal stability.³³ If Dryden's use of theater seeks to supplement or heighten the effects of his plays' language by way of the iconic emblem, Shadwell taps into performance's shape-shifting qualities, its scrappy scavenging of previous material, in order to challenge the values of permanence and transcendence increasingly understood to go hand in hand with textuality in the age of print.

If Dryden's emphasis on language as the essence of the English dramatic tradition is somewhat belied by his plays' use of wordless spectacle, Shadwell's less overtly verbal or textual understanding of dramaturgical succession—and of successful comedy—also remains, in some sense, a pose. In many instances, in fact, Shadwell's uses of material from previous plays turn out to replicate those plays' phrasings almost word for word—though he never acknowledges as much. As Paulina Kewes observes, throughout his dramatic prefaces Shadwell "shuns the admission of verbal borrowing and harps on hints, subjects, themes, and plots."³⁴ These protestations seem to reflect a growing sense toward the end of the seventeenth century that "only plots (ideas, themes, sentiments) can be borrowed legitimately, whereas the language (style, words, expression) must be altered if the work is not to degenerate into literary theft."³⁵ (This emerging definition of plagiarism may also account for Dryden's insistence that he was not just incorporating wholesale but improving upon the language of his dramatic predecessors.³⁶) Interestingly, then, Shadwell may actually admire his dramaturgical forebears' verbal style just as much as Dryden does, but this admiration is expressed more in practice than in theory. Moreover, as we will see, while Dryden uses stylistic imitation as a way of laying claim to literary propriety and authority, Shadwell's stylistic echoes arguably become part of a stealth operation by which he undermines the era's incipient conceptions of literary authorship and ownership.

Just as Shadwell may be more verbally aware than he cares to admit, he also proves to be more textually sophisticated than his protestations would lead us to believe. Indeed, his works are often marked by distinctive textual features, beginning with the abundant dedications and prefaces we have already glimpsed here. I argue, therefore, that even as Shadwell rhetorically downplays textual forms of heritage, these remain a core element of his work. Where he departs from Dryden, then, is in how he makes use of this textual attentiveness: Shadwell turns to the textual not for the purpose of shoring up his own legitimacy but for the purpose of confronting the print canon with conventionally "illegitimate" modes—including theatricality, femininity, and alternative notions of property.

Shadwell's more unorthodox models of dramatic inheritance could be viewed as having not just dramaturgical but political implications. Any late seventeenth-century discussion of patrimony and succession would clearly have resonated with the era's larger controversies surrounding the question of monarchical succession—and, more broadly, of arbitrary government, primogeniture, and sovereignty. Indeed, the strands of illegitimacy and femininity that Shadwell introduces into traditional concepts of inheritance could be said to have their literal counterparts within the iconoclastic succession plans pursued by the Whigs during the Exclusion Crisis (1679–81) and the Glorious Revolution (1688): as the Whigs attempted to keep England out of the hands of Catholic rulers, they sought to displace the Stuarts next in line (Charles II's brother James, and, after him, his son) in favor of their Protestant kin—namely, Charles II's illegitimate son, the Duke of Monmouth (in a failed rebellion), and later (successfully) James II's own Protestant daughter, Mary.[37]

As Ronald Berman and John C. Ross have shown—and as I touch on briefly in the discussion to come—*The Squire of Alsatia* in particular seems to speak to the period's ideological conflicts over what may be passed from one generation to the next. Whether Shadwell was familiar with the work of John Locke or whether he simply "share[d] a common cultural position," as Berman puts it, *The Squire*—and, I think, *The Lancashire Witches*—appear steeped in late seventeenth-century philosophical debates over how much power a father (or king) can wield, and how much freedom his children (or subjects) may exercise in laying claim to—or creatively renegotiating—the institutions he upheld.[38] The political overtones of both plays suggest that, for Shadwell and his contemporaries, the terms of the debates surrounding traditional inheritance models could be applied to discussions of the past and future of an emergent English literature—but also to arguments over the status of the expanding empire whose identity that literature was helping to define and question.

In the remainder of this chapter, I examine two plays by Shadwell that center on problems of inheritance. In *The Lancashire Witches*, two neighboring landowners conspire to marry their daughters to each other's sons in an explicit attempt to cancel out the sons' loutish qualities and thus "restore the [family] breed" (1.171).³⁹ This attempt is spectacularly thwarted by the young women, in collaboration with their even more spectacularly mischievous counterparts in the play, the witches. *The Squire of Alsatia* returns to this problem of unfit male heirs as it depicts the hoodwinking and near ruin of a hapless young scion. The scion ultimately emerges with his estate intact, but due only to the intervention of his younger brother, who, significantly, was raised separately from his sibling: having been taken under the wing of their father's own younger brother, this next-generation younger brother learned a different set of skills—one that privileges improvisation over strict replication, as well as a theatrical or entrepreneurial sense of timing over the two elder brothers' insistence on the imperviousness of inherited wealth to the passage of time. In its consideration of the different priorities that the father and uncle have shown in educating their respective wards, the play raises questions regarding what Michael Alssid calls "the kind of ideological heritage that is passed on from generation to generation."⁴⁰

At the same time, both comedies "inherit" many of their fundamental features from previous plays. *The Lancashire Witches* derives its premise, certain phrasing, several incidents, and a handful of character names from Thomas Heywood and Richard Brome's *The Late Lancashire Witches* (1634), and it borrows much of its remarkable annotative apparatus—both the concept and much of its content—as well as some wording within the play, from Jonson's *Masque of Queenes* (1609). Shakespeare's *Macbeth* likewise provides inspiration, as do what Shadwell calls the various "Witchmongers" (both "ancient" and "Modern"), who, as he explains, have supplied him with much of his witches' language and rituals (Shadwell, *To the Reader*, lines 90–91). *The Squire of Alsatia*, meanwhile, takes its basic plotline from Terence's *Adelphi*, and several specific passages are based on dialogue from that play. Yet the extent to which Shadwell acknowledges these sources varies greatly, troubling the boundary between imitation and misappropriation, and between inheritance and theft.

Finally, both comedies utilize textual elements in ways that enrich and complicate the questions outlined above regarding patriarchal and literary structures of succession. In *The Lancashire Witches*, this is done in two ways: first, through elaborate citations framing the witches' conduct within the publications of various relevant "authorities"; and, second, through italicized passages highlighting once-censored and now-restored material (mostly concerning the Anglican chaplain Smerk, who to certain eyes must have seemed to bear too many similarities to the play's villainous Catholic Priest, the aptly named Tegue O'Divelly). In *The Squire of Alsatia,* the most notable textual feature is Shadwell's "Explanation of the Cant," which provides a gloss for some forty-five terms or expressions used by the play's law-evading underclass (the residents of "Alsatia," a section of London in which debtors and other criminals could not legally be apprehended). The textual apparatus in both plays, then, hovers problematically between a kind of authoritative surveillance—cutting through the witches' mystique to reveal Shadwell's sources, decoding London's underworld argot—and a darker, anti-authoritarian defiance, whereby Shadwell circumvents official attempts at censorship, cites "proof" for superstition and magic, and celebrates the piquancy of contemporary criminal discourse.

In all of these ways, both *The Lancashire Witches* and *The Squire of Alsatia* posit a dramaturgical lineage that, in contrast to Dryden's, emphasizes the theatrical as much as the verbal, and, concomitantly, offers up a subversive, disruptive mode of appropriation in place of a more orthodox patriarchal inheritance. Shadwell thus helps to shape a nascent dramatic canon that upends accepted notions of cultural authority and male institutions of power, proposing instead, I suggest, a literary tradition that can accommodate the excessive, the supernatural, the aberrant, and the feminine.[41]

The plot of *The Lancashire Witches* can be said to focus on the problem of ancient aristocratic modes of male succession. On the one hand, the play is rooted in a nostalgia for a traditional England, the "Golden days of Queen Elizabeth" (3.5–8). In an essay on the play's political leanings, Jessica Munns explains that the Whigs of this era had claimed Elizabeth as a "potent political signifier"—namely, as "the English, Protestant Queen who defeated the Catholic, Spanish Armada and whose 'Golden' reign had been followed by that of the current Stuart monarchy with their foreign wives, foreign ways, and closet Catholicism."[42] As Munns points out, food and drink often served as "an emblem of moral character" in such rhetoric,[43] and indeed, Shadwell's play contains scenes in which his dramatis personae wax nostalgic for the days when "great Tables were kept in large Halls[,] the Buttery-hatch [was] always open," and the house was filled with "a good smell of Meat and March-beer" (3.28–31). Here the "lusty Appetites" of the English are implicitly contrasted with the effeminate, finical tastes of continental Europe (3.23), and the emphasis on plain, locally produced victuals (butter, meat, beer) likewise celebrates the English soil and English countryside. These values are seemingly epitomized in the character of Sir Edward Hartfort, whom Shadwell describes as "a worthy Hospitable true English Gentleman, of good understanding, and honest Principles" (dramatis personae, lines 1–3). Such principles are shown to be all the more precious in light of the imminent threat posed to them by Tegue O'Divelly, the play's lecherous, satanic Irish Priest, who is directly associated, in both the play's title and its action, with the witches.[44]

On the other hand, this traditional way of life is shown to be rapidly crumbling, perhaps due to inherent weaknesses: Sir Edward Hartfort's son and heir, Young Hartfort, is, according to the dramatis personae, "a Clownish, sordid, Country Fool, that loves nothing but drinking Ale, and Country Sports," most notably hunting and hawking (lines 4–6). In a sense, Young Hartfort represents everything that is pointless and obsolete about the vision of "Meat and March-beer" for which his father would seem to be a walking advertisement. The crisis of inheritance posed by this boorish progeny is overtly addressed in act 1, as Sir Edward expresses his dismay over his son's failure to interest himself in anything other than "Dogs and Horses, Peasants, Ale and Sloth," and, accordingly, his fear that the family "name [will] perish in him" (1.164, 1.174). Indeed, the play's main plotline could be said to center on this very problem: Sir Edward arranges to "match the unhewn Clown / To the fair Daughter of [neighboring landowner] Sir *Jeffery Shacklehead*," Theodosia, "who has all the perfections [that] can be wish'd / In woman-kind, and might restore the breed" (1.168–71). In order to make this bad bargain more palatable, Sir Edward sets up what he calls a "cross match," agreeing that his own daughter, the equally witty and beautiful Isabella, will be given in marriage to Sir Jeffery's son, Sir Timothy—another heir who, if not quite as hopeless as Young Hartfort, is nonetheless a "very pert [and] confident" yet exceedingly "simple Fellow" (dramatis personae, lines 10–12).

The play opens, then, with a situation in which the continuation of the two patriarchs' ancient family names and the consolidation of their ancient family estates (via the joining of the Hartfort and Shacklehead properties) are shown to depend entirely on the families' daughters. But these daughters—predictably—refuse to cooperate with their fathers' arrangements. They initially declare that, rather than settle for each other's doltish brothers, they will "be Husband and Wife to one another"—a plan that would certainly turn the old patriarchal system on its head (1.277). Needless to say, this plan does not come to pass. Or, at least, it does not come to pass at the play's most literal level: this initial female covenant, in combination with the local witches' coven, does enable the women to aid each other in a second strategy—namely, to marry two cosmopolitan young men, Bellfort and Doubty, whom they've recently met "at the *Spaw*" in the coastal town of Scarborough. They thereby circumvent their fathers' wishes, and the land-based power structure that those wishes represent (1.277–78). For despite Bellfort and Doubty's apparent subscription to a nostalgic, nationalist vision of England—they praise Sir Edward's hospitality as reminiscent of a time before the gentry were "grown Servile Apes to Forreign customes" (3.6–7; and see, more generally, 3.1–64)—their frequent allusions to sea travel, imperial conquests, and knight-errantry (all of which they mention only after Sir Edward is no longer within earshot) imply a much more flexible, less spatially circumscribed understanding of their British heritage (see, for example, 2.377, 2.379, 2.341, 2.398, 4.616).

Meanwhile, the play's male heirs, Young Hartfort and Sir Timothy, are essentially dropped both from the marriage scheme and from the plot of the play. No alternative matches are produced for them: act 5 ends with Sir Timothy threatening to "run mad, and hang myself and walk" (5.644), while Young Hartfort declares he "had rather not marry" anyway (5.660). In both cases, the male line seems to break off rather abruptly. Significantly, by contrast, Sir Edward has called Isabella the "truest Image / Of thy dead Mother," thus suggesting that, if anything, Isabella bears the marks of a matrilineal inheritance (1.141–42). The resignation expressed in Sir Edward's final speech may therefore most accurately express the state of patriarchal estate planning in the play: "Be ne're so wise, design what e're we will / There is a Fate that over-rules us still" (5.700–701).

The force that Sir Edward shruggingly attributes to "Fate," however, is actually being exerted by a much less comforting form of the supernatural—namely, the black magic practiced by the play's witches. And it is in these witches that the threat to land-based patrilineage is most vividly embodied. The witches help undermine the patriarchs' plans for their daughters by conjuring a storm that gives Bellfort and Doubty an excuse to shelter in the Hartforts' home; they then create such chaos in the household that the young women can play their own tricks with impunity—pelting Young Hartford and Sir Timothy with stones, boxing their ears, and kicking chairs out from under them, all the while insisting the men are victims of sorcery. By act 4 the witches have generated such fear that Isabella and Theodosia need only to dress up as witches in order to gain complete freedom of movement about the property, which allows them to marry their lovers in secret.

But, as this description implies, only a small part of the witches' function in the play bears on the plot: much of their import lies in the metaphorical resonances they enable. Most obviously, in helping Isabella and Theodosia thwart their fathers and brothers, the witches become closely associated with the young women. Indeed, as the two friends play tricks on their intended husbands and beguile their preferred suitors, the witches' simultaneous spells and seductions—the chief witch, Mother Demdike, fools the Irish Priest into sleeping with her at the same time that the young women are arranging their covert marriages to their lovers—suggest that the witches may be seen as direct analogues to their young comedic counterparts. Such analogies extend farther, too: to the Hartforts' maid, Susan, and to the leering Lady Shacklehead, both of whom are casting their own spells, as it were, on the men on whom they've set their sights. Thus, the witches' presence not only helps derail the play's immediate structures of male inheritance but suggests, at a figural level, that such structures are likewise under threat from "ordinary" women who know their own minds and can use sexuality to control the men in their midst.

Traditional male inheritance is further undermined by the symbolically evocative language in which the witches describe their antics, a language that frequently alludes to perverse or inverted cycles of reproduction. The witches depict themselves as gathering up "screech-owls eggs" and "sail[ing] in Egg-shells"; they collect "that which falls from a mares Womb / When she's in Lust" along with the "flesh from a black Foles head, / Just as his Dam was brought to Bed" (3.611, 2.505, 2.490–91, 2.487–88). They claim to manufacture flying ointment from dead babies' fat, to "suc[k] the breth and blood" from as-yet-unchristened newborns, and to "*Cause barrenness where e're we will,*" gleefully slaying "Brat[s] in the[ir] Mothers' Wombs" (2.447, 2.517, 2.466). Not only do they gruesomely impede the usual course of procreation, however; the witches pursue alternative modes of generation as well—modes that, significantly, do not involve men: they lift "cry[ing]" mandrake roots from the earth and fashion human effigies from "wool and wax" (1.436, 2.607). These acts of creation blur the line between human and non-human, and between life and death (2.443): the witches raid "Charnel houses," "Graves," and "Tombs," amassing "Sinews and shrunk Veins. / Marrow and Entrails," "And the blood of murder'd men" (2.461, 2.473, 2.453–54, 2.475).

Although most of these activities are ostensibly performed in service to the Devil—a figure of masculine authority—many of them also invoke either literal or symbolic castration: the witches recount how they've gleaned "from dead mens Eyes the glewy Stuff, / Their Eye-balls with [their] nailes scoop'd out / And pieces of their Limbs [have] brought" (2.463–65). Their trophies likewise include severed "Fingers" and "Noses," in addition to "A Wolfs ... Yard," or penis (2.444, 2.474, 2.484). Moreover, the witches' pranks seem aimed as much at their own satisfaction as the Devil's; the scene just described ends with the witches dancing and singing, celebrating their power and liberty:

> *What joy like ours can mortals find?*
> *We can command the Sea and Wind...*
> *We Sail in Egg-shells on rough Seas,*
> *And see strange Countries when we please!*
> ....
> *When we're on Wing, we sport and play,*
> *Mankind, like Emmets, we survey.* (2.495–515)

Indeed, the Devil seems less a stern supervisor than an indulgent patron sponsoring these terpsichorean revels: he reacts to their boasted accomplishments not with brisk nods of approval but with jolly guffaws ("Ho, ho, ho" [2.459, 2.469, 2.482, 2.494]); the witches may refer to him as their *"Master the Prince of the Flies, / Who commands from Center all up to the Skies"* (2.520–21), but his role remains distinctly passive, less patriarchal than avuncular.

To the extent that Shadwell's witches short-circuit traditional modes of inheritance—engaging in spectacular acts of creation that largely spurn any overarching legacy or institution—they may serve as apt figurations of Shadwell himself. For while Shadwell's deployment of the works of his predecessors appears at first to limit his witches'—and his own—powers of subversion and theatricality, his play ends up exceeding these sources, exposing their shortcomings, and turning them on their heads.

I will start with Shadwell's acknowledged sources. In his preface to the reader, he writes,

> For the Magical part, I had no hopes of equalling Shakespear in fancy, who created his Witchcraft for the most part out of his own imagination (in which faculty no man ever excell'd him) and therefore I resolved to take mine from Authority. And to that end, there is not one action in the Play, nay scarce a word concerning it, but is borrowed from some antient, or Modern Witchmonger. Which you will find in the notes, wherein I have presented you a great part of the Doctrine of Witchcraft, beleive it who will. For my part, I am (as it is said of Surly in the Alchymist) somewhat costive of beleif. The evidences I have represented are natural, viz. slight, and frivolous, such as poor old Women were wont to be hang'd upon. (Lines 85–96)

These invocations of "Shakespear" and "antient, or Modern Witchmonger[s]" would seem to insist on both the witches' and Shadwell's harmlessness. If the witches are nothing but figments of imagination, and if Shadwell's own powers of imagination pale in comparison to those of both previous playwrights and witch-hunting zealots, then it seems that the play's supernatural actions are mere echoes of echoes. Likewise, the "Authority" Shadwell openly cites from the "Witchmongers"—in an extensive system of endnotes and margin notes, tracing the witches' magical rites and recipes to Roman-era poets and Renaissance-era demonologists—serves not to justify or even testify to the witches' magic but to assert its textual (or metatextual) basis, and to emphasize Shadwell's own skeptical remove (for someone so "costive of beleif" must necessarily rely on others to supply the "Magical part"). For example—to cite only two of Shadwell's thirteen endnotes to the first act, all crammed into a single, densely printed page—the witches' use of spindles or spinning wheels is traced to Martial, Lucan, Ovid, and Propertius, and precedent for their scraping of holes with their fingernails is drawn from Horace, as well as from Heinrich Kramer's *Malleus Maleficarum* (1487), Jean Bodin's *Demonomanie* (1580), Nicholas Rémy's *Demonolatreiae* (1595), and Martin Delrio's *Disquisitiones Magicae* (1599 and 1600), among others ("Notes upon the Magick," notes *b* and *d*). Such annotations—and Shadwell's prefatory remarks concerning them—thus appear to create a situation in which the witches' spectacular volatility in the play is rendered lifeless or static, tethered to a list of dry textual tradition.

The preface's very next paragraph, however, immediately contradicts such reassurances: "For the actions, if I had not represented them as those of real Witches, but had show'd the ignorance, fear, melancholy, malice, confederacy, and imposture that contribute to the beleif of Witchcraft, the people had wanted diversion, and there had been another clamor against it, it would have been call'd Atheistical, By a prevailing party who take it ill that the power of the Devil should be lessen'd" (lines 97–103). If the previous passage had suggested that the play's supernatural elements were merely copies of copies, here Shadwell acknowledges that these elements are also real within the world of the play. Though Shadwell has just finished casting himself as a skeptic, he now appears intent on providing "diversion" at the cost of a more principled exposure of ignorance. For all his citing of "Authority" a moment ago, it now emerges that he is equally if not more concerned about the desires of "the people." Indeed, in his preface's first paragraph Shadwell explains that "the reason of my introducing of Witches" was "to make as good an entertainment as I could, without tying my self up to the strict rules of a Comedy" (lines 8–10). Shadwell's use of the witches, in short, far from establishing his reliance on the texts of other authors, actually provides him with a method of bucking literary convention and prioritizing popular illusion and amusement above all. (Indeed, the play is considered to be the earliest of Dorset Garden's famous "machine farces," and no doubt the witches offered many opportunities to showcase the theater's cutting-edge staging capacities: John Downes described it as "having several *Machines* of Flyings for the Witches, and other Diverting Contrivances in't."[45])

How does this rhetorical pivot on Shadwell's part change our understanding of how he uses his sources? The quotation just cited may prove the most telling in this regard: "For the actions, if I had not represented them as those of real Witches . . . , [the play] *would have been call'd Atheistical*." Here Shadwell contends that to represent his play's black magic as fictitious would be to risk undermining the existence of the ultimate Author of all. Consequently—perversely, and in contrast to the asseverations he has just finished making—the more powerful his witches become, the stronger the claim he can make for his play's conformity to the one true, universal "Authority." In a similarly perverse twist, Shadwell's own moral credentials—his status as no "Atheist"—are no longer proven by the fact that he is simply recycling others' fancies, but, rather, by his own force of impresarial imagination. As we will see, the witches' "real" existence derives not from the lore he has lifted from the work of others (namely, the details of the witches' potions, spells, and rituals) but from the fact that Shadwell has thoroughly integrated them into the rest of the play as a play—has expanded their presence beyond mere set pieces and managed to assimilate them into what is otherwise, in many ways, a typical Restoration comedy.

In other words, by executing this fleet-footed reversal in his preface, Shadwell begins to redefine authority. If "Authority" at first seemed to refer to ancient and modern predecessors in print, it is now associated with theatrical spectacle. If moral rectitude initially appeared to depend on skepticism, it is now proven by an active imagination—one that works in concert, significantly, with principles of popular entertainment. And if the work of textual scholarship and annotation seemed, a moment ago, effectively to counteract the power of female witches, it now seems that this apparatus exists merely to be cast aside, or overwhelmed, by "real" witches, whose theatrical presence adds up to much more than the sum of their textual parts.

Shadwell's revised definition of authority is further revealed in the way he uses those textual sources that he does not acknowledge (indeed, this nonacknowledgement is itself evidence of Shadwell's subversive redefinition). These unacknowledged sources may include Thomas Potts's *The Wonderfull Discoverie of Witches in the Countie of Lancaster* (1613), an account of the 1612 witch trials that had taken place in Lancashire, centering on a woman named Demdike,[46] and Heywood and Brome's *The Late Lancashire Witches*,[47] which many scholars have deemed almost journalistic in its faithful treatment of another witch-related, Lancashire-based scare in 1633–34.[48]

If, as Shadwell initially claims, his goal in the play is to satirize superstition, then surely a reference to the actual persecution of witches in Lancashire would aid him in his purpose: such a reference could point his audience to the practical consequences of fantasy and delusion, while advertising the playwright's own avoidance of these. By not mentioning the historical context, however (and the texts that surround it), Shadwell gives the impression that the witches (if not their every spell, potion, and rite) are essentially of his own making, thus implicitly celebrating (and boasting of) the very powers of fantasy that he claims to disown. Of course, the irony is that Shadwell actually does hew closely to his sources, and does so on a specifically textual level, lifting not just basic concepts or premises but proper names (Demdike, Doughty, etc.), phrases,[49] and even rhyming words (e.g., "duggy"/"puggy," used when the Devil-turned-dog sucks at the witches' teats).[50] A topsy-turvy dynamic emerges here, in which Shadwell claims a textual lineage at one level, implicitly disavows it at another level, but then—at yet another level—also participates in it surreptitiously. In short, sources are acknowledged only where they can best serve a protective role, and only to the extent that they do not detract from Shadwell's own claims to dramaturgical imagination.[51]

This complex position can be discerned most clearly, perhaps, in Shadwell's use of Jonson. Although Shadwell alludes to Jonson's *Alchemist* in his preface, this reference serves as a kind of red herring.[52] His real debt to Jonson consists in his extensive borrowings from both the main text of, and the annotations to, Jonson's 1609 *Masque of Queenes,* which, of course, go unmentioned: Borgman traces some twenty-seven of "the learned comments" in the endnotes to Jonson, many of which are taken essentially verbatim, suggesting that Shadwell had "an open copy of the *Masque of Queenes* before him" while writing[53]; in addition, many of the witches' incantations directly echo those of Jonson's witches.[54] Not only do the unacknowledged borrowings from Jonson serve as yet another illustration of Shadwell's privileging of appropriation over inheritance, but the particular way in which he uses these borrowings helps to reveal—perhaps more clearly than any other piece of evidence—the transgressive (rather than dutiful) ways in which Shadwell engages with authority.

As much scholarship has documented, Ben Jonson himself seems to have associated textuality—as opposed to theatricality—with authorial control. The playwright's heavily annotated masques, in particular, have been viewed as deploying scholarly citation as a way of staking a claim to authority. As Evelyn B. Tribble writes, "Ben Jonson's career can be read as a series of attempts to exploit the potential of the press to order and contain."[55] In the case of *The Masque of Queenes*—for which, as with most of his masques, Jonson marshals the full force of "the humanist page, with its battery of marginal notes and Latin glosses"[56]—this effort to "order and contain" begins with the textual assertion of ownership. Tribble explains that "any number of parties could be said to have interests" in court masques: "the king, the queen, the prince, the masquers, the buyers of the printed masque." *The Masque of Queenes,* according to a warrant issued by James for expenditures toward the production, came about after "The Queene our dearest wife ... resolved for our greater honor and contentment to make us a masque this Christmas."[57] However, in a move that quickly becomes part of a recurring pattern, Jonson usurps this female act of "mak[ing]" by "repackaging the masque on the ... page and presenting [it] to the court as his gift."[58] Indeed, Jonson casts the citations themselves less as outside sources than as refractions of his own internalized, consummate knowledge: in his dedication to Prince Henry, he describes "retrieu[ing] the particular *authorities* ... to those things, w[hi]ch I writt ovt of fullnesse, and memory of my former readings."[59] Finally, the annotations will protect the masque from readers' rival interpretive claims: Jonson writes that the notes will serve to "decline the stiffness of others originall Ignorance, already armed to censure."[60]

As Lynn Sermin Meskill has demonstrated, these same concerns regarding ownership and fame—particularly, the safeguarding of these against the forces of femininity and ill will—constitute major themes within *The Masque of Queenes* itself. Essentially, the masque celebrates King James's heroic rise to power in spite of "the witches and queens who once threatened his accession": James's triumph owed to "the death of a powerful queen with no heir [Elizabeth] and ... a beheaded mother [Mary Stuart]," and had ostensibly come to pass only after a "self-publicized rescue from a group of witches."[61] At the same time, Meskill contends, the masque metaphorically depicts Jonson's own rise to fame in spite of similar threats: "in both cases," Meskill adds, "the problem of 'succession' is at issue,"[62] and both men are able to take up their rightful succession only after thwarting the "envy," or evil-eye, associated with female power and willful acts of misreading.

Accordingly, the plotline of *The Masque of Queenes* bears witness to several competing types of creation and self-constitution. On the one hand, Jonson's witches, "midwives to 'Dame Earth,'" are "involved in a frustrating and antithetical process of midwifery": having "gathered exotic ingredients and materials," the witches "bury ... them in the ground [and] hope [thereby] to give birth to something new"; however, "their effort ends in abject failure and rage."[63] This attempt is then abruptly "cut off and completed by a male figure, referred to as 'Heroic Virtue,' who ... gives birth to his own Fame."[64] By thus representing the Athena-like "birth of Fame out of her male parent," the masque evokes "the male fantasy of reproduction without women."[65]

The annotations, Meskill explains, help to extend this project of fending off envious, effeminate bids for power: "By erecting a barricade of ancient authorities, . . . the writer can hide himself from the envious gaze of judging posterity."[66] The notes thus become a "monument" or "emblem" that replaces the more accretive "romance"- or "narrative"-based forms of creation that the witches symbolize.[67]

By contrast, Shadwell may borrow wording, scholarly sources, and even the very concept of annotation from *The Masque of Queenes*—but in doing so he departs radically from Jonson's ideological project. Indeed, his borrowing is perhaps less an homage than a hijacking. Rather than distinguishing himself from his witches, he aligns his work with theirs, and rather than depicting the women's performances as thwarted and futile, he represents them as abetting his own theatrical creativity: recall that the witches' dancing and chanting bolster his efforts to "make as good an entertainment as I could," while their shape-shifting and gravity-defying antics allow him to refuse to "ty . . . my self up to the strict rules of a Comedy" (Shadwell, "To the Reader," lines 8–9). Moreover, if Jonson's annotations are intended as a barricade and lasting "monument," Shadwell intentionally exposes his own apparatus as awkward and inflexible, unable to keep up with the witches' more insidious effects.

A detailed look at *The Lancashire Witches'* patterns of annotation will illustrate how Shadwell rejects Jonson's association of textuality with authority. Perhaps the clearest example of how Shadwell uses his citations to reveal textuality's limits can be seen in his references to the "Witchmongers." These quoted sources appear initially to fence in the witches' power, but they turn out to possess several blind spots when it comes to accounting fully for the women's influence in the play. As already mentioned, the witches perform various spells and ceremonies throughout; these tend to be concentrated at the end of each of the first three acts, and include generating a storm, bringing together various offerings to the Devil, and initiating a new witch, Madge, into their ranks. All of these activities are thoroughly annotated. Yet, as we have seen, the witches' influence in the play extends beyond the structural bounds of these capstone scenes, and infects the behavior of several of the play's non-witch characters. To some extent, these behaviors are also annotated, but where the witches' influence is arguably most dangerous, the apparatus seems almost conspicuously absent.

Among the non-witch characters, Shadwell's annotations tend to cling most frequently to the words and actions of Tegue O'Divelly and the Hartforts' maid, Susan. For example, the various bizarre antidotes to witchcraft offered up by the Priest—he advises the Shackleheads (in his exaggerated Irish accent) to avail themselves of "Conjur'd shalt" and "shome Holy-Wax" as defenses against the witches, and to "spit three times upon deir Boshomes, and Cross demselves" (5.445–46, 5.450–51)—are shown in Shadwell's notes to appear in Heinrich Kramer, Tibullus, Theocritus, and Theophrastus. Susan's enumeration of the lengths to which she has gone to seduce the household's protestant chaplain, Smerk—including putting her "Hair and Nails in Powder in [his] Drink" and placing "a live Fish in a part about me till it died, and then [giving] it [to him] to eat" (2.134–36)—likewise receives annotation (in an asterisk prefacing the "Notes upon the Second Act"[68]). It is not only through his textual apparatus, then, but also through verbal parallels—the "Hair and Nails" used in the aphrodisiac, as well as the "Holy-Wax," echo the ingredients of the witches' spells, which include "Wolves Hairs" and "Wax and Wooll"[69]—that Shadwell draws a link between the witches' black magic and these characters' corrupt, distinctly irreligious, bids for power. The Priest combines Christian symbolism with sorcery in a kind of unholy amalgam (crossing himself, but also spitting—and doing so "three times," a number central both to Christianity and to magic), and Susan uses the power of her body to seduce a man as supposedly spiritual as the chaplain. (As further proof of the connections between the witches and O'Divelly, in particular, a character declares in act 4 that "I do not know what to think of his Popish way, his Words, his Charms, and Holy Water, and Relicks, methinks he is guilty of Witchcraft too" [4.299–301].)

O'Divelly and Susan remain on the margins of the play's main plot, however, and where the witches' connections to the non-witch characters prove most central—and most consequential—the annotations either cease altogether or, in one case, function in the wrong way. As stated earlier, the words and deeds of Isabella and Theodosia, like those of Susan and O'Divelly, can be seen as direct extensions of the witches' own. If the Maid's and Priest's bizarre rituals echo those involved in the witches' charms, then Isabella's and Theodosia's physical brutalization of their would-be suitors mirror the witches' attacks on all of the play's male characters. The young women may not metamorphose into cats and attack Sir Timothy and Young Hartfort until their faces are "all of a gore blood" (5.298), but by dragging Sir Timothy by the ears and pelting him with stones, or yanking a chair out from under Young Hartfort (acts that end up being erroneously blamed on Mother Demdike and her coven [4.10, 4.75–76]), the young women practice an over-the-top, slapstick violence closely akin to the witches'.

These similarities extend not just to the women's actions, moreover, but also (as with the Priest and the Maid) to their language. Isabella declares that Sir Timothy has "a hollow Tooth would Cure the Mother beyond *Arsa fetida* or burnt Feathers" (2.318–19). His face, she says, appears to have "Rickets," so that it approximates the "Lines and air of a Piggs face": she adds that "*Baptista Porta*"—or Giambattista della Porta, a Renaissance physiognomist—"would have drawn thee so" (2.302–5). So hideous is Sir Timothy's visage, she claims, that it "would give a vomit beyond *Crocus* . . . to one [who was] fasting" (2.325–26); indeed, it is "uglier than any Witch in Lancashire" (2.308). Interestingly, although Isabella refers directly to the witches here, she does so in order to draw a parallel between them and Sir Timothy, not herself. And yet, of course, her vocabulary mirrors that of the witches' ritual offerings and incantations. Her references to various forms of bodily decay (hollow teeth, rickets) call to mind the charnel-house corpses and dead infants from which the witches collect the ingredients for their magic. At the same time, her mention of medicinal herbs—asafetida, crocus—recalls the witches' frequent references to botanical pharmacology (including smallage, nightshade, poplar leaves, aromatic reed, water parsnip, cinquefoil, aconite, seaweed, henbane, hemlock, moonwort, fig tree, cypress, and yew [3.588–605]). In addition, Isabella's allusion to "Cur[ing] the Mother"—asafetida and other remedies were used to treat postpartum women—fits well with the witches' repeated references to fertility and childbirth. Finally, Giambattista della Porta, in addition to practicing physiognomy, worked as a magician (and, interestingly, in a connection that may bind Shadwell himself even more closely to his witches, as a playwright). Yet no annotations track Isabella's language here, as if her invective were merely the witty rallying—the "pretty jest[ing]" (1.246)—of the "dear little Rogue" Sir Timothy tries to believe she is (2.292).

In short, Shadwell initially appears to have contained or tamped down the witches' power through his annotative apparatus: their magic, he repeatedly suggests, is not truly their own—much less his own—rather, it derives from textual sources, many of which are the work of "demonologists" and others whose goal, throughout the centuries, has been to pin down and circumscribe the apparently uncanny capabilities wielded by women. Thus, every time a witch mentions an animal or plant—every time a witch murmurs a spell or plans a prank—Shadwell cites several precedents, from Johannes Wier's *De Lamiis* to Virgil's *Eclogues, Georgics,* and *Aeneid;* and from Ovid's *Metamorphoses* to Horace's *Epodes*. But what Shadwell's apparatus does not track—even as it seems to pose much more of an actual danger to the patriarchal order within the play—is the way in which the witches' power seeps into the young women's speech and actions. Isabella's language here is eerily conversant with the same concepts of a darkly insurrectionary natural world, of debased and manipulated bodies, and of beings on the threshold of life and death. Indeed, Isabella's own waywardness proves much more of a blow to male power structures in the end, as she ultimately chooses her own marriage partner, and thus dictates the future of the family line, in spite of her father's wishes; in contrast, the witches themselves are carted away. However, whereas Shadwell keeps detailed annotative track of the witches' mutinous ways, Isabella's parallel conduct is allowed to float free of any editorial supervision.

Isabella and Theodosia are not the only central characters who show signs of the witches' influence: the witches seem to affect even those characters who would appear (at least initially) to stand against everything the witches represent. Isabella's lover Bellfort, for example, spends the play speculating detachedly about what might be causing the locals to believe in the witches' existence, refusing to assign a supernatural explanation to even the strangest events: upon his and Doubty's arrival on the Hartforts' land, the estate's retainer, Clod, falls from a treetop, where he had been placed by the witches; his exclamations about the witches' involvement, however, are dismissed by the young men, who remark how odd it is that someone would be climbing a tree on a stormy night, and wonder aloud if Clod is mad or drunk (although, perhaps tellingly, Bellfort's first response upon seeing the poor man is "What [the] Devil" [1.566]). Likewise, when several local men gather later in the play to testify to the witches' various misdeeds, Bellfort declares, "'Tis so extravagant, that a man would think they were all in Dreams that ever writ of it" (3.504–5).

Strikingly, though, at other points in the play Bellfort's own language approximates O'Divelly's, who, as we have seen, is very much implicated in the play's black magic. For instance, one of the Priest's anti-witchcraft recipes calls for "Taak[ing] one of de Tooths of a dead man ... and burn[ing] it, and taak[ing] de smoke into both your Noses, as you taak Snufh" (3.412–19), a gruesome prospect that Shadwell's margin note (citing a similar remedy in Reginald Scot's *Discoverie of Witchcraft* [1584]) hastens to defuse. However, when Bellfort teases Sir Timothy by describing his customary treatment of romantic rivals, using strangely similar (and almost equally bizarre) terms—"I rip out their Hearts, dry 'em to Powder, and make Snuff on 'em.... I have a box full in my pocket Sir, wil you please to take some"—the remark is left to stand on its own (3.197). Indeed, Sir Timothy's deadpan reply—"I will have nothing to do with such a cruel man"—does not so much reveal him to be lacking a sense of humor as it reveals Bellfort to possess a rather macabre notion of what is apparently meant to be clever raillery (3.200–201).

Even more directly than that of O'Divelly, however, Bellfort's language recalls the witches'—especially their collections of body parts (Bellfort's "rip[ped] out Hearts" echoing the "Marrow and Entrails," "Bones" and "Eyeballs" that the witches gather) and their anthropophagic recipes (Bellfort's heart-derived snuff, soon to be inhaled through the nasal passages, brings to mind, for example, the "Drink" that the witches concoct from the boiled-down "flesh and fat" of "unchristen'd Brat[s]" [2.456–51]).[70] But whereas the witches' words are hedged with textual precedents, we are left to conclude, somewhat unnervingly, that Bellfort's speech originates simply from his own bizarre imagination—or, perhaps more unnervingly, that his imagination has been infected by a power untouched and unnoticed by the text's apparatus.

Such a suggestion becomes particularly troubling in the context of the young suitors' rhetoric of romance, which, while generally conforming to clichés of courtly love, occasionally veers into more surreal territory. Bellfort, for example, exclaiming to Doubty over his depth of feeling for Isabella, describes his "excess of Joy" as so extreme as to have "become a pain[:] I cannot bear it" (4.507–8); "My Blood is chill," he adds, "and shivers when I think on [Isabella]" (4.511). Later, when Sir Edward learns that the couples have married in secret, Bellfort seeks to exonerate himself by saying that, "had there been any other way for me to have escap't perpetual misery, I had not taken this [way]." Doubty likewise confirms, "I must have perisht if I had not done it" (5.652–56). Again, while suffering and dying for love are common enough tropes, the level of desperation expressed here is striking, and the oddly specific physiological symptoms—"chill[ed]" and "shiver[ing]" blood—suggest that Smerk is not the only man in the play whose inclinations have been affected by love potions and black magic. Compare Smerk's similar complaints of mortal pains and violent changes in temperature after drinking Susan's "admirable... Caudle" [3.305]: "I am all on fire.... [I] burn in love.... A minutes absence is death to me.... I am struck in my Bowels.... I have a Thousand Needles in me.... Oh! I dye, I dye, oh, oh" (4.203–61). Smerk's language is more graphic, but it expresses the same basic conceit. Here, then, even the part of the play that seems most conventional and straightforward—the lovers' marriage representing, of course, the classic comic ending—carries the taint of the witches' effects.

In sum, the witches arguably contaminate characters and plotlines where they otherwise seem to have no place. But whereas the notes keep track of the witches' actions, they fail to capture their larger, second-degree effects, possibly suggesting a larger failure of textual authority—namely, the failure to rein in the witches' theatrical, subversive impact. This shortfall is perhaps illustrated most clearly through Sir Edward Hartfort. Despite apparently symbolizing everything in the play that is most patriotic and patriarchal, at moments Sir Edward speaks a language that echoes the witches' lexicon. When, for instance, Sir Edward learns that his son plans to go hawking on the morning of his intended wedding day, the otherwise even-tempered patriarch—he elsewhere explains that he "call[s] Philosophy to [his] aid" when having to face his son's recurring stupidities—launches into a rant whose level of descriptive detail seems oddly off key:

> Thou most incorrigible Ass..., to have a good Estate setled upon thee, and to be married to a woman of... Beauty,... Wit and Wisdom..., would have transported any one but such a clod of Earth as thou art: thou art an excrement broken from me, not my Son.... [S]uch drones serve not the ends of their Creation, and should be lopt off from the rest of men.... Thou most excessive blockhead, thou art enough to imbitter all my sweets; thou art a Wen belonging to me, and I shall do well to cut thee off. (5.375–97)

Interestingly, this language will be echoed in *The Squire of Alsatia,* when Sir William finally realizes the extent of his eldest son's prodigality: "I look upon this Rascal as an Excrement, a Wen, or Gangren'd Limb, lop't off" (5.3.23–24). Perhaps, then, a vocabulary of growth gone wrong—of disease and disfigurement—is simply the lens through which Shadwell views patrilineal inheritance in late seventeenth-century England. Yet, specifically within the context of *The Lancashire Witches*, these images of excess matter ("drones" or "wen[s]") being "lopt off" or "cut . . . off" from its living source may be said to directly evoke the witches, with their collections of hair, nails, dogs' foam, and urine, as well as their harvesting of severed extremities (including, in fact, "Fingers, Noses, and a Wen" [2.474]).

Such parallels would seem to suggest the witches' role as a kind of subconscious for the play's more standard comic characters—as a dark, suppressed fantasy, perhaps even a kind of Freudian id. Indeed, this connection may prove more relevant in regard to Sir Edward than to the women of the play: the young women, to be sure, make the most strategic use of the witches' presence, and even become witch-like themselves to varying degrees of literalness, but they do so only in pursuit of a particular goal (marriage to the men of their choice); once this goal is reached, the women may presumably move on, reabsorbed into the traditional structures of comic closure. The same might be said of their suitors. In the case of Sir Edward, however, no comic closure is forthcoming: yes, by the end of act 5 his daughter has married a "m[a]n of ample Fortune and worthy Famil[y]"; his own male heir, however, has been "lopt off" from both the family and the plot. Like the witches, then, Sir Edward must look to alternative means of reproducing and continuing himself—means that now depend entirely on a (transgressive) female body. It seems no coincidence, therefore, that the witches have been holding their revelries in Sir Edward's cellar (as indicated at 2.430): in many ways, they represent the subterranean desires and anxieties, the internal chaos, haunting the play's most archetypal patriarch.

Understanding the witches as a kind of subconscious to the men in the play may help us to analyze not only the operations (and limits) of the play's annotative system but also the manner in which texts are wielded within the world of the play itself. Repeatedly within the play (as in the apparatus), we find men using texts with confidence but without control—a failure that, again, owes at least partly to the fact that the witches influence the men in ways that they cannot (or will not) discern. The causes behind the breakdown of male textual authority within the play, moreover, may add another layer to this complex gender dynamic: not only does female power constitute the blind spot in the men's use of texts, but it actually reveals the men's texts to be insightful in ways that the men do not (consciously) realize. Just as importantly, the methods by which the female characters shore up textual legitimacy in the play turn out to be rooted in the women's powers of theatricality. In short, if the textual apparatus surrounding the play is revealed to be less illuminating than expected, the use of texts within the play suggests that, to the extent that books can shed light on the world, their ability to do so may depend, paradoxically, on those forces—femininity, sexuality, the body, theatricality—that epitomize everything male textual authority seeks to restrict and repress.

An early sign of the dependency of male texts on female performance occurs near the beginning of act 1. Here, Sir Timothy, ineffectively attempting to woo Isabella, declares, "Mother *Demdike* and all her Imps were abroad [this afternoon], I think; but you are the pretty Witch that enchants my heart" (1.208–9). Isabella immediately calls out this blandishment as mere boilerplate—"*Academy of Compliments,* you are well read I see"—which Sir Timothy acknowledges: "who would have thought she had read that!" The exchange exposes Sir Timothy (perhaps unsurprisingly) as a lazy reader: *Academy of Compliments* appears to refer to a compendium of such remarks, a reference work presumably intended to save its user the effort of having to read widely and deeply in search of that perfectly apt turn of phrase.[71] Yet what initially seems an inept usage of texts actually turns out to be oddly on point: as we have seen, Isabella does turn out to be a "pretty Witch," in many ways. The accuracy of Sir Timothy's remark, however, owes neither to the sagacity of the volume he is citing nor to that of its user but, rather, to the spectacular antics of both Isabella and her "real" witch counterparts. Indeed, as the play progresses, Isabella may actually be inspired by Sir Timothy's uninspired compliment to model her behavior ever more closely on that of the witches.

This exchange between Sir Timothy and Isabella posits a complex relationship between performance and text—but also, perhaps more broadly, between actions and words, body and mind. Sir Timothy's figuration of love as a bewitchment is not just a quotation from a popular compendium but, more generally, a cliché—a dead metaphor. Indeed, we could say that it is this dead metaphor that lies behind Shadwell's entire play, binding the "enchant[ing]" young women to their enchantress counterparts, and thus unifying what would otherwise seem to be two completely separate plays of two completely separate genres. And, significantly, it is only these women's extravagantly embodied, anarchic actions that, as it were, reinfuse this "dead metaphor" with life force: it is the young women's physical bullying, their disguising themselves as witches, and their marrying of unauthorized suitors—in parallel to the witches' stranding of men in trees, their hobbling of horses, and their sexual involvement with clergymen—that reanimate the trope, that transform a verbal formula into corporeal reality. If a poetic cliché about women's "charms" could be said to underpin the whole play, we are nonetheless forced to admit that its verbally based concept only succeeds to the extent that its actresses (and, to a lesser extent, its actors) can bring it to life.

A second example of this same phenomenon takes place about 150 lines after the one just described, comprising a kind of pendant piece to the first. This example, moreover, serves uncannily as a kind of mirror to Shadwell's own use of texts, and thus reinforces the continuities between the forms of male textual authority being exercised around the play and those being exercised within it. Attempting to convince Sir Edward of the witches' existence, Sir Jeffery Shacklehead reels off a list of required reading: "No Witches? why[,] . . . Read *Bodin, Remigius, Delrio, Nider, Institor, Sprenger, Godelman,* and *More,* and *Malleus Maleficarum,* a great Author, that Writes sweetly about Witches, very sweetly" (1.359–62). The reference to *Malleus Maleficarum,* of course, alludes not to a "great Author" or even to an author at all but, rather, to a title (translating literally as "mallet" of "female evildoers"). Indeed, *Malleus Maleficarum* was written by two of the authors Sir Jeffery has just finished citing—namely, "Institor" (the Latinized name of Heinrich Kramer) and Jacob Sprenger. The fifteenth-century work was so famous—historians have called it "the virtual bible of witch-hunting"[72]—that even the insistently unsuperstitious Sir Edward catches the error immediately ("*Malleus Maleficarum* a Writer, he has read nothing but the titles I see" [1.365]), further emphasizing the extent of Sir Jeffery's ignorance. Yet it remains irrefutable that witches do "exist" within the diegetic world of the play: that is, the witches and their magical powers are not simply figments of certain characters' imaginations; they seem fully to inhabit the same plane of reality as the other characters. Their magic has real effects on the play's plot, and the stage directions describe their actions as actually taking place onstage: immediately following this exchange, for example, we are told that "*Mother* Demdike *rises out of the ground*" (1.384).

Confusingly, then, the books Sir Jeffery cites do turn out to bear some relation to the truth. In fact, they are more accurate in their depiction of reality than is Sir Edward's ostensibly more reasonable explanation of the witch's appearance: "Yes, I see 'tis almost dark, ... and here is a poor old Woman gathering of sticks" (1.387–89). Yet the texts' reliability operates in defiance of Sir Jeffery, whose mastery of them is clearly only superficial. As in the example of Sir Timothy's quotation from the compliments compendium, the authority of the texts here depends not on their (incompetent) user, or even on the men who wrote them, but on the women whose dramatic exploits provide their most direct corroboration.

One final instance of Shadwell's use of print helps elucidate the ways in which he may ultimately be anchoring his text's authority in the theatrical body. As Shadwell explains in his preface, he uses an italic typeface, throughout *The Lancashire Witches*, to restore and highlight politically controversial material that had been "expunged" in the play's original performances. This move seems to have two separate implications for concepts of centralized male power. On the one hand, it serves to undermine the institutional power structures represented by the Master of the Revels (who at this time was Charles Killigrew), enabling the reader to second-guess the censor's judgment. Thus, Shadwell declares that he has "printed [the play] just as I first writ it ... in my own vindication" (lines 29–33), so that the reader "may easily see ... how strict a scrutiny was made upon the Play" and exonerate the playwright accordingly. On the other hand, the italicized passages could be seen as bolstering Shadwell's own power, as they reveal his ability to override official rule and to bring the reader over to his side. (In this way, his use of typography would seem to associate Shadwell closely with Jonson, who was intent on touting the printed edition of *The Masque of Queenes* as the masque's most authoritative version, and thereby insisting on his own status as the masque's sole author, fending off the competing claims of those who financed, produced, acted in, or attended its performances.) Importantly, however—and in a move antithetical to Jonson's practices—Shadwell gives the last word on the play's text not to himself, or even to the reader, but to the production's original cast: as Shadwell goes on to assert, "I ... [have] Print[ed] the whole Play just as I writ it (without adding, or diminishing), as all the Actors who rehers'd [*sic*] it a fortnight together, before it was reviewed, may testify" (lines 81–84). Here, Shadwell stakes the accuracy of the text we are reading not on his own position as the text's writer but on the memories of those who performed and embodied it in rehearsal.

By suggesting that textual authority depends on theatricality, Shadwell is also making an additional, related argument about the nature of literary legacy—one that connects, of course, to his larger critique of traditional aristocratic male succession in *The Lancashire Witches*' plot. Shadwell's treatment of texts inverts Jonson's own textual practices in *The Masque of Queenes*: where Jonson insists on an alliance between his annotated masque and institutions of male power (declaring, in his dedication to Prince Henry, that he has added his citations in accordance with the prince's request), Shadwell uses his textual apparatus to cast doubt on the potency of such institutions. And where Jonson uses his text to corral his readers, Shadwell, to a large extent, seems to invite his readers to notice the inadequacies in his text, and to form their own opinions of it—with the aid of a group of individuals (the actors) whose knowledge of the text derives from their efforts to free themselves of its pages: to go, as the modern idiom has it, "off book." In all of these ways, then, Shadwell not only overturns Jonson's own textual strategies but works to redefine what Jonson imagined a literary legacy might look like. Rather than viewing this heritage as manifested in tightly controlled, male-authored texts, he posits a model of legitimacy and posterity that depends on a decentralized, feminized, performative revamping of the work of previous writers.

Seven years later, in *The Squire of Alsatia*, Shadwell again takes up questions of inheritance: of property, of worldviews, and also (or perhaps especially) of literary bequests. As in *The Lancashire Witches*, traditional male primogeniture is held up to scrutiny, and the play's relationship to its dramaturgical predecessors—in this case, primarily Terence's *Adelphi* ("The Brothers")—privileges theatricality over a strictly textual inheritance, even within what would seem to be yet another scholarly apparatus: a glossary of the cant terms used by the play's criminal-underworld characters. Where *The Squire of Alsatia* differs from *The Lancashire Witches*, however, is in the degree to which it manages to integrate its subversive, alternative inheritance structures into the very fabric of the play's more traditional patterns of succession.

In *The Lancashire Witches,* the witches' theatricalized, short-circuited modes of reproduction deliver severe blows to an already weakening model of patriarchal inheritance: as a result of the witches' conduct (both literally and figuratively, as carried out by the play's young women), Isabella and Theodosia end up marrying men of their own choosing, leaving their male-heir brothers out in the cold. However, the witches ultimately remain relegated to their role as a kind of id to the main characters of the play, and even their young-women counterparts cast aside their initial notion of becoming "Husband and Wife to one another" in order to marry highly suitable spouses, if not their fathers' first choices.

By contrast, in *The Squire of Alsatia,* the play's ego and id are folded into a single character: Belfond Junior. Belfond Junior is at once a more loyal heir than his foolish elder brother—Belfond Senior—and yet also the more libertine of the two (he has added at least one illegitimate branch to the family tree before the play even begins). Likewise, while he is the hero who preserves the family's fortune, he is also an unsavory profiteer, the majority of whose wealth, it seems, will come in the form of a carefully orchestrated (and in many ways fraudulently based) nuptial windfall. This amalgamated character, as I will show, points to a template for literary inheritance related to, but also in some ways more nuanced than, the one modeled in *The Lancashire Witches.*

The Lancashire Witches posited a mode of literary inheritance in which dead literary tropes depend on performance for reanimation, and in which textual precedence—in the form of the annotative apparatus, as well as the male characters' use of books within the play—fails to control the theatrical antics both of the witches themselves and of the non-witch counterparts for whom the witches serve as a kind of repressed subconscious. By contrast, in *The Squire of Alsatia,* Belfond Junior's irreverent, libidinous subconscious receives little suppression. As a result, this complex character ends up epitomizing a form of succession that simultaneously melds fidelity with improvisation, and careful stewardship with revaluation and misappropriation.

Like *The Lancashire Witches, The Squire of Alsatia* immediately confronts us with an heir apparent, Belfond Senior, who clearly lacks the insight and judgment required to steer his intended legacy into the future. Shadwell's critique of traditional inheritance structures goes further here than in the earlier play, however, as Belfond Senior's inadequacies are not simply a matter of unlucky genetics (as were Young Hartfort's) but of bad education: if Sir Edward Hartfort hoped a marriage between Young Hartfort and Theodosia might "restore the breed," debates abound in *The Squire of Alsatia* over two competing models of "breeding."[73] In other words, the problem of Belfond Senior's unfitness points not just to the dangerous arbitrariness of male primogeniture but to the values that undergird this system, and that have been inculcated in him by his father, the family patriarch, Sir William Belfond. The play juxtaposes these priorities, meanwhile, with a set of equal and opposite priorities, as articulated by the self-made merchant Sir Edward Belfond (who is Sir William's younger brother) and his nephew and adopted son, Belfond Junior (who, likewise, is Belfond Senior's younger brother).

As Ronald Berman and John C. Ross have elucidated, the colliding sets of values articulated by Sir William and Sir Edward correspond, respectively, to the period's Tory and Whig ideologies. More specifically, they align with the dichotomies John Locke poses between patriarchal authority and human reason (in *Some Thoughts Concerning Education*) and between absolute power and mercantile freedom (in *Two Treatises of Government*[74]). Although Ross cautions against interpreting *The Squire*'s 1688 debut as a sign that it was simply a mouthpiece of the 1688 Glorious Revolution—he notes that the Revolution did not occur until late in the year, and then, "even in the months following William of Orange's unresisted invasion..., there was more debate than agreement about 'Revolution principles'"—he joins with Berman in understanding the play as very much a "Whig fable," one that echoes Locke's rebuttal (in *Two Treatises*) of Sir Robert Filmer's 1680 *Patriarcha: A Defence of the Natural Power of Kings against the Unnatural Power of the People*.[75]

My own reading of *The Squire* does not center as squarely on its political orientation: I focus more on what I see as the play's parallel concern with artistic inheritance. Yet the values at issue in each of these inheritance problems share much in common. Indeed, given the years in which these plays were written, it may be impossible to divorce questions of artistic succession from debates around the monarchy and its fate. In the discussion that follows, then, I trace competing sets of ideologies that implicate both social and aesthetic concerns. Specifically, I argue that the values espoused by the two generations of elder brothers include a belief in asset consolidation and in the male line's insusceptibility to the passage of time, principles that they (mistakenly) associate with texts—specifically, with wills and articles of marriage. By contrast, the alternative values voiced by the two generations of younger brothers include, first, the dispersal (or disbursal) of assets and, second, a sense of "good timing" useful in theatrical and entrepreneurial contexts alike; both of these articles of faith are also associated with the play's gang of Alsatian thieves. At stake in the debates between Sir Edward and Sir William, however, is not just the question of how best to accrue, protect, and bequeath familial wealth but also the question of how best to manage literary legacies—a question that Shadwell likewise considers in terms of the unification versus the distribution of property, and the treatment of time as static versus progressive.

As Sir William and his younger brother Sir Edward debate the merits of the educations they have given their respective wards (both of whom, again, are Sir William's sons by birth), one of the questions that arises first is the importance of consolidating power as opposed to spreading it out over multiple sites and roles. For example, whereas Sir Edward has encouraged Belfond Junior to immerse himself in foreign travel and military service, Sir William contends that Belfond Senior "has travell'd to better purpose: for he has travell'd all about my Lands, and knows every Acre and Nook, and the value of it"; he claims that Belfond Senior will thus be much better off than Belfond Junior, who "will know nothing of his own Estate, but how to spend it" (2.1.410–12).[76] In short, Belfond Senior's movements have been contractive whereas Belfond Junior's have been expansive. Accordingly, when Sir Edward teases his elder brother that he has raised Belfond Senior to be a well-qualified "Gentlemans Baily" (or "bailiff," "one who superintends the husbandry of a farm for its owner" [*OED*, s.v. "bailiff," def. 3]), Sir William retorts that, indeed, his son will now be able to serve as "his own Baily," thus keeping all decisions in his own hands and collapsing two roles into one (2.1.361–62). Belfond Junior, meanwhile, plays multiple roles in succession—scholar, lawyer, traveler, soldier—so that, rather than obsessively reviewing his own landholdings as owner and overseer, he will be able "to serve his Country in any Capacity" he may be called upon to fulfill (2.1.416). These distinct worldviews may be most clearly put to the test in act 3, when Sir William unsuccessfully attempts to rout the Alsatians in the name of a single, consolidated authority: the king (enlisting the royal Tipstaff and Constable). Sir Edward and Belfond Junior, by contrast, effectively overpower the criminals by calling upon multiple authorities with overlapping mandates—a constable, the Lord Chief Justice, a sergeant, and a company of musketeers.[77]

Concepts of time are the second category separating Sir William's educational philosophy from Sir Edward's. Sir William's understanding of inheritance assumes a cyclical or eternal temporality: he boasts that his son "knows a sample of any Grain as well as e're a fellow in the North: Can handle a Sheep or Bullock as well as any one: Knows his seasons of Plowing, Sowing, Harrowing, laying Fallow: Understands all sorts of Manure" (2.1.356–59). In this world, just as the season for "Plowing" turns to the season for "Sowing," so, too, will "Manure" convert, eventually, into new samples of "Grain." If Sir William's outlook emphasizes a kind of timelessness, Sir Edward's emphasizes the good use of time (the importance of which he has likely experienced firsthand in his business dealings). As Sir Edward explains to his brother, "most of our Youth are ruin'd by having Time lye heavy on their hands." He has sought to counter this effect by teaching Belfond Junior to "love Musick"—an interest, he believes, that "helps . . . young Gentlemen . . . to spend their time alone," rather than "run[ning] willy-nilly . . . into any base Company to shun themselves" (2.1.421–24). In addition to helping him learn to be the master of his own time, Belfond Junior's musical background seems to have made him a master of good timing: his success in thwarting the Alsatians' plans to siphon off the Belfond wealth owes not just to his ability to recognize their designs upon Belfond Senior but also to his (and Shadwell's) ability to reveal his insights at just the right instant—to intercede at just the moment when doing so will have the most effect. Thus, he instructs his servant as to the precise juncture at which he should divulge Belfond Senior's follies to Sir William: "do not discover him to my Father yet" (3.2.251). Similarly, he bursts in on the extortionary wedding between Belfond Senior and Mrs. Termagant just as the bride and groom are about to take their vows (5.5). Clearly, Belfond Junior boasts not just musical skill but theatrical flair—the implications of which I explore more fully below.

By presenting two contrasting models of heirship embodied by Belfond Senior's and Belfond Junior's respective upbringings, Shadwell offers a redefinition of inheritance itself. It might initially appear that Belfond Senior's education has epitomized the very concept of the familial legacy, molding him into the estate's consummate steward, so that his identity begins and ends with the ancestral property itself. Likewise, we might think at first that Belfond Junior's education has prioritized the opposite: his cultivation of new experiences and diverse responsibilities, as well as his sense of improvisatory, theatrical timing, would seem to epitomize a kind of "anti-inheritance." Yet this "anti-inheritance" is precisely Sir Edward's bequest to his nephew. That is, to the extent that Belfond Junior's education will allow him to make his own way in the world, he will be doing so in imitation of his merchant-guardian, who is himself, of course, "self-made." In this sense, Belfond Junior is much more heir-like than his brother: whereas Belfond Senior's inevitable rebellion against his restrictive education comes close to obliterating the family holdings, Belfond Junior rescues it at the last minute. By the same token, however, Belfond Junior inhabits his heirship in such a way as to defy it, too—to inherit without ever actually claiming his inheritance. As we will see in greater detail below, by turning traditional structures of inheritance inside out, *The Squire of Alsatia*'s hero thereby serves as a kind of stand-in for its playwright.

Just as significant as the similarities I will delineate between Belfond Junior and Shadwell, however (and very much informing these similarities), are the resemblances linking Belfond Junior with *The Squire of Alsatia*'s chief villain, Cheatly—and I would like to consider these first. Cheatly's world, like the educational model Belfond Junior has been exposed to, operates according to a paradigm of expenditure and reallocation. The "Alsatia" of Shadwell's title refers to the Whitefriars neighborhood of London, which offered legal immunity to its residents: dating back to the time when actual friars lived there, the district had been considered to lie outside of the king's authority. By the seventeenth century, Alsatia had become notorious as a haven for debtors (indeed, Shadwell tells us in his dramatis personae that it is precisely "by reason of Debt" that Cheatly himself is there [line 27]). Consequently—in the play at least—it is a place that is founded upon the passing of financial deficit from one person to the next: as each debtor undertakes to fleece his next victim, he seeks to create a new debtor in his own image—in a precise inversion of traditional patterns of succession. Shamwell, the Belfonds' renegade cousin, perfectly illustrates this dynamic: originally "a most silly Bubble" who lost all his money to Cheatly, he has had to take up Cheatly's own ways to survive. By the time the play's action begins, he and Cheatly together have succeeded in "ruin[ing]" over "two hundred... young Heirs" (3.2.187–89). Accordingly, Cheatly's mock-affectionate references to Belfond Senior as "my sprightly Son," "my noble Heir," "my brisk Lad," and "my Heir in Tail" (1.1.69, 3.2.96, 1.1.219) may be interpreted almost literally: Belfond Senior is on the brink of becoming—like his cousin before him—this con man's "Heir" and successor.

Indeed, a few days in Alsatia are enough for Belfond Senior to have nearly completed a similar inversion of the usual order of inheritance. Throughout the first two acts of the play, reports about the drunken vandalism of a certain "Squire *Belfond*" have been reaching Sir William (2.1.278–85, 3.1.73–82), but Sir William, falsely assuming that Belfond Senior is still safely ensconced in the country, believes the reports must pertain to his younger son, and confronts Belfond Junior accordingly. Belfond Junior replies that the Alsatians must "have gotten some body to Personate me, and are undoubtedly... carrying on some Cheat in my Name" (3.1.102–3). Having resolved to go directly to Alsatia to "discover this Imposture" (3.1.110), he arrives at the tavern where the reputed hooligan is said to be spending his time, and demands to know "Who [it] is... in this House here, who usurps my Name, and is call'd Squire *Belfond?*" (3.2.105). Although Belfond Senior steps from the tavern's shadows to declare he "is called so without usurping," such a claim no longer seems entirely accurate: by placing himself in the hands of the Alsatians, Belfond Senior has set himself up to lose the very inheritance that defines him as the Belfond heir—whereas Belfond Junior, via an enterprising marriage, is poised to become, in more than one sense, the true heir to the "great Estate" his uncle has accrued "by Merchandize" (1.1.391). The topsy-turvy form of succession symbolized by Alsatia has, in a very real sense, transformed the elder Belfond into the "[im]personat[or]," the "impost[or]," and the "usurp[er]" of the family "Name."

The Alsatian model of inheritance can thus be seen as a parody of the traditional model—bequeathing liabilities rather than assets, turning eldest sons to usurpers while their younger brothers become the rightful heirs. In addition—and in this regard the Alsatian model comes disconcertingly close to the ideological outlook on which Belfond Junior has been weaned—it is a system that relies as much on the self-made as the handed down. Put another way, it depends on the very same sense of good timing and improvisation that underpins Belfond Junior's success. For Cheatly's schemes to swindle "his" heirs require resourcefulness, creativity, and, perhaps most importantly, theatrical aptitude. Recall that, at the heart of his plan to trap Belfond Senior is the marriage Cheatly arranges between him and one of the female members of the play's criminal underclass, Mrs. Termagant (who also happens to be Belfond Junior's cast mistress, suggesting yet another way in which Alsatia becomes a site of reverse primogeniture, with the elder brother inheriting the younger brother's hand-me-down lovers). This arrangement calls upon all of Cheatly's powers of dramaturgy and stage management: along with Shamwell, Cheatly directs Termagant to "personate a Town Lady of Quality, and be as Haughty and Impertinent as the best of 'em," and provides her with a convincing-looking "Lodging," "Plate," and "Furniture" (3.2.74, 3.3.51). After being filled in on the details, Mrs. Termagant comments admiringly on the "rare design" of Cheatly's ploy (3.3.54).

Indeed, in engineering the near marriage between Belfond Senior and Mrs. Termagant, Cheatly proves similar to Belfond Junior in a number of ways: not only does the scheme require the theatrical skills that Belfond Junior displays throughout the play but, more specifically, the scheme functions as a (highly unflattering) mirror to Belfond Junior's own marriage, in act 5, to Isabella, which also depends on artifice. After all, Belfond Junior can only marry Isabella if he can first extricate himself from a marriage to Lucia—another woman he has recently seduced. And the only way he can do this is by testifying falsely to Lucia's virginity (5.7.15–30).

Both of these deception-reliant marriages, moreover, are essentially cunning profit schemes. Belfond Junior has apparently rejected Lucia in favor of Isabella due to financial considerations[78]—a fact that links Belfond Junior directly, of course, to his con-artist counterpart. For whereas Lucia's attorney father may be able to provide a reasonable dowry, Isabella comes with a fortune of 20,000 pounds—a veritable bonanza for the Belfonds. (To put that amount in perspective: although we never learn the exact amounts accrued by Sir Edward via his "lucky hits" as a merchant, we are told that Sir William commands "3,000 *l.* per annum" [dramatis personae, line 1].) The outsized scale of Isabella's fortune thus evokes the kind of breathtaking windfall associated with new forms of capitalist speculation—or perhaps (as the parallels with Cheatly suggest) with outright theft. The marriage may thus hint (again, like Cheatly's matchmaking between Belfond Senior and Mrs. Termagant) at sources of wealth that undermine the traditional inheritance structures.

The significance of Belfond Junior's achievement in winning Isabella and her dowry is heightened by the contrast between his own methods of acquisition versus his father's. At the beginning of the play, Sir William is hoping for Isabella to become Belfond Senior's wife, but, in adherence to his conventional understanding of inheritance, he has agreed to a 5,000-pound payment to her guardian, Scrapeall, in order to secure the match. By contrast, the end of the play sees Belfond Junior circumventing patriarchal figures altogether (recognizing, after all, that the money is in Isabella's hands: it has been left to her by an uncle, and is thus fully her own) and, consequently, getting the better deal. The only other character in the play actively exhibiting this degree of financial savvy is Cheatly.

The various connections between Cheatly and Belfond Junior that I have just outlined may ultimately culminate in the play's title. The titular phrase refers primarily, it seems, to Belfond Senior, the country landowner-to-be who, ridiculously, finds himself in the gritty urban underworld of Alsatia (and, while there, is referred to constantly—mockingly—as "the Squire"). But "squire" can denote not only a country gentleman but also a "gallant or lover" (*OED*, s.v. "squire," def. 4a), a description that certainly fits Belfond Junior as he juggles the attentions of three women at once. (And of course, as we recall, Sir William himself believes at one point that references to "Squire Belfond" are denoting his younger son.) Moreover, perhaps to a greater extent than his elder brother, Belfond Junior is "of" Alsatia, showing himself to be remarkably familiar with its ways: it is he who identifies Shamwell as "a most silly Bubble"—a term that Shadwell seems to have deemed specialized enough to require explication in the printed play's cant glossary.[79] (Likewise, it is he who describes Cheatly as "fit for no places but *Ram-alley*, or *Pye Corner*," showing his familiarity with two of the seediest locations in London [3.2.207–8].[80]) Then again, of course, it is Cheatly himself who could be said to be the neighborhood's chief "Squire" (something akin to Gay's "Captain" Macheath), the powerful proprietor of the Alsatian demesne.[81] The ambiguous meanings of Shadwell's title thus invite us to consider further the blurring between the younger Belfond son and the play's chief criminal.

By closely associating Belfond Junior and Cheatly in all of these ways, Shadwell crafts an even more subversive critique of traditional inheritance structures than he did in *The Lancashire Witches*. In the earlier play the female characters may have exposed the weakness and haplessness of the intended male heirs—and pointed toward alternative modes of reproduction—but their challenge to traditional patterns of succession is ultimately disposed of: the witches are dispensed with and the young women are married appropriately, if not exactly as intended by their fathers. Moreover, if the earlier play suggested parallels between these mutinous women and the law-enforcing patriarchs, these parallels remain mostly subliminal. By contrast, in *The Squire of Alsatia* the subversive characters' challenge to patriarchal inheritance models is not so easily dismissed. Rather, Shadwell suggests that the new, "anti-inheritance" structure he is depicting—the new profiteering of mercantile capitalism—actually works by cannibalizing the older sources of wealth, just as the Alsatian gang seeks to swallow up the Belfond family fortune. The Alsatian criminals may be routed by the end of the play, and the Belfond estate may be preserved from ruin just in the nick of time, but by this point Shadwell has strongly hinted that Cheatly's most salient skills—his canny use of assets and time—live on in Belfond Junior and his ilk, whose self-made fortunes will continue to grow as England's outdated, land-based forms of wealth continue to dwindle.[82]

At the same time that Shadwell depicts a shift in traditional inheritance structures, he enacts a similarly unorthodox model of literary inheritance. As dramaturgical heir to Terence (or perhaps his anti-heir), Shadwell displays many of the traits that we see in Belfond Junior—and in Cheatly. Like both the play's hero and its villain, Shadwell turns concepts of inheritance upside down via a wide dispersal of assets and an improvisatory or theatrical sense of timing. He annexes a second space, Alsatia, to Terence's unified setting, and he multiplies the play's dramatis personae—first, by importing all of the characters associated with Alsatia and its conflicts (gang, rabble, musketeers, etc.) and, second (perhaps more significantly), by dividing Terence's Pamphilia into three characters: Mrs. Termagant, Lucia, and Isabella.[83] As previous critics have pointed out, the addition of Alsatia in particular infuses the play with a notable theatricality: it is the scenes in Alsatia that supply the play with its most vital characters, as well as its most ebullient moments of stage business.[84] It is also the Alsatian scenes that best showcase Shadwell's canny sense of timing, for not only is Shadwell the ultimate mastermind behind Belfond Junior's perfectly cued interventions and revelations, of course, but he specifically designs the play's cultural references to be acutely of the moment. As Shadwell's near-contemporary John Dennis observed, "Shadwell's *Squire of Alsatia* took exceedingly at first as an occasional play," offering audiences vicarious access to the "nest of villains" who (as rumor seems to have had it) were plaguing the Whitefriars neighborhood: although Dennis's claim that "the story is built on . . . a true fact" cannot be easily substantiated, the play does have a distinctly "documentary" feel,[85] and Ross finds several "contemporary references to the fleecing of moneyed young men by confidence-tricksters, corrupt usurers or gamblers," suggesting that Shadwell was reflecting a broader set of concerns, or at least anxieties, surrounding urban life at the time.[86] Of particular interest to original audiences, it seems, was the play's incorporation of cant: according to Dennis, *The Squire of Alsatia* "discovered the cant terms that were before not generally known, except to the cheats themselves"; Albert Borgman cites a contemporary report ascribing the play's initial success to its amusing use of these terms.[87]

Just as Shadwell's timing enables him to enhance his play's impact and appeal, however, he also grafts this same "live" or "theatrical" understanding of time onto the sense of quasi-permanence, or timelessness, that tends to be associated with texts. Indeed, many of *The Squire of Alsatia*'s individual lines of dialogue function as essentially literal translations from *The Adelphi*, preserving a direct line of descent, as it were, from literary father to son. (Ross counts twenty-one "ostentatiously close verbal" echoes.[88]) In thus integrating textual and theatrical prowess, however, Shadwell is also not necessarily straying from the alternative inheritance models put forth by Belfond Junior and Cheatly. They, too, have a way of joining improvisation with bookish knowledge.

I will turn first to Belfond Junior: Sir Edward explains early on that he "instructed him to read the Noble *Greek* and *Roman* Authors," and we see this education reflected in Belfond Junior's frequent allusions to such literary touchstones as Ovid's *Metamorphoses* and Horace's *Odes* (2.1.377). Significantly, however, such references often end up becoming intertwined with performativity: Belfond Junior, for example, asks that his singing master set one of Horace's odes to music (from which his friend Truman gives a sample); a few lines later, he cites a joke from Buckingham's *Rehearsal*, while also quoting Shakespeare's "If Musick be the Food of Love, play on," suggesting not only that his reading is allied with playgoing but that this reading and playgoing serve to reinforce his interest in musical performance (2.1.118–31). A remark by Sir Edward is telling in this regard: he notes to Sir William that he has taught Belfond Junior to read widely in order to "make him wiser and honester," but also to make him "fit for the Conversation of Learned Gentlemen" (2.1.380–81)—a statement that seems to dovetail with Shadwell's assertion, in his preface to *The Humorists*, that the "reading of Books is conversing with men."[89] In other words, reading, for both generations of younger Belfond brothers, as well as for Shadwell himself, is closely associated with live, interactive, social, and communal art forms.

By contrast, Sir William, perhaps in keeping with his own understanding of time and property as solid and unchanging, seems to have raised Belfond Senior to view texts in a much more static way. For him, texts—specifically, the last will and testament of Sir William's brother-in-law, as well as a number of documents relating to Belfond Senior's planned marriage to Isabella—function not as the basis for performance and sociability but as a means for the further consolidation of assets and the strict preservation of those assets into a predictable future. But this trust in the written word's stability soon leads Sir William into trouble. At first, the brother-in-law's will, and Sir William's handling of it, seem to conform to—and to confirm—Sir William's outlook: apparently, the brother-in-law (whom we never meet) has no children of his own, meaning his fortune will add further to the Belfond family assets. In attending so single-mindedly to this text, however, Sir William is called away from his estate prior to the opening of the play, allowing Belfond Senior to escape his watchful eye and unwittingly to place himself—and, indeed, the recently enhanced family holdings—at the mercy of London's underworld.

Likewise, Sir William overestimates the stability of the documents facilitating the hoped-for marriage between Belfond Senior and Isabella: he seems to believe that his "Seal" upon the "writings" is all that is needed to lock their financial stipulations permanently into place (1.1.340–42). Yet such textual assurances do not stand up to Belfond Senior's simplest whims: when he balks at returning to the country, Sir William exclaims, "Thou most ungracious Wretch to break from me, at such a time, when I had provided a Wife for you, a Pretty Young Lady, with fifteen thousand Pound down, have setled a great Jointure upon her, and a large Estate in Present on you, the Writings all sealed, and nothing wanting but you . . . !" (4.6.65–67). By contrast, the other characters' more figurative definition of "sealing" seems to reflect more accurately the reality of the play's world: they speak of sealing vows with kisses, as well as with other "Mutual Enjoyments," further reinforcing the notion that the universe they inhabit revolves more around impulse and action than writings and signatures (4.3.74, 5.7.62).

Another definition of "sealing" in the play likewise exposes Sir William's beliefs as naïve: as Shadwell's "Explanation of the Cant" clarifies, a "Sealer" is "One that gives Bonds and Judgments for Goods or Money" (line 4). Thus, Sir William's attorney warns him that Cheatly is "that most audacious Rogue . . . who has drawn in so many young Heirs, and undone so many *Sealers*" (1.1.305–6), and Cheatly himself calls Belfond Senior "the hopefullest *Sealer* that ever yet toucht Wax among us," for he has agreed early on in act 1 to pledge portions of the family estate to Cheatly and Shamwell in exchange for ready money, clothes, a coach, and other such "Outragious Splendor[s]" with which to "dazle the whole Town" (1.1.81–95). Belfond Senior's acts of "sealing," then, do not shore up the value of his family estate; they liquidate it: as Cheatly forecasts, "Thou shalt make thy fruitful Acres . . . to fly, And all thy sturdy Oaks to bend like Switches!" (1.1.82–84). Here, all that seemed solid and enduring—down to the hardwoods of the Belfond acreage—is shown to be up for negotiation. Sir William's failure lies not just in his believing sealed documents to be unimpeachable, then, but also in his belief that words themselves—"sealing," ironically, being a prime example—could retain a single, stable, unchanging meaning.

If Sir William's understanding of texts and words provides a telling contrast to Belfond Junior's, Cheatly's provides (unsurprisingly) an illuminating parallel—and, again, one that pertains to Shadwell and his mode of literary inheritance. In addition to being singled out in the dramatis personae for being "very expert in the *Cant* about the Town" (lines 32–33), Cheatly also proves adept at "University" speech, or sophistry: "Why look you Sir," he declares to Sir William, "you must be forc'd to grant that whatsoever may be, may also as well not be, in their own essential differences and degrees" (2.2.120–22). Similarly, he asks Belfond Senior's bewildered servant, Lolpoop, "Your Master being in this matter, to deport his Count'nance somewhat obliquely, to some principles, which others but out of a Mature Gravity may have weigh'd, and think too heavy to be undertaken; what does it avail if you shall precipitate or plunge your self into affairs, as unsuitable to your Physnomy as they are to your Complexion?" (1.1.180–84). This pseudo-scholarly idiom extends to a bastardized legalese, such as the one with which he threatens Lolpoop: "you are indebted to me 20 *l.* upon a *Scire facias:* I extend this up to an Outlawry, upon Affidavit upon the *Nisi prius:* I plead to all this matter *Non est inventus* upon the Pannel; what is there to be done more in this Case, as it lies before the Bench, but to award out Execution upon the *Posse Comitatus,* who are presently to issue out, a *Certiorari*[?]" (1.1.187–92). Such phrasings suggest some degree of familiarity with written documents of various kinds, and, accordingly, Lolpoop exclaims that he understands nothing of what has just been said, for "I am not Book-learn'd" (1.1.185). However, the ultimate effect of Cheatly's reading (like Belfond Junior's) is to enhance his theatrical skills. While Cheatly has clearly produced the effect of "Book-learn[ing]" on Lolpoop, Belfond Senior applauds the artistry of what he recognizes to be nonsense: "[you] *Banter* . . . the best of any man in the World," he declares; "I protest Sir you do it Incomparably"—to which Cheatly replies with all the false modesty of a leading man greeting his admirers: "No, no, I swear not I . . . Faith you make me blush" (1.1.197–200).[90]

This is the difference between Cheatly and the men whose speech he imitates: as Belfond Senior and Shamwell agree, Cheatly "would run down the best Scholar in *Oxford,*" or, indeed, "in *London*"; for whereas the denizens of the universities "are all Scholar Boys, and nothing else, as long as they live there," Cheatly can shift easily between languages (1.1.45–52). University students, in other words, despite the fact that "they are as confident as if they knew every thing," actually "understand no more beyond *Magdalen-Bridge* than meer *Indians.*" Cheatly, by contrast, in addition to being able to "*Cut a Sham or Banter* with the best Wit or Poet of 'em all," is fluent in the slang spoken beyond the campus grounds (1.1.53–56). Indeed, at one point he may even utter an *"Indian"* phrase: "If you meet either your Father, or Brother, or any from those Prigsters," he advises Belfond Senior, "stick up thy Countenance, . . . [and] we'll all pull down our Hats, and cry bow wow" (3.2.94–97). Scholars have speculated that this phrase may derive from an early seventeenth-century transliteration of a Native American chant, sung during a ceremonial dance witnessed by British voyagers to Virginia.[91] Cheatly has several verbal modes at his disposal, then: when his "literate" sophistry proves less effective, he can switch to an incantatory, performative cry.[92]

Indeed, the function of many of *The Squire of Alsatia*'s cant words, I argue, is not unlike the role played by Cheatly's "bow wow": typically reeled off in rapid succession, the effect of these words depends as much on sound as on sense. Early on in the play, Cheatly gleefully relates how a drunken Belfond Senior "*lugg'd out* in defence of his *Natural;* the Captain *whipt* his *Porker* out, and away *rubb'd Prigster* and call'd the Watch" (1.1.134–35); Hackum likewise laments that he "lost all [his] *Ready*" at the gaming table, and was left without "a *Rag* or a *Sock:* Pox o' the *Tatts* for me: I believe they put the *Doctor* upon me" (1.1.140–41). In both of these instances, the sheer number of gutturals—lug, pork, prig, rag, sock, pox, doc—give the lines an almost physical force, again suggesting that the main effect of the cant is more somatic than semantic, its interest more theatrical than philological.

I want now, finally, to turn back to Shadwell, who himself sustains a tension between faithful reproduction of, and improvisatory deviations from, his source text, and in ways that might best be described in terms of the bilingualism that both Belfond Junior and Cheatly exhibit—a dual fluency in seventeenth-century England's classical (and readerly) heritage as well as in its modern, popular (and theatrical) trends. This bilingualism could be said to be exemplified, in fact, in *The Squire of Alsatia*'s most striking textual component, its "Explanation of the Cant." The "Explanation" not only mediates between two idioms (cant and standard English) but also straddles, on one side, the kind of scholarly print culture best able to preserve classical learning and, on the other, an ever-evolving oral culture reflective of a world completely foreign to that of ancient Rome. Such commodities as beaver hats or pocket watches, for example, in addition to various forms of English currency, clearly signal our remove from Terence's world.

Like the annotative apparatus that accompanies *The Lancashire Witches,* the "Explanation of the Cant" seems at first to deploy print in the interest of providing a kind of ideological containment for amoral, folkish energies: by rendering the Alsatians' cant transparent to everyone, it saps the criminals of one major source of their power—and it does so in a way that is (apparently) orderly, rational, and comprehensive. Shadwell's glossary thus promises to expose to the light of day a world that thrives on business conducted under the table, in back alleys, and after dark.

However, other aspects of the "Explanation" disrupt any such attempts at encyclopedic order. For instance, the organization of the glossary's entries might appear alphabetical upon first glance—this impression is created by the giant drop capital used in the word that heads the list ("Alsatia")—but the entries that follow jump all around the alphabet. Nor are the terms arranged according to the order in which they appear in the play—another schema that, like alphabetization, would presumably be most useful to readers wanting to look up words as they encounter them. Rather, the list's (somewhat loose) organizing logic is one that the Alsatian residents themselves might have chosen, privileging the categories that are most important to their work and world. Thus, "Alsatia" is followed by a kind of miniature dramatis personae—with a *"Prig"* denoting a "Pert Coxcomb," a *"Putt"* referring to "One who is easily wheadled and cheated," and so on. This cast of characters is followed in turn by a series of terms for money: *"Rhinocerical"* is glossed as "Full of money," while a *"Meg," "Smelt," "Decus," "George," "Hog,"* and *"Sice"* refer, respectively—and in declining order of value—to a guinea, half-guinea, crown piece, half-crown, shilling, and six-pence. Next come a set of definitions relating to pickpocketing and thieving—watches, rings, expensive clothing—and, later, a group of words associated with cheating at dice. Notably, too, whereas in a typical glossary the unfamiliar terms are outnumbered by the standard-English synonyms, here the ratio is reversed—so that, for example, *"Coale, Ready, Rhino,* [and] *Darby"* are all glossed, tersely, as "Ready money," while *"Blowing, Natural, Convenient, Tackle, Buttock, Pure,* [or] *Purest pure"* are all names for "a Mistress, or rather a Whore" (lines 6, 20–21).[93] Again, the result is a list that, rather than serving as a tool to help readers quickly navigate the criminal ecosystem of the play, seems almost to initiate us into it. We come away with a growing understanding of the Alsatians' own priorities, while also sensing that our standard-English synonyms for the Alsatians' vibrant vocabulary are somehow inadequate, impoverished.

To engage substantively with this list, then, is to wade into the play's underworld and its values: there is no efficient way for the reader to single out any one term and go back to her reading—no way to settle a word's meaning without interrupting the teleological plotline in which the Alsatians are ultimately routed: instead, the reader ends up detained, as it were, within the borders of Alsatia. In this way, the user of the glossary is put in a position not unlike that of Belfond Senior, marveling at the curios in the criminals' linguistic cabinet: "*Prigster, lugg'd out, Natural, Porker, rubb'd,* admirable! This is very ingenious" (1.1.136–37). Perhaps, then, the "Explanation" is best thought of not as a key—giving its possessor the power to enter into Alsatia's secrets at will—but as a trap door through which we find ourselves dropped into the play's criminal domain. (Indeed, the position of the "Explanation" within the text—just following the title page and preceding the dedication, prologue, and dramatis personae—suggests that it provides a primary entry point into the play and its universe.) Shadwell's glossary thus turns out (like *The Lancashire Witches*' scholarly apparatus) to be a highly equivocal document, intermixing the stereotypically "print-cultural" values of clarity and comprehension with the theatrical-leaning values of trickery and wonder—balancing a concern for translating between classical and modern traditions against a contrary interest in simply plunging the reader, cognitively and sensorially, into a whole new world.

If Shadwell demonstrates the same ability, shared by Belfond Junior and Cheatly, to shuttle between print traditions and theatrical innovations, does he also manifest these characters' entrepreneurial—and larcenous—models of "anti-inheritance"? Interestingly, in the material that precedes his 1669 play *The Royal Shepherdess*, we see Shadwell emphasizing these same connections—joining theft, capitalistic enterprise, and a dual fluency in texts and theatricality—as he seeks to justify his borrowings from John Fountain's 1661 closet drama, *The Rewards of Virtue*. In the play's prologue, Shadwell paints himself as the "bold Purloiner of the Play," and boastfully contrasts his crime—that of having "stollen a whole Play"—to the sins of "petty Thieves," who "steall small things" only.[94] Yet in his preface to the reader, Shadwell justifies this theft as nothing but the honest labor of the self-made professional.

"This Play, before I took it in hand, was wrote by one Mr. *Fountain* of *Devonshire*," he explains, "a Gentleman" who dabbled in playwriting merely "as a slight diversion from his more serious Studies."[95] In keeping with these scholarly origins (for Shadwell suggests that playwriting still constituted a kind of "Stud[y]" for Fountain, even if an un-"serious" one), the play was "never ... intended for Action" and, accordingly, "had ... many long, uninterrupted Soliloquies, some of fifty lines together, which perhaps might give some delight in the reading, but could afford little diversion to the Hearers." What may serve as "diversion" for the gentleman-amateur, in other words, does not necessarily prove diverting for actual playgoers: the task of making it so, Shadwell implies, ultimately falls to the commercial playwright, who, by contrast, is habituated to the business of the theater and the demands of paying customers, and can thus translate the verbose products of the study into a successful theatrical production. Creating a profitable play, however, requires an investment of time and labor (as opposed to the gentleman's "slight diversion"); consequently, it is only "with some pains" that Shadwell has been able to transform the play into "a pleasant entertainment for the Audience," by "represent[ing] that in Action, which was expressed by [Fountain] in long Narrations."[96] Once again, then, Shadwell associates thievery with entrepreneurship and enterprise—undertakings specifically defined here as the theatricalization of a readerly text (translating "long Narrations" and "Soliloquies," which can make for good "reading" only, into "Action[s]" that can please the "Audience").

Moreover, Shadwell links these (mis)appropriations to a kind of alternative inheritance structure. Returning to *The Royal Shepherdess*'s prologue, we see Shadwell again contrasting aristocratic playwrights with the non-aristocratic: whereas "In our times / Small Faults are scorn'd," he writes, "Great [Faults]" are often celebrated as "worthy Crimes"—and yet "Onely for Noble Sparks."[97] A double standard is thus revealed: thefts are condemned in "the base Vulgar," but when the nobility go ahead and steal a "whole Play"— Kewes thinks Shadwell may be alluding to Sir William Davenant, whose Shakespearean adaptations were being performed in the 1660s—such thefts are considered to be their birthright, as it were.[98] (Shadwell adds that such crimes may be "safely" committed "When the Author's dead"—thus implying not only that the original author is no longer around to object but also that his writerly estate is now up for grabs.) But Shadwell goes on to suggest that he will simply make himself into the heir of these "Noble Sparks": the audience, he notes, by excusing "some great malefactors heretofore," have, "for each Thief you've pardon'd, made Ten more."⁹⁹ In short, the public's indulgence toward previous literary larceny has allowed the thieves to reproduce—and Shadwell, the prologue suggests, is among these offspring, simply following in the footsteps of his "great" predecessors.

Through a highly complex series of rhetorical moves, then, Shadwell equates his professional-playwright status with that of a resourceful thief, who makes his own opportunities—and yet he also suggests that, in committing his literary thefts, he is heir to an illustrious aristocratic tradition.¹⁰⁰ In a sense, we might say that what Shadwell is laying claim to here is not the individual literary property of Fountain or anyone else but, rather, an ancient heritage—of which stealing is, he implies, a longstanding component. He thus substitutes a new inheritance model for the old one. According to the new model, heirs are not born but made. Each heir must prove his legitimacy, and he may do so only (paradoxically) by taking that which is not his.

This seems to be the model at work in Shadwell's adaptation of Terence. Unlike in *The Royal Shepherdess* (or *The Humorists,* in which he confesses to borrowing "hints" from Molière; or even *The Lancashire Witches,* in which Shadwell lists—if very incompletely—his dramaturgical debts), nowhere in *The Squire of Alsatia*'s front matter does Shadwell acknowledge his reliance on Terence. Gerard Langbaine, whose plagiarism detector is usually set on high, insists that no acknowledgment is necessary, as Shadwell "is not beholding to the *French,* or *English* for his Model; and [because] those for whom he chiefly writes, are Persons that are well acquainted with Poets of Antiquity, and need not be informed."¹⁰¹ But it is difficult to judge how watertight Langbaine's reasoning here is, or would have been considered to be: Kewes lists Sophocles and Euripides as two of the models invoked most often by playwrights, suggesting that the classical canon was not always deemed so ingrained as to require no citation; indeed, she argues that "the acknowledgement of sources" had become "so frequent" by the late 1660s that "the foregrounding of the original author and/or source must have been seen as a commercial asset."¹⁰² Why, then, does Shadwell not admit to his borrowings from *The Adelphi?*

It is important to distinguish here among the various types of borrowing in which Shadwell is engaged. Whereas he owns up to his use of "hints," storylines, and scenarios from other playwrights (such as the ones he takes from Molière, or Fountain, or—in *The Lancashire Witches*—Shakespeare), Shadwell is much less likely to confess to his borrowings when it comes to verbal imitation: he neglects to credit Jonson and Brome for the phrasing he incorporates into *The Lancashire Witches* and its notes, and in *The Squire of Alsatia,* despite the fact that the play includes many direct translations from Terence, these go unmentioned. Such a pattern seems to accord with what Kewes shows to be the emerging consensus on plagiarism in the Restoration: as noted earlier in this chapter, whereas plots and stories were considered "common property," "verbatim copying" was derided as morally and aesthetically suspect.[103] Correspondingly, Shadwell seems quick to acknowledge dramaturgical debts when it comes to sourcing his plays' narrative premises—which were seen as fair game anyway—but never mentions his use of his predecessors' individual words and phrases, the appropriation of which was viewed as theft.

We might conclude, then, that Shadwell is simply coy about which debts he owns up to, so as to exculpate himself from accusations of plagiarism. However, it is also necessary to view Shadwell's conduct here against the backdrop of his larger rhetorical positioning vis-à-vis verbal borrowings. As noted at the beginning of this chapter, he seems to subscribe to a larger vision of dramaturgical succession in which language per se is not the primary site of inheritance and improvement. Rather, he repeatedly asserts that the plays of the pre- and post-Commonwealth eras are united by a shared interest in representing human nature as vibrantly and compellingly as possible. Of course, as we have seen, in practice Shadwell's debts to his predecessors may be as textual, or language-based, as any other playwright's (including Dryden's). However, as he does in his broader claims regarding the late seventeenth century's dramaturgical legacy, when it comes to acknowledging these verbal debts Shadwell prefers to discount this type of textual heritage. Such a move dovetails well with Shadwell's larger critique—as manifested in both *The Lancashire Witches* and *The Squire of Alsatia*—of traditional models of property inheritance, which, like the Drydenian conception of literary inheritance, tend to emphasize unity and timelessness. Rejecting such paradigms, Shadwell implies that what makes him a worthy heir to his dramaturgical forebears—like Belfond Junior (and, indeed, Cheatly)—is a theatrical entrepreneurialism whose improvisatory creativity (and consequent success) make up for its occasional dependence on sleight of hand.

By allying himself—as a kind of literary anti-heir—with witches and con artists, Shadwell raises larger moral questions: if drama—and literature more broadly—could be said to embrace misappropriation and theft, how can we understand the place of these art forms within the larger value system of our society and culture? The debate surrounding the moral effects of the stage on its audience—but also the moral effects of texts on their readers—is one that was becoming increasingly high pitched in the 1680s, though Shadwell alludes to it only indirectly in the plays I have examined here. By contrast, as I show in the next chapter, Aphra Behn engages head on with the question of how drama—whether onstage or on the page—may guide, or misguide, our judgment (and treatment) of others.

2

"CAN MY IMAGINATION FEEL?"

Reading, Theatricality, and the Mind-Body Problem in Aphra Behn's The Luckey Chance *and* The Emperor of the Moon

THE PUBLICATION OF BEN JONSON'S 1616 *Works* has often been seen as a turning point for English dramaturgy: both implicitly, in its design, and explicitly, in its critical remarks, the volume elevated the printed text of plays over their live performance. The result, writes Jonas Barish, is that, for the first time in history, drama "moves formally into the domain of literature."[1] Such a dualistic understanding of drama—the separation of script from show—may have depended, in part, on a dualistic understanding of human nature: if a play can be divided into words and action, then this division seems to mimic the split, within each of us, between mind and body. Jonson himself famously articulates this analogy in his introductory remarks to *Hymenaei*, explaining that the reason he is presenting the masque in printed form is that "things subjected to understanding have... a noble and just advantage... [over] those which are objected to sense; that the one sort are but momentary, and merely taking; the other impressing, and lasting: else the glory of all these solemnies had perished like a blaze, and gone out, in the beholder's eyes. So short lived are the bodies of all things, in comparison of their souls."[2] Jonson draws a parallel here between the "bodies" and "souls" of masques, on the one hand, and, on the other, the faculties through which these elements are apprehended. Printed language will persist because it makes its appeal to our spirits, or "understanding[s]"—to an inward wisdom or intelligence that transcends our mortal frames. By contrast, theatrical spectacles, however brilliant, lodge themselves in our "eyes" only, and therefore, like bodies—indeed, just like the bodily organs through which they are perceived—are subject to decay. Accordingly—returning to Barish's assertion—it seems that drama becomes "literature" not simply when it is regarded as something to be read (as per the etymological root of the word) but when it is regarded as something that, in being read, is also able to engage our "souls" rather than our "sense[s]" alone.

Jonson's distinction between a play's literary and theatrical sides—and in particular his alignment of a play's language with the human soul, and of a play's performance with the human body—retains its currency into the later seventeenth century. Indeed, each of these categories could be said to take on an even more insistent significance starting in the middle of the century, when, of course, plays could be read but not publicly performed and, at the same time, debates about mind and body were becoming increasingly central to the era's philosophical projects. In this chapter, I argue that the playwright, poet, translator, and novelist Aphra Behn, during a period in her career in which she is actively thinking and writing about problems of epistemology and the New Science, deliberately utilizes drama as a way to reconsider Jonsonian assumptions regarding mind and body, imagination and experience, reading and spectating. Through a close examination of the final two of her plays staged during her lifetime—*The Luckey Chance* (1686) and *The Emperor of the Moon* (1687)—I contend that Behn works to overturn basic philosophical distinctions crucial both to her era's evolving literary-critical discourse and to its incipient empirical discourse, each of which relies, in many ways, on a separation between material and immaterial, sensation and understanding. Specifically, in *The Luckey Chance* Behn suggests that our experience of the external world may be shaped as strongly by our imaginative conceptions (such as those involved in reading) as it is by our sense perceptions (such as those involved in playgoing). Inversely, in *The Emperor of the Moon,* she insists that the imaginative operations involved in reading can involve our bodies as much they do our minds, and that theater's effects on us may owe less to its materiality than we might expect. In this way, Behn questions much of the intellectual groundwork underlying the New Science—groundwork that is also fundamental to an emergent conception of literature as defined by a canon in print.

The ambitions of Jonson's 1616 *Works* notwithstanding, one might argue it is not until the Interregnum period that the division Jonson posits between plays as literature and plays as theatrical entertainment truly comes to the forefront of critical awareness in England. Marta Straznicky contends that it is only in 1642, with the theaters closed, that "reading becomes an imagined substitute for playgoing rather than an extension of it."[3] Peter Berek sees this shift as taking place a few years later, but concludes, similarly, that "by the 1650s the ... printed text [is no longer] a record of performance [alone]"; rather, it emerges as its own autonomous work of art.[4]

Presumably, once plays could be performed again, in 1660, the chasm between stage and page would have become less pronounced: audience members could once again purchase the text as a reminder of the production (as Samuel Pepys often did, for example). However, the discursive distinction between a play's printed and theatrical manifestations appears to persist—and, significantly, the distinction continues to be figured, as it was by Jonson, as a mind-body divide. Thus, Dryden, in his dedication to *The Spanish Fryar* in 1681, writes that, although "'tis my Interest to please my Audience ... 'tis my Ambition to be read." "That," he adds, "I am sure[,] is the more *lasting* and *nobler* Design," a phrase that precisely reproduces Jonson's diction in the preface to *Hymenaei*.[5] A play's true artistic value, he continues, consists in its "purity of phrase, the clearness of conception and expression, ... the significancies and sound of words"—of which the live staging allows us only the most "transient view"[6]: indeed, Dryden notes, he now considers the more "extravagan[t]" elements of his earlier plays to be mere "*Dalilahs* of the Theatre."[7] Here, then, a play that is written to be read—quite literally, a literary play—is associated with that which is "lasting," "noble," or "pur[e]"; by contrast, a play that is written to please an audience is associated with sensuality, seduction, and debasement.[8]

At the same time that Dryden was insisting on a "dualistic" conception of drama's constitutive elements, however, dualistic understandings of the wider universe were being energetically debated. On one side, the newly formed Royal Society operated on the assumption that knowledge about our world could be gleaned through experiment and the observation of physical evidence. On the other side, a variety of thinkers, from Thomas Hobbes to Margaret Cavendish—and implicitly, I suggest, Aphra Behn—contended that the physical apperception of external phenomena could never yield an adequate degree of certainty about our world. This inadequacy arose in part from the difficulty of identifying what counts as objective or external evidence, as opposed to subjective belief, or even imagination.[9]

As much recent scholarship has shown, Behn's prose from the 1680s reveals her to be actively participating in the debates sparked by the new philosophy. We know that Behn was familiar with the work of Lucretius, Hobbes, Sprat, Creech, and Fontenelle, and, as Karen Gevirtz notes, Behn seems to have been particularly intrigued by the way that Lucretian thought dealt with the interaction of the physical with the mental.[10] Problems of epistemology, eyewitnessing, and the mind-body relationship all emerge repeatedly in Behn's translations, novels, short stories, and poetry from this decade.[11] Indeed, as historians of the early novel have long asserted, questions of the real, of the strange but true, remain central to the genre's development during this period.[12] Yet critics have been slower to recognize that similar issues are also being aired in Behn's plays from the same juncture. And indeed, drama—with its basis in illusion—seems ready made, even more than the novel, for exploring problems of perceiving and believing, body and mind, epistemology and hermeneutics.

As discussed in my introduction, the 1640s and 1650s saw the beginning of a coalescence of a print canon. It is thus no surprise that Dryden—following Jonson—explicitly tethered his own dramaturgical legacy to print. However, as chapter 1 suggests, Thomas Shadwell pushed back against a notion of dramaturgical succession based so squarely on textuality (as opposed to theatricality). Behn, in turn, explodes the dichotomy separating print from performance—thus undermining the Jonsonian-Drydenian divisions between high and low art forms, and between intellectual and sensual modes of artistic engagement. She thereby questions the prestige of the nascent print canon by stressing the inextricability of "imaginative" processes—such as reading—from "physical" experiences such as theatergoing.[13]

One of the two main plotlines in *The Luckey Chance* centers on a pair of reciprocal bed tricks, which pose overlapping sets of complex philosophical questions for characters and audience alike.[14] Both tricks involve Charles Gayman and Julia Fulbank, who, though they have long loved one another, have had their courtship cut short by Julia's apparently financially motivated marriage to the aging City banker Sir Cautious Fulbank.[15] Both of the bed tricks are therefore intended to unite Gayman and Julia without (supposedly) imperiling Julia's honor. In the first, which Julia engineers, a disguised servant offers the cash-strapped Gayman a large amount of gold (which Julia has stolen from her husband) in exchange for sleeping with an unknown woman (who will of course turn out to be Julia). Taken aback by the sum, Gayman assumes his propositioner to be an aging harridan "past all Hopes of Courtship and Address" (2.1.189),[16] but accepts anyway. In the second trick, Sir Cautious agrees—after Gayman has beaten him at dice in the "lucky chance" of the play's title—to allow the young lover secretly to take his place in bed, thus leaving the unsuspecting Julia theoretically innocent of adultery.

Significantly, the tricks share what would seem to be a fairly major obstacle to their success: in each, the expected bedfellow is far older than the actual body in the bed—a discrepancy, one would think, that would be almost immediately apparent. Yet, oddly, in both instances the covert identity of the "aged" participant goes undiscovered for several minutes—possibly, in the first trick, for the entirety of the encounter. As a result, both bed tricks end up raising a number of philosophical conundrums: to what extent do our preconceived ideas determine our bodily perceptions? And if one of these sources of information contradicts the other, which—internal or external—can be considered more "real"?

At the same time, of course, the bed tricks raise questions about the epistemology of drama: how does an audience member gain knowledge of a play's diegetic reality? In attempting to discern what the characters themselves believe to be true, can we trust our physical senses—what we see and hear in the theater—more than, or less than, the intellectual comprehension we can gain from a printed text? Or—and I argue that this is the side toward which Behn ultimately leans—does the act of spectatorship draw as much upon the imaginative powers as does the act of reading? (And, concomitantly—as Behn asks more pointedly in *The Emperor of the Moon*—does the act of reading draw as much upon bodily experience as does the act of spectatorship?)

I will begin by analyzing the two bed tricks of *The Luckey Chance* in the order in which they occur in the play. As I have already noted, in many ways the tricks are symmetrical, or reciprocal. Yet they can also be seen as exploring separate philosophical problems, in part due to the different outcomes of each. In the first trick (just following 3.4)—in which the identity of the disguised lover (Julia) is not revealed until two acts later (5.4.78–82)—imagined preconceptions are shown to contradict sense perception; crucially, however, the imagination proves able to access a kind of truth that sense perception fails to apprehend. The second bed trick (5.5–7) further extends the notion that imagination might yield a more reliable connection to reality than sense perception: the outcome of the trick initially seems to mirror that of the first, as imagination appears to override, at least momentarily, physical sensation.

In this case, however, the identity of the disguised lover (Gayman, this time) is soon revealed. I argue that the revelation of this identity does not necessarily owe to the fact that sense perception has reasserted its epistemological priority over the imagination (as previous critics have assumed). Quite to the contrary, I believe we might understand the second trick's revelation as, again, tinctured by imagination.

I then consider how Behn uses strategic staging in order to reinforce these philosophical quandaries for her audience. Just as the lovers discover that their physical perceptions cannot necessarily be trusted, the audience is made to realize that our senses alone are not sufficient to yield a full understanding of what has gone on in the play (indeed, we are denied a basic grasp of some of the play's most fundamental plot points). In this sense, the audience may find themselves disadvantaged in comparison to Behn's readership: the ambiguities of the play are such that casting choices, and the cast's interpretation of events, become especially consequential in determining the playgoers' understanding of the story. In the end, I argue, theatergoer and reader alike are left to try to patch together an unstable combination of evidence and speculation, fact and insight—yet also to acknowledge the limitations of these elements. The ultimate implications of this process that Behn induces in us, of course, are not only epistemological—and ethical—but also, finally, literary: what role should our physical senses—and physical pleasure—play in the interpretation and evaluation of art? Can a work of literature ever fully succeed if it appeals to our minds alone?

The Luckey Chance's first bed trick is engineered by Julia as a kind of test of Gayman's fidelity to her (despite the fact that she, hypocritically, is the one who—as far as we can tell—has betrayed him in order to marry Sir Cautious). She arranges for her former suitor, bankrupted by his lavish courtship of her, to be offered a sum of money (which she has stolen from her husband) in exchange for agreeing to sleep with an unknown partner. Gayman, reasoning that no one but the superannuated would need to resort to such methods, assumes that his intended bedmate must be an old woman (2.2). Behn carefully sets up the incident in such a way as to leave a number of points ambiguous to audience and reader alike: although we follow Gayman as he enters Julia's disguised bedchamber, our only information about what happens next derives from Gayman's subsequent account, as he attempts to defend himself to Julia the next day. This account ends up being quite detailed because, notwithstanding the fact that Julia knows (or thinks she knows) what has happened—given that it was she who was in the bed—she proceeds to interrogate Gayman closely. Perhaps she hopes to discover that he has actually, at some level, "passed" his fidelity test—in other words, that, despite agreeing to the initial solicitation, he realized at some point in the course of the encounter that his bedfellow was in fact his beloved.

Far from clearing up the issue of his fidelity or infidelity, however, Gayman's account ends up raising more questions than it answers. He begins by relating how he was led to the mysterious bed by "Young, Dancing—singing Fiends innumerable!" (4.1.73), which is itself a problematic statement. On the one hand, the audience's experience corroborates this account to some extent, for we saw these dancing and singing figures, too (though we understand that they were Julia's servants in disguise). On the other hand, we know that Gayman categorically rejects superstition, as he affirms when the mysterious invitation is first proffered:

> Spirits, Ghost, Hobgoblings, Furys, Fiends, and Devils
> I've often heard old Wives fright Fools and Children with,
> Which once arriv'd to common Sense they laugh at.
> —No, I am for things possible and Natural,
> —Some Female Devil old, and damn'd to Ugliness,
> And past all Hopes of Courtship and Address,
>   Full of another Devil call'd Desire,
> Has seen this Face—this—Shape—this Youth
> And thinks it worth her Hire. It must be so. (2.1.184–92)

To the extent that he is dealing with "Devils," Gayman transforms the term here into a figure of speech ("another Devil call'd Desire"), connoting mischief and unnatural lust. He again affirms his lack of superstition as he is about to enter the chamber: "Nor Fiend, nor Goddess can she be, for these I saw [i.e., Julia's disguised servants] were mortal! No—'tis a Woman—I am positive" (3.4.69–71). His persistence the next morning in describing the evening as enchanted, then, already leaves us wondering about the sincerity of his narrative to Julia.

From this moment on, the audience and reader must nonetheless rely on this unreliable narrator, as Behn ceased to allow us any "firsthand" knowledge of the scene as soon as Gayman entered the bedchamber. "[As] for the Amorous Devil," Gayman relates, "the old *Proserpine*... she was a silent Devil—but she was laid in a Pavillion, all form'd of gilded Clouds, ... whither I was convey'd, after much Ceremony, and laid in Bed with her; where with much ado, and trembling with my Fears—I forc'd my Arms about her" (4.1.75–81). At this point in the relation, Julia interjects, in a confident aside, "And sure that undeceiv'd him" (4.1.82). Yet Gayman resumes by describing "such a Carcase," so thoroughly "rivell'd, lean, and rough," that "a Canvass Bag of wooden Ladles were a better Bed-fellow" (4.1.83–84). Can Gayman possibly be conveying his experience truthfully here?

Several critics have proposed that Gayman is dissimulating his own real pleasure in the liaison so as to make his "infidelity" seem less reprehensible. However, as Jane Spencer notes in her edition of the play, there is another defense, nearer to hand, that seems a much surer bet: given the fact that (false) cries of political unrest ended up raising the household not long after Gayman reached Julia's bed (though the timeline here is left deliberately fuzzy), he could easily have cited this interruption (whether or not it really did prevent the act of intercourse) and thus wound up with a much more solid excuse.[17] Consequently, it seems unlikely that Gayman is using his "Carcase" description as a way of exonerating himself. What's more, the fact that he doesn't even mention the false alarm and resulting household confusion suggests that the encounter may well have continued, uninterrupted, beyond the initial "embrace" he describes—in which case it becomes even harder to understand Gayman's insistence that the body he caressed was as knobbly and harsh to the touch as "a Canvass Bag of wooden Ladles." Finally, if the "Carcase" is indeed a conscious fabrication of Gayman's, his description is oddly emotional: he describes himself as "trembling with [his] Fears" while in the bed. At one point, this tremulousness even enters into the act of narration itself, as he cuts himself off midsentence to invoke heaven's aid: "such a Carcase 'twas—deliver me—so rivell'd, lean and rough—" (4.1.83).

Assuming, then, that Gayman is honestly relating the encounter as he understands it to have happened, we are left to conclude that his imagination—his belief about whom he would find once he reached the bed—has somehow effectively superseded any information he was gathering through his senses, once he was actually under the covers. How and why did this happen? Catherine Gallagher has influentially contended that the mistake symbolizes a larger cultural mindset, according to which women's sexuality is denied its own reality and becomes, for all intents and purposes, the imaginative construct of men.[18] Without entirely refuting this interpretation, I would argue that Gayman's perceptions must be contextualized not just within the gender dynamics of the play and its time period (and also, perhaps, our own) but also within the play's other overarching themes—namely, of the mind-body problem, and, very much relatedly, of old age.

The play's plot centers on two May-December marriages (Julia's to Sir Cautious and Leticia's to Sir Cautious's fellow alderman, Sir Feeble Fainwou'd). But even as Behn leverages the contrast between young and old bodies for its comic effects, she also suggests that this contrast is not as straightforward as it might seem. Interestingly, Gayman makes this very point as he is about to embark on his surreal assignation with "the old *Proserpine.*" As he is taking leave of Julia in order to keep his appointment (he of course hedges around his actual reasons for needing to go, believing that she knows nothing about the rendezvous), she presents him with a final opportunity to pass her fidelity test. Insisting that the two of them cannot sleep together because she cannot possibly endanger her honor as a married woman, she requests Gayman's patience: "afford me a Lease of your Love," she asks, "'Till the Old Gentleman my Husband depart this wicked World" (2.2.195–96). But Gayman replies,

> Unreasonable *Julia,* is that all,
> My Love, my Sufferings, and my Vows must hope?
> Set me an Age—say when you will be kind,
> And I will languish out in starving Wish.
> But thus to gape for Legacies of Love,
> 'Till Youth be past Enjoyment,
> The Devil, I will as soon—farewell—(2.2.195–205)

As this speech makes plain, Gayman is haunted by the fear that, when he does finally clasp Julia in his arms, their youth will be spent. Indeed, given that the characters ultimately do end up striking the very bargain described here (5.7.185), with Sir Cautious "bequeath[ing] [his] Lady to [Gayman]" in his will (quite literally a "Legac[y] of Love"), Gayman's fear is one that may very well be borne out: such an agreement puts the lovers in the position of waiting for death as a condition of their love's fulfillment. And when Sir Cautious finally does die, who is to say what "Enjoyment[s]" will remain to the no-longer-young lovers?

As much as Gayman's inability to perceive Julia's body may owe, then, to women's place in (or displacement from) a patriarchal culture, that which he does perceive has a striking kind of logic to it: given the very real impasse that the lovers face, the "Carcase" Gayman takes into his arms becomes a kind of skeletal memento mori, a nightmarish foreshadowing of mortality itself—the condition of their eventual love, and, possibly, its rapidly ensuing corollary. Nor does Gayman's grim vision focus itself solely on the aging female body. In the passage above, as we have seen, Gayman's concern is for the evanescence of "Youth" in general, and, later, at the opening of act 4, he laments more specifically the passing of his own: as Julia berates him for his alleged infidelity and charges him with "lov[ing] me not," he exclaims, "Not love you! / Why do I waste my Youth in vain Pursuit, . . . / Unheeding, and despising other Beauties?" (4.1.10–15). Gayman's own salad days—and the physical attractiveness that attends them—are also of limited quantity: at some point, he implies, he will no longer be invited to sample the charms of those "other Beauties"; this is a privilege extended only to young men (especially if, like Gayman, they are in debt). Gayman's misapprehension of the body he encounters in the bed, therefore, is not necessarily the sign of his own failure of interpretation, nor need it be the sign of a larger cultural failure; rather, it reflects what is actually a deeper reality. If Gayman's physical perceptions cannot discern the difference between a "rivell'd" body and that of a rich banker's trophy wife, this is because his senses have conformed themselves to his imagination's unempirical—but arguably superior—grasp of the lovers' shared situation.[19]

Indeed, the intensity of Julia's distress upon hearing Gayman's description of her body suggests that, at some level, he has confirmed what she herself secretly believes may be true: "[*Aside.*] Now tho I know that nothing is more distant than I from such a Monster—yet this angers me . . . 'S'life after all to seem deform'd, old, ugly—[*Walking in a fret.*]" (4.1.86–97). The use of the phrase "I know" seems telling, as this is precisely the question: what does she "know" of herself at this point? Is she in some sense a "Monster" for abandoning her beloved for the sake of money? Might her preference for an old decaying businessman also constitute a choice in favor of a deeper kind of moral decay? And might this moral decay (or her anxiety about it) be manifesting itself physically—etching worry lines on her face, sapping the color from her cheeks?

Julia alludes to just this possibility near the beginning of act 1:

> Had I but kept my sacred Vows to *Gayman*
> How happy had I been—how prosperous he!

> Whilst now I languish in a loath'd Embrace,
> Pine out my Life with Age—Consumptious Coughs. (1.2.32–35)

The preposition "with," in the final line, is marked by an intriguing ambiguity. Most basically, perhaps, it connotes adjacency—Julia pines alongside of, in the shadow of, Sir Cautious's decrepitude. But it also connotes affliction: she "Pine[s] . . . with Age," and "Pine[s] . . . with . . . Coughs," in the same way that a person might pine with envy or longing. The line thus seems at once to suggest Julia's dread that her life will be spent beside the senescing banker, but also her sense that the choice she has made is eating away at her—"Consum[ing]" her. Gayman's misapprehension of Julia's body may thus reflect not only his own intuition about the likely consequences of Julia's decision but, indeed, the workings of a sympathetic imagination—his half-conscious insight into Julia's own, inner sense of mourning and loss.

With the first of *The Luckey Chance*'s bed tricks, then, Behn depicts the ability of imagination to override physical perception, but also possibly to improve upon it—to allow us to reach truths unavailable to empirical observation alone. Indeed, she suggests that, at times, imagination (pining, regret) may actually determine physical reality, as Julia's disquiet "ages" her prematurely.

In some ways, Behn seems to be issuing a warning here, a warning that the play's other storylines help to develop. Thus, for example, in the scene in which the guilt-ridden husbands believe that the ghost of Sir Feeble's wife's lover has come to seek revenge (3.5), Behn cautions against elevating our anxieties to the same epistemological plane as bodily reality: doing so may allow one's fears to foil one's best-laid plans. Yet Behn also seems to gesture toward the benefits of refusing to draw a line between sensory-based knowledge and the dream logic of imagination: by declining to distinguish too sharply between fancy and fact, we may become capable of a kind of sympathetic understanding—one that a more vigilant enforcement of the mind-body division would never allow us to attain. Just like Gayman's mistaking of Julia for a riveled bag of bones, Sir Cautious's and Sir Feeble's sightings of Belmour's "ghost" provide another example of how a hyperactive fantasy might actually help a person to see more clearly the emotional or moral truth of a situation.

This notion of imagination's peculiar capacities for insight is one that echoes throughout Behn's writing. As G. Gabrielle Starr notes in relation to Behn's prose narrative, "the status of an experience as fact (is it true that . . . ?) is [frequently] pushed aside in favor of its imaginative conception, its potential for pleasure, or particularly ... its moral uses."[20] Discussing one of Behn's shorter tales, "The Unfortunate Bride, or the Blind Lady a Beauty," Starr concludes that "physical sight" in the story proves to be "in no way superior to imagined vision," as the blind character's "fancy" is shown to "exceed ... the certainty of [the other characters'] ... sight."[21] Maura Smyth likewise asserts, in regard to *Oroonoko* in particular, that Behn "uses Fancy to talk back to ... [a] culture that privileges only that which can be experienced through the senses," deploying the "strange but real space" of the New World to "illuminate an experiential quality of reality that empiricism cannot capture."[22]

The epistemological efficacy of the imagination was not necessarily an outlandish concept among Behn's contemporaries. For example, although Thomas Hobbes subscribed to a strict materialism—explaining that "there is no conception in a mans mind, which hath not at first, totally, or by parts, been begotten upon the organs of *Sense*"—he also insisted that sense itself is ultimately a *"seeming,* or *fancy,"* which "consisteth, as to the Eye, in a *Light,* or *Colour figured;* to the Eare, in a *Sound.*"[23] Accordingly, those "qualities called *Sensible*," he notes, are located "in the object that causeth them, ... [b]ut their apparence to us is Fancy, the same waking, that dreaming."[24] (Indeed, Hobbes adds, it thereby "cometh to passe, that it is a hard matter, and by many thought impossible, to distinguish exactly between Sense and Dreaming."[25]) In short, "Sense in all cases, is nothing els but originall fancy, caused (as I have said) by ... the motion, of externall things upon our Eyes, Eares, and other organs."[26] It is assertions such as these that prompt Todd Butler to declare that, for Hobbes, "encountering and understanding the external world becomes a fundamentally imaginative experience."[27] In fact, the conclusion that all sensation is essentially a form of fancy leads Hobbes to insist that thought alone—or what he calls ratiocination—is what allows us to access genuine knowledge. And such ratiocination, proceeding, as it does, via a kind of *"Mentall Discourse,"* must essentially come down to a sequence of imaginings.[28]

Margaret Cavendish's unorthodox philosophical career differed quite a bit from Hobbes's, yet both thinkers insisted on the insufficiency of empiricism alone when it comes to knowing our world.[29] "Experimental philosophy has but a brittle, inconstant, and uncertain ground," declared Cavendish, for

> most men ... consider not so much the interior natures of several creatures, as their exterior figures and phenomena[,] ... supposing that sense and art can only lead them to the knowledge of truth. ... But, nature has placed

> sense and reason together, so that there is no part or particle of nature, which has not its share of reason, as well as of sense ... and therefore it is fit we should not only employ our senses, but chiefly our reason, in the search of the causes of natural effects: for, sense is only a workman, and reason is the designer and surveyor; and as reason guides and directs, so ought sense to work.[30]

As the quotation above suggests, it is ultimately Cavendish's materialism that leads her (as it does Hobbes) to declare mental processes to be as epistemologically valuable as sense perception: just as all of nature is infused by both "reason, as well as ... sense," so too the mind partakes just as fully of matter and the material world as do our faculties of sight, hearing, and touch.[31] As Starr summarizes, not only reason but "fancy" or speculation becomes for Cavendish—as for Hobbes—a "tool of inquiry."[32] What's more, the "utility ... [of this] fancy or imagination" is far from "phantasmatic"; rather, it is able to access the world around us just as penetratingly as—or, indeed, more acutely than—our bodies.[33]

According to Cavendish's vitalist philosophy, the soul or mind is bound up inextricably with the body. This means that reason "perceives [along] with the sense, ... for surely the rational part of matter, being intermixed with the sensitive, must perceive as well the original, as sense doth."[34] Thus, although "it seemeth as if the rational did take copies from the sensitive"—in other words, as though our physical perceptions are essentially being relayed or translated through the body for use by our mental faculties—"this doth not hinder [the rational] from making [its own] perception also of the original."[35]

Quite to the contrary, Cavendish continues, our rational perception "is not so involved within the sensitive, that it cannot peep out, as a jack-in-the-box," from time to time, and thus even supplement or improve upon the information our senses are receiving.[36] Consequently, "whatsoever the sensitive perception is either defective in, or ignorant of, the rational perception supplies," being "much purer and subtler than the sensitive."[37] Refusing simply to "rest in the knowledge of the exterior figure or object, ... [rational perception] penetrates into its interior nature, and doth probably guess and conclude what its interior figurative motions may be."[38] Indeed, it is only through speculation or fancy that we are able to apprehend the minute underpinnings of our world, too small for our outward vision to discern. How else can we understand the work of atoms, for example—"as small, as small as can bee"—or magnetic force: "What *Eye* so *cleere* is, yet did ever see / Those little Hookes, that in the Load-Stone bee, / Which draw *hard Iron?*"³⁹ While Cavendish is convinced that our senses can access truth directly, she still prioritizes imagination as the superior epistemic tool, capable of entering inner chambers of reality that sense perception alone cannot infiltrate.⁴⁰

Such deliberations have consequences not just for epistemology but for drama as well. If our imaginations are capable of accessing truths that our physical perceptions cannot, is not reading, perhaps, a more penetrating mode of dramaturgical consumption than spectating—allowing us to assess a character's motivations, or to puzzle out ambiguities in the plot, with greater clarity? Despite drama's dual status as both words on a page and events on a stage, ought we not to privilege the text as the more effective means by which drama might make its larger artistic contribution?

Certainly there were writers of Behn's era who asserted just that. In his dedication to *The Spanish Fryar* (already partially quoted in this chapter), Dryden insists that "a judicious reader will discover, in his closet, that trashy stuff, whose glittering deceived him in the action": whereas our physical senses are easily misled, our readerly acumen is able to weigh the merits and faults of a play more accurately. He explains that what we see in the theater actually hampers rather than helps our powers of discernment: "In a playhouse, everything contributes to impose upon the judgement: the lights, scenes, habits, and grace of action . . . surprise the audience, and cast a mist."⁴¹ By contrast, the reader's closet permits this mist to be cleared away, allowing our inward vision to detect what the dazzled eyes could not.

But, as I demonstrate further below, Behn seems never to have privileged reading over sensation in the way that Dryden did; indeed, she repeatedly complicates the distinction between the two. While she does seem to champion the epistemological force of the imagination, she also insists (in a further parallel with Cavendish's thought) that imagination cannot operate in isolation from the body; in fact, far from suggesting that drama is most fully realized in one mode or another, she finds drama to be the perfect medium for emphasizing the intertwinedness of body and mind, witnessing and reading, "low" entertainments and the literary canon's Parnassian heights.

I turn now to *The Luckey Chance*'s second bed trick. While previous critics have viewed this second trick as essentially reversing the mind-body dynamic of the first, I argue that it ends up reinforcing many of the concepts raised in the earlier encounter. Recall that, in this second installment of the deceit, Gayman and Julia are again in bed together, but this time Gayman is the one fully aware of what is happening (he has won a night with Julia in a bet with Sir Cautious), whereas it is Julia who believes she is about to receive the attentions of an aged bedfellow (this time her husband). And mental preconceptions clearly play a similar role at the outset of both tricks—namely, in maintaining the illusion of old age despite what would seem to be physical evidence to the contrary. Thus, when the trick is finally revealed, and Julia fumes (somewhat hypocritically[42]) over having been made an "Adulteress," Gayman replies, "Oh! Calm your Rage and hear me; if you are so, / You are an innocent Adulteress. / It was the feeble Husband you enjoy'd / In cold Imagination, and no more, / Shyly you turn'd away—faintly resign'd" (5.7.24–31). At least according to Gayman, then, Julia's "cold Imagination" governed her experience even in the midst of active "enjoy[ment]." (To "enjoy," of course, can simply mean "to have the use of benefit of"—without, necessarily, feeling "joy"-ful about doing so.[43]) However, if both tricks begin with imagination prevailing over bodily sensation, their trajectories soon diverge: we learn that Julia remained "faintly resign'd ... [only] ... Till my Excess of Love—betray'd the Cheat," as Gayman puts it (5.7.31–33). Most scholars seem to understand this phrase as referring to Gayman's sexual potency. As Gallagher concludes, "Unlike Julia's body, only Gayman's [can] undo the misrepresentation: no mere idea can eradicate the palpable sign of identity, the tumescent penis itself."[44] According to this reading, Behn is critiquing a society in which the male body becomes the ultimate fact, around which all other realities orbit. And for my own purposes here, such a reading suggests that, if the first trick illustrated the imagination's ability to override, enhance, or adjust empirical fact, the second, inversely, illustrates the ability of empirical fact (or, at least, certain empirical facts) to put imagination back in its place.

Unlike Gallagher, however, I do not interpret Gayman's "Excess of Love" as necessarily alluding to his superlative sexual capacity. Indeed, in what is surely its most striking deployment in Behn's oeuvre, this same phrase refers to the opposite phenomenon in her well-known 1680 poem "The Disappointment." Here I quote the relevant stanza and the one preceding it:

> Ready to taste a thousand joys,
> The too transported hapless Swain,

> Found the vast Pleasure turn'd to Pain:
> Pleasure, which too much Love destroys:
> The willing garments by he laid,
> And Heaven all open'd to his view,
> Mad to possess, himself he threw
> On the Defenceless Lovely Maid.
> But Oh what envious God[s conspire]
> To snatch his Power, yet leave him the Desire!
>
> *Nature's Support,* (without whose Aid
> She can no Humane Being give)
> It self now wants the Art to live;
> Faintness its slack'ned Nerves invade:
> In vain th' inraged Youth essay'd
> To call its fleeting Vigor back,
> No motion 'twill from Motion take;
> Excess of Love his Love betray'd:
> In vain he Toils, in vain Commands;
> The Insensible fell weeping in his Hand.⁴⁵ (Lines 71–90)

"The Disappointment" is, of course, like Rochester's *Imperfect Enjoyment,* a poem very much about the mind-body relationship. And, as soon becomes evident, the participation of "Love" in this relationship—and, therefore, of "Excess of Love"—proves quite vexed.⁴⁶ In lines 71–72, we see a tension introduced as the male lover (elsewhere identified as Lisander) is thwarted in his attempts to "taste" the delights of intercourse by his "too transported" state: in other words, physical delectation is impeded by mental rapture or ecstasy. Line 74—where "Love" first appears—seems to reiterate this tension: "too much Love" is pitted against "Pleasure," thus aligning "Love" with the mental transport of 72 and "Pleasure" with the "tast[ing]" of sensory joys in 71. Yet Behn refuses to retain this neat binary, and her use of a kind of double chiasmus, in lines 87–88, sows a deliberate confusion: "No motion 'twill from Motion take; / Excess of Love his Love betray'd" (lines 87–88). In line 87, the word "motion" can mean both "physical ... movement" but also "perturbation, agitation (of the mind or feelings)" (*OED,* s.v. "motion," def. 2). Thus, while the line expresses an apparent tautology at one level, at another level it articulates a classic version of mind-body dysfunction: Lisander's affective frenzy cannot stir his penis into action. In line 88, this interpretive ambiguity becomes intensified. We are first presented with the tautology (love betraying love), but then we detect the mind-body opposition: too many thoughts of love undercut the lover's ability to make love. (Dizzyingly, Behn has inverted the order of the contrasting terms in line 87—body/mind—in line 88: mind/body.) To make matters even more complicated, the phrase "his Love" here could also refer to Lisander's beloved (Cloris), who also has been "betray'd" by his immoderate passion. And the poem's surrounding stanzas contain twelve additional instances of the word "Love," all of which possess shadings of these various connotations, plus more (a reference to "Love and Fate," for example, evokes Love as Cupid [line 92]).

The stanzas' topsy-turvy wordplay shows Behn to be exposing the all-too-slippery divisions between psychological and physiological, metaphorical and literal, when it comes to "Pleasure," "Motion," and, of course, "Love." In this sense, the poem is really about the impossibility of locating an experience strictly in the body or in the mind, in physical reality or in the ways we think and talk about reality. Nonetheless, the trajectory of the verse's narrative makes clear that "Excess of Love" refers to an imaginative surfeit rather than a physical one. That is, even as it alludes, in crucial ways, to the inextricability of mind and body, the phrase most expressly denotes a mental state that undermines bodily action.

One could obviously still argue that "Excess of Love" refers to something different in *The Luckey Chance* than in "The Disappointment": certainly, we need not conclude that the second bed trick ended in impotence.[47] The various references to "enjoy[ment]," "Adulter[y]," and Gayman's having "possess[ed]" Julia seem to point fairly clearly to sexual consummation (5.7.59). But I hope the above analysis has also suggested that Gayman's "Excess of Love" could plausibly refer to a bewildering spectrum of events, in which mind and body play varying roles in varying ratios.[48] That is, even assuming that the sexual act between them is in fact consummated, what if it is not this act that gives Gayman away? Could the "Excess of Love" that "betray[s] the Cheat" not still be, at least in part, a mental phenomenon—as it is in the poem? In this construal, might Julia's doubts be raised not by Gayman's body, but by the way he inhabits it—by her bedfellow's hastiness, for example, or (inversely) by his pausing to luxuriate in this long-awaited moment? It seems worth noting here that it is only just prior to embarking on the second bed trick that Gayman finally learns the truth about the first trick (5.4.78–82); the realization that he has already joined Julia in bed, but that he has ludicrously failed truly to experience it, likely spurs in Gayman a kind of frantic resolve to savor now, as fully as possible, what he missed the night before.

The notion that it is Gayman's mental state that has entered into a condition of "Excess" is reiterated by Gayman a few lines later:

> Heavens! [Prior to tonight] I ... ador'd you,
> But now I rave! And with my impatient Love,
> A thousand mad, and wild Desires are Burning! (5.7.37–39)

The "rav[ing]" state of "mad[ness]" depicted here is, by definition, one in which imagination has outstripped external realities—so that, even having just completed the act of intercourse (as far as we can tell), Gayman's love remains "impatient," rendering inadequate any physical attempts to slake it. Again, I do not mean to insist that Gayman's body plays absolutely no part in the revelation of his identity. But what Gayman's words here suggest is that the central responsibility for breaking through Julia's mental preconceptions cannot be assigned to the "tumescent penis"—which, after all (and as Behn's verse so eloquently conveys), seems a curiously unsteady symbol for anything like stable selfhood. Rather, I would argue that Julia's "cold Imagination" has been corrected, at least to some extent, through its confrontation with Gayman's own fiercely "Burning" fancy—that Gayman's body becomes recognizable to Julia only once it has been animated by his unique accumulation of long-pent-up desires.

The philosophical systems of Hobbes and Cavendish again provide a useful context in which to consider how seventeenth-century thought could accommodate such a possibility. In the model of perception that Gallagher seems to be positing, Julia's physical senses register an external object (Gayman's body) and deliver the news to her mind. But, as I have noted already, neither Hobbes nor Cavendish understood perception to work in this dualistic (or essentially Cartesian) manner, in which physical facts are registered upon our physical beings and are then relayed to the spirit or soul, as the seat of judgment. Rather, in Hobbes's view, sensation and fancy are virtually indistinguishable, and in Cavendish's, the two are so enmeshed as to prohibit the kind of sequential messaging that Gallagher's scenario implies. As Cavendish insists, "there is sense and reason, or sensitive and rational knowledge, ... in every part of every particular creature,"[49] and thus it is a mistake to "believe that all knowledge lies in the head"—after all, "the heart, liver, lungs, spleen, stomach, bowels and the rest, know as well their office and functions... as the eyes, ears, nostrils, tongue, etc. know their particular actions."[50] According to Cavendish's system, Gayman and Julia are properly understood as bodies suffused throughout by spirit or mind, simultaneously imparting and receiving information by way of both their physical and imaginative capacities.

By recognizing the complex questions that *The Luckey Chance*'s bed tricks pose regarding sensation, imagination, and epistemology, we can become more attuned to the questions the play raises about sensation, imagination, and drama. On the one hand, Behn suggests that imagination may yield richer understandings than sense perception alone. Yet, on the other hand, she thwarts our attempts to schematize too starkly the respective epistemological contributions of our minds and bodies. Of course, as a medium divided between page and stage, drama inherently combines text (which depends, for its "sensory" elements, more fully on the imagination) with live performance (whose medium is, of course, the bodies, voices, sights, and sounds of the stage). But which associated activity, Behn asks—reading or spectatorship—might be said to be the keener mode of apprehension, if we acknowledge imagination's "realities" as rivaling those of physical sensation? Which of these allows us to grasp most fully what an individual play means, or, indeed, what drama can be? In a context in which drama had recently been elevated to an incipient print canon, and had recently begun to be taken more seriously by book buyers as stand-alone reading matter, these questions were more relevant than ever.

The Luckey Chance poses its questions of medium and perception not just thematically but structurally—forcing readers and theatergoers alike to share in the characters' basic factual confusions. I have already mentioned the ways in which Behn makes us (both readers and audience) privy to the arrangements preceding her bed tricks, and to some of their aftereffects, but not to the events themselves. However, as we will see, multiple additional performance-based strategies compound these problems: strategies of staging and casting, theatrical in-jokes, and scenes in which, depending on how the actors interpret their roles, we might suspect the characters themselves to be "acting" for one another's benefit.

I will start with the first bed trick. In the scene in which Gayman narrates his encounter with the "old *Proserpine*" to his increasingly unamused young lover, we might say that Behn creates not merely a dramatic irony but also a visual one: as Julia Fawcett has pointed out, in the first production of the play, Julia Fulbank was played by Elizabeth Barry, whose "plump and pleasing body" would, Fawcett posits, have allowed Behn's audience to feel a distinct hermeneutic superiority over Gayman at this moment.[51] Yet, as I have suggested above, Julia's angry aside after hearing Gayman's description—"'S'life after all to seem deform'd, old, ugly"—also hints, perhaps, at some glimmer of psychological (if not also physical) truth behind his apparent misprision, her joyless marriage to Sir Cautious having taken its toll. And in fact, by the mid-1680s, it seems that Barry had gained a reputation for being "mercenary" and even "heartless"—attributes that resonate with Julia's own guilty sense of having married for money.[52] Curiously, moreover, despite her status as the most celebrated actress of her time (and as the longtime mistress of the libertine par excellence John Wilmot[53]), Barry was, according to contemporary accounts, a "plain woman": the author of *A Comparison between the Two Stages* (1702, attributed to Charles Gildon) called Barry "the finest Woman in the World upon the Stage, [but] ... the ugliest Woman off on't."[54] The audience, then, may find Gayman's mistake to be visually absurd: he has just compared Elizabeth Barry, the stage's most irresistible woman, to a canvas bag of clanking ladles. But how much credit can the audience grant to optics here? And to what extent—either due to what they know of Barry's offstage reputation, or due to Julia's own possible self-doubt—might they begin to question their sense perceptions?

The staging of the second bed trick's aftermath may introduce even more ambiguities. Here, as Gayman tries to justify what has just happened, Sir Cautious's reactions—which he reveals in asides following each of Gayman's statements—serve as a guide to our own interpretation; yet this guide turns out to be somewhat dubious. Most crucially, perhaps, when Gayman says that his "Excess of Love—betray'd the Cheat," Sir Cautious's response is one of dismay: "[*Aside*] Ay, ay that was my Fear—" (5.7.33). This reaction appears to confirm Gallagher's interpretation of what has occurred behind the bedroom door—namely, that Gayman has proven so virile as to make glaringly obvious that he is not Julia's aging husband. However, depending on how the character is played, and how the lines are spoken, each of Sir Cautious's inferences could be made to seem either more or less legitimate.

Is Sir Cautious looking on gravely at this moment, sobered by what has just happened, or is he comically clasping his head and shaking his fists without pausing to reflect? As Robert Markley points out, the casting of famed comic actor James Nokes as Sir Cautious may well suggest that the character was interpreted almost as a kind of buffoon, rather than as the sinister hoarder of money and women that readers might envision.[55] Sir Cautious's next aside—in which he infers that, despite her indignant excoriations, Julia is "well enough pleas'd I fear"—could likewise be more or less accurate depending on how the actors were playing the scene (5.7.46).

Indeed, it seems possible that the characters themselves may be playing in a scene: given Julia's expert stage management of the night before (the pageant she produced of dancing nymphs and shepherds), might not part or all of the exchange between the lovers here be strategically performed as a way of manipulating Sir Cautious? After all, as Gallagher has noted, a well-executed scene of outrage would allow Julia to exploit her injured-wife status, making Sir Cautious more likely to guiltily accept her "vow—by all things Just and sacred, / To separate forever from his Bed" (5.7.64–65).[56] Likewise, the revelation, in the closing moments of the play, that Gayman is aware—but has somehow failed to mention—that his uncle has died and left him two thousand pounds a year (5.7.204–5) suggests that Gayman is certainly capable of keeping secrets, if not putting on elaborate acts of his own.[57] (Note, too, that, if Julia is performing for Sir Cautious, and if Gayman is an active participant in this performance, then the speech about his "Excess of Love" takes on further ambiguities: to what extent do Gayman's words—however we interpret them—align with what actually happened, and to what extent might they simply be calculated to rub salt into Sir Cautious's wounds?)

Here again, the casting may inform the scene's meaning: as Markley notes, the fact that Julia was originally played by Barry, and Gayman by Thomas Betterton, suggests that many of the characters' lines throughout the play could have carried parodic overtones, with the actors spoofing their own well-known tragic personas (Markley cites Gayman's lofty pledges of fidelity in 4.1.23–28, for example: "By all the Powers above! . . . / I never had a Wish or soft Desire / To any other Woman, / Since *Julia* sway'd the Empire of my Soul!").[58] Similarly, as Barry's Julia rants in blank verse about her injured "Honour"—citing her husband's "barbarous[ness]" in bringing "so shameful and so base Revenge" upon her—the lines' pathos may be tempered by metatheatrical humor (5.7.45, 5.7.57, 5.7.55).[59]

And yet, given the warnings that Behn has been sending us, throughout the play, about the unreliability of human perception, how much stock should an audience place in these theatrical cues? To what extent can an audience member rely on observations regarding staging or casting, body language or vocal inflection, to gain insight into a character's "true" motivations? After all, theater depends, as an art form, on the willing suspension of disbelief.

These epistemological conundrums prove crucial to an interpretation not just of what has "happened" in the first and second bed tricks but, even more disarmingly, of how the play ends. Here, as Sir Cautious "bequeath[s] [his] Lady to [Gayman]—with [his] whole Estate" (5.7.186), and Gayman asks, "Do you consent my *Julia?*," she replies (teasingly? resentfully?), "No Sir—you do not like me—a canvass Bag of wooden Ladles were a better Bed-fellow" (5.7.188–90).

Fawcett beautifully articulates the ways in which these uncertainties around the play's ending force us to heed Julia's body in a way that Gayman, in the first bed trick, seemingly has not—rectifying both his error and its gendered implications: "By leaving her script ambiguous, Behn puts the responsibility for narrative closure into the hands—or rather, onto the body—of the actress portraying Julia, which the audience must attend to and interpret in order to know how the story ends. Thus Behn not only cajoles her spectators into drawing meaning from the movements of a woman's body.... She also emphasizes how crucial these movements are: to interpret them incorrectly is to suffer an unsatisfying night at the theatre, to be marked as a poor critic of plays."[60] Yet I would argue, with Gallagher, that our interpretation of the play's final moments (and, perhaps, of the play as a whole) ultimately hinges upon a question that transcends the physical—namely, the question of Julia's desire. Is Julia more delighted than dismayed to have an excuse to abandon her husband's bed? And, now that Sir Cautious has accepted her choice, does she intend to continue engineering covert liaisons with Gayman? The answer to each of these questions lies, significantly, "on the other side of what we see and hear."[61] That is to say, although various physical components of the play's theatrical production may encourage our suspicions one way or the other, the final determinant of the story's outcome is not corporeal—or, at least, not merely corporeal—but psychological, emotional. To return to the word that has already caused so much epistemological tumult in the play, we might say that the question of Behn's ending depends on the question of Julia's "love." To believe that we could find an answer simply by watching Julia for physical clues—and, accordingly, to believe that we could interpret a play simply by way of careful spectating—is to disregard the serious challenge to the authority of the senses that Behn weaves throughout *The Luckey Chance*.

As seventeenth-century commentators would have been quick to point out, the question of how or whether to assign epistemological authority to sense perception is one with broad implications not just for the kinds of hermeneutic questions outlined above but for moral questions as well—and, by extension, for debates surrounding the moral effects of the theater. Historians have argued that the 1680s marked a new phase in dramaturgy, reflective of what appears to have been a growing concern regarding the theater's social benefits—or, depending on one's perspective, dangers. As Robert Hume writes, "By the later seventies, ... both heroic drama and sex comedy were dying a natural death," and, by the eighties, "two basic developments are unmistakably plain": "serious drama becomes increasingly *affective*," while "in comedy," we see "a gradual move toward a new, purer type," signaling "the beginning of what ultimately becomes defined as 'exemplary' comedy."[62] Hume points to comedies such as John Crowne's popular (and distinctly chaste) 1685 play *Sir Courtly Nice,* in the epilogue to which Crowne explicitly announces his abandonment of "all that lewdness" found in so much current fare.[63] Likewise, the prologue to Edward Ravenscroft's good-natured *Dame Dobson* (1683) describes the play as "the Poets *Recantation*" for his naughty *London Cuckolds* of the year before.[64] Hume writes that here, as in many other defensive statements made by playwrights (including Behn's preface to *The Luckey Chance*), "The Ladies" are increasingly used metonymically to refer to a newly squeamish public, now a full generation removed from the "coterie" audiences that greeted the theaters' initial reopening.[65]

Frances Kavenik considers Behn's late comedies to fit fairly well with the trend Hume describes: she sees both *The Feign'd Courtesans* (1679) and *The Second Part of the Rover* (1681) as "avoid[ing] the kind of sexual confrontations which comedies and their audiences of the 1670s thrived on," and observes that, likewise, *The Roundheads* (1682) and *The Luckey Chance* present us with lovers who are no longer "licentious" but who "focus [their] passion ... on ... single, suitable lover[s]."[66] In contrast to the wives gleefully cuckolding their husbands in plays like *The Country Wife*, for example, here "the women often feel guilty about their adultery," while at the same time Behn "create[s] husbands who are seditious, cowardly, or avaricious," so that the husbands' younger rivals—all, significantly, "former lovers" to the women—become "wit heroes" rather than "rakes," "rescu[ing]" their beloveds from villainy.[67]

As we will see in a moment, both the dedicatory epistle and the preface to *The Luckey Chance* would seem to affirm Behn's interest in contributing to the emerging moral emphasis that was distinguishing both theater and theatrical discourse in the 1680s: in the preface, Behn defends herself against accusations of lewdness, while in the epistle she praises the power of theater in general to provide tangible moral exemplars. Ultimately, however, the play's larger skepticism regarding the epistemological utility of sense perception seems to undercut such paratextual protestations. Even if we accept the premise that the theater engages more of our senses more intensely than other art forms (a premise Behn proceeds to reject in *The Emperor of the Moon*, one year later), the philosophical questions raised within *The Luckey Chance* cast serious doubt as to whether such sensory engagement offers any more immediate access to ontological or moral truth.

Behn's dedicatory epistle to Lord Hyde, Earl of Rochester, draws a direct connection between the theater and a society's moral and political rectitude: "Cardinal *Richilieu*, that great and wise Statesman, said, That there was no surer Testimony to be given of the flourishing Greatness of a State, than publick Pleasures and Divertisements—for they are, says he—the Schools of Vertue, where Vice is always either punish't, or disdain'd" (lines 10–14 [roman and italic type reversed]). Behn proceeds to explain why public spectacle specifically, as opposed to mere words, may provide "secret Instructions to the People": "'Tis Example that prevails above Reason or *Divine Precepts*," she writes, for "Philosophy [is] not understood by the Multitude" (lines 14–16). It is therefore "Example alone"—rather than the rhetorical persuasion of treatises or sermons, it seems—"that inspires Morality, and best establishes Vertue" (lines 17–18). Accordingly, Behn goes on to say, it was only upon "beholding in our Theatre a Modern Politician set forth in all his Colours" that an unnamed man of her acquaintance finally "renounc'd his [erroneous] Opinion," after "neither Conscience nor Religion" had succeeded in "perswad[ing] [him] to Loyalty" (lines 18–21).

The Luckey Chance's preface would seem at first to support the views laid out in the dedicatory epistle regarding the importance of theater's power of example: Behn begins in a position of indignant self-defense, complaining that the play has been "charge[d] ... with the old never failing Scandal—That 'tis not fit for the Ladys" (lines 11–12). As she proceeds to respond to such charges, however, she sketches an increasingly complex relationship between moral instruction and live theater, and contradictions soon arise that echo the philosophical doubts raised by the play's themes.

The first of these contradictions can be seen in the preface's privileging of page over stage—reversing the hierarchy posited only a few pages earlier, in the dedicatory epistle. Prior to *The Luckey Chance*'s performance, Behn insists, the play had been "nicely look't . . . over [by] . . . Dr. *Davenant*," "read . . . and licens'd . . . [by] Sir *Roger L'Estrange*," and "perus'd . . . with great Circumspection [by] . . . Mr. *Killigrew*," all of whom found "no such Faults as 'tis charg'd with" (lines 40–46); moreover, "the Play was read by several Ladys of very great Quality, and unquestioned Fame, and received their most favourable Opinion, not one charging it with the Crime [of indecency], that some have been pleas'd to find in the Acting" (lines 101–4). Here, it appears that the play's moral rectitude is best discerned in its textual version, rather than "in the Acting" of it. Indeed, according to Behn, the most strident remonstrations against the play seem to have arisen from elements of performance: detractors reportedly objected "*That Mr.* Leigh [Sir Feeble] *opens his Night Gown, when he comes into the Bride-chamber*" to join Leticia on their wedding night (3.2). But this "Jest," Behn insists, was "of [Leigh's] own making," and, as for herself, she "never saw [it]" (lines 53–55). Whereas in the dedicatory epistle Behn praises the advantages of live performance over texts in the teaching of virtue, here she warns against the way in which live actors—no doubt with the encouragement of a live audience's laughter—can corrupt a text that had (allegedly) been morally pure prior to its theatrical premiere. If this is the case, can the public theaters really serve as the "Schools of Vertue" she touts them as?

But here Behn introduces yet another twist into her argument (and it is here, too, that the thematics of the play enter into what had initially seemed an unrelated debate): the real reason for the critics' objections seems to be less what they have witnessed in production than what they imagine themselves to have witnessed. Behn scoffs (lines 55–58) that Leigh surely "ha[d] his Cloaths on underneath" the gaping gown—she cites a production of *Oedipus* in which "the Gown [is] open'd wide, and the Man shown in his Drawers and Wastecoat"—and, if this was the case here, then "where [was] the Indecency," other than in the minds of the over-excited onlookers? A second objection to the production appears to have been sparked, similarly, not by what happens onstage but by what the audience envisions happening off of it: Behn ventriloquizes her censurers, "*Why we know not what they mean, when the Man takes a Woman off the Stage, and another is thereby cuckolded*" (lines 59–61). Again, it is not what the playgoers have observed but what their fancies have filled in—beneath the gown, between the acts—that has raised their moral hackles. Indeed, Behn goes on to bemoan that it is simply the "Business . . . [of]

obstinate Criticks... to find Fault[s]," or, "if not," then "by a loose and gross Imagination to create them": "for they must either find the Jest, or make it" (lines 90–92). Just as for the characters within the play, so, too, for the observers of the play: sense perception is all too easily overridden by imagination.

But if it is inward conception rather than outward perception that leaves the stronger impression upon us, then, by implication, the theater can hold no more sway over us (moral or immoral) than reading can. Indeed, this notion seems to have been one that other writers were also expressing as the century came to its close: Elkanah Settle's response to Jeremy Collier, *A Farther Defence of Dramatick Poetry* (1698), insists that, in fact, it is reading that affects us more deeply than theatergoing. Rebutting Collier's insinuation that "the *playing* it self" exerts some particularly "extraordinary" force upon us, Settle asks whether performance really could "imprint the subject of the History, or Fiction, too lively in the Fancy, more than the bare Reading it can do?"[68] Answering this question firmly in the negative, Settle continues: "For he that Reads a History, or Romance, if a sensible Reader, raises in his own Fancy some *Idea* of this or that *Hero* or *Heroine*, or perhaps *Libertine* or *Lover*, which he shapes to himself more or less lovely; chiefly from the personal Description of the Character, the Bravery, the Adventures, and Distresses, &c. which he reads in the History; and partly from his own Humour or Inclinations which possibly may recommend one particular Character, more to his Favour then [*sic*] another."[69] As suggested by his description of the reader as "sensible," Settle seems to understand the reading process as blurring mind and body: his reader is prone both to an overactive "Fancy" and, therefore, to acute bodily sensation (the reader "shapes" a character to his or her liking).

Behn's preface to *The Luckey Chance* thus makes a similar point, it seems, to the one that Settle will articulate a decade later—but she takes it one step further. That is, the problem here does not necessarily lie in her detractors' strength of imagination—after all, in certain cases (as we saw with Gayman's skeletal memento mori), imagination may be capable of yielding valid insights of its own. Rather, error arises (as it does for Gayman) from the critics' inability to recognize and respect imagination's power—from their failure to understand that what seems to be reality (an actor's nakedness, a character's act of adultery) is informed as much by fancy as by fact. Such a state of affairs, of course, once again complicates the dedicatory epistle's claim that the theater edifies by way of its sensorially striking "Example[s]" (line 16).

For not only can what we observe (or think we observe) in the theater turn out to be far less morally uplifting than what we read in the script alone, but it is precisely by setting so much stock in (what we think are) our empirical perceptions that we are led into epistemological, hermeneutic, and, indeed, moral error—"creat[ing]" monstrosities upon the stage where a solitary reader would have detected only minor mischief.

Perhaps it is not theater we should be looking to for moral instruction, then, but drama. After all, it is drama that—as a medium innately straddling the performative and the readerly—always requires us to pay equal attention to body and mind, spectacle and speculation. As Benjamin Bennett writes, "When I read a novel in book form, I know that I am doing exactly what is meant to be done with the work. When I read a play in a book, I am much less confident in this regard; I recognize that the work's present mode of being, for me, is secondary or subordinate with respect to another mode of being ... [which] the very idea of drama compels me to envisage."[70] Reading a play thus erodes our self-assurance as readers, making us feel that we are being forced to work with faulty, flawed, or partial information. At the same time, however, "dramatic *performance,* while in a strong sense indispensable to the very existence of the work, is still, in every particular instance, strictly detachable from the work, as an interpretation of it."[71] In this sense, drama, as an eternally neither-nor sort of art form, forces us to be "conscious" of our limited perspective, and our interpretive limits, in ways that other art forms do not.[72] Perhaps it is the humility that comes with this conscious limitation, and the self-questioning it initiates, that ultimately provides the only truly adequate basis for moral education.

Before I pursue this suggestion further, it is important to note that at least some of Behn's statements regarding morality in *The Luckey Chance*'s preface seem disingenuous,[73] if not outright hypocritical: as the Cambridge editors point out,[74] Behn's tone of righteous indignation on the topic is complicated by her own stage directions, which call for Sir Feeble to "*Throw ... open his Gown*" (3.2.13 sd)—prior to which, moreover, Sir Feeble has explicitly announced his intention to "throw open my Gown to fright away the Women" (3.1.85–86). Indeed, far from being merely a comic flourish, the gesture is a key element in the scene's mounting plot tension: it causes Leticia's serving women to "*run away,*" depriving her of further ways to postpone the marriage's unwelcome consummation (a moment earlier, she had reproached Sir Feeble, "For shame of Modesty Sir; you wou'd not have me go to Bed before all this Company" [3.2.13 sd; 3.2.3–4]). Likewise, it is hard to see how we could impute any truly innocent "*mean*[ing]" to a man's "*tak*[ing] *a Woman off the Stage, and . . . thereby cuckold*[ing]" her husband. To be sure, Anthony Leigh was almost certainly not stark naked beneath his gown, and, as we have seen, what happens offstage between the lovers in this play is not always as straightforward as we might assume. It does seem, then, that the critics' purported shock speaks as much to their suggestible imaginations as it does to the suggestive content of the play. Nevertheless, we might legitimately ask at this point, Is Behn's stance of moral umbrage anything more than a pose?

On the one hand, it seems safe to assume Behn is mocking the notion that a play could serve unproblematically as a "School . . . of Vertue." On the other hand, despite her mockery (or by way of her mockery), I also think she is forcing us to acknowledge that questions of mind, body, and interpretation are never without moral implications. This latter project can be seen in the preface's oft-cited remarks on female dramatists, in which Behn raises many of the same issues surrounding corporeal "fact" and imagined realities.

Pointing to the different moral standards applied to men and women playwrights, Behn again taps into questions of imagination versus sense perception: she insists that many of the contemporary stage's most objectionable elements "are never taken Notice of, because a Man writ them," when the same things, "from a Woman," would be "blush[ed] at" (lines 20–21): "Right or Wrong," she writes, "they must be Criminal because a Woman's" (lines 28–29). Each of the apparent empirical datapoints here—the female dramatist's purported "Crim[es]," her critics' flushed faces—turns out to be of questionable ontological status: when the critics feel their faces turning hot, this may be the sign not of something amiss in the play but of something amiss in their minds; indeed, as Behn says, the "Wrong[s]" of her plays may just as well be "Right"—but the critics' sexism has predisposed them to judge otherwise.

Of all of these empirical "facts," moreover, it is Behn's own sex (and also, therefore, the critics' sexism) that seems the least objectively grounded of all. "Had I a Day or two's time," she writes, "I would sum up all your Beloved Plays, and all the things in them that are past with such Silence by because written by Men: such Masculine Strokes in me, must not be allow'd" (lines 81–86). This resonant phrase can be read at least two ways. First, Behn's writing is the result of "Strokes" ("movements of the pen" [*OED*, s.v. "stroke," def. 16a]) indistinguishable from those made by a man: indeed, ten lines later she ventures that if she had written under a man's name, she would have been credited with writing "as many good Comedies as any one Man that has writ in our Age" (lines 97–98). Second, and even more fundamentally, Behn herself appears to comprise manly "Strokes" in the sense of "mark[s] traced by the moving point of a pen" or the "component line[s] of a written character" (*OED*, def. 17a): we see this latter connotation reinforced in the preface's closing rhetorical move, in which Behn writes, "All I ask, is the Priviledge for my Masculine Part the Poet in me, (if any such you will allow me) to tread in those successful Paths my Predecessors have so long thriv'd in" (lines 127–30). Of what, exactly, does Behn's femaleness consist, if she also contains this "Masculine Part"—one that has such a corporeal presence to it, indeed, that it is capable of walking off by itself, "tread[ing]" the same laurel-strewn "Paths" as any of Behn's writer-predecessors? Behn's critics may point to her female body as an irreducible fact of her writing, but here she insists that sexual difference is not as categorical as it appears to the observer's eye.[75]

For Behn, then, the question of when to trust sense perception as opposed to imagination is a question with moral stakes. Where these stakes become particularly critical, however, is not only in how we understand and respond to plays but in how we understand and respond to one another. Of course, Behn is using a play—and the discussion surrounding that play—to make her point, and, in doing so, she makes a strong case for plays' moral significance. But—to return to the suggestion I made a few moments ago—this is not the same as making the claim (as she does in the epistle) on behalf of theater. Rather, I would argue that for Behn it is drama—in its double capacity as both text and performance, with all of the interpretive unease that that doubleness can cause—that is the moral medium. Yet she does not suggest that this moral function serves simply to inculcate virtue: rather, precisely by compelling us to ask how we know what we know—and by forcing us to try to understand the relationship, in this regard, between our bodies and our minds—drama can effect in us a process of moral questioning by which, with any luck, we might begin trying to define what "Vertue" is in the first place.

Within the context of *The Luckey Chance,* to engage in this process means that, before we can decide whether Julia is a pattern of wifely devotion or a scheming adulteress, and before we can decide whether Gayman is a liar or an honest man, we are obliged to exercise every hermeneutic resource we have to its maximum capacity—our eyes and our ears, but also our psychological intuition and our powers of sympathy, even our knowledge of the actors' previous roles or offstage reputations. And indeed, the play as performed nearly begs to be read and reread, even as reading the play makes us yearn to see it performed. But in the end, we are left simply to confront the fact of each of these interpretive methods' inadequacy—and to conclude that perhaps the most serious error, more grievous than any of the play's characters' possible missteps, is to judge our world, and the people in it, without ever doubting our ability to know them fully.

Al Coppola has suggested that Behn's concern, in the late 1680s, with overcredulity—with an excessive readiness to believe in what Coppola calls the "immediate intelligibility" of our surroundings—is as much a political concern as it is a moral or ethical one.[76] Contextualizing Behn's late plays amid a "spectacular politics" of royal pageants, public punishments, executions, demonstrations, and riots,[77] Coppola contends that Behn is pushing back against an "endemic abuse of spectacle for political ends" and, at the same time, against a "troubling appetite for uncritical wonder" in late seventeenth-century Britain.[78] He sees these abuses and appetites epitomized, in many ways, in the events surrounding the Popish Plot (1678–81), a fictitious conspiracy to assassinate Charles II and replace him with his Catholic brother, the Duke of York (later King James II). (Though fears of the plot had receded by 1681, the original "informant," Titus Oates, had not formally been discredited until a 1685 trial, after which he then, according to his sentence, stood in the pillory five times per year in five locations across London.[79])

Coppola focuses on depictions of overcredulity in Behn's *The Emperor of the Moon*, in which the gullible Doctor Baliardo's lunar investigations are at moments compared to spying and treason,[80] but *The Luckey Chance* actually contains several direct references to the Popish Plot itself, starting in the very first scene.[81] Throughout the play, Behn uses the alderman-husbands' anti-Catholic paranoia as a way to ridicule and mock them; their political frenzy directly aids in the cuckolding of Sir Feeble, whose attempt to consummate his marriage with Leticia is interrupted when he becomes convinced that he must immediately depart for the Guildhall so as to prevent the government's imminent overthrow (see 3.2). The symbolic emasculation that ensues is further affirmed in Julia's chiding of both men: "Away, I'm asham'd to see wise Men so weak"; "the Whimseys of the Brain for want of Rest . . . play'd you this Trick" (3.5.175–78). Yet, of course, absurd as they may have been, delusional beliefs in the Popish Plot, in the years preceding *The Luckey Chance*'s premiere, resulted in very real acts of violence. (Moreover, as the confusion around the play's central bed tricks demonstrates, such imaginative suggestibility is clearly not limited to foolish cuckolds.) Behn thus implies that a refusal to examine carefully our epistemological assumptions—a refusal to question how we know what we think we know—is a trait both deeply human and, in its effects, deeply inhumane. It is a problem, she implies, that is not limited to the privacy of the bedchamber but that extends to the most public of political actions.

Interestingly, historians have suggested that the epistemological issues raised by the Popish Plot centered (as they do in Behn's play) around questions of media: the sheer volume, variety, and intricacy of the messaging by both parties during the crisis forced Britons to reexamine by what means they received information, and to attempt to discern which of those means could be deemed more or less trustworthy. Although Coppola mainly views the pageantry surrounding the Popish Plot as part of the era's broader "culture of spectacle,"[82] other scholars have emphasized the way in which the Plot's multi-platform media construction—consisting of forged letters, show trials, highly theatricalized processions, sermons, public executions, broadsides, and even illustrated playing cards—represented, in some ways, the first sustained mass-media event.[83] As Claire Walker notes, the lapse of the Licensing Act in 1679 allowed an "emergent print media" to "flood... the streets, coffee houses, and other venues for public discourse with newspapers, broadsheets, and pamphlets full of the latest news and comment"; these, in turn, would have often been read aloud in groups, merging with oral discourses of gossip and public debate.[84] Indeed, Walker notes a kind of reciprocal translation between Plot-related public processions and print publications: popular demonstrations often served to convert text into performance, bringing "texts, images, and memorabilia to life as public spectacle." Walker describes the parades of 1679, 1680, and 1681 as "living tableaux of the broadsheet attacks on papists."[85] Yet these processions would, in turn, be rendered back into text: "those who did not witness the spectacle were still able to access its messages through newspaper accounts, the printed pamphlets and broadsheets which described it in detail."[86] Moreover, text and image often combined within single publications: Margaret Ezell discusses the illustrated publications that, in combining "a series of pictures with captions and explanatory text below," served essentially as "elaborate cartoons," creating a shared iconography in the public consciousness that continued to be reinforced by extravagant effigy burnings attended by thousands in the London streets.

Behn's meditations, in *The Luckey Chance,* on how we know what we think we know—on the complex relationship between what we witness and what we read, and the ease with which our sense of reality can be manipulated by interlocking modes of information—clearly reflect not just the philosophical context of her time but also her political context. Behn was living in an era when an excessive quickness to believe what one saw, read, or read about others seeing—or, indeed, what one heard someone read about others seeing—could result in innocent people being imprisoned and executed.[87] As Walker points out, the difficulty of separating fact from fiction in the increasingly confused media landscape of the late 1670s and early 1680s was becoming ever more urgent as the public was cast as "the principal arbiter of affairs of state."[88] Behn's references to the Popish Plot make clear that questions of perception and imagination, knowledge and interpretation, are as topical as they are philosophical, as public as they are private.

If *The Luckey Chance* suggests that bodily sensation can be superseded by the imagination, then Behn's *The Emperor of the Moon* suggests, even more radically, that imagination can be experienced bodily—so that there may actually be no distinction between our perceptual and conceptual realities. At the same time, Behn uses this self-proclaimed farce—with its *commedia dell'arte* elements and its over-the-top, machine-made special effects—to continue to challenge the division not just between mind and body but between the theatrical and readerly halves of drama, and to point out the possible hermeneutic and moral misprisions that result from attributing too much interpretive authority to either component. Even as *The Emperor of the Moon* depicts the imagination, and its deployment in the reading process, as more embodied than we might think, it likewise depicts the theater, in all its spectacular materiality, as less fully corporeal than we would tend to expect. As in *The Luckey Chance,* Behn questions the cultural assumptions forming around an increasingly authoritative print canon, undermining the implicit claims embedded in publishers' marketing techniques—whether the inclusion of frontispiece portraits, the creation of a collectible series, or the gathering of a writer's complete works—that aligned print with prestige. She reminds theatergoers and readers alike that books do not hold an artistic monopoly on imaginative abstraction, and that reading, indeed, is not always as refined as Humphrey Moseley, and now Jacob Tonson, were urging the public to believe.[89]

Again, seventeenth-century philosophical discussions provide a useful context for Behn's explorations of the role of body and mind in our experience of different art forms. Of particular interest are the debates surrounding the role of language in how we apprehend and know our world. As Bernard Gert has noted, although Hobbes emphasized the primacy of our senses in piecing together our reality—"there is no conception in a mans mind, which hath not at first, totally, or by parts, been begotten upon the organs of *Sense*"—he notably diverges from standard empiricism in contending that language ought to be included among these fundamental sensory stimuli.[90] This idea is evident in Hobbes's definition of something that he calls "compound imagination." Whereas *"simple Imagination,"* he explains, is that which is produced when we call to mind a "whole object, as it was [originally] presented to the sense," compound imagination results from two separate sensory experiences becoming combined—as when, for example, "from the sight of a man at one time, and of a horse at another, we conceive in our mind a Centaure."[91] This distinction seems straightforward enough, except that, interestingly, "sight" in this case appears to extend to readerly as well as physical vision. Hobbes further illustrates the concept of compound imagination with the example of a man who "compoundeth the image of his own person, with the image of the actions of another man ... as when a man imagins himself a *Hercules,* or an *Alexander* (which happeneth often to them that are much taken with reading of Romants)."[92] Here the lived, real-time sense of one's "own person" becomes ontologically equivalent to reading about a heroic character in a book: our minds combine the two experiences in the same way that they would combine the memory of having seen a man with the memory of having seen a horse.

Hobbes's particular choice of example further blurs the division between corporeal reality and linguistic or readerly experience: Hercules, of course, is synonymous with physical vigor; the name referred as early as the sixteenth century both to the actual "celebrated hero ... represented as possessed of prodigious strength" and to "one who resembles Hercules in strength; a man of prodigious strength; a big man" (*OED,* s.v. "Hercules," defs. 1a. and 2). Thus, Hobbes's "Romants" devotee has not just conflated the idea of himself with the idea of a hero, but has, even more specifically, conflated his own physique with a hero's brawn—all, counterintuitively, by becoming imaginatively wrapped up in a verbal fiction.

Perhaps even more surprisingly, it was some of the foremost proponents of experimentalism who seem to have been most convinced of reading's equivalency to physical experience. As Steven Shapin and Simon Schaffer have documented, "virtual witnessing," or the process by which a given experiment could be "produc[ed] in a *reader's* mind," became "the most powerful" tool that the Royal Society had at their disposal for "the crediting of their [experiments'] outcomes as matters of fact."[93] If, according to empiricist thought, the validity of an experiment depended on its ability to be witnessed by multiple observers, then the "multiplication of witnesses" became the key factor in establishing the scientific authority of the Royal Society's activities; print, of course, allowed this multiplication to take place on a vast scale, essentially uncurtailed by time and space. Adrian Johns likewise affirms,

> If there is one thing that everyone knows about the experimental philosophy, it is that that philosophy was indeed experimental. It depended on *doing* things, and on showing the things that were done to other people.... But experimental philosophy also rested on repeated acts of writing, printing and reading.... [It] thus depended on a widening network of correspondence and printed communication in order to build up the international acceptance of both particular "matters of fact" and experimental conduct in general which its proponents sought. And the outcome of this circulation was reckoned to be knowledge.[94]

As Shapin and Schaffer note, not only did the Royal Society's Robert Boyle embrace the potential power of print through his numerous publications, but he sought to enhance this power via a specifically "literary technology"—namely, a writing style intended to replicate the immediacy of an object presented to the eye. As Boyle explains in his "Proemical Essay" to *New Experiments,* he "knowingly and purposely transgressed the laws of oratory ... in making sometimes my periods [i.e., complete sentences] or parentheses overlong: for when I could not within the compass of a regular period comprise what I thought requisite to be delivered at once, I chose rather to neglect the precepts of rhetoricians, than the mention of those things, which I thought pertinent to my subject, and useful to you, my reader."[95] In instances where the "laws of oratory"—designed for speakers and listeners—would require that information be conveyed sequentially, Boyle insists that his readers should instead have their evidence "delivered at once," in the same way that a scientific specimen or apparatus would strike an observer. Boyle's publications also included engravings: actual images were crucial to the multiplication of witnesses as well. Notably, however, as the remarks above suggest, it is specifically the reading experience that converts the casual book buyer into a corroborator of empirical fact and a guarantor of scientific truth. Reading, then, becomes not just a process of rational ideation but a process by which the laws of the physical world are verified; the reader's imaginative work becomes foundational to the Royal Society's materialist, empiricist project. Intriguingly, despite their different beliefs about how knowledge is best attained—Hobbes insisted that ratiocination was the path to truth, while Boyle proclaimed experiment to be the basis of discovery—both philosophers ultimately depict reading as epistemologically equivalent, in many ways, to sense perception.

Similarly to Hobbes and Boyle, Behn blurs the line between readerly imagination and embodied experience—with implications for the era's philosophical debates as well as its debates regarding the cultural significance of drama and, ultimately, an emergent print canon. *The Emperor of the Moon* centers on the "Don Quick-sottish" Doctor Baliardo, driven mad by his "reading [of] foolish Books" regarding the moon and its supposed inhabitants.[96] This obsession, despite its being based in reading, is soon revealed to be just as somatic as it is intellectual in its nature: as we will see, Baliardo proves a bit too eager for firsthand knowledge of the various "shapes" in which the moon's "Nymphs" appear (1.2.55). Ironically (or fittingly), Baliardo's sensually tinged studies provide an opportunity for his daughter and niece to be pursued by their own lovers, one of whom, by posing as a *"Eutopia*[n] . . . Caball[ist]," has offered Baliardo the prospect of pleasant "Conversation" with the lunar demigoddesses (1.2.25, 1.2.94). What was seemingly the most abstract and distant of pursuits, then, has become the most inextricable from bodily desire.

At the same time that Behn suggests that reading can have corporeal correlatives, she implies that theater can yield mental insight. The play's plot reaches its conclusion when, in a pageant staged by the lovers in the final act, the young people arrange to be married (a "real" priest is playing the role of the pageant's priest) while simultaneously "curing" Baliardo of his delusions. (The idea seems to be that, by raising Baliardo's madness to its most dizzying heights yet, the pageant can cause his delirium to "break" like a bad fever—but I will explore this in more detail in a moment.) The pageant thus becomes both the most fantastical and the most pragmatic moment of the play—at once sheer caprice yet also a true turning point for the characters. In this way, in a pointed reversal of antitheatrical discourse, the theater—even in all of its spectacular artifice—is depicted as sharpening our intellectual and epistemological faculties (our ability to know what is real), whereas reading resulted in the sacrifice of mental acuity to physical desire.⁹⁷ With her play's themes, then, but also in her unique use of physical comedy—as well as a set of elaborate stage directions specifying these slapstick effects—Behn compels us to rethink the relationship between mind and body, textuality and performativity, "high" culture and pandering spectacle.

I want to begin my discussion of *The Emperor of the Moon* by examining a seemingly trivial bit of stage business at the end of the first act, which introduces several of the theoretical questions I have begun to describe. Baliardo's niece, Bellemante, noting—in her comically French-inflected speech—that she is "in a *Belle* Humor for Poetry," declares that she will "make some Boremes on Love" (i.e., *bouts rimés,* or "rhymed ends"); she writes one couplet and starts the next but, pausing to think of a rhyme, sets down her notebook on a table and paces about the room (1.3.24–25, 1.3.31). Harlequin (a servant), who is hiding under the table, jumps out and fills in the second couplet; this pattern repeats itself until the eight-line poem is complete.

Although the scene is perhaps most explicitly one of writing, it is also, of course, one of reading: indeed, writing itself is figured here as a kind of reading, insofar as when Harlequin and Bellemante take turns adding to the poem, each line they inscribe is also a way of processing the previous line. This dynamic is present even in the poem's opening couplet, in fact, which is framed as a reactive gesture, the response to a question that has been posed (according to the verse's conceit) prior to the lines' composition: "*Out of a great Curiosity, / A Shepherd this implor'd of me. / Tell me, said he*" (1.3.48–50). Although the speaker within the poem proceeds to address her lover's inquiries only silently ("*I blush'd, and veil'd my wishing Eyes, / And answer'd only with my Sighs*"), it is, of course, the poem itself—the narration of these silent signs—that is also a way of making sense of the originating question.

But as much as the scene depicts writing as a kind of reading, it also depicts reading as a kind of writing—that is, as an active and creative reshaping of the text in front of us. For reading here is depicted as literally kinetic: Bellemante takes up the book and lays it back down, she paces restlessly to and fro, and—in a telling combination, directly joining mental processing with bodily movement—she "*Studies and walks*" (1.3.44 sd). Harlequin, meanwhile, moves even more hectically, ping-ponging comically out from and back under the table before Bellemante can spot him. Reading, it seems, is an intensely physical exercise.

As Bellemante and Harlequin perform this comic pas-de-deux, Behn reminds us not only of the corporeality of reading but also that this corporeality can edge into the realm of the specifically sexual. It is this fact that sparks the jealousy of Bellemante's suitor, Don Charmante, upon finding the finished verses: "Whose is this different Character?" he demands; "The Ink's yet wet, the Spark is near I find" (1.3.60, 68). As Harlequin's and Bellemante's handwriting intertwine on the page, the acts of writing and reading are figured as acts of physical intimacy. This trope is literalized, of course, by the poem itself, which—as alluded to above—depicts a lover who must read (as it were) his beloved's body for evidence of affection: blushes, an averted gaze, and carefully calibrated sighs substitute for "*Tell*[ing]" and "*answer*[ing]." Both within the poem, then, as well as in the circumstances of its composition, writing and reading are transferred to the surface of the flirtatious body.

It is precisely this sense of reading as embodied—and, more specifically, as sexually embodied—that permeates the play's characterization of Doctor Baliardo. These links to Baliardo are announced in the first line of Bellemante and Harlequin's poem, where the shepherd's "*Curiosity*" echoes Baliardo's own inquisitiveness. The only other use of the word *curiosity* in the play occurs when Baliardo declares he is "fill'd with Curiosity" to see a lunar map referred to by a certain sesquipedalian apothecary (the disguised servant Scaramouch)—a map that, the apothecary claims (with an allusion to one of Baliardo's favorite books), serves to supplement missing information in Gonzales's *Cosmographia of the Lunar Mundus* (3.2.61–62, 44–45).[98] Significantly, Scaramouch is posing here not just as a lunar expert but as a suitor seeking the hand of the family maid, Mopsophil—or, as he puts it, seeking to effect the "Conjugal Circumference of a Matrimonial Tye" with her (3.2.27–28). Baliardo's "Curiosity" in this moment, then, is simultaneously readerly, bookish, and vaguely salacious ("Hum—A sweet-heart for *Mopsophil!*" he exclaims, upon hearing his visitor's intentions [3.2.31]).[99]

The bodily component of Baliardo's reading comes across much sooner than this, however, revealing itself in the very first scene of the play, when the doctor is described as "infected" with his lunar fixation (1.1.94). For while his lunar research is initially evoked in strictly textual terms—as we have seen, he is called "Don Quick-sottish," driven mad by "reading foolish

Books"—the second scene indicates the distinctly material form that this reading-induced obsession takes: when we first see the doctor, he enters "*with all manner of Mathematical Instruments hanging at his Girdle,*" while his servant Scaramouch "*bear[s] a Telescope twenty (or more) Foot long*" (opening stage directions of 1.2). The telescope thus becomes a symbol of phallic sexuality—but also, equally importantly, of reading. As Baliardo prepares to spy on "the great Monarch of the upper World [as he] enter[s] ... into his ... secret Closet" (1.2.3–8), he likens his lens to "a States-man's peeping-hole, thorow which he Steals the secrets of his King" (1.2.13–14), thereby emphasizing both the illicit, voyeuristic nature of his intentions and their readerly overtones: Baliardo's intentions will not, presumably, be fulfilled simply by watching the king as he peruses the private documents in his "Closet"; rather, they will be fulfilled by reading these documents himself. (It is hard to imagine how else the king's "secrets" could be revealed, under these circumstances.)

The priapic voyeurism of Baliardo's telescopic reading assumes even more fleshly implications when, moments later, an unexpected celestial guest (a "*Fantastic*[ally]" attired Charmante) provides an opportunity for further inquiries into the lunarians' private lives (1.2.23 sd). This "Caball[ist]" from the land of "*Eutopia*" informs Baliardo that the moon is populated by "Persons of a Form and Species more Divine than Vulgar Mortals": salamanders, nymphs, gnomes, and sylphs (1.2.25, 1.2.39–44). Yet these beings, "when in Conjunction with Mortals"—the salamanders and gnomes with women, and the nymphs and sylphs with men—may "beget Kings and *Heroes*" whose "Spirits" resemble those of "their Deietical" parents (1.2.45, 1.2.41–42). Indeed, the "Love and Conversation" of these beings has the power to "Immortallize" those privileged humans with whom they have chosen to "Conj[oi]n" (1.2.50, 1.2.49, 1.2.45). "Most admirable Philosophy and Reason," Baliardo declares sagely, yet then follows up immediately: "But do these Silfs and Nymphs appear in Shapes?" (1.2.54–55). The "Love and Conversation" of purely "Deietical" beings, it seems, is not where Baliardo's interests lie—though the bodily status of the (masculine) gnomes and salamanders also apparently concerns him very little. As this discussion with Charmante quickly makes clear, Baliardo's telescopic reading and, by extension, the long hours spent in his library, are as motivated by sexual inclinations as they are by rational inquiry.

Indeed, these desires are brought to a kind of climax when, moments later, Charmante takes out a painted "*Glass with a Picture of a Nymph on it, and a light behind it,*" which he then places over the back of Baliardo's telescope—leading Baliardo to exclaim that he is "Astonisht, Ravisht with delight . . . , all Rapture, Sir, at this rare Vision" (1.2.78 sd, 1.2.86, 1.2.93). Baliardo's language of sexual possession[100] becomes all the more explicit when the disguised Charmante reminds him that such nymphs "love not like the Vulgar, 'tis the Immortal Part they doat upon" (1.2.111–12). The contrast between, on the one hand, the "Prayer" and "Refine[d] . . . Thoughts" with which Charmante tells Baliardo he must fill his mind in order to glimpse the lunar inhabitants (1.2.121) and, on the other hand, the pleasure that Baliardo expresses upon seeing them, comically reveals the distance separating the abstruse intellectual pursuits to which Baliardo claims to have been dedicating himself and the mind-blown physical delight that he now experiences.[101] Yet Behn is careful, as we have seen, to align this sexual excitement with Baliardo's scholarly reading sessions (whether enacted in the library or through the lens).

In this way, Behn extends one of the key conclusions of *The Luckey Chance*. If, in the earlier play, Behn suggested that the imagination can overpower sense perception, here she implies that the imagination (whether employed in the act of reading or in other activities) can take on its own sensory manifestations. A scene early in act 2 establishes this notion when Baliardo, having been knocked upside the head by (a concealed) Harlequin, becomes convinced that the blow might easily have been caused by "Imagination" alone. In this scene, the young lovers and servants, who were in the midst of holding a masked ball when Baliardo unexpectedly burst in on them, have disguised themselves as figures in a tapestry so as to avoid being caught. We might fairly describe Baliardo's ensuing encounter with the tapestry as another scene of sexualized telescopic reading: convinced by Scaramouch that this never-before-seen piece of décor in his home is a gift from "some of the Caballists" (2.3.89–90), the doctor proceeds to inquire specifically into its narrative content—"Prithee what Story's this?" (2.3.99)—and uses a "*Perspective*" (or magnifying glass) to follow its plot more closely (which in this case, of course, entails the detailed scrutiny of the lovers' physiques [2.3.101 sd]). Absorbed once again, then, in a readerly study of ripe young bodies as facilitated by optical instruments, Baliardo fails to notice Harlequin's truncheon. Yet, given the already very physical nature of his text-based (or textile-based) analysis, Baliardo can easily assimilate the resulting injury into his readerly experience:

Doctor: What was that struck me?
Scaramouch: Struck you, Sir! Imagination.
Doctor: Can my Imagination feel, Sirrah?
Scaramouch: Oh, the most tenderly of any part about one, Sir!
Doctor: Hum—That may be—
Scaramouch: Are you a great Philosopher, and know not that, Sir?
Doctor (aside): This Fellow has a glimpse of Profundity— (2.3.103–9)

The fact that Behn stretches this exchange two to three lines beyond what is necessary for Scaramouch to tell his fib suggests that she is signaling something more here than Baliardo's mere gullibility—that there may, in fact, be something "Prof[o]und[ly]" philosophical in Scaramouch's words. For what has Baliardo's reading throughout the play demonstrated, if not that imagination can affect—indeed, infect—the body?

The events of the next few moments reinforce this mind-body confusion, when, in an inversion of what we might expect to happen, it is only after Harlequin darts out a second time and "*The Doctor sees him*" that Baliardo begins to suspect "a Plot upon my Daughter and my Neece" (2.2.111 sd, 2.2.113–14). Imagination, of course, is usually linked more closely with the eyes (or "images") than with the other senses—and, accordingly, what we perceive visually can often be dismissed as mere illusion where a jolt to our muscles or bones cannot. Here, however, the hierarchy is reversed: "feel[ing]" can apparently be attributed to nothing more than fantasy, while "*see*[ing]" is taken as proof of reality. In other words, for Baliardo in this scene, the more fully embodied the sensation, the more likely it seems to be the product of the mind. And although we might initially be tempted to write off Baliardo's view of the mind-body relationship as the ravings of a literal lunatic, I argue that the play as a whole ends up reinforcing such notions, implying that imagination can feel, while bodily sensation, conversely, can convey abstract truths.

Baliardo's musings—"Can my Imagination feel?"—resonate almost uncannily with Margaret Cavendish's writings on perception published thirty years earlier (but which we have no evidence that Behn would have read). Cavendish compares physical touch to mental activity: "touch is like a thought in sense," she asserts in *Observations upon Experimental Philosophy,* "and thought like a touch in reason."[102] But as Cavendish clarifies in her *Philosophical and Physical Opinions,* this "like"-ness carries more weight than that of mere simile: in accordance with Cavendish's vitalist system, haptic and ideational experience are both generated by "motions" in our bodies. Thus, she writes, "the *touch* in the heel, or any part of the body else, is the like *motion,* as the *thought* thereof in the head; the one is the *motion* of the *sensitive* spirits, the other in the rational *spirits,* . . . for thought is onely a strong *touch,* and *touch* a weak *thought.* So sense is weak knowledge, and *knowledge* a strong *sense,* made by the degrees of the spirits."[103] If "thought" is a "strong touch," while "touch" is a "weak thought," clearly Cavendish would agree with Scaramouch in positing that the "Imagination [can] feel . . . the most tenderly of any part about one, Sir!" As spoken in the play, the line strikes us as whimsical and perhaps deliberately misleading: it is employed, after all, in humoring and deceiving a madman. Yet, as the parallel with Cavendish suggests, it also seems possible that Behn may be using such statements to level a serious epistemological critique—one that questions the growing empiricist dogma of her age, and at the same time undercuts Jonsonian and Drydenian distinctions between rationality and sensuality, dramatic "literature" and live theater.

The Emperor of the Moon is obviously not unique among Behn's writings (or those of her contemporaries) in its assertion that reading, and the imaginative work it entails, can also involve our bodies. Ruth Perry, Ros Ballaster, and William Warner have pointed to the persistence of this association within the period's amatory fiction in particular (of which Behn was a prominent practitioner, of course).[104] More generally, Adrian Johns and Michael Schoenfeldt have outlined seventeenth-century notions of a "physiology of reading."[105] However, I contend that, by exploring this concept within the specific forum of a play, Behn is able to add several layers of complexity: if she shows reading to be more fundamentally physical than is often acknowledged, she also shows theater to possess more of an imaginative component than its spectacular nature would lead us to suppose. As we have seen, in *The Luckey Chance* Behn suggested that if we hope to interpret our world with any kind of accuracy, we must draw upon all of our physical and mental faculties, while recognizing the limits of both types. One year later, Behn stated this notion even more forcefully, implying not only that the skilled interpreter must consider all of the kinds of information at his or her disposal—empirical, speculative, and everything in between—but that, indeed, some of the most valuable knowledge may derive from the least promising sources (whether the minds of "madmen" or the bodies of *commedia* clowns).

To understand better how Behn is complicating common assumptions about both reading and theatergoing in regard to the mind-body problem, it may be helpful to return for a moment to Elkanah Settle's response to Collier. I have already quoted Settle's query as to whether playgoing can really "imprint the subject of the History, or Fiction, too lively in the Fancy, more than the bare Reading it can do" and his conclusion that, on the contrary, the "*Idea*" that a reader conceives of a character may at times have a much stronger effect on him or her than would a character already brought to life upon the stage. However, I now want to examine more closely Settle's analysis of the role of mind and body in this comparison. Just after relating how the reader constructs an idea of a favorite character, he goes on to describe the effects of this idea in physical terms: "The [reader's] *personal Idea* of this Historical or Romantick Favourite, he carries with him from his Closet to his Bed, and can rise with it to morrow: For as 'tis a Form of his own Creation, his Scene of *Fancy* gives it an Air of *Truth* and *Life*."[106]

The reader's "*personal Idea*" of the character draws much of its power from the reader's ability to internalize and customize this figure to his liking, yet this imaginative work also has physical effects: as the eager reader dreamily conducts his beloved character "from his Closet to his Bed," it seems that the page—though seemingly a less sensory medium than the stage—may actually have the potential, paradoxically, to create the more sensual experience.

So far, Settle's arguments accord with Behn's. However, the mind-body confusion that Settle describes seems to operate only in one direction. That is, if reading's imaginative flights can engage the body, the theater's physicality actually obstructs imaginative engagement. Settle goes on to explain that, in contrast to a reader's experience with a character in a book,

> when you see the *Hero* or *Heroine,* or any other *Darling* in a *Play,* 'tis in the person of the *Actour* or *Actress*.... No sooner is the Curtain faln, [therefore,] but both the *Hero* and *Heroine* are no more to you, than the *Betterton* and *Barry*.... And all for this plain reason, *viz.* you want that darling *personal Idea,* which the Reading only can give you, not the *Playing.* 'Tis true, you'l say, the seeing a *Play* may raise an Affection in us for the *Virtues, Honour* or *Bravery,* or possibly for some worse *Qualification* in some darling *Character*

in a Play, abstracted from the Person in the Play, *viz.* the Comedian that presents it: However the *History* or *Romance* does all this, rather more . . . [because] the personal Charms . . . in the forementioned *Idea* . . . strengthen and heighten the forces of *Reading,* by a more lasting Image of Reality above those of *Actions.*[107]

In short, whereas a reader's "Image" of a favorite character is capable, essentially, of seducing him, Settle appears not to believe the inverse to be true: the "person of the *Actour* or *Actress*" may impede our ability to respond emotionally or intellectually. It is only when we "abstract" a character's qualities from the body of the actor that we are able to experience any "Affection" toward him.[108] But the theater's corporeality is ultimately irreducible: inevitably, the performance must end, and the actors must exit the stage as mere "*Betterton*[s] and *Barry*[s]."

By contrast, although Behn, like Settle, questions the ability of physical experience to affect us more intensely than imagination (as in *The Luckey Chance*), she does not conclude that reading makes a stronger impact on us than live, embodied performance. Rather, the power of both playgoing and reading, she suggests, lies in their ability to enlist both our bodies and minds in ways we would not expect.

Behn brings this argument to a head in the spectacular pageant that caps off *The Emperor of the Moon*. We might describe the premise of this pageant as distinctly "Setttlean," in a way, as it would seem that Elaria, Bellemante, and their suitors believe that their pageant can "cure" Baliardo's readerly delusions precisely by way of its physicality—that is, whereas Baliardo appears to have been suffering from his reading-induced delusions for some time now, with no sign of relief, the young lovers seem to think that only theater—or, more precisely, the tangible fictitiousness of theater, in which (to return to Settle) the most heroic of "abstract[ions]" must always be reduced to flesh-and-blood "Persons"—can make visible the illusive nature of Baliardo's lunar fantasies. Scaramouch need merely drop his disguise as a lunar prince—declaring himself, while "*Put*[ting] *off his Helmet,*" to be "Your humble Servant, Sir, and *Scaramouch*"—for Baliardo to understand instantly that he is "undone and cheated every way," his niece and daughter having married against his will and under his nose (3.3.194 sd, 3.3.196–97). For Scaramouch, once revealed as "himself," cannot also be a lunar prince—just as Settle's "*Betterton* and *Barry*" cannot also, once they stride off into the wings, remain the heroic figures they played onstage. In other words, the fact that the theater must use actual persons and things to stand in for imaginary figments means that—unlike with prose, whose claims to truth must be checked more laboriously against confirmed histories, biographies, geographies, and so on—theater's counterfeit status can be confirmed by the mere lifting of a helmet, or (as Settle has it) the "fall[ing]" of a "Curtain."

Or so it would seem. In practice, the young people's pageant is much more mimetically complicated than the schema described above. Note that the lovers have designed the pageant very specifically so as to bring about a "real" event. Thus, by the end of the staged wedding between Baliardo's female relations and their celestial suitors, a genuine wedding has taken place between the women and their actual suitors. Far from reinforcing the distance between corporeal fact and abstract imagination—the concept the lovers were attempting to teach Baliardo—the pageant has served to equate the two. To extend Settle's example: it is as if, say, the Pericles we've been following onstage turns out to be Betterton, but Betterton turns out to have survived an actual shipwreck and been reunited with his actual long-lost daughter in the course of the three-hour timespan in which we've been sitting in the theater.[109] The mask has melded with the man; the representation of an action has fused with the action itself. Possessing no separate reality of its own, the stage is suddenly much more like the page, a space in which actual and virtual are all too easily intermingled.

Behn's erosion of the physical distinctness of the stage is not limited to the final moments of act 3, moreover; arguably, it takes place throughout all three acts. Not only do we struggle to separate the wedding in the pageant from the wedding in the outer play, but we struggle throughout all three acts to define where, precisely, this outer play leaves off and where the play within the play begins: the pageant itself could very well be said to span *The Emperor of the Moon* in its entirety. Of course, it is only in act 3, scene 3 that the scheming lovers and servants mount a full-on production, including the dozens of dancers, singers, and machines called for by Behn's stage directions; however, they have been laying the theatrical groundwork for the pageant's central fiction since act 1 (so that, as the play nears its end, Baliardo describes having been "Cozen'd ... by ... degrees" [3.3.234–35]). As we have seen, Charmante and Scaramouch anticipated their roles in the pageant early on, appearing in the guises of an otherworldly cabalist and a collector of rare celestial maps, respectively; at a later point, Harlequin pretended to be a lunar ambassador

(3.1). Moreover, Elaria and Bellemante contributed to this setting of the scene, as it were, by staging a dumbshow for Baliardo in which they appeared to receive visits from invisible lunar suitors (2.4). It is fair to say, indeed, that the young people's play-acting—even before the pageant—is what constitutes much of the play's action.

The confusion between the outer play and the play within the play could be said to extend to Behn's very title, which would apply equally well to either, or both. Officially, the pageant possesses its own title: Scaramouch calls it *The World in the Moon* (1.1.108–9). Yet the title of the outer play—*The Emperor of the Moon*—also derives from the young people's theatrics. As discussed above, Baliardo's own readerly fantasies have posited a lunar ruler, but he refers to this somewhat shadowy figure as "the great Monarch of the upper World" (while likening himself to a statesman spying on a "King" [1.2.3–4, 1.2.14]). By contrast, it is Charmante, in his guise as "Caball[ist]," who first christens this "Monarch"/"King" more specifically as "the Emperor of the Moon, Sir, the mighty *Iredonozar*" (1.2.118–19). It is this same *"Emperour"* (according to the stage directions following line 122) whom the cabalist then shows to Baliardo through the telescope (via the painted transparency that he inserts over the back), and who will appear as a central figure (played by Don Cinthio) in the final pageant. As a result, Behn's title could be said to refer not to her own play's dramatic premise (that is, to Baliardo's lunar fantasy) but to the play within the play, which has been designed to take advantage of this fantasy (and which, in turn, confers on that fantasy an increasingly vivid reality).

Behn's subtitle—*A Farce*—proves just as slippery. It would seem to refer most immediately to the play's *commedia dell'arte* elements, exemplified by the physical antics of Harlequin and Scaramouch (as in Harlequin's ping-pong-like poetizing, in the boreme scene, or his slapstick wallops to Baliardo's head, in the tapestry scene). Again, however, the term turns out to be closely tied to the pageant. As the play opens, Scaramouch reports to Elaria that he has just visited Don Cinthio's lodgings, where, he says, "I found him with his dear Friend *Charmante,* laying their heads together for a Farce":

> *Elaria:* A Farce.—
> *Scaramouch:* Ay a Farce, which shall be called, *The World in the Moon.* Wherein your Father shall be so impos'd on, as shall bring matters most magnificently about.... In order to this, *Charmante* is dressing himself like one of the Caballists of the *Rosacrusian* Order, and is coming to prepare my credulous Master for the greater imposition....

> *Elaria:* But the Farce, where is It to be Acted?
> *Scaramouch:* Here, here, in this very House; I am to order the Decoration, adorn a Stage, and place Scenes proper.... (1.1.105–19)

Once again, we are left to wonder at what point Behn's play simply becomes her characters' play, especially given the shared territory in which the two are enacted. Indeed, Scaramouch's repetition—"Here, here"—seems significant, reflecting the iterative process by which stage becomes house becomes stage. Where does one space ebb away and the next begin its encroachment? Where does one fiction end and the next take over? If Settle insists that the theater grips our imaginations less tightly than a book because of the material contingencies of the stage—because our affective response is always mediated by, for example, an actor's body—then *The Emperor of the Moon* asks to what extent we can ever truly draw a line between thespian and character, between "real" play-acting and a character's diegetic mummeries.

I have now described a handful of ways in which Behn alludes not just to the embodiedness of reading but to the surprising "disembodiedness" of the theater: she creates a scenario in which many of the physical components of theater—components that we might expect to impede its traversal of the border between fiction and reality—turn out to be less of an encumbrance than we might think. Behn thus questions not just whether the theater's physical basis is really quite as definitive as we might assume, but also whether theatergoing is really quite as far removed from the experience of reading as we might believe. At the same time—as I demonstrate in more detail below—Behn questions whether theater is really as incompatible with "the literary" as we might otherwise suppose.

Behn's 1671 prologue to *The Amorous Prince, or, The Curious Husband* articulates what seems to have become a conventional divide, in the late seventeenth century, between literary drama and farce. The speaker warns the audience that the comedy they are about to see fits into neither of these categories:

> First then for you grave *Dons* who love no Play
> But what is regular, Great *Johnson*'s way;
> Who hate the *Monsieur* with the Farce and Droll,
> But are for things well said with spirit and soul;

> 'Tis you I mean whose judgments will admit
> No Interludes of fooling with your Wit;
> You're here defeated, and anon will cry
> S'Death! wou'd 'twere treason to write Comedy.
> So! there's a party lost; now for the rest,
> Who swear they'd rather hear a smutty jest
> Spoken by *Nokes* or *Angel*, than a Scene
> Of the admir'd and well-penn'd *Cataline;*
> Who love the Comick Hat, the Jig and Dance,
> Things that are fitted to their Ignorance:
> You too are quite undone, for here's no Farce,
> Damn me! you'l cry, this Play will be mine A—[110]

Whereas the basis of a "regular" play consists in its immaterial qualities ("things well said with spirit and soul"), farce centers on bodily action ("the Jig and Dance") and bawdy humor ("smutty jest[s]"). The admirers of "regular" plays expect their personal tastes to align with governmental regulations and the law (so that they can imagine a world in which "'twere treason to write Comedy"). Fans of farce, by contrast, express their preferences in relation not to state prescript but to their own anatomies (a play not to their liking "will be mine A—").[111] Finally, if serious drama is identified primarily with the authors who write it ("*Johnson*," and his "well-penn'd *Cataline*"), farce is identified with the actors who perform it (so that the evening's highlights include jokes "Spoken by *Nokes* or *Angel*").[112]

This distinction between mind and body—between the written word and live speech—is of course one that we have already seen highlighted at the beginning of this chapter: Jonson's insistence on separating his own plays' poetry from their performance was deemed by Jonas Barish to be crucial to the seventeenth century's new emphasis on drama as "literature."[113] But I will now spell out more precisely what "literary" drama seems to mean during this period, especially in relation to the larger themes I have been outlining in Behn's plays.

Robert Hume has argued that Dryden's critical oeuvre grants unprecedented centrality to "style or stylistic problems" in its discussion of plays. Indeed, Hume deems these questions of style to be Dryden's "most abiding concern."[114] Thus, although Dryden essentially preserves Aristotle's six categories for analyzing dramatic works, he significantly reprioritizes them according to this focus. Here is Aristotle:

> Every Tragedy... must have six parts, which parts determine its quality—namely, Plot, Character, Diction, Thought, Spectacle, Song....
>
> The Plot... is the first principle, and, as it were, the soul of a tragedy... For Tragedy is an imitation, not of men, but of an action and of life, and life consists in action....
>
> Character holds the second place... [because it] comes in as subsidiary to the actions....
>
> Third in order is Thought—that is, the faculty of saying what is possible and pertinent in given circumstances...
>
> Fourth among the elements enumerated comes Diction; by which I mean... the expression of the meaning in words; and its essence is the same both in verse and prose.... Of the remaining elements Song holds the chief place among the embellishments.... [And] [s]pectacle... of all the parts, is the least artistic, and connected least with the art of poetry. For the power of Tragedy, we may be sure, is felt even apart from representation and actors.[115]

Dryden's fellow Restoration writer Thomas Rymer, in his *Tragedies of the Last Age* (1677), retained Aristotle's hierarchy, explaining that, in each of the tragedies he was examining, he "chiefly consider'd the *Fable* or *Plot*, which all conclude to be the *Soul* of a *Tragedy*."[116] By contrast, Dryden, in his response to Rymer, insists (citing the French critic René Rapin) that words—or *dictio*—are the most important element of all. (Indeed, he speculates that Aristotle may have ranked words where he did—that is, in fourth place—only because the playwright arrives at them last chronologically: they are "the Last Product of the Design."[117]) Accordingly, Hume notes, when Dryden quarrels with Rymer's assessment of Shakespeare and his contemporaries, he "does not attempt to defend the Elizabethan playwrights against Rymer's strictures on their plots—rather, he upholds the beauty and effectiveness of their expression."[118]

Interestingly, both Aristotle and Rymer (in his direct echo of Aristotle) refer to a play's "Plot" as its "Soul": Aristotle explains that this is so because drama is, at root, "an imitation of an action and of life, and life consists in action."[119] Dryden, by contrast, seems instead to position a play's "soul" within its words (and thoughts), and to understand "action" to be fundamentally corporeal. This outlook can be seen most clearly, perhaps, in his Dedication to the *Spanish Fryar* (already partially quoted earlier in this chapter):

> But as 'tis my Interest to please my Audience, so 'tis my Ambition to be read; that I am sure is the more lasting and the nobler Design: for the propriety of thoughts and words, which are the hidden beauties of a Play, are but confus'dly judg'd in the vehemence of Action... The purity of phrase, the clearness of conception and expression, the boldness maintain'd to Majesty, the significancie and sound of words, not strain'd into bombast, but justly elevated, in short, those very words and thoughts, which cannot be chang'd, but for the worse, must of necessity escape our transient view upon the Theatre; and yet, without all these, a Play may take. For if either the Story move us, or the Actor help the lameness of it with his performance, or now and then a glittering beam of wit or passion strike through the obscurity of the Poem, any of these are sufficient to effect a present liking, but not to fix a lasting admiration; for nothing but Truth can long continue; and Time is the surest Judge of Truth.[120]

The primary denotation of the word "Action" in this passage—as in the phrase "the vehemence of Action"—is almost certainly performance, or acting, rather than plot (*OED*, s.v. "action," def. 17). Yet there seems to be some meaningful overlap here between the concept of a plot's "action," or incidents, in the Aristotelian sense, and the "action" of the actor: both create their effects physically, so that the skillful actor can make a play appear graceful and brisk despite its inherent "lameness," while a "Story [may] move us" with its ups and downs and twists of fate, despite its lack of any grounding in "Truth." A play's "thoughts and words," by contrast (or "words and thoughts," as Dryden puts it the second time), are its "hidden beauties"—internal as opposed to external. Well-chosen words ultimately endure because of their "clearness of conception" and the "significancie" they convey to our minds, whereas the events occurring onstage—whether as part of the plot's events or the way that the actors' bodies enact those events—will disappear once our own "pleas[ure]"-seeking bodies have left the theater.

Hume posits that Dryden's emphasis on thought and words over plot stems in part from what he views as Dryden's revolutionary shift in focus from writer to reader. Whereas Renaissance theorists had focused on "prescriptive, composition-oriented criticism"—a kind of criticism that would necessarily highlight such questions as a plot's unity, arc, and pacing—Dryden's essays, Hume believes, represent a move toward the "appreciative criticism later crystallized by Addison."[121] Thus, although Hume acknowledges that much of

Dryden's "attention [is] still directed (like Renaissance critics') to the craft of writing," he also sees Dryden's criticism as more "explanatory," "descriptive," and "analytic"—aimed at enhancing the reader's experience of a text as opposed to determining what makes for good writing.[122]

As we are about to see, Behn's use of farce in *The Emperor of the Moon* reinforces Dryden's readerly conception of drama while also overturning (as she does in the play's thematics) traditionally held assumptions regarding the immaterial, soulful, lasting, noble qualities of reading. In other words, even while embracing a Drydenian notion of plays as a literary mode—and thus (in the late seventeenth century's emerging definition) as a mode that rewards careful reading—Behn looks to expand our understanding of what careful reading might mean. As I will show, she ultimately suggests that the most comprehensive "literary" analysis of a play may require not just a scrutiny of its words but an understanding of its performative elements as well.

Behn begins her blurring of the readerly and performative qualities in *The Emperor of the Moon* in her adoption, and adaptation, of the Italian *commedia* tradition. As Robert Henke observes, *commedia dell'arte* typically employs what are essentially two types of characters: "mimetic" and "anti-mimetic." The mimetic characters are the ones who draw the plot forward, whereas the anti-mimetic characters—essentially clown figures (or *zanni*)—show off "a range of skills and routines rather than imitating a fictional character or world."[123] In the context of productions that were mainly improvised, these skills were displayed during what were traditionally the only "scripted" elements of a production—namely, the *lazzi,* or interpellated interludes, in which stage fighting, acrobatics, sight gags, and other antics were offered up to the audience, usually with no direct relation to the main plot. (Jennifer Meagher adds that certain routines gained such a completely autonomous stature that audiences could reasonably expect, at any given performance, to see the trademark *lazzi* of a particular actor or troupe, regardless of the show's narrative scenario.[124]) By contrast, the mimetic characters' actions tended to be more diegetically motivated.

Behn alters this formula, however, so that (as we have begun to see) the interpellated clowning scenes in *The Emperor of the Moon* are linked to the rest of the play thematically; by connecting them in this way, she allows the antics of Scaramouch and Harlequin to serve as a kind of commentary on the other characters' behavior. The structural coherence Behn thereby creates might be said to accord with the neoclassical unities, which emphasize principles of dramatic composition. Yet it is also a coherence that (in keeping with Dryden's more "reader"-oriented critical priorities) seems aimed at an interpretive payoff, rather than at some ideal architectonic integrity. That is to say, the parallels linking the clown characters to the play's more firmly "mimetic" characters do not actually reduce or eliminate the clowns' subplot (their rivalry for Mopsophil's hand), and do not, therefore, solidify the play's unity of action in any truly meaningful way. Rather, the effect of the parallels is to help those interpreting the play to understand the central characters' actions from new perspectives.

The first instance of such paralleling can be found in the interlude that caps off the telescopic "reading" scene in 1.2. (It is no coincidence, moreover, that this scene, as well as two of the three others that I am about to cite, is a scene of reading, which I explain further below.) In this slapstick interlude, Harlequin, having overheard Baliardo's plans to marry off "[his] Mistriss *Mopsophil*" to a neighboring farmer's son, declares, "If I have Honour, I must die with Rage" (1.2.163, 1.2.165). After listing various modes of death, however, Harlequin cannot settle on one that is "uncommon" enough as to "leave behind me an eternal Fame" (1.2.173). Finally, he recalls "hav[ing] somewhere read in an Author, either Antient or Modern, of a Man that laugh'd to death.—I am very Ticklish, and am resolv'd—to dye that Death" (1.2.164, 1.2.171–74). He then proceeds *"to tickle himself, his Head, his Ears, his Arm-pits, Hands, Sides, and Soles of his Feet; making ridiculous Cries and Noises of Laughing several ways, with Antick Leaps and Skips; [and] at last falls down as dead"* (1.2.178 sd). The episode plainly epitomizes the broad humor typical of *commedia*'s *lazzi*: although Harlequin's fit is technically motivated by the narrative, its main purpose is essentially anti-mimetic, to return to Henke's phrase. Yet Harlequin's absurdist—and, significantly, reading-induced—bout of self-tickling also clearly evokes the sexual, almost onanistic pleasures in which Baliardo was indulging only moments before, during his telescopic reading session.

We could point to any number of additional instances in which Harlequin's and Scaramouch's comic routines could be said to echo the "mimetic" characters' actions. The boreme-writing episode, of course (1.3), represents another such interlude (occurring only moments after the self-tickling), in which the doctor's sexualized reading practices are mocked and rendered in comically literal terms. The scene in which Harlequin dons a disguise in order to win over Mopsophil (3.1), though certainly affording an opportunity for the display of fancy special effects—as a calash turns into a workaday baker's cart and back again, twice—also serves, at another level, to parody Charmante's and Cinthio's elaborate stratagems to pose as lunar dignitaries in order to gain their own mistresses' hands in marriage. The interlude in which Harlequin pretends to be the pregnant mistress of Scaramouch in order to turn Mopsophil against his rival (2.5) likewise parallels, in certain key ways, the episode just preceding it (2.4), in which Baliardo watches his daughter and niece (pretend to) receive the silent, invisible attentions of their ostensible lunar lovers:

> [*Elaria and Bellemante*] *put themselves in Postures of Sleeping, leaning on the Table,* Mopsophil *lying at their Feet. Enter* Doctor, *softly* . . .
> Bellemante: (*speak*[*ing*] *as in her Sleep*) Ah, Prince . . .
>
> How little Faith I give to all your Courtship, who leaves our Orb so soon. . . .
>
> But since you are of a Coelestial Race,
>
> And easily can penetrate
>
> Into the utmost limits of the Thought,
>
> Why shou'd I fear to tell you of your Conquest?
>
> —And thus implore your Aid.
>
> [*Bellemante*] *rises and runs to the* Doctor. [*She*] *Kneels, and holds him fast. He shews signs of Joy.*
> Doctor: I am Ravish'd!
> Bellemante: Ah, Prince Divine, take Pity on a Mortal—
> Doctor: I am rapt!
> Bellemante: And take me with you to the World above.
> Doctor: The Moon, the Moon she means, I am Transported, Over-joy'd, and Ecstasy'd. (*Leaping and jumping* . . .) . . . Heaven keep me moderate! lest excess of Joy shou'd make my Vertue less! (2.4.2–34)

Here, although technically Bellemante is placing Baliardo in the position of her celestial prince ("*Kneel*[ing]" to him and "*hold*[ing] *him fast*"), it is Bellemante into whose position Baliardo is placing himself: as Bellemante pleads with the prince to "take [her] with [him]," we see the results on the body of Baliardo, who is once again (as in the telescope scene) "Ravish'd" and "rapt" (with its implications of sexual abduction), as well as fearful for his "Vertue." Baliardo may stop short of strapping on a faux pregnancy belly and donning women's clothes, but he is arguably more overtly feminized in this moment (and more overtly deflowered) than is Harlequin a moment later. What seems merely an instance of broad physical clowning on Harlequin's part, then, turns out, on closer inspection, to reflect pointedly on the play's central characters, central plot, and central themes.

As these examples make clear, Behn manages *The Emperor of the Moon*'s slapstick elements in such a way that they participate in, but also actually epitomize or enact, the play's overarching themes: comic moments we might otherwise regard as simple buffoonery actually contribute—via their very physicality—to the play's abstract philosophical claims regarding the indistinguishability of body from mind, and of corporeal from intellectual stimulation. In this way, Harlequin's and Scaramouch's antics help to break down the divide between physical farce and "literary" drama, between plays that bring us immediate "pleas[ure]" (to come back to Dryden's wording) and plays that reward our interpretive efforts with "significancie."

In challenging these distinctions between farce and literary drama, moreover, Behn is also breaking down the separation between playgoer and reader. Whereas in a play such as *The Luckey Chance* we could pinpoint which aspects a reader might be more likely to discern than a member of the live audience (and vice versa), in *The Emperor of the Moon* these aspects are very much bound up together: whether we are more aware (as spectators are likely to be) of the play's ridiculous bodies or (as readers are more likely to be) of its thematic treatment of reading, each point of entry brings us to a similar conclusion regarding reading's fundamental embodiment and the body's centrality to reading.

If Behn reveals to us the tenuousness of the separation between mind and body, between farce and "regular" drama, and between playgoer and reader, does she allow her characters to benefit from the same insights? As we have seen, the play's scheming young lovers—Elaria, Bellemante, Cinthio, and Charmante—seem to have a one-sided view of theater's power, believing it can "cure" Baliardo by dint of its fundamental embodiedness: like Settle, they seem to assume that the doctor's fantasies can be shattered if they align them with a theatrical performance and then bring that performance to an end—revealing hero and heroine to be (as in Settle's example) mere Bettertons and Barrys. Yet the lovers strategically use the final act's pageant to generate "real" events (their marriages to one another), implying a more nuanced view of theater, in which, as it were, one can carry a play's heroes and heroines—just like the heroes and heroines in Settle's Romances—into one's (marital) bed. In this deployment of theater, the line between actuality and fantasy becomes as indeterminate as it is for Settle's excitable reader.

But what about Baliardo? Does his reaction to the pageant reinforce or disprove the Settlean notion of theater's fundamental entrenchment in material reality? He seems, after all, to have been effectively disabused of his illusions precisely through the process that Settle describes, whereby the persons of the actors are finally made to obtrude upon the personas they have been playing: as soon as Scaramouch *"Puts off his Helmet,"* Baliardo shouts, "Ha,—*Scaramouch*—"; he then proceeds to recognize "Keplair" as his physician, to understand that Cinthio and Charmante "are not . . . the Emperor of the Moon . . . and . . . Prince of *Thunderland*," and to conclude that there is, accordingly, "No Emperor of the Moon,—and no Moon World!" (3.3.194–222). Yet Baliardo also seems to have been made aware of the material power of reading: "Burn all my Books," he commands, "and let my Study Blaze, / Burn all to Ashes, and be sure the Wind / Scatter the vile Contagious Monstrous Lyes" (3.3.227–29). The doctor now perceives his reading-induced fantasies to be not just mental conceits but sources of "Contagi[on]" and disease—to be misshapen or "Monstrous" aberrations, whose misleading notions can be physically dissipated like dust. If the pageant's curative effect is shown to be rooted in its corporeality, then, reading's vitiating force is seen, in this moment, to be equally so rooted—thus, once again, confusing the boundary between performance and text.

Baliardo's final words of the play may offer the most conclusive—or conclusively inconclusive—statement about what Behn's characters (as well as her audience members and readers) may have learned from everything they have just taken in. Paraphrasing the famous Socratic paradox, Baliardo declares, "He that knew all that ever Learning writ, / Knew only this—that he knew nothing yet" (3.3.239–40). Similarly to the ending of *The Luckey Chance*, then, the ending of *The Emperor of the Moon* effectively challenges playgoers and readers alike to continue trying to understand our world, even while recognizing the slipperiness of the tools available to us: our physical senses are influenced by our imaginations while our minds are more tethered to bodily needs and desires than we would care to admit. At the same time, Behn does not allow us simply to throw up our hands; if the line attributed to Socrates expresses the scholar's knowledge of his own lack of knowledge, Behn has Baliardo express a more conditional ignorance: we know nothing "yet." In this way, Behn seems to be daring us to try to know more, even as we acknowledge all of our potential sources of knowledge—whether "writ[ten]" texts, embodied performances, or both—to be continually resistant to any one method of interpretation.

3

TEXTUAL TIMELESSNESS, PERFORMATIVE TIME

Posterity in William Congreve's Love for Love *and* The Way of the World

IF RESTORATION DRAMATISTS' HISTORICAL POSITION made them acutely conscious of their relationship to the past, this consciousness likewise led them to question how their own achievements might survive them. For as much as the era's playwrights insisted on a continuity between their work and that of earlier seventeenth-century writers, they were also keenly aware of all that separated them—culturally, socially, politically—from the world in which those plays had been written. How well, or badly, would their own work translate for later generations, viewing them from a similar temporal remove? What was the best way to ensure a stable and abiding literary bequest? And is this project not, to some degree, a contradictory one for dramatists, given that a play must also speak to live audiences, and that theater is, by definition, transitory?

Scholars have long considered William Congreve to be a consummate wielder of print in the furtherance of his own cultural legacy. Specifically, he is seen as having effectively teamed up with publisher Jacob Tonson in a bid for readerly posterity over and against theatrical popularity. In this chapter, however, I demonstrate that Congreve does not, in fact, draw a firm line between textual permanence and theatrical ephemerality—that he reveals texts (both his own play-texts and his characters' legal, financial, and other documents) to be riddled with instability and irrationality. At the same time, he suggests that a text's true permanency, its ability to remain relevant to our lives, consists in its incorporation of a kind of theatrical language: of verbal repetition, redundancy, and excess—of linguistic ambiguity, and even anarchy, only barely contained within the rectilinear dimensions of the page.

Congreve's longstanding association with print as a medium of timeless monumentality may have originated alongside his very first play. John Dryden, in "To My Dear Friend Mr. Congreve, on his Comedy, call'd, *The Double-Dealer*" (1694), anointed Congreve as his successor by celebrating the younger writer's transcendence of the theater's mercurial ways. Depicting himself as "just abandoning th' Ungrateful Stage," Dryden figures Congreve's accomplishment as gloriously unaffected by the fickle tastes of theatergoers.[1] After a sweeping account of the monarchy's return and the reinstatement of wit's "Empire,"[2] Dryden casts the up-and-coming dramatist as Vitruvius, the ancient Roman architect:

> Our Age was cultivated thus at length;
> But what we gain'd in skill we lost in strength.
> Our Builders were, with want of Genius, curst;
> The second Temple was not like the first:
> Till you, the best *Vitruvius,* come at length;
> Our Beauties equal; but excel our strength.
> Firm *Dorique* pillars found Your solid Base:
> The Fair *Corinthian* Crowns the higher Space;
> Thus all below is Strength, and all above is Grace.[3]

What Congreve has achieved with *The Double-Dealer,* it seems, is a lasting classical edifice: as a "Temple," it is a site of communion with the eternal, but it is also durable itself (the word "strength" appears twice in four lines). Here current Britons will come to worship, and future Britons will return to marvel. So "firm" and "solid" is Congreve's work that even its most playful wit and charm assumes lapidary substance: the very "Grace[s]" of his comedy—signaled, in Dryden's verse, by a leaping triplet—are comprised of carved "*Corinthian*" capitals. Thus, Congreve's writing, already endued with an almost archaeological significance, will prove immune to the vagaries of popular trends and ticket-sales.

Congreve's plays, of course, did not actually take the form of Roman temples, yet many scholars have come to understand his highly intentional deployment of the print medium as a kind of architecture. Indeed, as Harold Weber points out, "To My Dear Friend Mr. Congreve on . . . *The Double-Dealer*" was first published in the prefatory matter to the quarto edition of *The Double-Dealer* itself—which also included two strategic dedications and a number of carefully assembled commendatory verses. Weber thus sees Dryden's poem, and the context in which it appeared, as central to a larger campaign on Congreve's part to "formulate a history of the seventeenth-century English theatre and to position [himself] as the fulfillment of its most important traditions"—and to do so, specifically, through print.[4] Indeed, Weber believes that, in its insistently text-based claims to legitimacy, this campaign "inscribe[s]" within itself, as a "foundational trope, . . . the playwright's alienation from the spectator."[5]

The 1694 quarto of *The Double-Dealer* represented only the beginning of a long and sustained effort to constitute Congreve's legacy in a series of deliberately designed editions. In particular, the three-volume *Works* of 1710—by way of its use of page layout and its position within Tonson's larger publishing agenda—sought to prove that English poets might credibly rival the Greek and Roman authors and that, on this basis, one could (in the words of John Barnard) begin "constructing [an] eighteenth-century canon" for posterity.[6] As D.F. McKenzie has shown, such design elements as engraved headpieces, ornamental drop capitals at the beginning of each act, printers' ornaments designating scene divisions, and letter-spaced roman capitals for headlines declared Congreve's *Works* to be of a piece with the great classical tradition: typographical treatments of this kind had been hitherto mainly reserved for editions of Terence and Plautus (with the exception of Ben Jonson's 1616 *Works*), and, more recently, the French neoclassicists.[7]

Barnard likewise contends that Tonson's longer-term publishing strategies were targeting a new "reading public"—"leisured" and "middle-class"—whose "taste [the editions] helped define."[8] As Barnard explains, in the period spanning from 1679 to 1720, Tonson adopted a number of groundbreaking practices. He asserted the continuity between ancients and moderns in his poetry anthologies by printing classical translations side by side with modern compositions. Likewise, he insisted on a uniform English literary lineage by devoting multivolume single-author editions to older and more contemporary authors alike. Finally, he gave as much attention to aesthetics—including uneconomic uses of white space, engraved title-pages, and authors' portraits—as to his volumes' literary contents, marking these texts as definitive objects of cultural heritage.[9] Barnard thus concludes that, "in their format and typography" but also in the broader historical context within which they were being presented, Tonson's editions—including Congreve's *Works*—"look to the future."[10] McKenzie likewise affirms that Tonson utilizes "the resources and conventions of print," as well as his savvy understanding of the book trade,[11] "to make conscious a concept of the reader[,] and offer opportunities to direct his responses in [new] ways."[12] He thereby "defin[ed] and exploit[ed] . . . a market for 'polite' literature" to an extent no one had done before.[13]

In many respects, the use of print seems the most obvious method by which to preserve a play for posterity. Print, after all, had been the means by which the plays of the sixteenth and early seventeenth centuries had been remembered during the Interregnum's closure of the theaters, and their stage revivals after 1660 depended on printed copies. Print outlives the individuals whose memories and anecdotes would otherwise provide the only continued existence of a play in performance. Moreover, to invoke again the common scholarly wisdom surrounding Jonson's 1616 *Works,* it was arguably the publication of plays with all the gravitas afforded to classical masterpieces that first allowed readers to regard them as "literature"—not as fleeting entertainments pitched to the latest fashions, but as works of art worthy of being read and reread.

However, in this chapter I hope to suggest that, especially in his last two comedies, Congreve shows the printed (or written) page to be less effective than we might think in staving off elements of mutability and decay. Partly through his own stylistic choices, but also through the use of characters who themselves marshal texts in their bids to control the future, Congreve ultimately reveals texts to be as shot through with desire and whim, uncertainty and error, as the appetitive, unruly bodies upon which they are purportedly imposing order. And yet, paradoxically, Congreve also suggests that it is this very metamorphic quality—a kind of theatrical, sensual shape-shifting, rooted in language itself—that allows the written or printed word truly to endure.

The classicizing, canonizing strategies that Congreve undertook in his 1710 *Works* went beyond page design and typography, extending into his plays' structure and diction. Critics have argued that these choices, too, served to align the plays more firmly with scholarly "rules"; with an official, print language; and with "literary" values privileging readerly regularity over aural vitality. As McKenzie and Peter Holland have shown, the 1710 *Works* systematically removed vulgarities and blasphemies found in the quarto editions—such as "Pox," "Jesu," "Hell," and "Whore"—while regularizing slang or dialect ("a" becomes "he"; "an" becomes "if"; and so on). These revisions conferred on Congreve's text what Holland calls a "solemn dignity," enabling it to "conform to canons of literary perfection."[14] They were also in line with the revisions Tonson was making to the work of other authors in his series. But, Holland believes, by favoring the "eye" over the "voice," such emendations were ultimately detrimental to performance.[15]

Similarly, in what Barnard calls an "extremely unusual" move for the time, the 1710 edition reorganizes the plays' scene divisions to highlight better their conformity with the neoclassical rules, and, in so doing, minimizes stage directions. As McKenzie explains, because neoclassical scene division legislated that a new scene begin each time a character entered or exited, once Congreve had adopted this system, he no longer had to denote "movements on and off stage . . . per se"; instead, such movements were implied by the insertion of a new scene number, underneath which would appear "a kind of roll-call of everyone [who would be in] attendance" during that scene.[16] Likewise, at the end of an act, instead of using "*Exeunt*" to indicate the actors' departure from the stage, Congreve could simply announce the "*End of the [nth] Act.*" Again, onstage action is de-emphasized in deference to the literary "structure of the play."[17] The plays' status as aesthetic forms, their ambitions to persist as monuments of a sort, seem to necessitate the erasure not just of the bits of vernacular so deeply "of their time" but, likewise, of the shuffling, changing, time-bound bodies that speak them.

Although McKenzie argues fairly persuasively that Congreve had originally written his plays with neoclassical scene divisions in mind (so that signaling the scene changes typographically doesn't actually change the plays that much[18]), Holland complains that the new scene divisions do, in fact, create quite a few awkward stagings: characters are occasionally compelled to remain onstage when we feel, instinctively, that they should have stormed off several beats earlier; in other instances, two characters must either enter or exit simultaneously when, theatrically, it would make more sense for one to follow the other.[19] What the revised scene divisions add up to, Holland insists, is a "theoretic straitjacket,"[20] in which theatrical effectiveness is sacrificed to principles of aesthetic elegance, and in which movement—specifically, we might add, the ephemerality of movement—is rejected in the interest of abstract literary ideals and, concomitantly, the permanence of texts.

Indeed, one could make the larger argument that the aim of neoclassical dramaturgy more broadly is to minimize theatricality, and theatrical temporalities, in order to cultivate a sense of what one might call textual time: as John D. Lyons explains, "the world of the [neoclassical] play" should, according to contemporary theorists, "exist . . . in apparently complete independence of the world of the spectator."[21] This effect is achieved via the unities, which, by "try[ing] to bring scenic space and fictional place close to a ratio of one-to-one" (i.e., the unity of place), while likewise attempting to make "the time of performance . . . the . . . same length of time [as the] time of the . . . story" (i.e., the unity of time), ostensibly lead to the creation of a "radically separate space" for the play's story to transpire in: spectators, by being encouraged to focus on the play's own internal sequencing, are prevented "from [noticing] the 'objective' passage of time."[22] Indeed, in this sense "the *reader* may actually be the perfect audience to fulfill the wishes of the [neoclassical] dramatic theorists," writes Lyons, for it is the reader for whom "the barrier . . . between characters and spectators" that the unities are meant to erect is, ultimately, most fully operative.[23] Congreve, by underscoring the unities typographically, seems to have these ideals in mind, arguably seeking to construct an oeuvre that is elevated not only above the bustle of individual performances and performers but also—in his nod to the ancients—above the distractions of the present day.[24]

In addition to the texts of Congreve's plays, the texts within them also seem to be attempting to forge a "time out of time"—a world set apart from somatic or lived time. The characters' wills, deeds, and other documents are intended to preserve a particular reality—usually a particular financial reality—from the welter of impulse and passion that could otherwise lead to dynastic downfall and economic ruin. In *The Way of the World* (1700) especially, the various texts used by the characters would seem to succeed in this undertaking, leading Holland to conclude that "the immutability of contracts" in the play effectively causes the plot's "facts" to become "fixed" in place,[25] impervious to the dramatis personae's complex series of intrigues and counter-intrigues. Yet, as I argue below, Congreve ultimately suggests that texts are not exempt from movement and transformation. For while texts do provide some sense of order for the language that comprises them, they are ultimately shown to create a space that is not "out of time" but, rather, in which language may come to life in accordance with its own (often theatrical) timing.

Before turning to Congreve's plays, I first want to explain in more detail how I am thinking about performance, or theatricality, and time. Theorist Bert O. States identifies two central, complementary definitions of "performance": on the one hand, performance can be understood—as in the famous formulation of Richard Schechner—as "twice-behaved behavior," or "ritual."[26] On the other hand, performance can be seen in terms of what States refers to, citing Peggy Phelan, as an "aesthetic of presence."[27] Whereas Schechner deems performance to be something that "can be stored [and] transmitted,"[28] Phelan insists it "cannot be saved, recorded, [or] documented.... Performance's only life is in the present."[29] And where Schechner emphasizes "repetition," writing that "performance means: never for the first time,"[30] Phelan maintains that performance is unique to a particular instant, location, and body (or group of bodies). Of course, these two notions of performance overlap in many ways (making it possible, for example, for Mircea Eliade to assert that "Every ritual has the character of happening *now*, at this very moment. The time of the event that ritual commemorates or re-enacts is made *present*").[31] Nonetheless, I believe these two respective concepts—performance as ritual and performance as presence—can help us to gain a better understanding of what Congreve is doing in his final two comedies.

Specifically, my contention in this chapter is that Congreve activates each of these separate concepts within the language of each play, in order to create a sense of time that runs counter to the (literally) prescribable future we would normally associate with texts. Thus the stylized dialogues of *Love for Love* evoke the repetition of ritual—particularly (as I will show) the ritual of late seventeenth- and eighteenth-century masquerade—while the superlative, almost surreal wit of *The Way of the World*, by embodying a kind of bewildering fertility, creates a sense of present-tense emergence (or what performance theorist David Cole might call "presencing"[32]). Moreover, the fact that Congreve achieves both effects specifically through language—as opposed to through action or plot or another kind of dramatic tool—allows him to produce something unique: not just a play, but a play-*text,* into which performance is embedded. Accordingly, as I will explain, the typographical immaculacy of Congreve's printed *Works* serves not to hamper the plays' theatricality, as one might surmise, but to reinforce it.

In his last two comedies in particular, Congreve presents two seemingly opposite but ultimately mutually reinforcing models of posterity. On one side, as we have seen, he posits a form of posterity in which a printed or written document supposedly ensures that a certain vision of the world (artistic, generational, class-based, or otherwise) will continue unchanged into the future, invulnerable to the fluctuations in values, tastes, and appetites endemic to human existence. On the other side, he celebrates an alternative notion of posterity, in which dynastic and literary continuance into the future is guaranteed not by static rigidity but by constant and unceasing flexibility—a flexibility associated with spoken dialogue and performance. And texts, seemingly paradoxically, can actually be seen to nurture this shifting, mobile model of posterity as well.

In *Love for Love* (1695), this conception of posterity as continual change (rather than frozen permanence) is achieved through a kind of Schechnerian ritual—specifically, through a set of repeated refrains borrowed, I contend, from the masked balls of the late seventeenth and eighteenth centuries. As Terry Castle explains in her definitive study of masquerade in this period, the conventions of the masked ball posited a world in which who we are is "perennially open to reconstitution."[33] Correspondingly, despite the fact that *Love for Love* is almost obsessively preoccupied (as are most of its characters) with problems of knowing and being known, the play's masquerade motif ultimately implies that full knowledge of one another is neither possible nor desirable.[34] Likewise, the documents wielded by the characters (which include legal contracts as well as magical prophecies), despite seeming to guarantee a particular set of future outcomes, are revealed to be just as subject to error and decay as the mortal bodies their textual authority appears to be policing.

The Way of the World, which premiered five years later, can be read in certain ways as a kind of sequel to *Love for Love*. If the earlier play's thematic and stylistic motifs center on knowing and uncertainty—problems (in part) of courtship—the latter play's language alludes to, and performs, a darkly luxuriant fecundity and procreation.[35] Consequently, where *Love for Love* lends itself to a Schechnerian notion of performance as ritual, *The Way of the World* could be said to exemplify a Phelanian definition of performance—one that depends on emergence and live, or living, presence. More than providing a thematic extension from courtship to new birth, however, the latter play offers an answer to a question posed but never fully resolved within the plot of *Love for Love*—namely, the question of what it would take for a text to be able to shape the future, and how. For where *Love for Love* simply shows texts to be open to contingency—to be less controlling of posterity than their users would like—*The Way of the World* shows how texts might work with or within that contingency to create a different kind of posterity, inflected by a theatrical (and almost biological) mutability.

Finally, by using his own text to explore how a written or printed document might harness the temporality of performance—defined slightly differently in each play—Congreve ultimately produces what I see as a virtual theatricality on his own page, a kind of instability that, paradoxically, persists. And it is this unique combination of print and performance that is at least partly responsible, I would suggest, for the playwright's own literary legacy.

In *Love for Love,* three characters in particular (conveniently designated by their surnames) can be seen to articulate a belief in the stability of texts—in the power of texts to hold a certain version of reality in place over and against the vicissitudes symbolized by the human body. Mr. Foresight, who lives in fear of all kinds of misfortunes but especially of cuckoldom—and, by implication, the circumvention of his genetic posterity—is constantly "reading" ominous significance into the world around him, whether in the fact that he donned one of his stockings inside out that morning or in the fact that he accidentally got out of bed backward.[36] Sir Sampson Legend, meanwhile, harbors nearly as superstitious a faith in the capacity of legal documents (specifically, a signed "Bond," which we will examine more closely in a moment) to protect his own posterity—which he believes his libertine eldest son, Valentine, has jeopardized through both his economic and reproductive profligacy.[37] The last of the trio, Valentine Legend himself, starts out the play with a similar set of textual tenets, and, although he quickly abandons them,[38] his statements regarding his reading practices in the first few minutes of the play help define with particular clarity how it is that all three men understand texts and their relationship to time.

Valentine begins act 1 vowing to abandon his hitherto disastrous pursuit of sensual pleasures and to pursue books instead: having wooed his beloved, Angelica, with "Coaches and . . . Liveries; [with] . . . Treats and . . . Balls" more numerous than he could afford (1.1.40), he now enjoins his servant Jeremy, "Read, read, Sirrah, and refine your Appetite; learn to live upon Instruction; feast your Mind, and mortifie your Flesh; Read, and take your Nourishment in at your Eyes; shut up your Mouth, and chew the Cud of Understanding. So *Epictetus* advises" (1.1.10–14). Texts, it seems, are meant to counteract that which is all too mortal within us: our "Flesh" (which will eventually decline and die), but also our appetites and our reliance on our "Mouth[s]," whether used for eating or, perhaps, for speaking—that mode of communication that (unlike books) disperses and disappears even as we perform it. Valentine appears to believe that the written word can provide a kind of stoic "refine[ment]" and lasting source of value where the body must necessarily fail us.

Foresight's attempts to overcome the weaknesses of the flesh seem at first to take a less textual form. However, Congreve links Foresight's methods directly to the act of reading when, at the beginning of act 2, the old man looks to a supposedly ancient "Prophesie" in his attempts (post facto, though he doesn't realize this) to prevent his young wife's infidelity:

> *When Housewifes all the House forsake,*
> *And leave good Man to Brew and Bake,*
> *Withouten Guile, then be it said,*
> *That House doth stond upon its Head;*
> *And when the Head is set in Grond,*
> *Ne marl, if it be fruitful fond.* (2.3.8–13)

We normally associate prophecies with oral lore, yet the one that Foresight recites here features a specifically scribal provenance: it is "written by *Messahalah* the *Arabian,* and . . . translated by a reverend *Buckinghamshire* Bard" (2.3.6–7).[39] Foresight's recitation exhibits a marked attentiveness, moreover, to what we might call the verse's textual integrity: he fastidiously retains the non-standard plural for "Housewife," for example, and the Middle-English "stond" instead of "stand," where a strictly oral transmission might have made updates. Such fastidiousness points to a conservative editorial mindset (perversely so, given that the text is, in any case, a "translat[ion]"), but, more specifically, Foresight's punctiliousness bespeaks a very particular understanding of how texts relate to reality. If we were to come upon Foresight's verse in any other context, we would likely characterize it as an adage or aphorism, rather than a prophecy per se: the lines' meaning seems to lie in their articulation of a general rule—something like "give her an inch and she'll take a mile." By contrast, the usefulness of a prophecy inheres in its ability not to transcend particulars but, quite the opposite, to tell us precisely what will happen when. It is this "prophetic" hermeneutic that infuses Foresight's textual approach (and, as we will see, Sampson's, too).

Foresight's interpretive system is really only a slightly exaggerated form of a larger belief we see repeated throughout the play (including, it would initially seem, in Congreve's own text)—namely, that a sufficiently careful attention to texts and their details could somehow shore up a person against loss, or, indeed, might hold at bay a larger, existential oblivion. Thus, although Sir Sampson Legend constantly draws distinctions between himself and the silly "old *Merlin*," as he calls Foresight, his entrance in act 1 (just moments after Foresight's "prophecy" scene) shows him to be as intent as Foresight on managing his posterity through the written word. Holding *"a Paper"* (elsewhere referred to by the characters as a "Bond"), Sampson glories in what he thinks is his revenge on his eldest son, Valentine, for the young man's extravagance:

> Here 'tis, I have it in my Hand . . . ; I'll make the ungracious Prodigal know who begat him . . . What, I warrant my Son thought nothing belong'd to a Father, but Forgiveness and Affection; no Authority, no Correction, no Arbitrary Power; nothing to be done, but for him to offend and me to pardon. I warrant you, if he danc'd till Doomsday, he thought I was to pay the Piper. Well, but here it is under black and white, *Signatum, Sigillatum,* and *Deliberatum;* that as soon as my Son *Benjamin* is arriv'd, he is to make over to him his Right of Inheritance. (2.5.1–12)

Like Foresight in his painstaking attention to nonstandard plurals and vowels, Sampson seems to believe that by ensuring that all his *t*'s are crossed and his *i*'s dotted—*Signatum, Sigillatum,* and *Deliberatum*—he can also ensure a document's direct correlation to (and, thus, his own control over) his domestic affairs going forward: "I'll make the ungracious Prodigal know who begat him. . . . I warrant my Son thought nothing belong'd to a Father, but Forgiveness and Affection; no Authority, no Correction, no Arbitrary Power." Like Foresight, Sampson believes that, by vigilantly supervising the specifics of a particular text, he can guarantee a proper familial dynamic, thereby protecting the future of the family name and family line (even, perhaps, until "Doomsday" itself). The "black and white" of the document reflects—or, even better, can effect—the proper distribution of punishment and reward to the prodigal and the pure.

Moreover, as I have already begun to describe, Congreve, too, appears to deploy text—that is, the text of his play—in similar ways, as if he might thus control the future reception of his work, irrespective of audience members' changing tastes, or the ever-changing bodies of an ever-changing series of cast members. As we have seen, Congreve's partnership with Tonson (and, more specifically, the various design choices manifested in the 1710 *Works*) suggests a bid for canonicity and classic status, while the replacement of idiomatic or dialect terms in the characters' speech suggests an attempt to extract Congreve's dramatis personae from their local social context and to preserve them as more universal figures. The elimination of the quartos' designated exits and entrances in favor of clearly demarcated scene divisions limits our sense of individual actors moving through a particular time and place, and Congreve's title pages further erase such particulars, replacing the conventional phrase (used in the quartos) "as it is acted at the theatre in Lincolns-Inn-Fields, by His Majesty's servants," with the phrase "Printed in the Year, 1710." Indeed, such strategies do appear to have helped assure Congreve's position within a specifically literary—rather than theatrical—firmament: as Julie Stone Peters points out, in the years following the publication of the 1710 *Works,* a number of poetic works were dedicated to Congreve, including Richard Steele's *Poetical Miscellanies,* of 1714, and Alexander Pope's *Iliad,* of 1720.[40]

However, *Love for Love* soon makes clear that texts—whether Valentine's books of philosophy, Foresight's omens and prophecies, Sampson's "Bond," or Congreve's own play-text—are not, in fact, invulnerable to the needs and desires of the human body in real time. Valentine abandons his "Paper Diet" as soon as practical concerns impinge, in the form of Trapland the scrivener. And Mrs. Foresight's dreaded infidelities, far from a hypothetical outcome, are already well underway before the play begins. So too, as we will see in more detail in a moment, Sampson's bond turns out to be suffused with his own self-love and erotic desire. Importantly, these outcomes do not point merely to a failure to use texts well—whether a failure to discern correctly the meaning of a prophecy or a failure to draw up a legal document free of loopholes. Rather, they point to a basic misconception that the universe can be summed up and managed through words on a page. The error of this assumption is exposed via the play's masquerade motif, which insists that the future is not written in the stars or in the codicil to a patriarch's will but, rather, is always inherently in flux—making it both unknowable and uncontrollable. Moreover, the fact that *Love for Love*'s masquerade motif is as thoroughly stylistic as it is thematic—that is, the fact that it inheres in a set of lexical patterns as much as it does in a recurring set of images—suggests that texts, because of their basis in language, will ultimately not just fail to pin down reality but will be obliged to participate in the metamorphic performances of which human experience inevitably consists.⁴¹

Significantly, despite its seemingly inherent conduciveness to the dramatic, masquerade plays almost no role in *Love for Love*'s plot per se. Indeed, in what would appear a contradiction, Congreve's only work to feature a masked ball as a central plot element is not a work for the stage at all but, rather, his prose fiction *Incognita* (1692). Yet perhaps there is no contradiction here: famously, Congreve wrote in his preface to *Incognita* that he had structured it like a play, writing that "*Since all Traditions must indisputably give place to the* Drama, *and since there is no possibility of giving that life to the Writing or Repetition of a Story which it has in the Action, I resolved in another Beauty to imitate* Dramatick Writing, *namely, in the Design, Contexture, and Result of the Plot.*"⁴² Accordingly, it seems that the conceit of the masked ball is meant to imbue *Incognita* with the kinds of ironies, misunderstandings, and coincidences that characterize dramatic storylines. (And it does do this, by preventing the novel's main character from realizing until the end that the woman his father wants him to marry is, in fact, the woman with whom he has chanced to fall in love.) Interestingly, however, while the masks in *Incognita* may make it dramatic, they do not make it theatrical. Indeed, Congreve acknowledges here that he has followed the principles of dramatic "*Design*" precisely because there is "*no possibility*" of endowing a prose fiction with the "*life*" that "*Action*" alone can provide.⁴³ Masquerade allows for complication and clarification, intrigue and revelation, but these intellectual or emotional ups and downs are meant to compensate for *Incognita*'s inability to present us with actual living bodies on a stage.

When Congreve sets out to write a play, then, perhaps he no longer feels a need to exploit masquerade's built-in tensions. But by drawing on the masked ball's distinctive phrasings (notably absent from *Incognita*), he may in fact have hit on a way of endowing a reading text with "*life*"—that very effect he had despaired of earlier. Through a series of verbal motifs, Congreve infuses his play, even for readers unable to attend a production, with a kind of ritual performance—with a kind of "*Action*"—that the most careful principles of dramatic construction could not provide.

Notwithstanding *Love for Love*'s lack of a literal masked ball, the play features two episodes that directly evoke masquerade, and these help reinforce the masquerade-based lexical patterns that pervade the play as a whole. The most straightforward of the two episodes is the (offstage) trick wedding between Mr. Tattle and Mrs. Frail, in act 5, during which they believe themselves to be marrying Angelica and Valentine, respectively. The hapless pair undergo the ceremony while dressed as a friar and a nun—personae that, as Castle explains, constituted two of the best known "types" circulating at the masked balls of the period. (Others included the "Oriental" costume, "occupational" garb such as that of shepherdesses and chimney sweeps, and "character dress," in which masqueraders would outfit themselves as Falstaff, Don Quixote, or the like.[44])

The other episode in which masquerade is evoked is Valentine's stint of feigned madness in act 4—a ploy that allows him to delay officially transferring his inheritance to his younger brother, while also serving as a vehicle for several satirical jabs, mostly aimed at his father and his father's attorney, Buckram ("Why does that Lawyer wear black?—Does he carry his Conscience withoutside?" and so on [4.6.16–17]). Despite the fact that (unlike the trick wedding) this episode involves no actual masquerade dress, Valentine later admits to having worn a "Masque of Madness" (4.18.6–7), and Angelica likewise refers to his "Disguise of Madness" (5.2.91). Moreover, Valentine makes his barbed comments to Sampson and Buckram while pretending to labor under the illusion that, as he puts it, "I am Truth, and come to give the World the Lie" (4.6.13–14). Not coincidentally, it seems, such allegorical figures constituted yet another type within the masquerade's established taxonomy; Castle notes that "Fortune, Day, Night, Temperance, Liberty, and a host of similar abstractions" all featured prominently among the favored guises of late seventeenth- and eighteenth-century masqueraders.[45]

Together, these references help to establish a pattern of allusion that, in turn, helps to develop what we might call the play's "masquerade epistemology"—or, perhaps more accurately, anti-epistemology. This destabilizing approach to knowledge receives its most vivid expression toward the end of act 4, in yet another of the play's invocations of the masked-ball tradition. Here, Valentine has just accused Angelica of cruelty as she prepares to exit the room without confirming her love for him—leaving him, as he complains, in "Uncertainty" regarding his future prospects with her. Angelica replies, "Wou'd any thing, but a Madman complain of Uncertainty? Uncertainty and Expectation are the Joys of Life. Security is an insipid thing, and the overtaking and possessing of a Wish, discovers the Folly of the Chase.

Never let us know one another better; for the Pleasure of a Masquerade is done, when we come to shew our Faces" (4.20.5–10). Angelica's declarations here seem to suggest that "know[ing] one another better" is made possible through the "shew[ing]" of "Faces"—that a "Wish" can be "possess[ed]" in the end. She also implies, however, that a wish once possessed is no longer the wish it once was: fantasy molders into "Folly." It is not "know[ledge]," then, that is given preference to, but "Joys" and "Pleasure"—and these, like wishes, are "done" once we obtain a sense of confidence about what awaits us. The recommended stance, in other words, is one not of complete detachment from reality (i.e., the stance of the "Madman") but of continued "Uncertainty and Expectation" regarding the future—a commitment to "Chas[ing] . . . Wish[es]" even when there is no reason to believe they can (or ought to) be finally captured.

Previous critics have dismissed this speech of Angelica's as mere teasing affectation, arguing that her words in the final act contradict these earlier remarks: moments before the end of the play, Angelica announces to Valentine that she "ha[s] done dissembling now," exclaiming, "Here's my Hand, my Heart was always yours" (5.12.97, 5.12.59). The only reason she did not reveal her love earlier, she explains, is because she had been testing him; apparently, now that Valentine's devotion has been proven, the "Masquerade" may be dispensed with. Yet Angelica's final remarks actually return us to her earlier philosophical position: singling out Valentine from the rest of his sex, she explains that most men are "Infidels"; they "pretend to Worship, but have neither Zeal nor Faith" (5.12.120–21). While the comparison of love to religious worship is obviously a conventional courtly trope, the pun on "Faith" here recalls Angelica's prior emphasis on the mysterious. "Faith" refers to constancy, of course, but also—more specifically—to devotion in the face of the unknown and unknowable.

This same resistance to epistemological closure might be said to define masquerade and, indeed, theater itself. Live theatrical performance, unlike Foresight's prophecy or Sampson's bond, takes as its grounding assumption the idea that reality is constantly being refashioned—that any current stability is temporary at best. This assumption is also fundamental, of course, to the eighteenth-century masked ball: as Castle notes, these assemblies allowed "anarchic, theatrical selves [to] displace . . . supposedly essential ones," resulting in "a material devaluation of unitary notions of the self, as radical in its own way as the more abstract demystifications in the writings of Hume and the eighteenth-century ontologists."[46] It is this conception of a shifting reality that *Love for Love* continually reiterates in its use of conventional seventeenth-century masquerade language.

As Castle describes, the masked ball was characterized by a set of highly "ritualized [verbal] gambits": before initiating conversation, she explains, participants would exchange a series of fixed phrases, "usually beginning 'I know you' or 'Do you know me?'"[47] Castle points out that this "obsessive verbal return to the question of identity . . . threw into relief" what she calls "the central enigma of masquerade phenomenology"[48]: such phrases, delivered in the masquerade's typical falsetto "squeak" (utilized, in part, to disguise one's sex), were meant not to answer the question of identity but, rather, to revel in its unanswerability. As I am about to show, these same phrases, or versions of them, constitute a veritable refrain throughout *Love for Love*—and they bring their ontological conundrums with them.

Perhaps the play's most prominent use of (and riff on) the language of masquerade could be said to occur in the scenes of Valentine's feigned madness. In 4.6, we witness the following interchange:

> *Valentine:* Answer me: who is that, and that?
> *Sir Sampson:* Gads bobs, does he not know me? . . . *Val, Val,* do'st thou not know me, Boy? Not know thy own Father, *Val!* I am thy own Father, and this is honest *Brief Buckram* the Lawyer.
> *Valentine:* It may be so—I did not know you—the World is full—There are People that we do know, and People that we do not know; and yet the Sun shines upon all alike. . . .
> *Sir Sampson:* Body o' me, I know not what to say to him.
> *Valentine:* Why does that Lawyer wear black?—Does he carry his Conscience withoutside?—Lawyer, what art thou? Dost thou know me?
> (4.6.4–18)

A similar exchange occurs at 4.16:

> *Tattle:* Do you know me, *Valentine?*
> *Valentine:* You? Who are you? No, I hope not.
> *Tattle:* I am *Jack Tattle,* your Friend.
> *Valentine:* My Friend! what to do? I am no married Man, and thou canst not lye with my Wife: I am very poor, and thou canst not borrow Mony of me: Then what Employment have I for a Friend? . . .

Angelica: Do you know me, *Valentine?*
Valentine: Oh, very well.
Angelica: Who am I?
Valentine: You're a Woman.... I know you; for I lov'd a Woman.
(4.16.52–69)

The compulsive concern with "knowing" expressed here is not limited to the scenes above, moreover, but suffuses the entire play—indeed, the word "know"—in various forms—is repeated no fewer than 166 times throughout *Love for Love*.[49] Yet the combined effect of these references, as we see here, is not an overarching preoccupation with "knowing" at all but, rather, with *not* knowing—or, perhaps more accurately, with the invention of ever more elaborate acts of disguise that, together, render full knowledge impossible.

Of course, *Love for Love* is, at one level, seriously invested in the problem of how to ascertain who we really are and, accordingly, how to predict each other's future behavior. After all, the main action of the play consists of (1) Sampson's attempt to make his son acknowledge his fatherly authority (or "know who begat him"), and thus to protect his legacy; (2) Angelica's attempt to adjudicate Valentine's dependability as a prospective spouse; and (3) Valentine's struggle to assert his own identity as eventual heir and husband/father. To attend to these themes as handled in the plot, however, is to assume that the play's problems of knowing are problems that are eventually worked out, in classic comic mode: Valentine's right of inheritance is reaffirmed; Angelica marries him; the old generation is replaced by the new. By contrast, to focus on the play's masquerade language is to see that the play also resists epistemological and temporal finality—to see it as a series of repeated performances with no clear beginning, middle, or end.

Moreover, recognizing *Love for Love*'s lexical borrowings from masquerade allows us to see the play itself as a kind of masquerade—that is, to understand the role of the masked ball not as a plot catalyst (in the vein of *Incognita*, or the various eighteenth-century novels that Castle analyzes in her book) but as a formal template for the work as a whole, producing an architecture of dizzying circularity. As Castle writes, "The masquerade . . . follows no plot; its spirit is profoundly antitemporal, and [it constitutes] a spectacular rebuff to all ordering forces, including those of historical encapsulation. The masquerade evokes a world of *temps perdu*."[50] In this sense, masquerade participates in the larger temporality—or "antitemporal[ity]," as Castle puts it—of ritual itself: as David Cole asserts, "the performance of . . . ritual" has the power to "ma[k]e present again . . . the *illud tempus*," or "time of origins."⁵¹ It is this return to the *illud tempus* that Cole sees as distinguishing theatrical performance from all other art forms.

But could this *illud tempus*—or *temps perdu*—of theater also be extended to drama as a written genre? I suggest that in *Love for Love* the answer is yes: for the play does not simply allude to masquerade but, as I have begun to show, takes on its stylistic—and even structural—principles. The scenic pattern of the play could be said to be defined by the masquerade's trademark verbal exchange, as Congreve pairs characters off in a series of teasing one-on-one encounters in which questions of "knowing" are raised with particular insistence (these include interviews between the Frail sisters, Ben and Prue, Scandal and Prue, and so forth).

Needless to say, these tête-à-têtes—presumably like many of those at a masked ball—do not ultimately add up to any real knowledge. Even (or especially) Angelica's and Valentine's supposed knowledge of one another turns out to be less definite than it appears. Angelica declares she has tested the Legend men satisfactorily by the end of the play: "I was resolv'd to try [Valentine] to the utmost," she explains to Sampson; "I have try'd you too, and know you both" (5.12.71–72). Yet this "know[ledge]" is in fact rather provisional. When Angelica proclaims she is "done dissembling," and thus advises Valentine not to "suspect" her love should her previous coldness now turn to "an extream Fondness" (5.12.97–99), Valentine explains that he'll "prevent that Suspicion":

> *Valentine:* For I intend to doat to that immoderate degree, that your Fondness shall never distinguish it self enough to be taken notice of. If ever you seem to love too much, it must be only when I can't love enough.
> *Angelica:* Have a care of large Promises; you know you are apt to run more in Debt than you are able to pay.
> *Valentine:* Therefore I yield my Body as your Prisoner, and make your best on't. (5.12.100–107)

Decisive as this dialogue is seemingly meant to be, it is also oddly unsettling. Valentine offers his body as security ("I yield my Body as your Prisoner, and make your best on't"), but the preoccupation with texts that pervades the play is premised on the body's instability and changeability: Valentine's libertine appetites have threatened to decimate the Legend fortune, and Mrs. Foresight's sexual proclivities have potentially undermined her husband's family line. Valentine's offer, moreover, also reminds us of what Angelica would call the "Pleasure" and "Joys" of uncertainty: Angelica's possession of Valentine's physical self may not ultimately guarantee his endless devotion, but it may well provide Angelica with delight as she seeks to detect her husband's love in his every bodily movement.

As in masquerade, *Love for Love*'s verbal returns to the question of knowledge yield little certainty but much pleasure—in addition to an important kind of liberation. (The fact that it is the husband, in this marriage, who cedes his body as property to his wife produces an intriguing—and also masquerade-like—inversion of the conventional roles.[52]) Accordingly, the characters who triumph in the end are those who seek not certitude but joy, and the characters left disappointed are those who persist in believing that the body's unpredictable appetites can be kept in check by texts—that a known future can be ensured by a letter-perfect prophecy or a bond signed and sealed according to protocol.

To understand this point more fully, it is useful to look in detail at the play's ending, which, at first glance, seems not to reward Valentine's masquerade antics. To be sure, Valentine's "Masque of Madness" postpones the contracted relinquishment of his inheritance to his brother Ben (if Valentine is *non compos mentis,* then he cannot sign the document that the bond obliges him to sign). Yet such counterfeiting cannot render the bond void—in part because, if Valentine wants to marry Angelica, he will need to show himself to be of sound mind. As absurd, then, as Sampson's and Foresight's belief in a prescribable future may seem, the fact of Sampson's bond remains. Is the power of texts to control the future not, therefore, reasserted?

In the end, the bond is thoroughly dispensed with: holding it aloft, Angelica *"Tears the Paper"* up, providing the decisive blow to Sampson's plans to disinherit Valentine and allowing Valentine to marry Angelica with both of their fortunes undiminished (5.12.54 sd). Richard Kroll sees this sequence as betokening the victory of "natural gesture" over the written word, but this is not quite accurate. The significance of Angelica's action does not lie in the material destruction of the bond, exactly—or in the silent eloquence of the gesture (as a testament to Angelica's love for Valentine).[53] Rather, to see this moment's true importance, we must set it against the events leading up to it: the reason Angelica has possession of the bond in the first place (and, thus, has the ability to tear it up) is not that she has simply snatched it out of Sampson's hands, as Kroll implies; rather, pretending to consider seriously

Sampson's proposal that she marry him, and claiming to want her own attorney's advice on the bond first, she has convinced Sampson to lend her the document for vetting purposes. In this sense, Angelica has outmaneuvered Sampson not through some impulsive performance but through a kind of textual savvy—beating him, as it were, at his own game.

Angelica's approach to texts differs from Sampson's, however, in a crucial way. If Sampson understands the bond as anchoring a stable future in defiance of the body's prodigal proclivities, Angelica discovers the errant desires encoded into the document: after leading Sampson to believe she might actually take him up on his marriage proposal, she points out that the jointure he has promised her is technically "not in your Power, Sir *Sampson;* for when *Valentine* confesses himself in his Senses, he must make over his Inheritance to his younger Brother" (5.2.101–3). This calculated probing leads to a key admission: "But, I warrant you, I have a Proviso in the Obligation in favour of myself," Sampson explains; "Body o' me," he adds—repeating what is (tellingly) his characteristic interjection throughout the play—"I have a Trick to turn the Settlement upon the Issue Male of our two Bodies begotten" (5.2.105–8). When Angelica says she must consult with her own lawyer on the matter, Sampson eagerly hands over the bond—which is, of course, a fatal error on his part. What makes this exchange so crucial, however, is not so much that it leads to Sampson's handing over of the document but, again, that it exposes the human weakness that has underlain the legal text all along. Even Sampson, it turns out, has never believed the future to be quite as firmly pinned in place by texts as his previous remarks have suggested: he has specifically drawn up the bond in such a way as to make allowance for the body's ability to surprise us—for the possibility that an old man might still fall in love, father an additional child, and thus, essentially, turn back time.

The corporeal frailty and temporal ambivalence built into the bond, then, are the reasons that Angelica is able to get hold of it and rip it up. But her destruction of the bond is ultimately effective not because the paper has been torn (presumably a replacement copy could have been drawn up based on the testimony of witnesses) but because, by this point in the play, none of the characters really want it to remain in force anyway: just as the document had had secret yearnings built into its very core, it turns out to be only as strong as the desires, wishes, and hopes for the future of those whose fates it appears to dictate. Valentine, most obviously, has changed his mind: having signed the bond under duress (in exchange for Sampson's bailing him out of debt), he naturally no longer wants to relinquish his inheritance. But, just as significantly, everyone else's thinking has evolved, too: indeed, if Angelica hadn't torn up the bond, Sampson might have done so himself, feeling no longer so charitable toward his younger son. This new stance owes partly to the fact that Ben himself has reversed course, deciding not to marry Foresight's daughter Prue, as the old men had planned—a decision based partly on Prue's own transfer of affections (she has been seduced by Scandal). In short, what Angelica's ripping of the bond reveals is that texts do not necessarily prescribe a particular future, but are ultimately shot through with, and answerable to, our mutable, mortal ways.

Congreve's own play-text may reinforce this same notion of texts' answerability to human weakness. As we have seen, Congreve's *Works* is designed in accordance with neoclassical principles of dramaturgy, which were meant to produce a "time out of time" quality—or what I have been referring to as a "textual" temporality. However, while one might expect this quality to foster critical remove, it was believed by the theorists of the period to bring about an experience of intense, immersive sensation. As Lyons explains, "the entire separation of audience and players" that the unities are intended to achieve is what—paradoxically—allows theatergoers to enter into the world of the play, for the strict differentiation of the two spheres is what facilitates the play's "status as a verisimilar autonomous object," and, consequently, the audience's ability to believe in it.[54] In other words, "by giving up reference to the world of the spectators, the play advances its truth status" and, thereby—contrary to what we might initially assume—helps the spectator or reader to invest all the more fully and affectively in the events portrayed.[55] The ultimate goal, Lyons emphasizes, is thus to heighten the audience's "pleasure at the vivid experiencing of a scene"—a pleasure that depends on their "emotional, libidinal, and perhaps transgressive participation" in the goings-on of the play.[56]

Not only does Congreve's adherence to the neoclassical rulebook make for a more "theatrical" play than we might expect, but so too does his use of the physical book that his printed drama constitutes. As we have seen, Congreve's 1710 *Works* seems to circumscribe, or place limits on, the kinetic human form: he minimizes stage directions and indicates characters' movements on and off stage implicitly, via an inert list of names, rather than denoting entrances and exits per se. At the same time, he insists on his plays' staid, architectural stability via his letter-spaced headings, drop capitals, and printers' ornaments. We might expect, then, that in securing his plays' position within a lasting print canon, Congreve sacrifices their connection to a living theatrical tradition. I would argue, however, that Congreve's carefully regimented text in fact creates a space—indeed, not unlike the carefully constructed parameters of the masquerade—in which a kind of virtual theatricality can endlessly, joyously, be performed.[57] That is, while the 1710 *Works* may curtail our awareness of the actual actors and actresses traversing the stage, it also focuses our attention on the characters' language, and, specifically, on the characters' masquerade-inspired verbal exchanges. These exchanges undermine the notion that we might ever know one another fully, while also suggesting that the process of trying to know each other—which it seems we cannot help but undertake—inevitably entails a kind of erotic tension and pleasure. What is actually being presented to us within the neoclassical walls of Congreve's text, then, is a carnivalesque world of uncertainty, and this world is stirred back to life in new ways each time a reader takes up the book and rereads its words.

Like *Love for Love*, *The Way of the World* is, in many ways, a thought experiment in how our bequest to future generations—whether in terms of blood, property, or art—might be controlled through texts. But if the fates of the characters in *Love for Love* seem, for much of the play, to depend on Sir Sampson's "Bond," in *The Way of the World* Congreve multiplies this dynamic several-fold, as a truly confounding number of interlocking documents (including wills, leases, licenses, and deeds) appear to determine the characters' futures. Moreover, whereas Sir Sampson's bond is spectacularly cast aside by the end of act 5, in *The Way of the World* texts seem never to lose their power over the proceedings: in fact, Peter Holland has argued that the play's most crucial document, the "Deed of Conveyance"—by which Arabella Fainall's (née Wishfort's) estate had been entrusted to Mirabell prior to her marriage to Fainall—proves so literally conclusive as to end the story essentially before it has begun. Put another way, because "the existence of the deed" constitutes "the play's [very] premise," *The Way of the World* has, in effect, "no plot[,] because it does not need to have a plot."[58] *The Way of the World* seems to depict a universe entirely predetermined by texts.

And indeed, texts in *The Way of the World* do, to some degree—and in a way that texts in *Love for Love* did not—succeed in shaping the plot's outcome. However, written documents are ultimately shown to be able to influence the future only to the extent that, at some level, they acknowledge their inability to do so: in the end, the Deed of Conveyance attains its power not because it is so carefully designed but, on the contrary, because it has been generated as part of a larger textual strategy of repletion, redundancy, merriment, and even mischief. Like Sampson's bond in *Love for Love,* the Deed of Conveyance turns out to be built upon mortal weakness. In the case of Sampson's bond, this weakness renders the text impotent; but, by contrast, Congreve's own text—the text of *Love for Love* itself—proves better able to accommodate change and transmutation: by incorporating a form of ritual language, the play-text creates a space in which timelessness and the temporary can coexist. The text of *The Way of the World* works similarly—though in this case, as I describe further below, the theatrical temporality is achieved through a language of presence as opposed to a language of ritual. Like the language of masquerade, but possibly even more so, this language "happens" before our eyes, inviting us into a world that is being made even as we apprehend it.

Before examining in detail either Congreve's own use of text or that of his dramatis personae, I want to examine a related phenomenon in the play—namely, the curious habit, shared by several of the central characters, of speaking as if reading aloud from a text, producing what we might call a kind of "documentese." (And, as we will see, the apparent purpose behind the characters' use of these "spoken texts" is the same as the one behind their use of written texts—to control their futures and manage their legacies.) The very existence of this "documentese" in *The Way of the World* seems to point to a new cultural regime in which the logic of the legal document has begun to exert an outsized power. And, to be sure, the looming reality Congreve alludes to is one that is increasingly mediated by contracts. Yet the logic of the document, as I will show, can also leave room for contingency and improvisation—as these moments of "spoken" or "performed" textuality rather aptly demonstrate.

The Way of the World's episodes of text-like speech are perhaps best represented by two parallel scenes in the play in which the speakers seek to protect their posterities: the famous "proviso" scene, in which Mirabell and Millamant playfully negotiate the terms of their hoped-for marriage (4.5),[59] and the scene that ends the preceding act, in which Fainall and his lover, Marwood, hammer out their own long-term plans (3.18). I will focus first on the less frequently discussed of these scenes: 3.18. Here, Fainall has just learned that his wife, Arabella Fainall, had carried on an affair with Mirabell prior to their marriage. This act of cuckolding *avant la lettre* automatically brings with it the hint of a tainted genetic posterity (suggesting that, even if no illegitimate children resulted from the earlier liaison, Arabella's sexual discretion may be in doubt). Newly aware that he may (potentially) be cheated out of producing his own heirs, and, thus, out of a reproductive future, Fainall seeks to avenge himself by cheating his wife out of her own inheritance, and, thus, out of her financial future:

> *Fainall:* Let me see—I am Marry'd already; so that's over—My Wife has plaid the Jade with me—Well, that's over too—I never lov'd her, or if I had, why that wou'd have been over too by this time—Jealous of her I cannot be, for I am certain; so there's an end of Jealousie. Weary of her, I am and shall be—No, there's no end of that; No, no, that were too much to hope. Thus far concerning my Repose. Now for my Reputation,—
> As to my own, I Marry'd not for it; so that's out of the Question—
> And as to my Part in my Wife's—Why she had parted with hers before; so bringing none to me, she can take none from me. (3.18.47–58)

The lovers' planned solution to this situation is textual: Marwood explains that she will "contrive a Letter" to be sent to Lady Wishfort (Arabella Fainall's mother) "as from an unknown Hand," revealing the premarital affair and threatening blackmail (lines 67–69); Fainall, meanwhile, reassures Marwood that "if the worst come to the worst,—I'll turn my Wife to Grass—I have already a Deed of Settlement to the best Part of her Estate; which I wheadl'd out of her; and that you shall partake at least" (lines 75–78). However, in addition to these references to actual documents, meant to secure the couple's future, the dialogue itself mimics such textual forms: here Fainall seems to have drawn up a sort of itemized list, or inventory, in which everything is organized under two categories—"Repose [and] . . . Reputation"—which are themselves then divided into subcategories (infidelity, absence of love, and so on). Indeed, the inverted syntax of the sixth and seventh sentences—"Jealous of her I cannot be"; "Weary of her, I am"—makes it seem as if Fainall is ticking his way through a grim kind of checklist: married?—check; in love?—no; jealous?—no; weary?—check.

Despite the fact that he is not actually reading from a sheet of paper in his hands, then, Fainall's language seems to conform to the logic of a document, in which—apparently—everything is summed up and tidied away ("I am Marry'd already; so *that's over*—My Wife has plaid the Jade with me—Well, *that's over too* . . . Jealous of her I cannot be, for I am certain; *so there's an end* of Jealousie" [emphasis added]). With the past written down and written off, all that is left is to plan calmly and deliberately for the future. Yet when we consider the above dialogue alongside the exchanges immediately preceding and succeeding it, we are confronted with some of the most untidy, undeliberate language of the play—language that, rather than running an audit on the past and plotting out a future accordingly, plunges us into a volatile, insistently "live" present. Moreover, as in *Love for Love,* this "theatrical" temporality is actually less clearly antithetical to the use of texts (either by Congreve or by his characters) than we might think.

Here is a fuller version of the exchange just quoted:

> *Fainall:* Why then, [Lady Wishfort's servant] *Foible*'s a Bawd, an Errant, Rank, Match-making Bawd. And I it seems am a Husband, a Rank-Husband; and my Wife a very Errant, Rank-Wife,—all in the Way of the *World*. 'Sdeath to be a Cuckold by Anticipation, a Cuckold in Embrio? Sure I was born with budding Antlers like a young Satyr, or a Citizen's Child. 'Sdeath to be Out-witted, to be Out-jilted—Out-Matrimony'd,—If I had kept my Speed like a Stag, 'twere somewhat,—but to crawl after, with my Horns like a Snail, and be out-stripp'd by my Wife—'tis Scurvy Wedlock. . . .
>
> Had you not made that fond Discovery . . . [of Mirabell and Millamant's attempted elopement prior to the opening of Act I], my Wife had added Lustre to my Horns, by that Encrease of Fortune [i.e., the half of Millamant's inheritance that she would have had to forfeit had she and Mirabell married without Wishfort's permission]—I cou'd have worn 'em tipt with Gold, tho' my Forehead had been furnish'd like a Deputy-Lieutenant's Hall.
> *Marwood:* They may prove a Cap of Maintenance to you still, if you can away with your Wife. . . . Well, how do you stand affected towards your Lady?
> *Fainall:* Why faith I'm thinking of it—[*Here follows the speech just quoted.*]
> *Marwood:* Besides you forget, Marriage is honourable.
> *Fainall:* Hum! Faith, and that's well thought on; Marriage is honourable, as you say; and if so, wherefore should Cuckoldom be a Discredit, being deriv'd from so honourable a Root?
> *Marwood:* Nay I know not; if the Root be honourable, why not the Branches? . . .
> *Fainall:* So, so, why this Point's clear—Well, how do we proceed? (3.18.1–66)

Through his invocation of the traditional iconography of cuckoldry, Fainall seems to relegate his wife's infidelity to the past: not only is the transgression irreversible ("My Wife has plaid the Jade with me—Well, that's over"), but his language casts it as meaningless, as the stuff of worn-out literary cliché. Yet the creative overabundance of Fainall's imagery here has the effect not of consigning the past to the past and charting a clear path forward, but of slowing or thickening time into an amorphous present tense.

Indeed, Fainall's metaphors here prove just as unpredictable—just as threateningly fertile—as the unfaithful wife who got him to this point: no ordinary cuckold, Fainall figures himself as a satyr, a stag, and a snail—and, a bit later, as a ram, goat, or bull (whose "Wife" may, at any moment, be "turn[ed] … to Grass"[60]). His horns are alternately lustered with mother-of-pearl, tipped with gold, and multiplied into a roomful of hunting trophies; they are transformed into a heraldic symbol (the "Cap"); and they burst forth like stems or stalks from the "Root" of matrimony. If Fainall's verbal "checklist" seems to seal the past in place and posit a knowable, legible future, the language surrounding it suggests a very different temporality—one in which past and future intersect in the present, and in which that present does not unfold according to plan but, rather, goes in unforseen directions, like the branches of the cuckold's "Antlers" (a telling elaboration upon the typical "Horns") or, indeed—concomitantly—like the branches of a family tree in which the lineage is not, as it were, entirely linear.

Perhaps the image that best emblematizes the formal attributes of the language in which it is couched, however, is not the cuckold's "Antlers" but the "Cuckold in Embrio." The immediate meaning of the phrase is clear enough: Fainall was a cuckold before he was a husband—he was a cuckold even while his plans for marriage were still gestating. But the image is also defiantly perverse: while an unexpected embryo may reveal an act of cuckoldry, the notion of an embryonic cuckold bizarrely jumbles together cause and effect, sign and referent. And it is precisely in its disruption of the usual temporalities of reproduction and representation that Fainall's "Cuckold in Embrio" so aptly epitomizes the scene's language as a whole. Metaphors, words, and even phonemes seem almost to reproduce themselves here: being "Out-witted," for example, leads to being "Out-jilted—Out-Matrimony'd," and, finally, "out-stripp'd." Meanwhile, the insistent alliteration ("'Sdeath," "Satyr," "Citizen's," "Speed," "Stag," "somewhat," "Snail," "Scurvy") reduces Fainall's lines, by the end of the scene, to a kind of satanic hissing: it is as if one kind of sound is breeding another—leaving Fainall as their mindless mouthpiece.

Of course, one might still argue that such verbal overabundance is nonetheless brought under control by Fainall's use of legal texts. The Deed of Settlement in particular seems to symbolize the way that texts can lock a certain state of affairs into place: it was signed upon Fainall's marriage to Arabella, and it is now too late for her to extract herself from it. However, the deed can also be seen as facilitating a kind of temporal flexibility. When it was first drafted, its primary purpose was to maximize Fainall's financial windfall in marrying Arabella; now that Fainall knows of Arabella's infidelity, however, he seeks to employ it as an instrument of revenge. Likewise, whereas originally the document would have benefitted Fainall alone, now it has the potential to benefit him in his new life with Marwood, should he end up seeking a formal separation from Arabella.

Far from serving as a time capsule, then—preserving a certain set of circumstances untouched into the future—Fainall's Deed of Settlement seems to accrue new meanings over time: its effects evolve and emerge before our eyes. In this sense, the deed could be said to operate within what Peggy Phelan might call a theatrical present: one in which reality is being made even as we apprehend it. And Congreve's own play-text, along with the typographical choices he makes, might be seen as working in the same way: with its tacit entrances and exits, its implied stage directions, and its absence of references to the original run, it refuses to situate itself either as a record of performance or as a blueprint for future performances. Rather, as in *Love for Love,* the text of *The Way of the World* creates a space in which a verbal theatricality can unfold here and now. If in *Love for Love* this verbal theatricality took the form of ritual repetition, then in *The Way of the World* it takes the form of a kind of linguistic mitosis—of language that, rather than tracing a linear path forward, grows out and over the page.

But if Fainall's language use in *The Way of the World* is erratic and disorderly—if he proves unable to control the future with words—does not Mirabell's speech provide a more watertight counterpoint? After all, critics have long insisted on a distinction between those characters in the play who "view ... proper[ly] ... [the] relation ... of language to ... ideas" (in the words of Richard Kroll) and those who, by contrast, employ a kind of language that "is not empirically grounded, and plays in its own nominalistic, freewheeling universe."[61] Indeed, Congreve himself famously proclaimed the incompetence of any critic who failed to spot this difference: writing his dedication to *The Way of the World* following its theatrical premiere, he sniffed that the play "had been acted two or three Days, before some of [its] hasty Judges cou'd find leisure to distinguish betwixt the Character of a *Witwoud* and a *Truewit*."[62] Accordingly, Charles Hinnant, like Kroll, maintains that whereas Fainall's linguistic practices reveal his inability to separate "false rhetoric" from "plain truth," the more successful characters in the play speak a language that "enabl[es] them to engage reality."[63] And indeed, when Mirabell saves the day with his Deed of Conveyance, or when the lovers trade stipulations in the proviso scene—all prefaced by contractual phrases such as "*Inprimis*," "I covenant that . . . ," "*Item*," "I article that . . . ," and so on—it would seem not just that they are using texts to pin down their own destinies but, more broadly, that they are announcing a larger historical future defined by the law and its texts: a rationalized society that rewards bourgeois forethought and prudence, documentation and cross-reference—and in which Fainall, and the decadent aristocratic culture he represents, will ultimately have no place.

Richard Braverman deems Mirabell's success in the play to bespeak what was to be, historically, the rise of contractual relations over older, feudal forms of social interdependence.[64] As he notes, the setting of the play's opening scene in a chocolate house seems significant in this regard: this space, in contrast to the "tavern" that would have been the traditional gathering place for rakes and other representatives of courtly power, symbolizes "a venue of new men and social equality."[65] And, in fact, the chocolate house's more historiographically famous sibling, the coffee house, has long been seen as the locus classicus for the textually mediated public sphere. With this literal change of scene, Congreve seems to be pointing toward a new reality.[66] Julie Stone Peters agrees: citing Mirabell's "well-edited, . . . symmetrical phrases," she contends that his "contractual, print-world mind" and language hold out "the promise of the future," heralding a new, modern "society that can trust only the inflexibly written."[67] In this new society, it seems, everyone's fates will to some degree depend on paper, on contracts—whether marriage settlements, property deeds, or written terms of service. This, one could say, will be the new "way of the world."[68]

Implicit within this new contractual culture is the "textual" temporality already mentioned: a time scheme in which a certain set of circumstances may be boxed up (as in Mirabell's "black box," in act 5) and opened again in the future, perfectly intact and unchanged. But along with this textual temporality comes a more general cultural stance: bourgeois prudence, for one—a kind of protestant ethic focused on future rewards and punishments—but also a kind of emergent middle-class morality. That is, in a world in which every action leaves a paper trail, we must constantly plan not just for the future but for how our past and present conduct will translate into the future. When everything is in writing, accountability for our behavior takes on new meaning, as everything can be recorded, archived, and exhibited in black and white to judge or jury.

Paul and Miriam Mueschke detect this middle-class ethos of accountability as much in the content of Mirabell's language as in the documents and document-like style in which he presents it. Focusing in particular on the proviso scene as a kind of ideological touchstone for the play, they see Mirabell's various stipulations for his marriage as an explicit way of casting aside a set of older, aristocratic practices in which future consequences were ignored in favor of instant gratification. For example, Mirabell adds a "proviso" banning the use of female friends as "Decoy-Duck[s]" to cover adulterous affairs, and another prohibiting corsets while pregnant (4.5.80, 4.5.103). The Mueschkes likewise posit that *The Way of the World* as a whole systematically works to reject "the *carpe diem* philosophy which permeates . . . the subplots of Etherege's comedies [and even] those of Congreve's three earlier plays." In this final play, "rake and wanton are held responsible for past and present transgressions"; "life is regarded . . . as a sequence of integrated experiences in which the present is invariably conditioned by the past and foreshadows the future."[69] This answerability is as much a moral outlook as it is, more practically, the corollary of a culture in which everything is put in writing.

I want to argue, however, that Mirabell's language embodies neither a nascent middle-class worldview nor the presumed textual time scheme that we might expect to accompany it. To be sure, the proviso scene does seem to function, at least in part, as a critique of a libertine culture in which long-term commitment is sacrificed to immediate impulse—in which, for example, married women "scrambl[e] to the Play in a Mask," attended by some "Fop," then "rail at [their husbands] for missing the Play" (4.5.82–84). When analyzed more closely, however, the scene's language reveals itself to abide by its own temporality, more improvisatory than prescribed, more pleasure-seeking than prudent—thus showing Mirabell's verbal practices to be more similar to Fainall's than they initially seem.

Consider, for example, Mirabell's list of prohibited beverages:

> to the Dominion of the *Tea-Table* I submit—But with *proviso,* that you exceed not in your Province; but restrain your self to native and simple *Tea-Table* Drinks, as *Tea, Chocolate,* and *Coffee.* As likewise to Genuine and Authoriz'd *Tea-Table* Talk—Such as mending of Fashions, spoiling

> Reputations, railing at absent Friends, and so forth—But that on no Account you encroach upon the Mens Prerogative, and presume to drink Healths, or toast Fellows; for prevention of which, I banish all *Foreign Forces,* all Auxiliaries to the *Tea-Table,* as *Orange-Brandy,* all *Aniseed, Cinamon, Citron* and *Barbado's-Waters,* together with *Ratafia* and the most noble Spirit of *Clary*—But for *Couslip-Wine, Poppy-Water,* and all *Dormitives,* those I allow—These *Proviso's* admitted, in other things I may prove a tractable and complying Husband. (4.5.106–20)

Richard Kroll (among others) takes seriously Mirabell's distinction here between "native" and "foreign" elements, a distinction he sees as participating in a larger "argument for a patriotic society that surfaces elsewhere in the play."[70] This distinction immediately breaks down, however: the "native" beverages include "*Tea, Chocolate,* and *Coffee*"—all colonial imports, but whose "home" has always been the tea table, thus apparently suggesting a definition of "native" that is metaphorical rather than strictly geographical. Yet the final list of permissible refreshments ("*Couslip-Wine,*" "*Poppy-Water*"—in other words, items indigenous to England but not to the tea table) shifts the categories back from metaphorical to literal.[71] In short, if this catalogue were actually to be employed as something like a contract—a document meant to guide future conduct, and against which future violations could be checked and corrected—it would be of very limited service beyond the specific drinks named, for its terms (by turns literal and symbolic) seem to redefine themselves as the list goes on.[72]

I would contend, in fact, that, rather than reflecting a reasoned resolution to depart from the current set of debauched norms, the enumerated beverages may be determined largely by the sheer joy of pronouncing them: it is as if Mirabell is himself intoxicated by the words' shapes and textures—"*Aniseed, Cinamon, Citron,* ... the most noble Spirit of *Clary* ... *Cowslip-Wine.*" These susurrous *s*'s, perhaps not coincidentally (as we will explore more fully in a moment), recall Fainall's own sibilant assonance of a few minutes earlier—the villain's hissings turned to the sweet lispings of the lover.

Just as striking as the pleasures of the phonemes here, though, are the pleasures of the immersive imagery, which, together with that of the surrounding lines, conjures a kind of bizarre barnyard tropics in which cinnamon trees grow alongside domesticated farm animals (invoked by the "Hog's Bones, Hare's Gall, Pig Water, and the Marrow of a roasted Cat" with which, a moment earlier, Mirabell teasingly accused Millamant of hoping to minister to her complexion [lines 92–94]). We might be tempted to explain the tropical allusions as a reference to empire and, implicitly, its bureaucracy—to a world of trade agreements, stocks, and bonds; of contracts, paper credit, and long-distance business arrangements that the written document alone makes possible. Indeed, Mirabell's evocations extend not simply to these regions' natural resources—their spices and fruits—but to their manufactured wares: he notes a few lines prior that he also forbids (but seems to relish describing) "Bauds with Baskets, and penny-worths of *Muslin, China, Fans, Atlasses,* &c."[73] Again, however, I would argue that these allusions to empire are less useful in reinforcing a rationalist, bourgeois world than in bodying forth a kind of dreamscape (and soundscape: "Bauds . . . Baskets") of delight.[74]

The larger temporality of this language, then, despite its "textual" style, is not one of preserved pasts and preplanned futures. Rather, the lushness of Mirabell's words suggests the very languors and "*Someils du Matin*" that Millamant so prizes but that Mirabell purports to frown upon: "My dear Liberty, shall I leave thee? My faithful Solitude, my darling Contemplation, must I bid you then Adieu? Ay-h, adieu—My morning Thoughts, agreeable Wakings, indolent Slumbers, all ye *douceurs,* ye *Someils du Matin,* adieu—I can't do't, 'tis more than impossible—positively, *Mirabell,* I'll lye a-bed in a Morning as long as I please" (4.5.30–36). This state of half-consciousness—this slowing and circling of time, in which leisurely wakings are followed once again by slumber—will not, it seems, be jeopardized by Millamant's marrying Mirabell: although Mirabell retorts that in that case he'll "get up in a Morning as early as I please" (line 37), his broader use of language throughout the scene suggests a distinctly less businesslike attitude toward time, one that allows room for words (and "Thoughts") to come to life slowly, in starts and stops.[75]

We have now seen, then, that Mirabell's "documentese" shares in common with Fainall's a sybaritic approach to sound and imagery, as well as a tendency to unfold within a temporality of immediacy or emergence—even as its text-based structures imply a reality that can be plotted out and controlled ahead of time. Perhaps the element that most clearly links the two scenes I am examining here, however, is the image of the unborn child. In a line that recalls Fainall's "Cuckold in Embrio," Mirabell's third "*Item*" stipulates, "When you shall be Breeding . . . I denounce against all strait Lacing, squeezing for a Shape, till you mould my Boy's Head like a Sugar-loaf; and instead of a Man-Child, make me Father to a Crooked-billet" (lines 97–105).[76]

At first glance, this proviso would seem to signal Mirabell's preoccupation with producing an heir (he assumes that the child will be male), and thus, again, with the notion of a guaranteed, stable legacy—one that contracts, deeds, and wills would seem to ensure. The choice of words, however (and even, as we are about to see, the figure of the embryo itself), implies an accretive rather than goal-driven dynamic. The "Sugar-loaf" anticipates the tea table Mirabell mentions in the next breath, and the "Crooked-billet," which was also a conventional name for taverns at the time, serves as an apt segue into the "drink[ing] [of] Healths" that Mirabell prohibits a few lines later. Moreover, while most editors gloss the word "billet" here as "stick," a billet can also refer to a figure from heraldry, understood to represent a bolt of golden or silver cloth, a brick, a metal ingot, or, interestingly, a folded-up piece of paper, such as a letter (which is, of course, the word's primary meaning in French). If we were to adopt this last definition, Mirabell's "Crooked-billet" hearkens back to the products of Millamant's own fanciful word use—namely, the rhymed love letters that, we learned in act 2, she likes to repurpose as curling papers. ("O ay, Letters—I had Letters—I am persecuted with Letters—I hate Letters—No Body knows how to write Letters; and yet one has 'em, one does not know why—They serve to pin up one's Hair . . . [but] only . . . those in Verse . . . I never pin up my hair with Prose. I fancy ones Hair wou'd not curl if it were pinn'd up with Prose. I think I try'd once" [2.5.34–42]).[77]

While the ban on straitlacing would thus seem to look forward to the future—Thomas Fujimura calls Mirabell "the first Truewit so sensible as to begin worrying about his offspring at the time he proposes to his mistress"[78]—the language in which the ban is expressed seems less concerned with the eventual products of the marriage than with a larger verbal pattern, manifested in the speech of various characters throughout *The Way of the World* (including Fainall). Indeed, throughout all five acts, we find myriad references to miniature or partially developed life forms: recurring allusions are made to unbreeched boy children and baby dolls,[79] to changelings, marionettes,[80] and anthropomorphic napkin-knots[81]; the play teems with half-men,[82] half-children,[83] the just-born,[84] and, of course, the embryonic or unborn. The word "breed[ing]" (in its multiple shadings, from procreation to upbringing to manners) is used fifteen times,[85] while pregnancy becomes a veritable leitmotif.[86] And beyond strictly human regeneration, a wider vocabulary of seeds and fruits, blooming and ripening, infuses the play.[87] The effect of this accumulation, moreover, is not just a thematic evocation of rampant fertility but the verbal enactment of this fertility, as fecund figures propagate and procreate at an alarming pace.

The image of the unborn child thus serves less as an emblem of the future than as an emblem of radical generativity. In the proviso scene, moreover, as in 3.18, this dynamic of verbal generativity seems facilitated, almost paradoxically, by the dialogue's document-like structure. The couple's uses of "*Inprimis,*" "*Item,*" and so on—just like Congreve's use of his own neoclassical text—may hold the scene's language apart in some way, but not for purposes of timelessness or petrification; rather, the lovers clear a space for their language to heed its own topsy-turvy temporality—its innately performative time schemes.

Here I would like to suggest that *The Way of the World* may be subtly looking to its own guiding metaphor, one that—though not nearly as explicit or extensive—plays a role similar to that of masquerade in *Love for Love*. This is the metaphor of the English landscape garden, in which order and disorder, containment and excess—conceptual pairings touched on by Congreve's language, of course, both lexically and structurally—play off of one another by turns. As John Dixon Hunt and Peter Willis explain, turn-of-the-century English gardens, rejecting what was seen as the French emphasis on "system," were marked instead by a "more flexible handling of the ratio of art to nature": garden pathways, for example, might follow "exaggeratedly wavy lines," so as to "announce a nature less controlled"; "enclosing walls should vanish," and instead, "by means of 'an easy, unaffected manner of Fencing,'" a more playful relationship was proposed between garden and countryside.[88] Thus, although gardens in the early eighteenth century "remained essentially geometric in overall design," and the "central axis remained strong," these decades saw the proliferation of "wildernesses" within the garden space—ornamental woods or shrubberies that encouraged "intimate encounters, exploration and discovery" as opposed to the types of "public display" embraced by court culture.[89] Classical statuary was placed conscientiously in clearings so as to indicate the owner's "taste, education and knowledge," yet, at the same time, plantings were no longer as classically symmetrical as they had once been.[90]

Richard Braverman has similarly suggested that Congreve's final comedy reflects concepts central to eighteenth-century garden design—specifically via "the figuration of Millamant."[91] He elaborates: just as "Mirabell loved Millamant not only with, but for, her faults, estate owners likewise came to appreciate the landscape for the irregularities that enhanced aesthetic pleasure by continually providing the unexpected."[92] Braverman sees these parallel preferences, moreover, as a sign of *The Way of the World*'s larger rejection of aristocratic, hierarchical worldviews—symbolized by the "absolutist" style of Italian and French gardens—in favor of liberty and spontaneity.[93] As Braverman has it, the new way of the world (as it were) favors "cultivation" over "domination."[94] I would like to propose, however, that the idea of the landscape garden provides a model not just for *The Way of the World*'s politics (or sexual politics), as Braverman argues, but for its overall vision of itself as a work of art.

Braverman writes specifically that Congreve "foreshadowed" the antiauthoritarian ethos of the landscape garden with his depiction of Millamant—but in fact, Congreve had direct connections to the thinkers who were first developing these aesthetic principles as early as the 1690s. Joseph Addison, whose *Pleasures of the Imagination* essays of 1712 are often cited as foundational to the landscape garden movement, wrote to Congreve from France in 1699—a year before *The Way of the World* premiered—in a letter that not only gestures toward a new model of horticultural design but essentially challenges Congreve to translate this model into literary terms:

> I dont believe, as good a poet as you are, that you can make finer landskips than those about the Kings houses or with all yor descriptions build a more magnificent palace than Versailles. I am however so singular as to prefer Fontaine-bleau to all the rest. It is situated among rocks and woods that give you a fine varietie of Savage prospects. The King has Humourd the Genius of the place and only made use of so much Art as is necessary to Help and regulate Nature without reforming her too much. The Cascades seem to break through the Clefts and cracks of Rocks that are cover'd over with Moss and look as if they were pil'd upon one another by Accident. There is an Artificial Wildness in the Meadows Walks and Canals and the Garden instead of a Wall is Fenc'd on the Lower End by a Natural mound of Rock-work that strikes the Eye very Agreeably.[95]

Here, the pinnacle of landscape design, according to Addison, is the use of only "so much Art as is necessary to Help and regulate Nature without reforming her too much"; his prefatory statement—perhaps a friendly throwing down of the aesthetic gauntlet—hints that Congreve (as a "poet") might do something similar, achieving the same balance of "Artific[e]" and "Wildness," but in words.[96]

I would contend that Congreve is indeed taking up a version of this challenge in *The Way of the World*—and exploring its possibilities further in the printing of his 1710 *Works*—and that the play's language of natural luxuriance specifically signals this project.⁹⁷ While at moments this language of fertility can seem overripe or overblown—especially in the mouth of Fainall, it seems to mark the culture of decadence that the play critiques—the play's strict neoclassical design both keeps this copiousness in check and sets it off to best advantage. In Congreve's play, "nature"—a term we might expand to include human nature and, concomitantly, the linguistic capacity that defines human nature—is not only "regulated" but also "helped" or enhanced, via Congreve's canny use of neoclassical and textual form.

We have now examined the parallels between Fainall's and Mirabell's use of document-like speech in *The Way of the World,* and its tendency not to freeze the past and control the future but to operate in accordance with a kind of theatrical time in the present tense. But what about the characters' use of actual texts, in addition to language that mimics text? There seems to be an important difference between Fainall's and Mirabell's respective textual practices: how is it that Mirabell is able to deploy his Deed of Conveyance triumphantly in the end, whereas Fainall's Deed of Settlement is dead on arrival?

The explanation given by previous critics for why Mirabell prevails—namely, that Mirabell has simply been more strategic than his nemesis—does not ultimately hold up under scrutiny. As we will see, some of the most significant effects of his Deed of Conveyance depend on events that Mirabell could hardly have anticipated. In fact, far from symbolizing and securing a lockstep future, the Deed of Conveyance may contain, embedded within it, the play's "original" instance of origination, as it were—the defining kernel of emergent, open-ended temporality. This kernel is, of course, also an embryo: recall that, when Arabella asks (rhetorically) why Mirabell arranged for her to marry Fainall, he responds, "If the Familiarities of our Loves had produc'd that Consequence, of which you were apprehensive, where cou'd you have fix'd a Father's Name with Credit, but on a Husband?" (2.4.13–16). While some critics have understood "apprehensive . . . of" to mean "fearful of" (as in our modern usage), I think the more likely meaning here is the now-archaic but then-current meaning of "conscious of," or "sensible of."⁹⁸ After all, if pregnancy had been a mere possibility, why not simply cease the affair, rather than take so dire a step as marrying a known scoundrel? (As Mirabell avers, "A better Man ought not to have been sacrific'd to the Occasion" [2.4.21–22].) Even if the pregnancy was never a reality, Arabella may have perceived it to be. What's more, Mirabell's phrasing does not preclude the possibility of an actual pregnancy that ended in a miscarriage. It is this pregnancy, then (perceived or real), that provides the foundation for Arabella's marriage to Fainall and, accordingly, for the Deed of Conveyance designed to block his access to her fortune.

To be sure, the Deed of Conveyance protects Arabella from Fainall's greed, which Mirabell correctly presumes he will act upon sooner or later; in this sense it is a predictive and prescriptive (and proscriptive) document. However, the deed's most immediate *raison d'être* is not a future prospect but a present emergency. Indeed, the present itself is oddly persistent throughout Mirabell and Arabella's exchanges: "You have been the Cause that I have lov'd without Bounds," she tells him, using the present perfect rather than the past tense we might expect (2.4.9). Does Arabella still have feelings for Mirabell? Foible suggests that these continued feelings may even be reciprocated when, discussing Mirabell with Arabella in the next act, she notes, "I find your Ladyship has his Heart still" (3.6.18–21). Congreve never reveals the precise nature of these characters' emotional entanglement at the time that the play takes place. But what is clear is that the Deed of Conveyance is built around a connection that predates, is coterminous with, and may even postdate the events of the play—one that refuses to be contained by time. This connection is aptly signified, then, by an embryo that, real or imagined, still haunts its parents' lives even after the implosion of the marriage meant to conceal the circumstances of its genesis. In short, far from presciently safeguarding the future, the Deed of Conveyance is in some ways a symbol of heat-of-the-moment passions, of "Familiarities"—and families—growing out of control, "without Bounds."

The deed's irrational fundaments are accentuated, I think, by what one could see as the document's parodic precursor in the play: a set of lyrics that Mirabell had written (prior to act 1) as part of his "sham Addresses" to Lady Wishfort, which he had undertaken as a way of spending time in Millamant's company without arousing suspicion. Exploiting the fifty-five-year-old Wishfort's desperation to appear younger than she is, Mirabell explains, he "was guilty of a Song in her Commendation. Nay, I got a Friend to put her into a Lampoon, and complement her with the Imputation of an Affair with a young Fellow, which I carry'd so far, that I told her the malicious Town took notice that she was grown fat of a sudden; and when she lay in of a Dropsie, persuaded her she was reported to be in Labour" (1.1.66–72). Though the Deed of Conveyance could not, on its surface, seem farther removed from this kind of prank, both the deed and Mirabell's "sham addresses" utilize texts to further an act of deception; and both center, crucially, around the figure of an embryo. Admittedly, Mirabell's tricks here remain blithely indifferent to later consequences—after all, he can only cover up his courtship of Millamant for so long—whereas the Deed of Conveyance, as we have seen, appears to be all about precaution. What I hope I have now shown, however, is that the deed turns out to manifest, at its very core, a similar heedlessness toward ultimate outcomes, and a similar focus on addressing only the most immediate contingencies. After all, Mirabell may succeed in keeping Arabella's fortune intact, but her heart and dignity—as well as, arguably, Mirabell's own—do not fare so well. Correspondingly, Congreve assigns to the deed the very same symbol of unchecked, unwilled fertility—the pregnancy out of wedlock—as he does to Mirabell's rakish literary hoax.

If the Deed of Conveyance responds to an immediate crisis as much as it may protect against a future one, so, similarly, we see that the later effects of the document (like those of Fainall's Deed of Settlement) are not locked in place from the beginning; rather, they evolve over the course of the play. If the Deed of Conveyance was initially meant to safeguard Arabella from Fainall's gold digging at the crudest level, it now safeguards her from an elaborate extortion plan. And if it initially worked in only a very general way to protect Mirabell's own financial interests—by preserving the fiscal well-being of the larger Wishfort family, into which he has been hoping to marry—it now benefits him directly: having saved Arabella from blackmail, Mirabell is suddenly restored to the good graces of Lady Wishfort, who, in her grateful relief, allows him and Millamant to marry with the full complement of Millamant's fortune (which Sir Jonathan's will prevented her from collecting should she marry without her aunt's express permission). Critics are perpetually praising Mirabell's far-sightedness, but it is impossible that he could have anticipated these eventualities upon first forming the trust (indeed, the fact that he attempted to elope with Millamant prior to act 1 proves he had essentially despaired of marrying her with her aunt's approval). In short, the Deed of Conveyance, though on its surface an example of how texts can "fix . . . facts" in place (to recall Holland's contention), is revealed, on closer examination, to serve as a complex symbol of language's essential instability: an instability that suggests, in turn, the inherent malleability—perhaps the inherent theatricality—of the social realm itself.

To return to our question, then, what is the difference between Mirabell's Deed of Conveyance and Fainall's Deed of Settlement? I would like to argue that the success of Mirabell's textual practices owes not to his superior ability to plan ahead but, rather, to his superior understanding (fully conscious or not) of texts' status as changing, shifting, "living" things.[99] Mirabell's grasp of this fact seems to be evidenced by the sheer redundancy of his textual strategies, which essentially layer one document atop the next. On the one hand, the Deed of Conveyance ends up being the only text necessary for the play's happy ending: it eradicates Fainall's threat and clinches Mirabell and Millamant's marriage in a single stroke. On the other hand, we also get the sense that Mirabell has spent a great deal of energy, over the last several weeks or months, curating texts that each contribute separately toward this satisfactory conclusion. In addition to (but independently of) the song and lampoon writing just discussed, he has arranged for his servant Waitwell to be married—complete with marriage license—to Wishfort's servant Foible, thus enabling Waitwell (in the guise of "Sir Rowland") to court an unsuspecting Wishfort without lasting legal consequence. (As Arabella sums it up, "if my poor Mother is caught in a Contract, you will discover the Imposture betimes; and release her"—in exchange for her consent to his marrying Millamant—"by producing a Certificate of her Gallant's former Marriage" [2.4.42–44].) Even this textual strategy is backed by another: as Mirabell reminds Foible early on, if the servants assist him in his plot, they will be rewarded by yet a further document—apparently some sort of property deed, as yet unsigned: "Go on and prosper, *Foible*—The Lease shall be made good and the Farm stock'd, if we succeed" (2.8.31–33).

Again, none of these texts (save the Deed of Conveyance itself) are entirely necessary in securing the play's ending. As we have seen, moreover, the Deed of Conveyance proves so effective precisely because it does not perfectly predict the future: its original purpose was to quarantine Arabella's fortune from a marriage meant to conceal the illegitimacy of her pregnancy, but its ultimate utility lies in its ability to stymie Fainall's blackmail attempts and (consequently) to procure Wishfort's consent to a different union. Put another way, the deed was originally meant to protect the respectability of Arabella's child, but it ends up ensuring the prosperity of Millamant's.

In short, what makes Mirabell's deployment of texts so successful is not his ability to control social dynamics through them but what seems to be his instinctive understanding that they do not and cannot control people—that their value and meaning will change over time. For, again, the various texts just listed—the song and lampoon, the marriage license, the property deed—are all tactically redundant; but it is their very superfluousness that is key, as they point to a broader principle underlying Mirabell's use of documents: a principle of play, of improvisation, of kaleidoscopic and contradictory impulses. Where Fainall's Deed of Settlement is coolly (mis)calculating, Mirabell's various squibs, licenses, leases, and deeds are bound up with, in tune with, the twists and turns of human desire.

And Congreve's own play-text exhibits a set of effects that are not dissimilar to these. On the one hand, the text seems a guarantor of order and stability: as we have seen, the 1710 *Works* deletes characters' movements to and fro in favor of further solidifying the plays' scenic divisions; it separates scenes and acts using engraved headpieces and printers' ornaments; it rescues the plays' bookly contents from their original performances (replacing the phrase "as performed at" with "printed in"). On the other hand, these refinements serve only to create more contrast between structure and style, between the art of the text and the wilderness of its language. Thus, even as the list of characters' names at the head of each scene seems fixed, their interconnections prove bafflingly ingrown, overgrown. And even as their dialogue seems to epitomize mannered wit, it contorts itself into erratic, erotic curlicues—into brambled branches, or branching antlers, of words. In this way, Congreve, like Mirabell, may draw up protections for one child—that is, for the play as he wrote it—but nonetheless simultaneously manages to make provisions for another child altogether: the play as it continues to take shape, unconstrained by temporal straitlacing (much less "theoretic straitjackets"), in the minds and theaters of future generations.

A striking piece of dialogue spoken in the climactic moments of act 5 may provide further evidence that Congreve understood texts—and, even more specifically, legal texts—to be less closely tied to timelessness or transcendence than we might otherwise deduce from his collaboration with Tonson. Here, Marwood makes one last attempt to reap financial and psychological revenge, threatening the Wishfort women with the prospect of a trial in which Arabella will be sued by Fainall for adultery, and Wishfort herself will be "ushered in [to the courtroom] with an *O Yez* of Scandal," upon which her "Case [will be] open'd by an old fumbling Leacher in a Quoif like a Man Midwife" (5.5.32–34). The entire family, Marwood warns, will become a "Theme for legal Punsters, and Quiblers by the Statute," while "provok[ing] naughty Interrogatories in more naughty Law *Latin*"—causing "the good Judge, tickl'd with the Proceeding, [to] simper . . . under a Grey Beard, and fidge . . . off and on his Cushion as if he had swallow'd *Cantharides,* or sat upon *Cow-Itch*" (5.5.35–43). The humiliation will not end with the trial itself, moreover, for the "young Revellers of the *Temple* [will] take Notes," and "after talk it over again in Commons, or before Drawers in an Eating-House" (lines 45–47): "Nay this is nothing . . . [for] it must after this be consign'd by the Short-hand Writers to the publick Press; and from thence be transferr'd to the Hands, nay, into the Throats and Lungs of Hawkers, with Voices more licentious than the loud Flounder-man's or the Woman that cries *Grey-Pease.* And this you must hear 'till you are stunn'd; nay, you must hear nothing else for some Days" (5.5.49–56). As John Loftis observes in his wonderful reading of this speech, Marwood here conjures a threat of public exposure whose shame centers on the body: as her pun on "Case" makes clear, the public examination of the family's private business amounts to fingering their genitals (and stimulating those of the "good Judge").[100] Worse, the family's most intimate selves are then physically ingested, as it were, by lower-class gullets: talked of in "Eating-House[s]," details of the trial will move from the "Short-hand" writers to the "Hands" and "Throats and Lungs" of the street vendors, mingling in their mouths with the fish and peas they hawk (both of these, Loftis points out, are wares that have sexual connotations as well).

Yet, as Loftis also emphasizes, the true horror of the situation appears to owe as much to its status in writing (and print) as it does to its degraded corporeality—indeed, the two are essentially inextricable. "Law *Latin*" may be the language of scholarly tomes, but it is also a medium for "naughty" insinuations: the specifics of the trial, after all, reach the hawkers' lungs by way of the notes taken in the courtroom, which are then relayed to the "publick Press." Congreve paints a picture in which it is futile to try to distinguish between lower-class orality and the texts of the educated—a picture in which little difference can be seen between the crush of the street and the hush of the courtroom.

I would contend, then, that this diatribe of Marwood's serves as Congreve's wry acknowledgement that—despite his close involvement in Jacob Tonson's larger project of forming an English canon, and, concomitantly, of creating a polite reading public to affirm it—it is ultimately impossible to isolate play-texts from performance. Indeed, as Congreve's characters' uses of texts seem to indicate—in both *Love for Love* and *The Way of the World*—all texts (not just play-texts, and perhaps most especially legal texts) may aspire to a kind of pristine posterity, yet they cannot help but also reflect a muddled, murky, and thoroughly embodied present.

The skepticism Congreve articulates regarding textual authority in his final two comedies is one that will become more fully developed in the plays of John Gay. Like Congreve's, Gay's critique of the inscribed or printed document stems in part from the recognition that such texts may be much more intertwined with "low" human impulses and pleasures than we tend to think. Gay, however, also advances this critique from the opposite direction: by the seventeen-teens and twenties, print's authority had become mistrusted more generally by a society nostalgic for a (mythical) pre-modern mode of communication, one less mediated by technology and the market, more in touch with the body. Yet Gay reveals this nostalgic tradition—of ballads and songs, pastoralism and rustic folkways—to be just as corrupted, by money and modernity, as print. Ultimately, I will argue, Gay shifts the debates around dramaturgy away from questions of its early heritage and its future legacy, urging us instead to understand drama—and literature more broadly—as a form that necessarily destabilizes the relationship between past and present.

4

"TAKE THIS SAD BALLAD, WHICH I BOUGHT AT FAIR"

Pastoral Performance and Print Capitalism in John Gay's The What D'Ye Call It *and* The Beggar's Opera

EARLY EIGHTEENTH-CENTURY BRITONS INCREASINGLY THOUGHT of their world as a "modern" one, sensing that a traditional, bucolic past had preceded their own reality but was now hopelessly inaccessible. Literary historian John O'Brien attributes this feeling of modernity to a number of contemporary cultural upheavals, including "the demographic shifts entailed in the migration from the country to the city and the expansion of the middling sort," but also, perhaps most importantly, "the spread in scope and availability of printed material," or what Benedict Anderson would call "print capitalism."[1] As Brean Hammond elaborates, the growth of the English book market was an integral component of "the 'commercial capitalism' that transformed pre-industrial Britain into a mass consumer society in the period between the English Civil War and the mid-eighteenth century."[2] While perhaps not enabling modernity per se, this emerging "mass market" in print—which by the 1690s had extended to the newspapers and periodicals that helped constitute the new public sphere, and which kept readers abreast of the latest developments in empire, trade, and post–Glorious Revolution politics—certainly contributed to the growing perception of "being modern" that was a defining feature of the period.

This turn-of-the-century awareness of an urban, commercial, imperial present—in contrast to a rural, land-based, regional past—manifested itself in a renewed interest in the pastoral mode. In William Empson's famous formulation, "Pastoral... impl[ies] a beautiful relation between rich and poor" by "mak[ing] simple people express strong feelings... in learned and fashionable language."³ In so doing, the pastoral evokes an idealized feudalism in which the shadow of global commerce, and the mercantile classes arising from it, are disavowed. Indeed, this shadow may always have haunted the pastoral mode, as Rome itself—where pastoral poetry originated—also benefitted, of course, from an expansive commodities trade belied by Virgil's rustic laborers.

The renewed vogue for pastoral may most famously have informed eighteenth-century verse, but it also permeated eighteenth-century theater, as well as critical discourses on the theater: as O'Brien documents, commentators lamented the passing of the old Stuart custom according to which public pastimes—including traditional English games, festivals, and revels, but also the stage—fell under the sponsorship and supervision of the monarchy, thus (supposedly) uniting rich and poor in just the way Empson describes.⁴ Accordingly, critics and practitioners alike frequently sought to reconnect the theatrical experience, now felt to be overly anonymized and commercialized, to "its imagined beginnings in ritual practice"—to its purported roots in "a language of gesture, physicality, and the body." This language was one that the rural, common "people" were believed somehow to retain.⁵

O'Brien goes on to illustrate how this nostalgic, pastoralist moment translated into an eighteenth-century fascination with pantomime and other "low" entertainments; however, as I will show, the same cultural contexts he describes can also help us to analyze John Gay's pastoral poetry and drama. Of course, it was John Rich, famous for playing Harlequin in the early century pantomimes, who later produced *The Beggar's Opera,* and this seems hardly a coincidence: like Rich's previous theatrical undertakings, *The Beggar's Opera*—and Gay's own previous "pastoral" works, including *The What D'Ye Call It*—emerged from a cultural juncture at which readers and audiences gazed wistfully back to what they perceived as a "pre"-print-capitalist world, embracing a concept of pure, embodied performance as a potential remedy.

As a satirist, of course, Gay ultimately regards any such remedy with skepticism, suggesting that the rustic, oral idyll envisioned by pastoralism was in fact always suffused by the mediation and commodification we tend to regard as a product of our own, "fallen" era. Yet this skepticism is not entirely cynical, either: at moments, Gay implies that by continuing to juxtapose written or printed text with embodied speech or song—by remaining aware of the ways in which they collide and interact—we can prevent ourselves either from being lulled into an oblivious nostalgia or from merely resigning ourselves to the notion that literate (and literary) culture can never transcend the commercial reality that enables its proliferation.

In this way, Gay joins the other playwrights in this book in raising important questions about drama's status as a hybrid medium, straddling the written and the performed. For Gay specifically, part of this hybrid status owes to drama's having one foot in the world of print capitalism and the other in what seems to be the organic immediacy of the body onstage. The era in which Gay wrote was quite different from the one that the other authors in my study had inhabited: between Congreve's career and Gay's, the universe of commercially lucrative writing had expanded. By 1725 (three years prior to the premiere of *The Beggar's Opera*), Daniel Defoe was declaring that writing had "becom[e] a very considerable Branch of the English Commerce. The Booksellers are the Master Manufacturers or Employers. The several Writers, Authors, Copyers, Sub-writers, and all other Operators with Pen and Ink are the workmen employed by the said Master Manufacturers."[6] This new state of affairs led Gay to pose a new kind of question vis-à-vis his chosen medium: can drama, through its use of performance—immediate, ritualistic, and communal—enable us to reclaim a set of shared values in which human expression is not merely another consumer product to be purchased? Or does drama, in its doubleness, reveal to us the extent to which even the most seemingly raw performance proves inextricable from the modern commerce of texts?

In asking these questions, Gay articulates a larger anxiety within the field of literate culture, and literature itself, in the early eighteenth century. Namely, he reveals his era's longing to set "literature" apart, to legitimate it by reference to universal human experiences untainted by the print marketplace that is, in the end, what allows for its existence. This longing occupied a central place in Gay's own career. For while Gay attempted to find patronage as a poet according to the "old" ways, he ultimately survived financially by becoming a popular dramatist—through the sale of tickets, but also, significantly, through the sale of the text of his plays: whereas Gay appears to have earned between 500 and 700 pounds from the theatrical run of *The Beggar's Opera,* and an additional 90 guineas for the publishing rights, he published the suppressed *Polly* one year later, by subscription, from which he earned 1,200 pounds.[7] Not only Gay's writings, then, but also his writerly career reflected a point in history at which the print medium—and any author whose work trafficked in print—was becoming increasingly dependent on market forces.[8]

Gay juxtaposes text and performance in several different ways over the course of his career. In *The What D'Ye Call It* (1715), commercialized literature's invasion of the pastoral idyll is symbolized by the appearance of print commodities that tend to stick out like a sore thumb in the homely, rural landscape in which the play is set. In *The Beggar's Opera* (1728), the incursion of printed and written matter is further punctuated (indeed, in some ways personified) by the tradesman characters, Peachum and Lockit, who, with their account books, seem to threaten the traditions of orality and a pastoral past—both of which are ostensibly represented within the play by a "feudal" ballad culture. (According to Mary Poovey, double-entry bookkeeping systems of the kind presumably used in the play would have relied on pre-printed books, into which a merchant's specific sums would then be inscribed. Peachum's and Lockit's books of business may thus combine printed and handwritten information.[9]) By setting up these (supposed) contrasts between a print-capitalist present and a nostalgic, voice- or performance-based past, Gay at once critiques the new way of life while also (increasingly, over his career) revealing the extent to which our idea of a pre-commercial mode of expression—embodied, tied to the land, and working in harmony with nature—has always been a convenient fiction.

I would like to add a quick note here about my use of the term "oral culture" in this chapter. In her book *The Invention of the Oral*, Paula McDowell explains that "oral culture," like "print culture," is a post-1960s category, and that the use of the word "culture" to signify a "total way of life" did not emerge until the nineteenth century.[10] Even concepts such as our modern, secular understanding of "oral tradition," she maintains, did not exist until the second half of the eighteenth century.[11] Significantly for my purposes here, she points to a growing interest in balladry as a key event in the development of such a concept—but she sees this interest as taking off only in the later century, citing as landmark publications Thomas Percy's 1764 "Essay on the Ancient Minstrels of England" (appended to his *Reliques of Ancient English Poetry*), in which he claimed that England's old heroic ballads were the work of "oral itinerant poet[s],"[12] as well as John Pinkerton's "Dissertation on the Oral Tradition of Poetry," which prefaced his *Scottish Tragic Ballads* (1781). In contrast to accounts such as Percy's and Pinkerton's, McDowell insists, early eighteenth-century discussions of ballads "took for granted the multimedia nature of balladry as both oral and textual," and "tended to understand the oral and print dissemination" of these songs "as working in tandem."[13]

Yet McDowell identifies no particular social or cultural turning point that would have ushered in a mid-century shift, and, in fact, the larger historical backdrop against which she situates her study pertains equally to the earlier part of the century. She writes that the concepts of "oral discourse, oral tradition, and what we now commonly refer to as 'oral culture' . . . began to crystallize in their modern forms [only] once it was ideologically useful for . . . authors to idealize a way of life that was separate from (and superior to) a world [of] . . . professional writing [and] print commerce."[14] These latter phenomena she traces specifically to the 1695 lapse of the Licensing (or Printing) Act, which replaced "an older guild-based model of printing" with "an openly competitive commercial model,"[15] and she includes "Augustan satirists such as Pope and . . . Swift" among the most "astute observers of" the ways in which "printing and letters" were becoming "unregulated trades," whose "only controls were, in effect, the market."[16]

Scholars such as Susan Stewart, meanwhile, point to an even earlier historical moment in which traditional modes of expression were romanticized as soothing correctives to print. Stewart notes that "folkloric forms such as the ballad" had been "collected artifactually since the sixteenth century."[17] The purpose behind these ballad collections, she explains, was partly to "'rescue' forms that seemed to be disappearing" in a world that was already witnessing the rise of literacy, urban life, and a print marketplace.[18] Indeed, Benedict Anderson cites the year 1500 as signaling "the onset of [Walter] Benjamin's 'age of mechanical reproduction,'" noting that an estimated twenty million books had already been printed by this juncture.[19] As a way of compensating for the effects of such print entrepreneurship, Stewart explains, ballads seemed to offer readers a vision of a "'minstrel' author completely immersed in a context of (imaginary) feudalism."[20]

A passage from Sidney's *Apologie* (1595) serves to justify Stewart's and Anderson's earlier timeline: "Certainly, I must confess my own barbarousness, I never heard the old song of Percy and Douglas [i.e., *Chevy Chase*] that I found not my heart moved more then [*sic*] with a trumpet; and yet it is sung but by some blind crowder, with no rougher voice than rude style; which, being so evil apparelled in the dust and cobwebs of that uncivil age, what would it work, trimmed in the gorgeous eloquence of Pindar?"[21] While Sidney makes no mention of print per se, he is clearly participating here in the nostalgia Stewart describes, whereby the ballad comes to epitomize everything that is unmoneyed, untutored, and unlettered (as in the "rude style" of the "blind crowder," whose failed eyesight precludes the reading of either song lyrics or musical notation). Yet it is precisely this (ostensible) naïveté that allows the ballad form to produce so viscerally powerful an effect, "mov[ing]" Sidney's "heart."

However, as Stewart notes in regard to the romanticization of ballads more generally, attitudes such as the one we see expressed here are informed more by the "imagin[ary]" than by the real. In fact, according to Adam Fox, although *Chevy Chase* was of course "a song . . . learned off by heart and carolled aloud," it was "probably the product of manuscript circulation in the first instance," and its robust cultural currency was "surely due to its dissemination in thousands of printed copies and the fact that people could also read it from the page, whether set above the fireplace at home or pasted on the alehouse wall."[22] Whereas Sidney associates ballads firmly with "barbarous" illiteracy, this association turns out to be based more on yearning than on fact. Indeed, it may be the resplendent "trumpet" of classical learning itself that produces the desire for the "dust[y,] . . . song[s]" that Sidney articulates here. Where Sidney believes these ballads to have been forgotten ("cobweb[bed]" over), they are in fact being invented in the very act of being reclaimed.

While eighteenth-century writers may not have used the phrases "print culture" and "oral culture," I nonetheless think these are useful terms for referring to clusters of concepts: namely, the economic, social, and discursive world that texts, and especially printed texts, in many ways defined; and, by contrast, a notion of a past in which our interactions were somehow less mediated by the commerce of letters. Just as importantly, as I argue in more detail below, I am convinced that we can trace these concepts to an earlier period than McDowell does: like McDowell, I see these ideas as operative within the history of British ballad collecting and "literary" ballad appropriation; however, unlike McDowell, I contend that this history begins prior to the Romantics, and is both reflected and elaborated upon in the work of John Gay.

I will begin considering Gay's juxtaposition of print and orality via a reading of *The What D'Ye Call It,* thought to be Gay's most successful play next to

The Beggar's Opera.[23] Here, Gay initially holds out performance as an apparent alternative to the world of capitalism, urban bureaucracy, global finance, and law, all of which written or printed texts seem intimately bound up in. That is, if literate culture is inextricable from an ethos of commodification, rationalization, and anonymization, then performance seems to offer the possibility of a mode of expression that is voiced, embodied, collective, and natural, ushering us back to the feudal values of pastoralism, in which an aristocratic notion of the "word as bond"[24] is joined to the vernacular traditions of unlettered laborers.

Performance is of course an inherent component of drama in general, but Gay brings it to the forefront of both *The What D'Ye Call It* and *The Beggar's Opera* by way of his overt framing structures, so that what we think of as the main storylines are in fact plays within plays. Inside these plays within, moreover, the characters perform for one another in various ways, through deception, melodramatic posturing, and, again—in what will become an increasingly prominent aspect of Gay's work—the singing of ballads. In the discussion that follows, although I argue that Gay does briefly give credence, in *The What D'Ye Call It,* to performance's nostalgic promise, I show that *The Beggar's Opera* reveals his ultimate skepticism of performance's ability to stand apart from the commercial reality symbolized by print.

Gay starts out in *The What D'Ye Call It* by contrasting performance with written or printed texts—linking performance to the pastoral, while associating texts with modern bureaucracy and trade. He proceeds to explode this contrast, however, by insisting that the embodied forms of representation at the heart of the play's dramatic action are in fact inseparable from writing technologies, merging in a hybrid art form in which books figure as theatrical props: characters may hold up a text, read from it, or declare a complete lack of any literacy whatsoever, all as ways of enhancing the rhetorical effect of their social performances. In this way Gay suggests that the body, as a representational form, can be just as mediated as a text—and, indeed, that each can mediate for the other. By the end of *The What D'Ye Call It,* however—though his optimism does not survive into *The Beggar's Opera*—Gay suggests that this hybrid mode might itself be capable of expressing human truths, and of bringing people together, to a degree unmatched by either performance or textuality alone.

Gay makes clear from the beginning that not all performance is raw and authentic. Indeed, the entirety of *The What D'Ye Call It* can be seen as a mash-up of recycled lines from other dramatists (from Ambrose Philips to Joseph Addison to William Shakespeare); and in case we are unable to find these allusions on our own, they are conveniently spelled out in the anonymously authored *Complete Key to the Last New Farce, The What D'Ye Call It*. (The *Key* is usually attributed to the actor Benjamin Griffin and the scholar Lewis Theobald, but may actually have been authored by Gay and Pope.[25]) The play's original status as an afterpiece—a farcical epilogue to Nicholas Rowe's *Jane Shore*—further emphasizes its role as theatrical parody or pastiche. Moreover, Gay, in critiquing the tired clichés of the theater, suggests that (as, indeed, the very existence of the printed *Key* reflects) much of contemporary dramaturgy's conventionality is tied up with print capitalism—that the commercial theater is all too dependent upon the print discourse that surrounds it, whether in the form of news, reviews, or advertisements.

Describing his new play to fellow Scriblerian Thomas Parnell (January 29, 1715), Gay comments that, as long as he proves unable to obtain a place at court, "I must rub on as well as I can in hope that Gazettes will some time or other be my friend."[26] Although Gay had not yet given up his dream of aristocratic support—he would continue to hang on at court for another ten years—here he acknowledges a shifting reality: the old system of sponsorship was giving way to a new one, dependent on a print-based public sphere (*The London Gazette*, the first regular newspaper in England, was issued in 1665); as a result, Gay needed the "friend[ship]" not of potential patrons but of the press. A few days after the play had opened, in a letter written with Pope to their mutual friend John Caryll (March 3, 1715), Gay notes, "The Parts in general were not so well play'd, as I could have wished, and in particular the Part of Filbert, to speak in the Style of the French Gazette."[27] Here, it seems, even as Gay gives his own opinion of the performances ("not so well play'd, as I could have wished"), he cannot help but also filter his response through the anticipated press coverage, wording his reaction so as to fit "the Style of the French Gazette." Gay thus registers an understanding that contemporary drama exists in a symbiotic relationship with a larger world of print.

If part of Gay's implication in *The What D'Ye Call It*, then, is that the stage has been influenced by its interaction with the press, this early play can in many ways be seen as an attempt to extricate the two, to liberate performance, as it were, from a print culture that too easily promotes the formulaic—even as Gay acknowledges, via parody, the theater's own routinized ways. There are moments in *The What D'Ye Call It*, as we will see, in which performance does seem to promise the release of genuine emotion rather than the repetition of familiar sentiments. Yet, in finally admitting the inseparability of performance from written and printed texts, Gay suggests that the only hope for dramaturgy to escape cliché is not to quit the world of print but to play performance and text off of one another in new and innovative ways.

In *The What D'Ye Call It*'s world of rural employments, raw emotions, and primal plot elements (crime and punishment, love and death, war and peace), the intensity of the characters' feelings at first seems to be captured most "authentically" by speech and gesture. In contrast, the technologies and technicalities of writing manifest themselves in texts that stand out like foreign objects—alien, reified, and strangely unassimilable into the play's primary action. Here, I discuss two instances in which texts appear in this way. In both, written language—and, specifically, printed language—is portrayed as an intrusive presence, oddly clumsy. Both moments emphasize textuality's obvious fabricatedness within the play's ostensibly "natural" world.

In the first of these scenes, we learn that Timothy Peascod, a young farmworker and one of the two central male characters in the play within a play of *The What D'Ye Call It*, was recently found guilty of robbing an orchard and stealing a hen. Under the Recruitment Act, also known as the Pressing Act or "Press-Act" (as it is referred to at 1.4.1), the penalty for such minor offenses could include conscription into the military.[28] And indeed, in what we learn of the backstory of the play within the play, Peascod was subsequently forced into the army, though he promptly escaped. Now, having been apprehended, he has been sentenced to death for desertion, and a concerned bystander hands him a copy of *The Pilgrim's Progress* to console him.

In the second scene I examine, print arrives in the form of an untitled ballad purchased by Kitty Carrot, the sweetheart of the inner play's other central male character, Tom Filbert (who has also been conscripted under the Recruitment Act). As we will see, the comic effect of both scenes relies on the texts' utter disparity with the dramatic situation—on their failure to engage with, much less represent, the surrounding events.

In the first example, Peascod, sentenced to death, has launched into a melancholy lamentation when, abruptly, he is handed John Bunyan's classic by a member of a group of onlookers—designated as "Countrymen"—to aid in his "repent[ance]" (2.1.22). However, the front matter alone causes Peascod to collapse with emotion:

> Lend me thy Handkercher—*The Pilgrim's Pro*—
> (I cannot see for Tears) *Pro—Progress*—Oh!
> —*The Pilgrim's Progress—Eighth—Edi-ti-on*
> *Lon-don—Prin-ted—for—Ni-cho-las Bod-ding-ton:*
> *With new Ad-di-tions never made before.*
> —Oh! 'tis so moving, I can read no more. (2.1.23–28)

As Howard Erskine-Hill has noted, the humor here arises in part from the "banal details of the imprint and the idea that Tim should call them moving."[29] But the scene's effectiveness inheres not just in the comic contrast between banality and pathos but, more specifically, in the striking disjunction between, on the one hand, the transcendent potential of the volume being proffered and, on the other, what this particular page more immediately depicts—namely, the commercial and technological aspects of print. Thus, the self-promotional language citing new and improved material ("new Additions, never made before"!), along with the reference to multiple editions or impressions of the type (this one is the "eighth"), contrasts starkly with the profound feeling with which Peascod reads them. The play's insertion of these phrases into the rhymed-couplet form of the recitation further empties them of meaning: the rhymes work only because the words are chopped up into nonsense syllables (e.g., "*Pro—*" and "*Oh!*").[30] Similarly, "*Edi-ti-on*" and "*Bod-ding-ton*" rhyme only if we pronounce the letters as they are spelled, and not as they would be voiced in communicative speech. Printed language in this scene thus appears incompatible with emotion, a commodified and inanimate artifact seemingly at odds with the terror and grief of death. Of course, this terror and grief is itself ironized by the play's flippant twists and turns of fate. Moreover, as we will see, one soon begins to suspect that Peascod and his fellow laborers are hamming things up. Nonetheless, the social injustices referred to—trumped-up charges invented to supply the army with young and politically disempowered bodies, death sentences for desertion—are very real. And the printed text, as portrayed by Gay, falls laughably short as a way of responding to the situation.

The second printed object to inject itself arbitrarily into the flow of the play's plot is a ballad—an art form that will, of course, become crucial in

The Beggar's Opera. At first, the scene in which the ballad appears can be viewed as epitomizing the ingenuous sentiment that (seemingly) characterizes the farmworkers' life and (supposedly) distinguishes it from the commercialized world associated with writing and print. Pitched into a suicidal anguish by Filbert's forced enlistment, staggering about the stage with her "hair loose," Filbert's lover, Kitty Carrot, invokes innocent nature: she bids farewell to the fields, flocks, meadows, and dew, and she pays tribute to "yon Tree" where Filbert first declared his love (2.8.76); she then pulls out the ballad and proceeds to sing from it, insisting that the ballad can help her to express herself in this time of tragedy. But, in contrast to the scene's images of flora and fauna, and of a pre-commercial life lived in harmony with nature, the ballad itself—which we might expect to complement such a culture—instead ends up importing values of buying and selling, its thoughts and feelings not arising organically, but rather purchased in the marketplace, printed and packaged for sale within a modern capitalist system.

The ballad is first introduced when Kitty, having contrasted her fate at length with that of happier maidens, concludes, "But I forlorn!" Within the same pentameter line she hastens to add, "This Ballad"—pulling out a sheet of paper—"shews my Care." She then hands the ballad to a woman named Susan (like the "Countryman" who offers Peascod *The Pilgrim's Progress*, she is another convenient nonce character, one of a group of "Haymakers" never mentioned again): "Take this sad Ballad, which I bought at Fair: / *Susan* can sing—do you the Burthen bear" (2.8.18–21).[31] Of course, the main purpose of this brief exchange is to set up the ballad singing; one could thus argue that it has little significance as dramatic dialogue. However, Gay's later use of ballads (as in *The Beggar's Opera*) forsook such preambles, incorporating songs directly into the fabric of the play. Here, on the contrary, Gay makes a point of the ballad's physical presence, its status as a material object with market value ("this ... Ballad ... bought at Fair").[32]

Not just highlighting the ballad's commodity status, however, the scene also seems to emphasize the ballad's use as a kind of substitute for the "natural" conveyance of Kitty's emotions. Like the copy of *The Pilgrim's Progress*, the ballad is plucked suddenly and arbitrarily from some pocket or other, thrust into the scene almost at random. Yet, like the buyer of a modern greeting card, Kitty feels that this piece of paper—composed, printed, and sold by others—will "shew ... [her] Care" better than she herself could. Replacing feeling rather than representing it, standing in for grief rather than facilitating it, the printed word here, too, is made to seem the product of an anonymous, commercial sphere that has nothing in common with the rural, homespun setting of the play's plot.

Both the play's *Pilgrim's Progress* scene and its ballad scene, then, portray writing or print technology as artificial—as having little bearing on "authentic" emotional experience (whether Peascod's despair over his impending execution or Kitty's sorrow over Filbert's conscription). But the play does not depict texts as merely oblivious or indifferent to the reality they are being asked to represent; rather, as the action unfolds, texts—and especially printed texts—are portrayed as increasingly and aggressively impinging onto situations where they are neither needed nor wanted.

One example of text's menacing presence can be seen in scenes 6 and 7 of act 2, just after the *Pilgrim's Progress* episode. Peascod, still unconsoled, has nothing more to do but await his death. Suddenly, however, a soldier appears with a "Reprieve," letting Peascod go free. Compounding this victory, and with equal abruptness, a constable then arrives to seize Peascod's original arresting officer, "for stealing Gaffer *Gap*'s gray Mare." The constable explains:

> Thus said Sir *John*—the Law must take its course;
> 'Tis Law that he may 'scape who steals a Horse.
> But (said Sir *John*) the Statutes all declare,
> The Man shall sure be hang'd—that steals a Mare. (2.7.7–10)

Here the entire discussion of horses versus mares—and, hence, of the arresting officer's escape versus his execution—depends (emphatically) on the authority of "Sir *John*." This is a reference to Sir John Holt, who served as Lord Chief Justice of England from 1689 to 1710.[33] Or, rather, the reference is to Holt's printed writings: if the events of *The What D'Ye Call It* can be assumed to be contemporary with the play's composition, Holt would have been dead for five years. His legacy, however, survived in the form of a bound collection of his judgments, first published in 1713 and reprinted multiple times thereafter, and it is presumably from these texts that the constable is quoting. Significantly, then, no legally trained mind is actually present to issue a verdict on this particular situation (despite the constable's emphasis on what Sir John "said"). A dead man's printed words must stand in.

Of course, the problem with these printed words, the scene suggests, is their disregard for "bodily" or "natural" categories in favor of their own linguistic constructions. Thus, while the difference between a male and a female horse would seem clear enough, the corresponding verbal symbols slip and shift: though not all horses are mares, all mares are horses. Horrifyingly, here the law has rendered this particular divergence between words and things into the difference between life and death. The statutes' dismissal of physical realities is echoed by the broken-up structure of the scene, as manifested by the arrival of the soldier with the "Reprieve" (another written or printed text), and by the introduction of the constable and Gaffer Gap (never heard from again in the play). As we are beginning to see, not only do texts become associated with "unnatural" outcomes, but they disrupt the action of the play, blocking its expected or "natural" sequence of events.

The cruel arbitrariness of the mare-horse distinction is highlighted in Peascod's triumphant reiteration of the constable's words, in which his rote replication of the man's exact phrasing is at once ludicrous and troublingly justified:

> A rare good sentence this—how is't?—the Laws
> No—not the Laws—the Statutes all declare,
> The Man that steals a Mare shall sure—be—hang'd,
> No, no—he shall be hang'd that steals a Mare. (2.7.13–16)

The "rare good sentence" is exactly that—a series of specific words in a specific order. Any syntactic tinkering, it seems, might result in semantic collapse. Indeed, Peascod's literalist quotation underscores the constable's own citation of Holt, and suggests the way in which a law, despite seeming illogical, could nonetheless survive via the mechanical repetition (or, perhaps more appositely here, mechanical reproduction) of language, carried forward with no regard to its application.

Not just in this scene, however, but throughout *The What D'Ye Call It*, the law is associated closely with the mechanical reproduction of language. The play's three justices of the peace, and their comically inept exercise of jurisprudence, perfectly illustrate this point. For example, when Tom Filbert's female relatives appeal to the justices in an attempt to save him from conscription, the trio do not explicitly cite a book of statutes or precedent in their response, as the constable does; they do, however, cite what they refer to as "the Press-Act" (or Recruitment Act): "I say the Press-Act plainly makes it out" (1.4.1). This language of "press[ing]" is present throughout the play. Filbert's uncle, for example, is said to have been "press'd" (1.1.35), a group of already deceased victims of the justices return as ghosts to bemoan their having been "press'd" (1.4.46), and Filbert is "press'd and forc'd away" (2.8.15). I do not mean to imply that the motif of "pressing" in *The What D'Ye Call It* is intended to function as a pun, exactly; rather, the term, in all of its multivalence, serves as a kind of emblem for the larger set of associations at work here. In other words, the Press Act (and, by association, the law more generally) is linked to the unthinking use, and gradual dehumanization, of language—a process in which writing, but especially print and the printing press, are also made to appear complicit.

Throughout *The What D'Ye Call It,* the Press Act and the legal institutions it symbolizes are tied to a literate and often print-based culture. It seems significant, moreover, that, historically, the Press Act was passed in order to provide soldiers not just for national defense, broadly defined, but for colonial conflicts: as Kevin J. Gardner explains, fronts such as America and the West Indies did not tend to attract volunteers; forced recruitment therefore became a necessary tool in protecting Britain's global commercial interests.[34] The laws that are threatening the play's rural laborers' way of life, then, are part of a larger system not just of print but of print capitalism, and the modern imperial project in which print capitalism plays an integral role. By contrast, the rural laborers seem embedded in a highly localized, ritualized, traditional order. The two can often be seen as coming into direct conflict. For example, Kitty laments,

> Happy the Maid, whose Sweetheart never hears
> The Soldier's Drum, nor Writ of Justice fears.
> Our Bans thrice bid! and for our Wedding Day
> My Kerchief bought! then press'd, then forc'd away! (2.8.12–15)

Here, the legal "Writ" thwarts and nullifies the spoken ("bid[den]") marriage banns: the passage reasserts the play's connection between writing technologies and arbitrary rules (indeed, they are joined in the single word "Writ"). By contrast, orality (the "Ban[n]s") is linked to community and consensus (banns are announced to a congregation, and it is this collective act of bearing witness that validates them). The momentary confusion that arises in the final line—in which "press'd" seems at first to refer to the kerchief ("bought! then press'd") but then turns out to refer to the conscripted sweetheart—further dramatizes the dismaying disjunction between the traditional, homely habits of the young lovers and the martial "Drum"-beat-like intrusion of the justice's writ.

But not only is the law portrayed as artificially imposed onto traditional ways of life; it is also depicted as antithetical to natural desires. Thus, Dorcas, another young farm girl finding herself at odds with official, written doctrine (she is pregnant and unwed), bewails her fate in a set of striking dualisms:

> Ah, Why does Nature give us so much Cause
> To make kind-hearted Lasses break the Laws?
> Why should hard Laws kind-hearted Lasses bind,
> When too soft Nature draws us after Kind? (1.1.95–98)

Here the passage's aural binary—"Laws" serves as a long-faced foil to the fanciful "Lass"—complements its rhetorical divide. Nature is associated with "kind"-ness (indeed, "kind" can refer to "nature" in the abstract, and the original adjectival meaning of "kind" is "natural"), but it is also linked to "kind-hearted[ness]" and to kinship (one's "kind"). In short, nature facilitates love's bonds; the law, by contrast, "binds." And indeed, the "binding" of young girls here is literal. Dorcas's outpouring comes just after the justices have ordered that Kitty must do penance in a sheet next Sunday (1.1.92–94).[35] And Dorcas herself later laments that, for her own transgressions, she, too, must "stand at Church . . . in a white Sheet" (2.3.4). In fact, the prescription of the penance sheet is the primary tool of punishment, other than "pressing," to which the justices consistently turn. And these two punishments are not unrelated. Each is aimed at a particular category of crime: natural instincts or excesses of the body. In sum, then, whether addressing erotic longings or literal hunger (illegally procured hares [1.1.37], trout [1.1.43], and fruit [2.1.13]), the penalties meted out by the justices seek (not unlike a printed text, it seems) to blanch, to flatten, to conscribe, or to bind up the most basic impulses of appetite. In associating print with a legal bureaucracy of "Statutes," "Writs," and double-indexed volumes of judicial decisions, *The What D'Ye Call It* depicts print culture as part of a larger, ever-expanding world order in which the desires of the body are subordinated to the logic of capital and empire.

The What D'Ye Call It initially appears to posit an alternative to writing and print, an art form capable of more accurately reflecting emotional and bodily reality: performance. Of course, I should add here that the word *perform* carries with it a whole host of connotations—to simulate, to feign, to put on, to imitate—that are very far from the allegedly simple modes of communication that, I have been contending, the play seems to attribute to the body in its "natural" state, unimposed upon by the principles of law, commerce, and text. And indeed, as I will argue below, Gay ultimately acknowledges and even celebrates these additional connotations, drawing upon them to expose all embodied expression as inherently mediated and constructed. However, at moments Gay also seems to gaze wistfully toward performance as a potential locus for emotional authenticity.

Of course, *The What D'Ye Call It*'s most central instance of representation via voice and gesture is, quite literally, a performance—namely, the yuletide pageant in which Peascod's, Kitty's, and Filbert's drama is played out. What's more, this performance is an insistently "pastoral" one, both in its setting—the country estate of Sir Roger—and in its social composition: the play within is a joint effort on the part of (on the one hand) Sir Roger and his fellow country squires—the introductory scene is set in *"A Country Justice's Hall, adorn'd with Scutcheons and Stag's Horns"*—and (on the other hand) the workers on the estate, whom Sir Roger calls "my Tenants" (line 66). In this sense, the pageant seems to embody the idealized feudalism to which the pastoral mode alludes (in its "beautiful relation between rich and poor").[36] And indeed, as we will see, what gives the pageant its power is the fact that it not only reflects but also actually precipitates a kind of utopian union between the aristocratic and laboring-class characters. In so doing, moreover, it responds to and even redresses various injustices in the participants' lives that the play's other representational models (writing, print) appear to ignore or ride roughshod over.

From the very beginning of the frame play, the yuletide theatricals are associated with truth telling: they are devised as a tool for exposing an attempted obfuscation of an inconvenient state of affairs. As the introductory scene establishes, Thomas (the son of Sir Roger) has been directing his attentions toward Katherine (the daughter of Sir Roger's steward), who is now pregnant. But Thomas disavows any responsibility. As a result, Katherine is left "debauched" (line 44), her "Reputation" in imminent danger (line 46). Her father, anguished on her behalf ("Poor Girl! . . . I cannot forget thy Tears" [line 46]), proceeds, in his role as steward, to engineer the impending pageant in such a way that the wedding that occurs in its final scene, between Tom Filbert (played by Thomas) and Kitty Carrot (played by Katherine), also constitutes the "real" wedding between the actors (a "real" parson, it turns out, has officiated at the ceremony). The pageant thereby serves to "reveal" the facts of Thomas's actions, and compels social and legal reality to reflect bodily reality.[37] This example also offers what is perhaps the play's most striking illustration of performance's ideal or utopian potential—its capacity to accurately relay, and respond to, situations that the other available representational models fail to address.

Certainly, to the extent that the pageant constitutes a kind of trick on the part of Sir Roger's steward, the performance itself could be said to be dishonest, and the resulting wedding obviously takes place under false pretenses. Nonetheless, the enactment of the ritual enforces a more fundamental morality: as John Fuller notes, when Thomas ultimately realizes what has happened, he "accepts the situation" of his marriage to Katherine "without demur."[38] Perhaps, Fuller speculates, this is because "the virtuous course has been presented to him"—because the thematic content of the theatricals has instructed him in, even guided him physically through, a more honorable code of behavior.[39] Thus, not only has the pageant brought social and legal reality into alignment with bodily reality, but it has also arguably brought Thomas's internal reality—his conscience, his feelings—into alignment with all three.

It would seem, then, that printed judicial decisions, writs, statutes, reprieves, title pages, and broadsheet ballads all drive a wedge between law and conscience, between written convention and human emotion. Contrastingly, the pageant—in its specific status as pastoral performance—has caused each of these pairs of terms to match up, in the same way that it literally "marries" rich with poor. Thus, if *The What D'Ye Call It* associates writing and print with legalese, with technology, with global capitalism and colonial violence, then performance, by contrast, operates in the service of a "natural" order of things, conveying the needs of the individual body and heart.

Yet this apparent opposition between urban and rural, commercial and communal, textual and corporeal, soon shows signs of collapse. The cracks in this orderly binary become palpable once we realize that the pageant's characters cannot be neatly slotted into categories of literate and illiterate, print-savvy and not. In fact, it gradually becomes clear that our presumption of the rural laborers' atextual existence stems, in part, from their own strategic protestations. In *The What D'Ye Call It* in particular, this revelation leads to another realization: that reading and writing alone do not confer power;

rather, the ability to *perform* literacy or illiteracy (according to the requirements of a given context) is what matters. And it is here that the concept of performance in the play begins to detach itself from notions of simply embodying or enacting, and instead takes on the connotations of feigning or putting on.

Of all the performed relationships to reading and writing that the rural laborers stage, Kitty Carrot's may be the most calculated, taking the form of a kind of public-relations campaign meant to broadcast her and her lover's lexical incompetency. Thus, as the sergeant comes to collect Tom Filbert for his army service, Kitty commences a lamentation, in which Filbert joins her:

> *Kitty:* When Gentlefolks their Sweethearts leave behind,
>   They can write Letters, and say something kind;
>   But how shall *Filbert* unto me endite,
>   When neither I can read, nor he can write?
>   Yet, Justices, permit us e'er we part [*sic*]
>   To break this Ninepence, as you've broke our Heart.
> *Filbert:* [*Breaking the Ninepence*]. As this divides, thus are we torn in twain.
> *Kitty:* [*Joining the Pieces*]. And as this meets, thus may we meet again.
> (1.2.14–21)

On a first reading, this passage seems to reiterate the divisions that the play has been laying claim to—at least superficially—throughout: "Gentlefolks" can overcome physical distance by writing, but the farm laborers can express their emotions only performatively, through gesture. Certainly, the ninepence serves as a kind of symbol or sign (if a somewhat imprecise one, representing both Kitty's broken heart and the forced separation of the lovers), but it remains stubbornly material and makeshift, signifying only through Kitty's hand motions. The lovers' illiteracy, Kitty maintains, bars them from the forms of communication with which one might hope to transcend the limitations of the detained and disciplined body.

However, other moments of the play directly contradict Kitty's protestations. For example, the question of who can read and write in the world of *The What D'Ye Call It* becomes particularly complicated when Filbert's grandmother pleads to the justices:

> Must Grandson *Filbert* to the Wars be prest?
> Alack! I knew him when he suck'd the Breast,

> Taught him his Catechism, the Fescue held,
> And join'd his Letters, when the Bantling Spell'd.
> His loving Mother left him to my Care....
> Come *Candlemas,* nine Years ago she dy'd. (1.2.25–31)

Here, we discover that Filbert in fact "*can* write": indeed, ironically, his writing abilities are the legacy of precisely that naïve, humble life—characterized by close family ties and marked by religious ritual—that one would otherwise associate with rural aliteracy. This short speech also shows that Filbert isn't the only one who can read and write; so can his grandmother (presumably born to an even more traditionally agricultural life, and female).

Likewise, Kitty herself, it appears, "can read." Her literacy is proven, I would argue, by her use of the ballad in the scene discussed earlier. Of course, Kitty could have purchased the ballad without being able to read it: the ballad seller might have sung the ballad to her.[40] But it also appears probable that she simply learned the song from the sheet of paper: her ability to do so seems confirmed by her blithe assumption that her fellow female farm laborer Susan will likewise be able to take up the broadside and sing from it on command. (And Susan seems to be up to the task.) The scene thus suggests Kitty's (and her cohorts') participation in the literate world, and, more specifically, in the print world, despite her statements to the contrary.

Moreover, the scene emphasizes Kitty's involvement not just with print as a physical fact but also with its concomitant cultural valences. As mentioned, the ballad has been "bought at Fair," and is thus a form of emotional expression mediated by a financial transaction. In fact, even apart from the ballad, the scene establishes Kitty's larger facility with commodity culture. In her valedictory elegy to the mortal world, she notes appreciatively, "And thou, my Rake, Companion of my Cares, / Giv'n by my Mother in my younger Years: / With thee the Toils of full eight Springs I've known, / 'Tis to thy Help I owe this Hat and Gown" (2.8.3–6). While we might imagine that the laborers are simple feudal tenants, inheriting their tools from their parents (as Kitty did) and working mainly in exchange for basic food and shelter, Kitty's rake has apparently earned her a sum of pocket money (such as the ninepence she holds in her hand) with which she can purchase apparel of her choosing: at the words "Hat and Gown" we envision Kitty making a little flourish or curtsy, perhaps, to show off her fashionable selections.

Why, then, does Kitty deny knowledge of the written word, of print and the commodity culture in which it participates? At least in part, Kitty makes her claims for rhetorical effect: they allow her to put on a convincing show for the sake of the justices. And perhaps the show is staged for her and Filbert's sake as well. Kitty's love of melodrama reveals itself in the way that she sandwiches her claim of illiteracy between two passages of absurdly exaggerated lovers' dialogue: "O rueful Day! / Rueful indeed, I trow. / O Woeful Day! / A Day indeed of Woe!" (1.2.13–16). She continues: "Yet one Look more—/ One more e'er yet we go [*sic*]. / To part is Death. / 'Tis Death to part / Ah! / Oh!" (1.2.22–27). More than simply sentimental, the interchange actually becomes so emotive that it loses all predicative power, starting with redundancy ("Woeful ... Woe") and ending in pure vocalization ("Ah! Oh!"). Indeed, if the lines can be said to "refer" to anything, it is to the dramatic (and, of course, Gay is using them to spoof contemporary stage conventions: the *Key* makes reference to *"Almeria's* repeated Sighs at the sight of her Father's dead body" in Congreve's *The Mourning Bride:* "Spouting Veins and mangled Flesh! Oh, Oh!—" [note to 1.2.23]). The centerpiece of the scene, however, remains Kitty's invocation (and disavowal) of literacy: reading and writing ultimately lie at the heart of her performance. In other words, Kitty's strategic use of texts—specifically, her strategic claim to textual ignorance—works in the service of a larger theatricality.

A similar synergy could be pointed to in the *Pilgrim's Progress* scene. For here, too, one of the play's laborer characters could be said to be manipulating his assumed inability to read (though this time the inability is seemingly emotional rather than educational in origin) in order to achieve a certain quality of affect. As we have seen, the incursion of *The Pilgrim's Progress* into the scene could be construed as interrupting Peascod's emotive display. Yet, significantly, it also augments it: Peascod "*Reads and weeps,*" and then dramatically "*Drops the Book.*" In short, printed texts are converted into the stuff of pure histrionics. Like Kitty, Peascod constructs his performance through a careful use of print and print culture.

The What D'Ye Call It's ostensible binary of print and performance further disintegrates upon a second examination of the way the play is printed. Howard Erskine-Hill has noticed several of *The What D'Ye Call It*'s print-dependent witticisms, observing that a number of the play's "surreal touches" would "not have been so apparent to the audience as to the reader."[41] He points to the "*Ghost of an Embryo*"—whose unwed mother has miscarried after being whipped (2.8.11)—as well as to the "Chorus of Sighs and Groans" who accompany Kitty in her lament (2.8.11). But of course the effect of these elements is not just "surreal" but critical—burlesquing tragic dramaturgy's penchant for the lurid. Somewhat ironically, then, the play as acted onstage is in some ways less capable of satirizing the contemporary theater than is the printed text.

In fact, many other comic effects in the play can likewise be apprehended solely by the reader. The tone of the stage directions, for example, frequently attains a kind of deadpan verging on mockery. For example, the directions that accompany the pronouncements of the country justices have the men "*Drinking,*" and "*Drinking,*" and "*Drinking also*"—the "*also*" serving, as it were, as the textual version of a raised eyebrow (1.1.91–94; the joke is repeated at 1.3.1–3). Another instance of the play's text-based humor can be seen in the interplay between the stage directions and the dialogue in the use of the term "Countrymen," a phrase designating what are essentially the play's "extras" (along with a number of "Haymakers" and "Soldiers" who appear from time to time). Of course, the term can mean "one who lives in the country, . . . a husbandman" (*OED,* s.v. "countryman," def. 3), and in the context of the play this definition seems the most fitting. Yet the word takes on a secondary meaning in Peascod's pseudo-Shakespearean speechifying (right before the *Pilgrim's Progress* interlude): "O Fellow-Soldiers, Countrymen and Friends, / Be warn'd by me to shun untimely Ends" (2.1.5–6). Here Peascod intends to apostrophize not humble rustics but "compatriots" (*OED,* def. 2)—fellow members of a nation, fellow fighters for a cause. As a result, subsequent references to these characters in the stage directions take on a kind of mock-heroic undertone. Thus, while *The What D'Ye Call It* suggests that print can yield an only ever mediated form of expression, it also renders much of its humor accessible via print alone. Indeed, such text-exclusive gags reveal the constraints innate to drama's "other" medium—namely, performance. The fact that these comic nuances are literally impossible to include in the staged version of the play not only implies but actually demonstrates, as it were, the limits of live voice and gesture.[42]

But perhaps it would be most accurate to say that those effects in *The What D'Ye Call It* that we might initially believe to be "text-only" actually rely, more specifically, on the dynamic between page and stage. That is, at least part of our enjoyment of the ironies just enumerated—the logical conundrum of the undead unborn, the drily mocking stage directions, the punning character identifications—stems from our awareness of their status as private jokes between us and the playwright, jokes that we know that the theater audience cannot access.

In this sense, *The What D'Ye Call It*'s print-only humor dovetails with the satiric effect of the subsequently printed *Key*. For the *Key*, while obviously highlighting Gay's parody of clichéd dramaturgy more generally, could be said to underscore his parody, more particularly, of the emotional heights that make sense only in live performance. For example (to return to a reference I have already mentioned), the "Oh, Oh!—" of Almeria upon confronting her father's blood-soaked corpse in *The Mourning Bride* would not necessarily strike a theater audience as absurd: when we, too, are seeing what Almeria is seeing, we are hardly offended to find language breaking down. It is arguably only the reader who, without the benefit of staged action, would think to expect verbal eloquence (indeed, perhaps as a kind of compensation for the missing visual tableau). Of course, one imagines that *The What D'Ye Call It* as performed would also prove quite effective in skewering emotional excesses such as these: Gay's use of rhyme, and his transposition of "high" tragic sentiments onto "low" comic characters, ensures that the parody comes through onstage as well as on the page. But the *Key*'s printed round-up of these moments also specifically emphasizes the gap between theatrical action and dramatic text. That is, the *Key* reveals how plays, once printed, often fall short of the pathos that a staged production might achieve, but it also suggests that much of the pathos that swept us up in a theater can, suddenly, appear silly when regarded from the cold distance of the printed page.

Both the *Key*, then, as well as the printed elements within *The What D'Ye Call It*, serve to exploit drama's doubleness—its status as both performance and book—to critique each of its components in turn. Both texts reiterate the dynamic that, I have been arguing, defines *The What D'Ye Call It* as a whole: as we have seen, the play creates a complex web of interconnection between print capitalism and pastoral performance, in which the two elements are initially made to seem antithetical but in fact depend upon and effect a critique of each other. In this way, Gay explodes his basic pastoral conceit: on one hand, he is suggesting, as Empson would say all pastoralists do, that the unlettered poor possess sentiments just as "beautiful" as those of the rich, and, accordingly, I think we should not underestimate the political import of *The What D'Ye Call It*'s treatment of the Press Act, of the harshness of the criminal laws, of wealthy cads who take advantage of their employees' daughters, and of other social inequalities. On the other hand, however, Gay also goes a step further, in revealing such pastoralism to be a myth: for the seemingly unlettered poor are never only simple victims; nor do the rich possess particularly exquisite or sophisticated sentiments in the first place (as seen both in Gay's "Booby Squire" characters and in his spoofs of "high" tragedy).[43] Yet this myth of a pastoral universality, Gay maintains, is fundamental to the way that much of imaginative writing in print seeks to legitimate itself in the modern era. The eighteenth century's nascent field of literature, he suggests, depends, for its sense of value, on a disavowal of the global capitalist economy in which it is complicit. In *The What D'Ye Call It,* Gay mobilizes the dramatic mode—in its incorporation of both the written and the performed—to reflect upon the illusory division between oral traditions and the world of print, but also upon the emergent canon's need to posit this division in the first place (indeed, to invent it), all so as to be able to take credit for bridging it over.

The Beggar's Opera may not at first seem to be a direct descendant of *The What D'Ye Call It.* Composed over a decade later, Gay's most celebrated play is not as overtly pastoral as his earlier play: although Swift's phrase "Newgate Pastoral" is often used in association with it,[44] the emphasis is usually on the first of the two terms—on the fact that, within the play's urban, criminal-underworld setting, any last vestiges of "nature" seem to have been turned completely inside out (so that, as Lockit famously puts it, "Every one of us preys upon his Neighbour, and yet we herd together"). I want to argue, however, that *The What D'Ye Call It,* and the dynamic that it sets up between print capitalism and pastoral performance, foreshadows some of the questions most central to *The Beggar's Opera.* Specifically, I want to demonstrate the ways in which the concepts that are so fundamental to Gay's 1715 farce become a crucial means by which to understand anew *The Beggar's Opera*'s use of ballads.

To consider more closely the way that print, orality, pastoralism and performance interact within the songs of *The Beggar's Opera,* we must look first at the way that these concepts operate within the play as a whole. The larger pattern that we see at work in the play's complex alignments of characters, as well as the arrangement of its dramatic episodes, is what ends up being reiterated—in compacted, explosive form—in its use of the ballads themselves.

In the pages that follow, borrowing my analytical framework from my reading of Gay's earlier play, I trace what at first seems to be an opposition, but is ultimately a blurring, between (on the one hand) the bureaucratic bookkeeping of Peachum and Lockit and (on the other) Macheath's claims to a "pastoral" ethos. Next, drawing a parallel between Peachum's and Lockit's books of business and the Beggar's playbook, I suggest that Macheath's final escape from hanging (as demanded by the "taste of the town") is not (as some critics have deemed it) an escape from a reading-and-writing-based commercialism in favor of traditional morality, or an escape from literary rules in favor of the impulses of the heart. Rather, it is a return to the very world of prescribed forms from which the master criminal had claimed to be exempt.

I then examine the songs in the play as microcosms of the paradoxes outlined above. While the play's sixty-nine airs may seem, at several points, to offer a haven from the world depicted in the rest of the play—that is, from a world mediated by money and by texts—in fact the songs insist on the inextricability of oral from literate, feudal from capitalistic. Finally, I look very briefly at the history of *The Beggar's Opera*'s publication and reception in order to illustrate how the printed play and its printed spinoffs likewise participate in Gay's repeated reminders that the mediating influences of commerce and writing have always been with us.

I want to start by looking at Peachum's and Lockit's account books. Few critics have mentioned these ledgers, despite what I argue is in fact their rather prominent structural placement in the play: Peachum's book of accounts is present onstage from the moment act 1 begins, and, as I will show in a moment, the books appear with what seems like very deliberate timing thereafter. Perhaps the critical neglect arises from the fact that, indeed, the ledgers seem too obvious to require comment: after all, as Maynard Mack notes, they seem to function as "the basic symbol of [the play's] price-society."[45] Serving as more than simply symbols of the society at large, however, they operate, I think, as symbols of how this society represents itself and its members—of how it mediates human interaction through a document-based system of contracts, laws, and bureaucratic procedure.[46] This textually mediated form of interaction comes to be associated, in the play, not just with the tradesmen's bookkeeping but with the Beggar-author's (implied) playscript. Both are tacitly contrasted with the "pastoral" ethos of the play's songs, and with those characters whose performances of the songs (most notably Polly and Macheath) are usually felt to serve as the play's emotional center of gravity. Over and against such apparent immediacy, the shopkeepers' ledgers and the Beggar's script quite literally prescribe the value, length, and shape of human lives, in accordance with a textual rather than "organic" order. However, as in *The What D'Ye Call It,* the apparent dichotomy between "organic" and "mediated" forms of expression in *The Beggar's Opera* quickly collapses under scrutiny.

Before examining in detail the role of Peachum's and Lockit's account books in *The Beggar's Opera,* it may be helpful to recall these books' historical resonance: for they serve as a kind of allusion to, or shorthand for, the famously elaborate accounting system used by the "Thief-taker General" Jonathan Wild (bap. 1683, d. 1725), generally understood to be the prototype for Peachum (though Empson points out Macheath's similarities to Wild as well). John Bender, articulating the larger historical significance of Wild's career, sees Wild as both benefitting from and, perhaps, contributing to—even perfecting—a set of bureaucratic principles whose full managerial potential was, at the time, only gradually becoming clear. Whereas the "old civic order had been lodged in personal operators," Bender explains, the early eighteenth century witnessed the displacement of this order by "the impersonality of written rules, regulations, and procedures"—and by "printed coordinates, advertising, and systematic reporting and dispatch."[47] It was precisely this new order—dependent, significantly, on the "written" and "printed"— whose power Wild both exploited and, thereby, confirmed.[48]

More specifically, as Bender explains, Wild made his fortune by "devis[ing] a system of indexed registers to keep track of London robberies." Himself the leader of a gang of thieves, Wild went about setting up a "lost property office," where he invited victims to come. Then, by "gaining detailed information about the circumstances of crimes from the victims" and correlating that information with his own careful records regarding his gang's yield, he was able to reunite stolen goods with their owners (for a price) and, at the same time, to learn immediately when a thief had "held back goods or otherwise betrayed him"—a circumstance that was itself profitable, of course, as disloyal thieves could then be "peached" in return for an informant's fee. By Bender's account, Wild's career thus becomes a spectacular testament to the power of "cross-referencing."[49]

Interestingly, given the specifically textual basis of Wild's methods, some of the most lucrative types of stolen goods, for Wild, were texts: account books, ledgers, receipt books, and records of transactions.[50] Such items fit perfectly with Wild's circular system (that is, of ransoming back the very items his gang had stolen) because, while the texts' market value was essentially null—and thus any punishment for their theft would be minimal—they were priceless to their owners, whose businesses (as Wild himself knew only too well) rose and fell on documents and documentation.[51]

In addition to profiting from such multifarious uses of hand-written business records, Wild deftly exploited print forms as well. As part of his work in the lost property office, according to Gerald Howson, Wild would "offer ... to advertise in the press for the [stolen] goods on [a] client's behalf."[52] The resulting advertisements—Howson finds "hundreds" in the newspapers of the time—served multiple devious purposes: citing, for example, an advertisement for a stolen account book, Howson explains that such a notice would have functioned to "allay ... the suspicions of the public, the authorities and, of course, the owner of the [stolen] books; it proved that Wild did not have the book himself; it served as a sign to the thieves that the owner was ready to come to terms; if Wild genuinely did not know who had stolen the books, it brought new thieves into his circle; and, finally, it made Wild's name familiar to the public in general."[53] Wild further managed his print-based public image via a "pamphlet-war" with former-collaborator-turned-Under-Marshal Charles Hitchen: when Hitchen attacked Wild and exposed his methods in a publication called "A Discovery of the Conduct of Receivers and Thief-Takers" (dedicated to the Lord Mayor), Wild replied with "AN ANSVVER TO A late Insolent LIBEL ... by *C—s H—n*. Wherein is prov'd in many particular Instances, who is Originally the GRAND *Thief-Taker*. ... Set forth in several Entertaining Stories, Comic Intrigues, [and] merry Adventures ... With a Diverting Scene of a *Sodomitish* Academy."[54] Here, in addition to answering Hitchen's accusations one by one and revealing Hitchen's own seamy past, Wild makes an unabashed claim for the pamphlet's "Entertain[ment]" value, clearly tapping into the popular market for criminal biographies and scandal sheets.

Even after finally being apprehended, Wild continued to exploit the print medium to his advantage. As Howson relates, upon his arrest, "pamphleteers began to circle round like vultures,"⁵⁵ and Wild agreed to an interview in *Applebee's Original Weekly Journal,* on condition that the journal also publish a list of the criminals Wild had most recently turned in to the authorities (that is, in his ostensible role as public servant). Meanwhile, however, lodged at the Old Bailey and awaiting trial, Wild seems to have taken matters into his own hands: he "went amongst the jurymen and others and gave out printed pamphlets whose purpose was to remind them of the great service he had done his country. Some of these pamphlets were copies of the list to be published by Applebee next day, [but] he was determined that the jury should read it in good time."⁵⁶ In a note appended to the list of criminals he had turned in, Wild insisted that his own current plight was merely the handiwork of those seeking revenge: "of the Numbers above convicted, some, that have yet escaped Justice," the pamphlet averred, were the very same men now lobbying for his death.⁵⁷ In the end this print campaign backfired: the editor of *Select Trials at the Old Bailey* later recounted that "The ... Council for the King took notice of the Prisoner's extraordinary Proceeding, in relation to the above-mention'd Papers," calling it an "unwarrantable" attempt to "prepossess and influence the Jury."⁵⁸ Unsuccessful as it may have been, this indeed "extraordinary" print campaign clearly speaks to the phenomenal textual cunning that defines every aspect, and every stage, of Wild's criminal career.⁵⁹

Although the specifics of Jonathan Wild's strategies do not turn up in *The Beggar's Opera,* they would seem to have been fundamental, in many ways, to the legend in which Peachum's character is embedded—a legend deeply familiar to both Gay and his eighteenth-century audiences. Gay needed only to place an account book in Peachum's hands and he had immediately conjured the whole world of text-based corruption that Wild pioneered. But Gay does more with the account books than simply use them as historically resonant stage-properties. He incorporates them into the dialogue that opens the play, and, indeed, builds them into the play's essential three-part structure. In this way Gay positions the account books at the crux of one of the play's driving questions: is all human experience inevitably mediated, scripted, and filtered through texts—whether in the form of commercial record-keeping or of literary conventions? Or is it possible to escape such textual prescription—through the embrace, instead, of a discretionary code of conduct, in which transactions are governed not by written forms but by one's word of honor, and of "natural" modes of expression? Or then again, Gay asks, might these two alternatives ultimately prove less divergent than they might seem?

In this section, I will trace the appearances of the account books over the course of the play: three times in all, once per act. I will then outline the apparent contrast Gay sets up between the account books' appearances and Macheath's three escapes in the play (also one per act). As this contrast builds, moreover, the account books become associated not just with writing and prescribed formula, but with the writing and literal "scripting" of the Beggar's (and Gay's) play; correspondingly, Macheath's final escape appears to be an escape not just from the death to which Peachum's accounting has sentenced him, but also from the reach of the Beggar's script, and indeed from all forms of textual mediation. Macheath's escape turns out to be less of an escape than it seems, however—and, likewise, the contrast between the impulsive freedom he claims to embody, on the one hand, and textual "bookkeeping," on the other (whether by Peachum or the Beggar-playwright), turns out to be less of a contrast than it had appeared.

In the next section, I go on to examine the role played by the songs of *The Beggar's Opera,* arguing that these songs epitomize, in many ways, the blurring of freedom and prescription, "natural" and capitalistic economies, that the rest of the play effects. In particular, by examining the songs' origins in a ballad tradition in which the notion of a pastoral past is already a nostalgic fiction, and from which print capitalism has seemingly never been absent,[60] we can come to understand the songs to be working in perfect parallel with Gay's satiric message.

As the first scene of act 1 begins, Peachum is seen *"sitting at a Table with a large Book of Accounts before him"*; following his famous opening song (in which he justifies his predatory worldview), he proceeds to embark upon a kind of dramatic reading from the account book, in the form of a roll-call of thieves and their thefts.[61] As Peachum reviews the data, it quickly becomes clear that the worth of a man's life, in Peachum's system, is calculated according to an algorithm: one thief has been "a Year and a half in the Service" and has yielded "one, two, three, four, five Gold Watches, and seven Silver ones"; another, "though he were to live these six months, will never come to the Gallows with any Credit" (1.3.4–19). In short, the profits that a thief brings in are divided by the amount of time served; and if the total is less than the forty-pound informant's fee that Peachum can earn for "peaching" his employees, then the thief will die. The account book thus symbolizes an approach to life in which formulae triumph over emotions, profit over morality. If, as we will see, Macheath's escapes seem to represent a victory for personal charm or charisma, then the account books represent the (apparent) opposite: a victory for anonymous, universally-applied principles that reduce persons to ciphers.[62]

As Michael Denning has pointed out, the direct counterpart to Peachum's roll-call of thieves—both thematically and dramatically—is Macheath's roll-call of prostitutes, in 2.4. As Denning notes, the contrast here is between "miserliness" and "prodigality," between "money" and "eros," and between "bourgeois" and "aristocrat" (though, as he points out, these "contraries" also prove entirely "interdependent" in the end).[63] But the apparent contrast is also a contrast between an ethos in which written information shapes how we relate to one another, versus an ethos in which direct personal relationships remain paramount. This latter outlook, like most of Macheath's purported values, resonates—in a distinctly "pastoral" manner—both with the notion of a tradition-steeped aristocracy and with the notion of an illiterate lower-class.

If Peachum assesses his employees according to their numerical data, Macheath reviews the prostitutes in the flesh (and by commenting on their fleshly attributes: "You look charmingly to-day," he greets Mrs. Coaxer [2.4.1–2]). If Peachum distinguishes individual thieves by a mark on the page—"set[ting] [their] Name[s] down in the Black-List" (4.4)—Macheath singles out each of the prostitutes with a kiss (although, as Jenny Diver will demonstrate, a kiss can constitute as acute a betrayal as Peachum's mark in the ledger[64]). And while Peachum's account book enforces a temporality cued to the larger administrative machinery that is the legal system—he grants his less profitable thieves "a Sessions or Two" longer to prove themselves—Macheath's timeframe is less regimented, cued instead to the women themselves and their (apparently unchanging) personalities: "are you as amorous as ever, Hussy?"; "Do you drink as hard as ever?" "As prim and demure as ever!"; "as careless and genteel as ever!" (2.4.3–17). While Peachum moves linearly down his row of entries, tallying his totals at the end of each term, Macheath watches the women swirl around him—they dance *"a la ronde"* in the ensuing song—circling, cycling back, "as ever."

This same set of contrasts may be expressed most vividly, however, not in the juxtaposition of these two individual scenes, but in the examination of the play's larger structure. As Denning has pointed out, *The Beggar's Opera* is in many ways punctuated by Macheath's three escapes, one per act. Yet a similar three-part structure is also provided by the appearances of the account books—also one per act. Interestingly, although Denning does not reference the three account-book scenes per se, he is already understanding the escapes to be working in contrast to everything that Peachum's books connote: thus, positing two types of law in the play, he sees Macheath's as a "discretionary system of law"—a law of "extravagance [and] personal favours," of "paternalism [and] ancient rights." This code of justice, he explains, stands opposed to Peachum's "rationalized law," which is instead a law "of counting and contracts."[65] And it is Macheath's "discretionary" law that forms the basis of each of his escapes, Denning avers—for all three, he suggests, "come from love": first Polly's love for Macheath, then Lucy's love for him, and finally that of the Beggar's projected audience (who, the Player thinks, could not bear to see a beloved character hang).[66] In the end, although Denning acknowledges that the play's heavily ironized final scenes do not constitute a "proper happy ending," he nonetheless deems these closing moments, via their privileging of "discretionary law," to be effecting a kind of "union"—I would add a particularly "pastoral" kind of union—"of the aristocracy and the people," over and against Peachum's bourgeois capitalism.[67] Gay forges this alliance, Denning believes, by giving the last word to the "rabble," who—in a twist on the topos of the royal pardon—are the ones who cry Macheath's "reprieve." Here, in contrast to the rigidity of Peachum's accounting system, a kind of democratic feudalism—a utopian alliance between aristocratic magnanimity and popular vote—carries the day, embodied by that high-class criminal, "Captain" Macheath.

However, by glossing over the specific role of the account books—by seeing them more as a general metaphor for Peachum's system of "counting and contracts" than as actual onstage objects whose appearances are carefully choreographed—I believe that we risk overemphasizing the differences between Peachum and Macheath, as well as the extent to which the play's ending favors the highwayman "hero."[68] To be sure, in acts 1 and 2 the account books and Macheath's escapes are neatly and carefully opposed, playing business off of pleasure, or (to use Denning's terms) money off of eros: thus in act 1 it is Peachum who pores over the account book, and it is his daughter Polly who first helps Macheath escape from the Peachums' house; when we next see an account book, in act 2, it is being consulted by Lockit (who holds it out for Peachum to see [2.10.4–6]), and, accordingly, it is Lockit's daughter Lucy who arranges for Macheath's escape from her jailor-father's domain. In the third pairing, however—the third consulting of the account books; the third escape—these clear lines of division begin to break down.

In act 3, as Peachum and Lockit again review the account books together (3.5), they no longer present a united front: whereas in act 2 they had agreed "to go halves on Macheath," now, following Macheath's escape from jail, Lockit has begun to suspect Peachum of plotting to keep all the profits to himself. Accordingly, Lockit has recently resolved, three scenes earlier, to "ply [Peachum with] . . . liquor, . . . get the secret from him, and turn this affair to my own advantage" (3.2): this is the intention with which he goes over the books with Peachum in 3.5. Interestingly, then, not only has Lockit diverged from Peachum at this point, but, in his plan to undermine his rival with liquor, he has now converged with his daughter, who, in a sequence following almost on the heels of this scene (3.7–10), is likewise attempting to overcome her own rival, Polly, with a stiff drink (this time a poisoned one). As scholars have pointed out, Lucy's ratsbane-laced cordial alludes directly to Handelian opera, with its heightened passions (such as the "Jealousy, rage, love, and fear [that] are at once tearing [Lucy] to pieces" [3.7]); by implication, then, the parallel between Lucy and Lockit in these scenes likewise associates Lockit with the emotive turmoil and frenzied passion which his apparent rationality and business-sense had previously seemed to oppose.

This same sense of subjectivity and instability, moreover, now seems to infect the whole accounting system: Lockit remarks that the account they are reviewing "is of so intricate a Nature, that I believe it will never be settled" (3.5.1–2). We might suspect this declaration to be serving merely as an excuse to start plying Peachum with brandy—except that Peachum agrees: "It consists indeed of a great Variety of Articles," he says (3.5.3). Peachum goes on to explain that the reason Lockit doesn't find any mention of "the Jewels" on the page they're perusing is that, being "so well known that they must be sent abroad," they have been "enter'd under the Article of Exportation" (3.5.12–15). In other words, it appears that a given item can be filed under any of a variety of different categories. Peachum reinforces this notion in his next sentence: "as for the Snuff-boxes, Watches, Swords, &c.—I thought it best to enter them under their several Heads," he notes, adding, a moment later, that "the Account of the last Half-Year's Plate is in a Book by it self, which lies at the other Office" (3.5.15–17, 3.5.23–24). In short, not only is the scene framed by Lockit's unbusinesslike (indeed, operatic and specifically feminized) passion, but the men's engagement with the account books themselves now exposes a system that is, in fact, rather dizzyingly amorphous: for although every item may be properly "sealed, numbered, and entered," the rules governing which goods fall under which heading, the number of headings, the number of books per account, even the number of offices in which to store the books, appear to shift before our eyes.[69] Where once the account books seemed to represent rationalized bureaucracy, they are now revealed to be much less rational: Peachum's accounting may be giving way here to an oddly Macheathian practice of "discretion," even "extravagance."[70]

If the third viewing of the account books shows them to be less clearly contrary to Macheath's worldview than they first appeared, so too, Macheath's third escape turns out to be less clearly contrary to Peachum's text-based ethos than we might expect. That is, his escape from the gallows returns him to a life entirely governed by contracts, strict accounting, and literally prescribed behavior. To understand how this comes to be the case, we first need to understand the confluence that occurs, in the second half of the play, between Peachum's account books and the Beggar-playwright's script.

Recall that, in act 2, as Peachum and Lockit perused the register together, they agreed "to go halves in Macheath," thus "booking" him (to use Peachum's phrase from act 1)—and, thereby, literally inscribing or scripting his capture.[71] I use the term "scripting" very consciously here: once marked for death in the account book, Macheath's fate is sealed by Peachum and Lockit, but also, we soon learn, by the play itself. "I hope you don't intend that Macheath shall be really executed," the Player says to the Beggar-playwright in the penultimate scene, but to no avail: "Most certainly, sir. To make the Piece perfect, I was for doing strict poetical Justice. Macheath is to be hanged" (3.16.1–4). Here the account book and the Beggar's (implied) playscript have become coextensive.

I should add that most critics have understood act 3's reference to "poetical Justice" differently: namely, as alluding to a set of common moral standards that the Beggar is then forced to jettison in a mercenary world. In this reading, it is not the Beggar's "poetical Justice" that aligns him with Peachum, but rather his abandonment of it when the "rabble" demands he do so. Such a conclusion is based partly on the Beggar's declaration that, after all, to implement the reversal (from tragic to comic ending) will be a task that is "easily" done, because "in [opera] 'tis no matter how absurdly things are brought about" (3.16.11–13): had he followed "poetical Justice," it seems, such injuries to good sense might have been avoided. However, Restoration-era commentators make clear that "poetical justice," too, can result in endings that are highly improbable: as Charles Gildon explained in 1692 (paraphrasing Aristotle in the *Poetics*), Euripides' dramas illustrated "poetic justice" by portraying incidents "as they ought to have" happened, whereas Sophocles' dramas "represented the Accidents of Human Life ... as they too often happen" in our own experience.[72] In other words, just like the happy endings of operas, poetical justice simply consists of its own set of conventions.

In this sense, poetical justice may be considered in light of the concept of the literary "contract" described by Jonathan Culler: the function of many writerly conventions, Culler explains, "is essentially to establish a contract between writer and reader so as to make certain expectations operative and thus to permit both compliance with and deviation from accepted modes of intelligibility."[73] Accordingly, the "justice" or fairness implied in "poetical justice" applies to a literary work's fictional characters, but also to the author and audience: as Culler elaborates, "The reader attends to characters in a different way if he is reading a tragedy or if he is reading a comedy": when, having given us comic cues, an author ends his story with a marriage, then he is not just rewarding his witty heroes; he is also rewarding us for having read his work in the way that he was implicitly asking us to do through his generic signaling. We agree to follow a certain set of interpretive rules, and, in return, the author must follow a certain set of compositional rules.

"Poetical justice," then, is simply a set of rules agreed to in advance. As such, it adheres to the same logic of contracts—over and against a logic of contingency or individual discretion—that governs Peachum's book of business. (For any thief who comes to work for Peachum has, essentially, already agreed to a set of terms whereby he will be hanged if and when his income falls short of the informant's fee: this contract is put into effect as soon as Peachum enters the thief's name into his book.)

Having understood both Peachum's ledgers and the Beggar's (implied) playscript as part of a larger system of score-keeping and written covenants, we can now view Macheath's final "escape" from a new angle. Although this third escape would seem to denote Macheath's circumvention of the destiny that both Peachum and the Beggar have prescribed for him, I would like to argue, instead, that the escape in fact represents Macheath's surrender to the logic of contracts and, even more broadly, the logic of the text. Recall that, having received his reprieve, Macheath returns to the stage not triumphantly, but rather with disgruntlement: "So, it seems, I am not left to my

Choice, but must have a Wife at last" (3.17.1–2). Turning to Polly's five rivals for this position—for, in addition to Lucy, four other women have just turned up, "with a Child a-piece," all claiming to be married to him—Macheath presents each with a dance partner (seemingly from among the "Rabble" in whose company he has reentered the stage), and then declares he'll "take *Polly* for mine," adding, in an aside to her, "—And for Life, you Slut,—for we were really marry'd" (3.17.9–10). Ironically, it is the very act of discarding the Beggar's playtext that has now scripted (as it were) Macheath's future, stripping him of his freedom of "Choice" (or the freedom not to have to make a choice).

The scriptedness of this new reality, moreover, is not just metaphorical but, most likely, literal: that is, it would seem that the legitimacy of Macheath's marriage to Polly—unlike that of the promises he made to Lucy (and apparently at least four other women)—lies in the fact that it has been textually ratified. Given the Peachums' horrified surprise upon learning of Polly's marriage to Macheath in act 1, we can assume that the ceremony took place in secret: according to Lawrence Stone, clandestine marriages of this sort, as long as they were "performed by some sort of clergyman, using the words prescribed in the Book of Common Prayer, . . . [were] recognized by both canon law and common law as legally binding"; they were usually further ratified by "a written entry into a marriage register (even if a private one), and often a written certificate."[74] Macheath's and Polly's marriage would seem to fit this description—not just in its secrecy, but also in what is apparently a grudging acknowledgment, on Macheath's part, that this marriage (unlike the others) is irrefutable: presumably the other "wives" have been joined to Macheath via "verbal spousals" only, which could rest on as tenuous a basis as a promise to marry someone in the future, provided that this promise was followed by physical consummation; while such marriages had been considered "culturally acceptable" since the Middle Ages, they were not recognized by the common law.[75] Significantly, then, the irrevocability of Macheath's and Polly's union seems to consist in its specifically textually-based—as opposed to orally- and physically-based—status: triply guaranteed by the Anglican liturgy, the written entry in the register, and the written certificate, the marriage has succeeded in "booking" Macheath, as it were, where Peachum's account book, and the Beggar's playbook, could not.

Going "off-script" would thus seem to have two sets of completely opposite ramifications for Macheath. On the one hand, dispensing with the playbook grants an escape from the letter of the law (both literary and jurisprudential). On the other hand, the reprieve that initially seemed to represent a victory of "love" over "counting and contracts" (to return to Denning's categories) now turns out to signal just the contrary—entrenching Macheath even more thoroughly within a logic of prescription, written records, and cross-referenceable documentation. In conclusion, if Peachum's and Lockit's third examination of the account books suggested that these texts' apparently rational authority was more subjective, emotional, and imprecise than we first believed, then Macheath's third "escape," likewise, suggests that the romantic extravagance we had attributed to him—epitomized, we may have believed, by his secret marriage to the daughter of his enemy—had in fact been governed by many of the same bookkeeperly principles we had associated (in the first two acts, at least) with Peachum and his ledgers.

Gay hints that not just Peachum and Macheath, moreover, but all of the characters in the play, keep a kind of script in mind—even those who would seem to harbor the play's last remnants of unmediated emotion and innocence. For example, one of Peachum's most recent recruits, Filch, despite descriptions pegging him as a kind of babe in the wood, turns out to be more textually adept than we initially realize. Mrs. Peachum, for her part, simultaneously infantilizes and feminizes him, declaring she is "as fond of this Child as though . . . he were my own," and praising him for having "as fine a Hand at picking a Pocket as a Woman" (1.6.1–3). But when Filch confesses his dread of being caught, her response is to advise him to "ev'n go to your Book, and learn your Catechism; for really a Man makes but an ill Figure in the Ordinary's Paper, who cannot give a satisfactory Answer to his Questions" (1.6.30–33). The Newgate Ordinary's (or chaplain's) "Paper," here, refers to the scandal sheet in which the chaplain infamously turned condemned criminals' confessions into tidy profits. Meanwhile, the "Book" Filch must study seems most explicitly to mean the Bible (prisoners able to read a biblical passage aloud—usually Psalm 51—could obtain benefit of clergy and escape execution). However, as Fuller speculates, the "Book" could also refer (again) to bound editions of the chaplain's "Paper," the careful study of which would allow Filch to fulfill generic expectations and thus cut the best "Figure" possible (note to 1.6.32). (Filch's hyperbolically precious declaration that he "fear[s] [he] shall be cut off in the Flower of [his] Youth" suggests, indeed, that he may already be fluent in the language of literary convention [1.6.20–21].) Of course, the term "book" can also denote a playbook, a connotation that encompasses the other two meanings as well: that is, for a thief to recite psalms, and/or to play up to the generic conventions of criminal biography, is also, quite literally, to learn his lines. Oddly, F.W. Bateson notes in own edition of the play that the actual Newgate Ordinary at this time was also a pastoral poet—suggesting an uncanny blurring between his "Paper," the Beggar's play, and Gay's own play; indeed, the Ordinary's paper thus becomes a potential rival not just to these play-texts but to Peachum's account book as well, in terms of determining the shape of the characters' lives.[76]

Polly is another character whose apparent ingénue status turns out, like Filch's, to be difficult to distinguish from her steepage in literary convention. Discussing with her parents the possibility of Macheath's death, she exclaims, "what is a Jointure, what is Widow-hood to me? I know my Heart. I cannot survive him"—to which Mrs. Peachum responds that "Those cursed Play-books she reads have been her Ruin," thus attributing Polly's sentiments not to a "know[n] Heart" at all, but to a well-studied text (1.10.52–53, 1.10.65–66). The notion that Polly's love is following a script (whether consciously or not) receives further support in Polly's famous speech in scene 12: "Now I'm a Wretch, indeed.—Methinks I see him already in the Cart, sweeter and more lovely than the Nosegay in his hand!—I hear the Crowd extolling his Resolution and Intrepidity! . . . I see him at the Tree! The whole Circle are in Tears!—Even Butchers weep! Jack Ketch himself hesitates to perform his duty, and would be glad to lose his Fee by a Reprieve. What then will become of Polly?" (1.12.1–9). Despite the fact that Polly stands alone onstage while speaking these lines—there is no directly rhetorical purpose behind them—the language obviously mimics a verbal style that *is* intended to move its audience (most immediately, perhaps, the "she-tragedies" of Nicholas Rowe[77]). Here we have the minor-yet-telling detail used for effect ("Even Butchers weep!"), as well as the (mock-) pastoral tropes invoking nature amidst a scene of crowded urban streets (yet another thief is linked, here, with delicate flowers). The archaic diction ("Methinks") and the use of the third person ("What then will become of Polly?") add further to the distinctly literary feeling of the oration.

The notion that Polly is somehow a character in her own story—or possibly in Macheath's—is echoed in the ensuing air, in which Macheath substitutes Polly's name for "Parrot" in the song "Pretty Parrot, Say": he thus suggests that Polly is both a reciter of empty phrases as well as a stock character or type. ("Polly" serves as a generic name for any parrot, just as the name "Jack Ketch" serves, in Polly's own speech, as a generic name for any executioner.[78]) When, as the song ends, Polly assures Macheath that "I have no Reason to doubt you, for I find in the Romance you lent me, none of the great Heroes were ever false in Love" (1.13.15–17), we receive a further indication that Polly is filtering her reality (and Macheath's) through literary models and literary language.

Polly's use of texts may seem different than that of the other characters: if her parents, Filch, and Macheath use books cynically—as instruments of calculation and manipulation—Polly would seem to wield her playbooks and romances more naively (depending on how the role is performed, of course). If the others use books as tools to control reality, Polly uses them (intentionally or not) to dream up alternative realities. In the end, however, Gay suggests there may be as little distinction between these textual practices as there is between Peachum's account books and Macheath's escapes. For, oddly, Polly's quixotic vision of Macheath at the gallows is, essentially, borne out in the penultimate moments of the play (right down to the reprieve): indeed, as has been pointed out, Polly's evocation of "the whole Circle ... in Tears" simultaneously denotes the gathered crowd at Tyburn—public executions serving as a form of free theater—and a tier of seating at the actual theater (perhaps even the Royal Theatre, where *The Beggar's Opera* was being staged). Polly's vision here, then, turns out—like her father's account books—to be yet another rival to the Beggar's (and Gay's) playscript. In short, the concept of raw emotion, uninformed by written genres, is shown to be a fantasy—indeed, a fantasy shaped by the literary conventions of pastoral.

I now want to suggest the several ways in which the songs in *The Beggar's Opera* emblematize, in condensed form, the same collapse of pastoral performativity and commercial textuality that we have seen borne out in Gay's characterizations of Peachum and Macheath. More acutely than any other element in the play, perhaps, the songs seem to raise the possibility (familiar to us by now from *The What D'Ye Call It*) of a performance that could break free of its text, thus unleashing an emotional truth unmediated by literate culture or market values: as Susan Stewart writes, "The ballad is ... a form continually marked by immediacy—immediacy of voice, immediacy of action, immediacy of allusion."[79] And many scholars have understood Gay's ballads as offering up just such an experience.[80] Thus Steve Newman asserts, "Unlike nearly every other action, linguistic and otherwise, in *The Beggar's Opera*, the songs resist being turned to advantage by the ... characters in the play."[81]

Yvonne Noble, similarly, declares that the play's ballads "serve powerfully to mitigate the divisive effect of Gay's satiric treatment of English society" by "their testimony to the culture that all Englishmen, of whatever class or occupation, have in common, 'by heart.'"[82] In this way, Noble believes, *The Beggar's Opera*'s musical airs create a "redeem[ing] ... circle of song" for characters and audience alike.[83] However, I argue that Gay prevents us from entering into this dream of generous, "heart"-felt immediacy in part by exploiting the inherent doubleness of the ballad form (again, a doubleness already hinted at in *The What D'Ye Call It*'s use of ballads). For like any modern pastoral (and perhaps like any pastoral ever), the ballad turns out to be inseparable from an imperial commerce of letters.

As Paula McDowell notes, the nineteenth-century belief that "traditional" ballads could somehow be separated from "vulgar" broadside ballads has remained stubbornly persistent even into the twenty-first century.[84] In fact, however, the two strands appear essentially undifferentiable: as she and other scholars have argued, the very notion of a "traditional" ballad culture seems actually to be the result of growing anxieties surrounding a newly market-driven, print-based literary world.[85] In their Janus-faced way, then, ballads come ready-made, as it were, for Gay's purposes—perfectly complementing his use of character groupings in his play: even as ballads conjure a pastoral harmony between aristocrats and manual laborers, they betray distinctly mercantile roots, as evidenced by their long association with print,[86] and thus with texts as market commodities. Of course, as is well known, Gay generates additional ironies by setting his own lyrics to familiar tunes, thus creating a juxtaposition between the "traditional" words and his often-satiric verses: again, however, upon further examination, most of the songs he employs actually come with their own alternative lyrics built in, which frequently (like Gay's) already function parodically. Accordingly, Gay's "pastoral" material is already, in a sense, "mock pastoral" before he even touches it (in the same way that Macheath is already a kind of parody of himself even without Gay having to belabor his parallels with Peachum—so that the parallels simply expose the instability that is already there).

The presence of opera in *The Beggar's Opera* has often complicated scholarly attempts to understand the ballads' role: Gay's playfully mocking stance toward the ballads themselves is often overlooked in the effort to see the ballads as a "grittily real" counterpoint to the "airy confections" of eighteenth-century London's Italian opera craze.[87] However, I would argue that Gay sees opera as simply another form of pastoral that already contradicts itself: although opera during this period in England seems to have catered to a super-elite audience for whom money was no object,[88] and although it depicted heroic and tragic worlds in which financial concerns are similarly disavowed, it also gained notoriety as a site of prodigious expenditure and jaw-dropping salaries. Thus Gay writes in his oft-quoted letter to Swift (1722): "as for the reigning Amusement of the town, tis entirely Musick.... Theres nobody allow'd to say I sing but an Eunuch or an Italian Woman.... People have now forgot Homer, and Virgil & Caesar, or at least they have lost their ranks, for in London and Westminster in all polite conversation's [sic] Senesino is daily voted to be the greatest man that ever liv'd."[89] Here, in contrast to truly "great" art forms such as the work of Homer and Virgil (whose own declarations of "I sing" convey all the heroic strength of their subject matter), opera's heroism is effeminate, dominated by castrati such as Senesino, whose incomes were perhaps as famous as their voices: Nokes writes that "the huge salaries paid to singers were a constant subject of newspaper gossip" and mockery[90]; and Hume attributes the astronomical sums to the same frenzy of speculative spending that led to the contemporaneous South Sea Bubble.[91] I would suggest, accordingly, that Gay is not so much holding up the ballad as a rebuke to the operatic aria as he is suggesting a parallel: both opera and the ballad tradition represent similar, "modern" endeavors to reclaim an elusive precommercial past, but both end up revealing themselves to be objects of commodification—a commodification just as unseemly in the fashionable cults surrounding the lavishly-paid castrati as it is in the demand for the ballad-mongers' cheaply-printed wares.[92] Ultimately, then, I propose that by understanding the ballads in *The Beggar's Opera* both as performances but also as print-cultural artifacts par excellence—both as pastoral relics and (therefore) as capitalistic commodities—we can better understand their relationship to the play's internal thematics, in which pastoral fantasy is revealed to be suffused with a "modern" account-book logic.

Ballad lyrics frequently posit the union between aristocrats and commoners that Empson identifies as central to all pastoral. Such a union can be seen in the high-low span of typical ballad subject matter: recurrent characters include not only King Arthur, Fair Rosamund, and Jane Shore, but also folk heroes such as Dick Whittington and Robin Hood.[93] However, this conception of the ballad as insistently "feudal" (joining rich and poor in a precapitalist, land-based world) seems almost calculated to dissimulate the ballad's embeddedness in commercial print. As Adam Fox points out in his book *Oral and Literate Culture in England, 1500–1700,* although we tend to imagine that "the ditties of women at their spinning[,] ... the lullabies of the nursery fire, or the catches of tinkers and the harmonies of harvesters" are simply "the stuff of unmediated oral tradition," in fact all "evidence suggests the permeating influence of print": printed broadsides could frequently be found pasted up on nursery chimneys and stuck onto the walls of country alehouses.94 Songs may have comprised part of a communal tradition, and may have been learned by heart, but this vernacular repertoire was, "in fundamental ways[,] ... being structured and determined by ... print," and thus by the larger literate and market-based culture to which it was central.95

This inseparability of ballads from print commerce was becoming particularly visible in the early eighteenth century: Dianne Dugaw identifies the 1723 *Collection of Old Ballads* as "the first antiquarian collection of ballads" in that it anticipates, in its self-conscious unearthing of "*the best and most Ancient Copies Extant*" (according to the full-length title), the so-called ballad revival of the Romantic period. The collection was anonymously published by James Roberts, "the largest job-printer in London at the time," according to Dugaw, and the publisher of "many of the pamphlets and novels of Daniel Defoe and Eliza Haywood."96 Volume 1 sold out and went into a second edition only two months after publication; a second volume was published later that year, and a third volume in 1725. A third edition of volume 1 was printed in 1727, and a second edition of the whole three-volume set came out eleven years later. As Dugaw points out, this venture was clearly a great "commercial success," appealing to what she calls "a mid-level readership"97—one presumably imbricated in Britain's growing trade economy.

Of course, ballad collections did not acknowledge this commercial basis outright. One of the most influential collections, the six-volume *Wit and Mirth, or Pills to Purge Melancholy* (published starting in 1698 but revamped by the poet Thomas D'Urfey in his own edition of 1719), provides a good example of this disavowal: in the front matter to the 1719 edition, D'Urfey lists the royalty whom he had previously entertained with his "Lyrical Performances" of many of the songs featured in the collection—including Charles II, James, William and Mary, Anne, and George I—thus hearkening back to an aristocratic patronage system, as well as a culture of court "Performance" in which art takes the form of ephemeral entertainments rather than material commodities. And although D'Urfey published *Wit and Mirth* by subscription, he is at pains to link the practice of subscription to this older model of patronage, by dedicating it to "*To the Right Honourable the Lords and Ladies, and also the Honoured Gentry of both kinds, that have been Generous to be Subscribers of these Volumes of SONGS,*" thus reiterating the elite status of his audience, and casting their financial support as "genero[sity]" rather than consumption. However, *Wit and Mirth* in fact draws in large part from a number of cheap printed sources: the scholar Cyrus Day speculates that many of the ballads had previously been printed as single-sheet songs, which would have sold "for a penny apiece, and were extremely popular"; he cites a 1701 advertisement for the first two (pre-D'Urfey) volumes, which assures potential buyers that here they "will find most of the single Songs that ha[ve] been Cutt on Copper for these Ten Years Past."[98] Even as D'Urfey's compilation seems to strive for a kind of pastoral performativity untainted by commerce, then—in which aristocrats patronize the "Lyric Performances" of communal folksongs—his edition is actually built on a foundation of popular print retail.

If the ballad as a genre simultaneously perpetuates a myth of precommercial roots while nonetheless owing its continued existence to the print marketplace, so too does the subject matter of individual ballads often reflect a similar contradiction. Many discussions of *The Beggar's Opera* often seem to assume that Gay was the first to invent "modern" parodic lyrics for older, "traditional" tunes; but as the examples below will demonstrate, he is in fact working within what appears to be a long history. For instance, the most widespread versions of "O the Broom" (whose melody Gay reuses in air 18) tell the story of a shepherdess seduced while milking her father's ewes; but other lyrics to the same tune enact satiric transpositions of this cliché. One seventeenth-century version, for example, tells of a man seduced by "Cards, Dice, and Queanes,"[99] thus turning the story of a rural loss of innocence into the story of a much more squalid, urban, and commercially-tinged kind of loss. Whether Gay knew of this version or not, he carries on the parodic custom in which it is written: thus, in Gay's rendering of the song, Macheath sings cynically of the sorrow of a "Miser" having to give up a "Shilling."

Gay's participation in a longer parodic tradition vis-à-vis familiar tunes can likewise be seen in his air 41, the melody for which is borrowed from "If Love's a sweet Passion" (from Purcell's 1692 opera-masque *The Fairy Queen*). Gay's lyrics mock the original song's courtly sentiments by comparing a young woman's granting of sexual favors to running up a tab "at the Bar," thus juxtaposing romance with lust, runaway passion with less lofty forms of intoxication. However, an earlier parody, from 1693, is titled—and the title alone gives a good sense of the song's contents—"The London Lottery: Or, Simple Susan, the Ambitious Damsel of Bishopgate-street, Who pawn'd her Night-rail and Smock, with other Apparel, for raising Money, in hopes to gain the Lot of three thousand Pound, or two thousand five hundr'd at least."[100] Here again, then, it would seem that Gay's own parody is part of an established practice of confronting fanciful love songs with the hard realities of urban life and modern finance.

The satirical dynamics become all the more complicated in a song such as Gay's air 16 (a duet by Macheath and Polly: "Were I laid on Greenland's Coast, / And in my Arms embrac'd my Lass; / Warm amidst eternal Frost, / Too soon the Half Year's Night would pass"). As Dugaw notes, the lyrics' reference to Greenland "connotes the innocent 'green-world' of pastoral literature, especially framed as it is in celebration of an all-saving love"; but when we recall the better-known lyrics to the same tune, "Over the Hills and Far Away"—which tell the story of a lover's betrayal—this green-world fantasy is punctured.[101] Then again, as Dugaw points out, "the realities of the actual 'Greenland' [already] intrude" on Gay's song—even apart from the echoes with "Over the Hills": Greenland would have evoked criminal transportation and the imperial project to which it contributed. And yet, Gay was not the first to pair "Over the Hills" with such associations: to cite just one example, D'Urfey's "The Hubble Bubbles" (1720), a song about the South Sea Bubble set to the same melody, transforms the original theme of a treacherous lover into one of corrupt colonial investment schemes.[102] In D'Urfey's version too, then, the rolling "hills" of the better-known lyrics are already replaced by the backdrops of imperial exploitation.

In using the ballad form for *The Beggar's Opera,* Gay thus imports into his play not a timeless culture of pastoral folksong, as many scholars have assumed, but a long lineage of mock-pastoral. As much as the songs may evoke a premodern world of rustic feudalism, the publication histories of the ballads Gay incorporates tend to reveal close ties to a global exchange economy. So too, the various extant versions of the ballads' lyrics reflect a long history of parody in which homespun sentiment is constantly being juxtaposed with urban venality. (The sheer number of ballads whose plots center around stolen virginity or romantic treachery hints, indeed, at a fundamental preoccupation, inherent to the ballad, with innocence lost.) The reluctance of scholars to acknowledge the doubleness intrinsic to the material Gay is appropriating suggests the striking durability, nearly three centuries after *The Beggar's Opera*'s premiere, of the pastoral desire to posit a prelapsarian culture from which modern society has parted ways—to believe in a purer world that preexisted our own debased reality.

But to acknowledge that the ballad tradition already contains its own parody within itself—and that Gay is drawing upon and compounding this dynamic—simply illustrates further what I have been describing, throughout this chapter, as the inherent doubleness of all pastoral literature. That is, all pastoral literature must inevitably include shadows of its own perverse parody, because its basic premise—the disavowal of its commercial elements—is innately unstable. Indeed, perhaps the same could be said of the modern print canon more generally, which must continually insist upon its aesthetic and moral value so as to prevent its capitalist origins from coming back to haunt it.

The history of *The Beggar's Opera*'s publication and reception further reiterates the layers of interrelations between print and pastoral that I have just been pointing to within the play and its ballad sources. For not just Gay, but publishers and audiences, too, it seems, embraced *The Beggar's Opera*'s own status as a print commodity. Interestingly, it is the songs of *The Beggar's Opera* in particular that, in the material history of the play's reception, appear most conducive to commodification in print. (This fact seems both unsurprising, given the inseparability of print from the songs' earliest iterations, and yet also counterintuitive, when we consider that it is the songs that seem to hold out the play's most palpable promise for redemption from the cynical commercialism of the London that Gay depicts.)

Perhaps the clearest illustration of the rapid embrace of Gay's songs as commodities can be seen in the second edition of *The Beggar's Opera*. First, this edition introduces a numbering system for the airs, from I to LXIX, thus hinting that purchasers of the play-text may have wanted to be able to identify and refer to the songs at a glance.[103] This edition in fact devotes three pages to a "Table of the Songs," a device that downplays the airs' narrative or dramatic context in favor of their status as stand-alone, endlessly repeatable favorites: although the songs are listed in the order in which they occur in the play, and are even divided by act, the provided page numbers allow the reader to skip over the surrounding scenes to arrive directly at the song itself; nor does the table provide any information about which character sings each song. Indeed, the Table of Songs precedes the dramatis personae, suggesting that the question of who sings what to whom (and when) is perhaps, in some sense, irrelevant: the whole point is that the reader him- or herself can now access them at will, in whatever context he or she chooses.[104]

Moreover, although *The Beggar's Opera* famously inspired numerous other artistic and narrative responses (mezzotints of Lavinia Fenton [who played Polly]; Hogarth's well-known images; further accounts of the life of Macheath), in many instances it is the songs themselves that seem to be turned, with the most ease and success, into what we might call the play's "spin-off" merchandise.[105] The *Daily Journal* for May 23, 1728 announces, "To-morrow will be Published, a New and entertaining Fan, consisting of the most Favourite Songs, taken out of the Beggar's Opera, with the Musick in proper Keys within the Compass of the Flute; curiously engraved on a Copper Plate. Sold for the Author, at Mr. Gay's Head, in Tavistock-street, Covent-Garden. Price Is. 6d."[106] William Schultz likewise describes a "set of playing cards apparently printed during the original run . . . , each [featuring] a different song" from the play: "The title of the air and the name of the character who sang it are given, followed by the music," scored for voice and apparently sometimes flute; "the words [are] printed as a verse stanza. . . . The actual playing card symbols are in small squares in the upper left-hand corners."[107] This product seems remarkable for a number of reasons: first (and no doubt the original purchasers would have enjoyed this, too), the very idea of the set raises the amusingly apt possibility of players using *Beggar's-Opera*-themed cards to gamble, bluff, and perhaps even cheat. But second, it is interesting to consider what happens to the status of the music here: while the purchaser might conceivably have used the cards as pocket-sized song sheets, to use them *as cards* would essentially necessitate treating the songs as little more than decorations (given that launching into a rendition of the contents of one's hand seems like a good way to lose the game). Here, then, Gay's airs, endlessly shuffleable, and prized not for their musical or verbal features but their monetary value—that is, in the context of the consumer market but also in the context of a game potentially being played for money—have come as close as they possibly can, it seems, to sheer print commodities.[108]

Print and performance; commerce and pastoralism: these terms appear less overtly in *The Beggar's Opera* than they do in *The What D'Ye Call It*. Yet subtle, repeated references to books—Peachum's and Lockit's account books;

the Beggar-author's implied script; the pages Filch studies; Polly's playbooks and romances—combine to create a sense of the oppressively prescriptive power of texts, and of the corrupt capitalistic system in which they play a central role. Performance, meanwhile, and the supposedly pastoral code of honor that Macheath appears to represent ("pastoral" because natural, ancient, and simultaneously aristocratic yet ingenuous), would seem, at first, to promise an avenue of escape from this system—and yet both the performative and the pastoral turn out to blur treacherously with everything they ostensibly oppose. However, it is finally in the ballads themselves (and, interestingly, their reception) that these concepts all come together: it is here that pastoral nostalgia and print capitalism, embodied performance and scripted words, form a kind of precarious, subversive whole. Through this explosive amalgam Gay at once tempts us with the notion of a ritualistic, premonetized mode of expression and exposes that notion as pure fiction; he at once offers up the prospect of a preliterary literariness yet at the same time sweeps it away. Most importantly to my own argument here, he does so by exploiting the fissures inherent to drama—by opposing script to performance, then showing the two to be mutually dependent; by setting text against body, then revealing the effects of each to rely upon, to have always relied upon, the other.

The Beggar's Opera premiered in the same year Alexander Pope published his first version of *The Dunciad*. Clearly Gay, like Pope, was expressing his growing concern that the field of literature—a category first made visible and coherent by booksellers, and with the support of a growing population of "polite" book buyers—was now being corrupted by those same forces (namely, the commercial interests of the print marketplace) which had once ensured the field's liberation from court politics and patrons' whims. However, while Gay shares these concerns with his fellow Scriblerians, he is unique among his generation—though at the same time he is also part of a venerable history, as my previous chapters have shown—in that he is attempting to wrestle with this problem through the dramatic mode.

For by harnessing not just print but also performance, Gay experiments with the possibility that "literary" value might be reclaimed through those elements of human expression that are not, in fact, "lettered": the oral, the somatic, the communal. In some ways, Gay's experiment fails, as the pastoral performances in his plays turn out to be just as susceptible as print to the forces of modernity, commerce, self-interest, and empire. In other ways, however, the experiment succeeds, as Gay reveals the opposite to be true as well—that is, as he reveals the extent to which printed reading matter is likewise inextricably bound up with a culture of embodied performance, and with a desire (even if that desire is never realized) to return to some more "natural," "authentic" version of human existence. By thus juxtaposing drama's twin components of textuality and theatricality, Gay—like Shadwell, Behn, and Congreve before him—seeks to complicate our understanding of "literature" as a category dependent solely on reading, books, and the print marketplace.

CONCLUSION

THE MID- TO LATE SEVENTEENTH century witnessed the formation of a distinct field of imaginative writing in English. Yet the crucial role of the book trade in curating and marketing this field meant that the emergent literary canon developed specifically in relation to a print-centric system of values, prioritizing cultural preservation and posterity, disembodied modes of consumption, and the notion of words as a commodity with an assigned price. Each of the dramatists featured in this study worked to second-guess these priorities, or even to redefine them, specifically by tapping into the inherently media-straddling, destabilizing potential of the dramatic form. Each playwright approached this task from his or her own angle. But together, Shadwell, Behn, Congreve, and Gay—and one could supplement this list, I believe, with a number of additional Restoration dramatists—contested the role of print, and of the specific kinds of cultural forces that print seemed to represent, in demarcating the concept of the literary. In this brief conclusion, I hope to sketch the ways in which the questions Restoration playwrights raised in their work would continue to guide ongoing debates about literature. Indeed, I suggest that it is these dramatists' influential contributions to the conversation that help to explain, in part, why the writer who came to be nearly synonymous with English literature in the following decades was, primarily, a writer of plays.[1]

To claim that Shakespeare's literary apotheosis owes ultimately to his status as a dramatist might seem counterintuitive: after all, scholars have tended to ascribe the Bard's cultural ascendancy specifically to an increasing emphasis on his plays as reading texts. However, I contend that, in fact, eighteenth-century readers' obsession with Shakespeare on the page was always shaped by the specter of the stage. Whether in their efforts to establish authoritative editions of the plays (thus shielding them from the variations introduced by iterative performances), or in treating his dramatis personae as quasi-novelistic figures (rather than as roles to be acted), those working to affirm Shakespeare's literariness in the eighteenth century were driven in part by their very awareness of his plays' inescapably neither-nor status—of the dangerous, shape-shifting force that the stage exerts on the page. And it is this cultural attunement to the complex doubleness of the dramatic mode that the Restoration playwrights had first worked to leverage in new and generative ways.

By most accounts, Shakespeare's elevation to National Poet had little to do with his having been a playwright per se; indeed, his literary beatification is typically said to have occurred simultaneously with his textualization—and, concomitantly, with his disassociation from the theater. As Fiona Ritchie and Peter Sabor point out, "Although David Garrick has been widely credited as the driving force behind Shakespeare's popularity in the eighteenth century, [in fact] Shakespeare had already achieved cultural prominence by the time the actor made his debut on the London stage on 19 October 1741," and a main reason for this prominence, they note, was Shakespeare's printed presence: by the late 1730s "the price war between publishers Jacob Tonson and Robert Walker [had] made cheap editions of individual Shakespeare playtexts readily available, increasing the public's access to his works."[2] This plethora of printed editions led to a situation in which by mid-century, as Jean Marsden puts it, Shakespeare's works "were as frequently read as seen," so that the "process of canonization" was one "in which the words themselves were sanctified,"[3] while editor after editor sought fervently for a "genuine text."[4] As evidenced by what Marsden views as the increasingly conservative attitude held by these editors, it was "the words of [Shakespeare's] text" that were "increasingly seen as the essence of his greatness."[5]

Michael Dobson's narrative of Shakespeare's rise differs from Marsden's history in that he sees Shakespeare's texts as undergoing quite frequent tamperings in the period. He points, for example, to John Bell's 1773–74 edition, which was praised in the *Monthly Review* for "expung[ing] ... the [plays'] deformities" in favor of their "beauties" so as to better "accommodate ... the taste of an age more refined than that in which the Author lived and wrote."⁶ Yet Dobson nonetheless sees such emendations as marks of, if not an increased sacralization of the text, then certainly a detheatricalization of it. Ironically, Dobson sees Garrick himself as a key figure in the transformation of Shakespeare's plays into "closet drama": in "marketing... Shakespeare to eighteenth-century theatre-goers as an exemplar of bourgeois morality," Dobson explains, Garrick may have "reclaimed the Bard for the stage in his own lifetime," but ultimately served to "domesticat[e] ... literature's last truly public sphere"—namely, the theater—by associating Shakespeare's oeuvre with the values of middle-class home life.⁷ Dobson sees the same impulse infusing later projects such as the Bowdlers' 1807 *Family Shakespeare,* which was "intended solely to be read in the home," as well as such editions as the Lambs' 1807 *Tales from Shakespeare,* which, as Dobson notes, seems bent on "rescu[ing]" the plays "from being drama at all."⁸

Despite Marsden's and Dobson's diverging views of how Shakespeare's texts were treated, they reach a similar conclusion regarding the plays' gradual sloughing off of their theatrical or even dramatic features in favor of the printed page. Transformed into objects of private study and thoughtful examination, the plays are purged of their association with entertainment and live performance. It is only a short step from this cultural attitude to Charles Lamb's notorious claim—to which we will return in a moment—that Shakespeare's great tragic characters are "essentially impossible to be represented on a stage."⁹

Yet I would argue that it is precisely because Shakespeare's plays *are* plays that critics' equation of him with "the literary" remains so insistent. In other words, it is drama's position halfway between page and stage, its complex relationship to the present and the past, its blurring of the line between material and immaterial, its split loyalties to immediacy and permanence, and its dual identity as a deeply human but also thoroughly commercial product that help to focus our attention on the elemental ambiguities with which, indeed, literature itself remains eternally occupied. More specifically, though, it is the Restoration playwrights who, I have been contending, first systematically mine these capacities within drama in order to disentangle print values from literary values, and it is therefore these playwrights' work that aids subsequent critics in apprehending the same tensions within the work of Shakespeare.

Several hallmarks of mid- to late eighteenth-century Shakespeare criticism may be shown to originate, I think, within the intellectual and historical contexts examined in this book.[10] These hallmarks include: (1) the perception of Shakespeare's relationship to his literary predecessors as non-classical, improvisatory, and even "feminine"—in contrast to more overtly "textual" and conservative modes of inheritance practiced by his authorial foil, Ben Jonson; (2) the perpetual but perpetually unfinished project to stabilize Shakespeare's texts—in certain cases surviving only in the form of actors' copies—into some permanent, authoritative version; and (3) the repeated synonymizing of Shakespeare with "Nature" to an extent that seems to offer an escape, to readers and audiences alike, from the commercialism of modern urban life. Each of these three critical concerns, I believe, can be traced back to theoretical cruxes I explore earlier in this study. However, the real signature of eighteenth-century Shakespeare criticism, which I will discuss in the most detail in the pages that follow, is (4) its concern with "character." This is a fixation that stems back, I suggest, to the Restoration's fundamental reconsiderations of the relationships between imagination and bodily sensation, reading and spectating.

I therefore echo, but also expand upon, Paulina Kewes's claim that Shakespeare's exalted cultural position owes to historical changes that commence within the world of Restoration drama.[11] Kewes stresses the economic structures during this period that allowed Restoration dramatists to become England's first proprietary authors, thereby pioneering a cultural role that Shakespeare would later inhabit so definitively.[12] What I hope to demonstrate here, by contrast, is that the plays being written in the late seventeenth century contributed to Shakespeare's unrivaled stature in English literature not just because of the monetary (and social) value attached to writing for the stage during this era but also because of Restoration drama's larger theoretical contribution—that is, (1) because of the continual efforts, by the period's playwrights, to question the growing sense that an emergent concept of "literature" was entirely reliant on concepts of print, and (2) because of their insistence, in so doing, on drama's unique ability (as a medium split between print and performance) to facilitate this questioning process. This contribution, I argue, provided the intellectual building blocks for

England's first Shakespearean scholars, while at the same time ensuring that the nation's poet of poets would—almost necessarily, as it were—be a playwright.

In the next few pages, I detail briefly the ways in which the print-based values of stability, mental abstraction, permanence, and proprietary authorship—values under pressure in the work of the playwrights I have been examining in this book—contribute to the deification of Shakespeare by the end of the eighteenth century. Counterintuitively, however, my argument is that these values contribute to Shakespeare's rise not because they had become increasingly and ineluctably entrenched in English culture over time, but rather because the playwrights in this book had called them into question—and because drama was their forum of choice as they undertook this questioning. I then turn to a well-known essay by Charles Lamb (1811) in order to discuss the ways in which "character," the critical focus most often associated with the eighteenth- and nineteenth-century reception of Shakespeare (and, more specifically, with Shakespeare's detheatricalization), can in fact be traced back to the Restoration and, thereby, to a Restoration-influenced appreciation of drama as the medium that—as a kind of hybrid creature—remains best suited to highlighting the particular fusion of mind and body, imagination and action, that defines who we are as human beings.

One of the attributes that helped make Shakespeare "Shakespeare" in the eighteenth century was his orientation toward classical source texts. Although Shakespeare's plays draw liberally on all kinds of earlier material for their plots, characters, and language—and although scholars in the eighteenth century were increasingly recognizing these borrowings—the fact remained that Shakespeare still seemed to have had (in Jonson's phrasing) "small Latin and less Greek."[13] This lack of classical learning placed Shakespeare in a different position vis-à-vis the past than other English contenders for canonicity. Moreover, when Shakespeare did avail himself of others' stories (such as in his use of Thomas North's translation of Plutarch's *Lives*), he tended not to draw attention to these borrowings—so that, as Stephen Orgel writes, "the only difference between [Jonson's] use of Tacitus and Shakespeare's of North is that Jonson liked to boast about it."[14] Whereas Jonson strategically advertised his relationship to previous texts as authorizing and legitimizing his own work, Shakespeare did not.

This apparent departure from the classical tradition of *imitatio*, however, aligned Shakespeare with a more modern understanding of authorship, in which invention and innovation figure centrally. Indeed, Jack Lynch posits that the very idea of "genius," so central to nineteenth- and twentieth-century conceptions of the artist, developed partly out of the eighteenth century's interest in how Shakespeare departed from practices of classical allusion.[15] Yet, as we have seen, the kernels of these concepts—that is, of the author as innovator, if not yet as "genius"—may be said first to emerge in the world of Restoration drama. Not coincidentally, the first writer to study Shakespeare's sources in detail was Gerard Langbaine, in 1691.[16]

Chapter 1 highlighted Restoration notions of literary property via the example of Shadwell—who acknowledged his sources only selectively, thus rejecting a Drydenian model of stylistic or textual succession in favor of one that prizes improvisation, creativity, and even the occasional misappropriation. Shadwell's use of textual apparatus underscored his departure from traditional notions of bookly authority in favor of theatrical éclat. But he also writes this tension into his plots: whereas *The Squire of Alsatia*'s Sir William Belfond advocates an inheritance model that emphasizes the conservation and consolidation of assets—and that relies, in part, on texts to effect these tasks—Sir Edward and Belfond Junior prefer (like Shadwell) a model that privileges dynamism and dispersal. Similarly, whereas *The Lancashire Witches*' Sir Edward Hartfort represents a form of power founded on patriarchal lineage (seemingly symbolized by the play's extensive annotative system, in which male authors seek to control female bodies through textual scholarship), the witches—again, more like Shadwell himself—short-circuit traditional modes of male inheritance via their own spectacular acts of creation.

Interestingly, this alternative mode of dramaturgical inheritance posited by Shadwell in the early 1680s—one in which a writer's legitimacy is proven through his ability to adapt the work of his dramatist forebears as a live audience demands, rather than through attempts to establish a strict textual lineage—had, as early as the 1670s, been associated with Shakespeare, too. In her preface to *The Dutch Lover* (1672), Behn defends her play against gender-based attacks:

> Plays have no great room for that which is men's great advantage over women, that is Learning; We all well know that the immortal Shakespeare's plays (who was not guilty of much more of this than often falls to women's

share) have better pleas'd the World than Johnson's works, though by the way 'tis said that Benjamin was no such Rabbi neither, for I am inform'd that his Learning was but Grammar high ... and it hath been observ'd that they are apt to admire him most confoundedly, who have just such a scantling of it as he had; and I have seen a man the most severe of Johnson's Sect, sit with his Hat remov'd less than a hair's breadth from one sullen posture for almost three hours at *The Alchymist;* who at that excellent Play of *Harry the Fourth* (which yet I hope is far enough from Farce) hath very hardly kept his Doublet whole.[17]

A play's true artistic legitimacy, it seems, rests not merely on its writer's familiarity with classical texts: indeed, Behn's use of religious terms such as "Rabbi" and "Sect" suggests that the (ostensible) learning on display in Jonson's work participates in a kind of sanctity—or sanctimoniousness—for its own sake. Rather, Behn locates dramatic authority in more immediate, material effects: whereas a classically correct play like *The Alchemist* produces a "sullen posture" in the playgoing supplicant, the strained seams of this same man's garments during a performance of *Henry IV* confirm the merits of that play (itself presumably stuffed full—if not "Farc[ically]" so—of physical, Falstaffian antics). Behn too, then, like Shadwell in *The Squire of Alsatia* and *The Lancashire Witches,* seems to advocate a relationship to our dramaturgical past that, rather than showcasing its steepage in classical scholarship and classical theory, emphasizes mobility and multiplication: *Henry IV,* of course—far from conforming stiffly to the classical unities—contains a number of subplots, takes place over several years, and ranges all over England in its setting.

As Paulina Kewes and others have noted, the post-classical, innovation-based model of authorship and authority toward which Behn is gesturing here was very much reinforced by the economics of the Restoration stage. But, as I hope to have demonstrated in chapter 1, this model was also enacted within the plays themselves. It is not just Restoration drama's remuneration structures, then, but the way that dramatists experiment with form and content that help to establish playwriting as a medium that can exercise a certain degree of liberty vis-à-vis earlier, textually preserved exemplars of the tradition. As we have seen, by the late seventeenth century, and certainly by the eighteenth, Shakespeare, too, was understood to be similarly straying from the norms set by print-based "Learning" and the classical rulebook.

If Restoration drama contributed to ongoing discussions around literary succession and its relationship to the printed page, it also helped conceptualize a model of literary posterity—of a work's future impact—into which Shakespeare likewise fit quite well. (Notably, Behn's preface already presumes this legacy, referring to "the immortal Shakespeare" even as she praises his plays' disregard for time-honored dramaturgical orthodoxies.) As Margareta de Grazia and others have shown, the continued process of English canon formation in the eighteenth century—the ongoing curation of a body of texts that would retain perennial cultural value—was substantially supported by the incipient fields of professional criticism and scholarly editing.[18] And early practitioners of these professions found their ideal object in Shakespeare—partly, in fact, because of the same idiosyncrasies that defined his relationship to the classical past. As de Grazia explains, eighteenth-century critical standards of aesthetic coherence, moral clarity, and linguistic uniformity did not come "ready-made" in Shakespeare's texts; rather, such standards "had to be worked into and out of his works by the editor's critical activity.... Shakespeare was [thus] used [by eighteenth-century editors], precisely because of his irregularity, to define and inscribe cultural codes that related to both value and action, style and manner, letters and probity."[19] As we explored in chapter 3, a similar kind of push and pull can be seen within the 1710 *Works* of William Congreve, where Congreve teams up with Jacob Tonson to deploy various bibliographical tools—printers' ornaments, engraved headpieces, ornamental drop capitals, and more—to call attention to his dramas' strict neoclassical forms; and yet these formal strictures only barely contain the kinetic energies of the plays' language. This deliberate tension, I have argued, lies at the heart of Congreve's bid for posterity, in which the static permanence of classical aesthetics is balanced against the constantly self-renewing, ritualistic temporality of masquerade, as well as the organic rhythms of (biological) emergence—motifs explored both thematically and stylistically within Congreve's final two comedies.

Significantly, in her account of the role of eighteenth-century editors in the canonization of Shakespeare, de Grazia explicitly singles out the work of the Tonson publishing dynasty: "By improving and rectifying Shakespeare," she explains, "the Tonson editions simultaneously cultivated English taste and manners, thereby creating a cultural need which its own publications could gratify."[20] Indeed, the Tonsons sought to make their name inseparable from Shakespeare's: "Shakespeare's image appeared sometimes on the title-page and sometimes on the colophon of the various Tonson publications," and through manifold legal and commercial tactics the family continuously "secured and retained their proprietorship of [Shakespeare's] works" throughout most of the eighteenth century.[21] But of course, the Tonson-Shakespeare association originates with what John Barnard describes as a collaborative venture by Tonson, Dryden, and Congreve—between 1679 and 1720—to establish a polite canon of poetry and drama.[22] Thus, the original 1709 Tonson Shakespeare (edited by Nicholas Rowe) was published as part of a series of collectible, small-format, multivolume sets, which ultimately included both Dryden's three-volume 1709 *Virgil* and Congreve's three-volume 1710 *Works*.[23]

These three authors shared more in common, moreover, than simply having their work published in the same series: all three came to symbolize a certain cultural position. As Barnard writes, Dryden and Congreve, from the very beginning of their careers, had each cultivated an authorial persona that suggested "a man educated in the classics, up to the minute with French literature and literary theory, and [thus] capable of creating a specifically English aesthetic which married the English virtues of variety and naturalness . . . with those of classical and contemporary, and, in particular, French, neoclassical ideals of correctness."[24] Barnard adds that "the English virtues of variety and naturalness" were thought to be "exemplified by Shakespeare," but here it seems useful to recall de Grazia's analysis of how editors worked to shape and curate these virtues: not content to leave "nature" undisturbed, Tonson and his successors aimed to civilize and regularize Shakespeare. We thus might even say that, in balancing Shakespeare's "variety" against the neoclassical uniformity to which polite print culture aspired, the 1709 Tonson edition (and those that followed) sought essentially to remake Shakespeare in the mold of Dryden and Congreve.

If Shakespeare ultimately came to epitomize the English canon in the eighteenth century, then, it is in large part because of the beguiling irreconcilabilities posed by post-Restoration editions of his works—where nature and art, irregularity and correctness, jostle against each other. And perhaps one of the most important of these irreconcilabilities is the simultaneous presence of a kind of theatrical verve alongside the fixity of the printed page. The collision between these two modes is commented on repeatedly by such critics as Alexander Pope, who, even as he decries the "faults" introduced into Shakespeare's works by dint of their theatrical origins, acknowledges the productive friction that arises between these "defects" and the eighteenth-century editorial project.[25] Pope accounts for Shakespeare's supposed lapses in taste by invoking the plays' earliest contexts: "It must be allowed that Stage-Poetry of all other, is more particularly levell'd to please the *Populace,* and its success more immediately depend[s] upon the *Common Suffrage,*" Pope writes in the preface to his 1725 edition of Shakespeare's works. Further infelicities must be ascribed to "the Author's being a *Player,* and forming himself first upon the judgments of that body of men whereof he was a member." Finally, Shakespeare's oeuvre has suffered from "those almost innumerable Errors which have risen from . . . the ignorance of the Players, both as his actors, and as his editors."[26] Yet it is these very faults, Pope holds, that enable Shakespeare, "of all *English* Poets[,] to be[come] the fairest and fullest subject for Criticism."[27] In other words, it is precisely the disparity between the irrepressibly performative elements of the plays and the stabilizing, systematizing effects of the rule-abiding text—a disparity that, I have argued, Congreve strategically builds into his 1710 *Works*—that allows Shakespeare and the eighteenth-century phase of canon formation to enter into a mutually defining symbiosis.

Eighteenth-century notions of Shakespeare as a poet of raw, untutored "Nature," lacking the discipline of classical learning, relate directly to a third hallmark of the era's Shakespearean criticism: a conception of Shakespeare's plays as hearkening back to a pre-print-capitalist moment in which writing remained untouched by market pressures.[28] Fittingly, it is Pope, followed by Samuel Johnson—each of whom depended upon the sale of their writing to make a living—who insist upon Shakespeare's naïve, uncalculating qualities: Pope wrote that Shakespeare was "not so much an Imitator, as an Instrument, of Nature"[29]; Johnson, more succinctly, called him the "poet of nature."[30] And indeed, according to David Fairer, it is at just the moment when letters are being increasingly professionalized that a notion of Shakespeare as "Nature's child," synonymous with "genuine poetry," is deployed in order "to re-identify poetry with its original sources in the heart and imagination": Shakespeare becomes a symbol of "poetry as a primal expressiveness, . . . capturing a fresh, instinctive voice" from his surroundings, a kind of Caliban and Ariel combined, at once earthy and unearthly.[31]

But the desire to embrace an ingenuous, vernacular Englishness as a bulwark against an expanding print marketplace is one that, as we saw in chapter 4, can be traced back as least as far as Gay, whose work speaks to a historical juncture at which the monetary worth of writing began to be perceived as a threat to its humanistic values. Of course, as Gay's satires imply, a pre-commercial past arguably never existed in the first place, and is rather a consoling figment manufactured by an alienated culture seeking some truer, more authentic means of defining itself. In many ways, Gay thus identifies a dynamic that became central to Shakespeare's reception at the very height of his cultural dominance, a point at which a nostalgic vision of a pre-print world became one of print capitalism's most canny commodities.

Kate Rumbold has analyzed a particular strand of eighteenth-century discourse that emphasized Shakespeare's role not just as national poet but, specifically, as poet of the people, associated with rural geographies and oral culture. She roots this discourse specifically in the publications surrounding the 1769 Shakespeare Jubilee—Garrick's elaborate, multiday, self-promoting celebration of the Bard, held in Stratford-upon-Avon and often seen as inaugurating the Shakespearean tourism industry. She examines a number of documents produced in connection with the Jubilee, including *Shakespeare's Garland. Being A Collection of New Songs, Ballads, Roundelays, Catches, Glees, Comic-Serenatas, &c. Performed at the Jubilee at Stratford Upon Avon* (written mostly by Garrick, with music by Charles Dibdin). Overall, Rumbold observes, the collection's lyrics "typically . . . load a wealth of critical ideas about Shakespeare onto the activities of serenading, marching, and dancing," invoking a language of childhood, myth, and folksong: "COME, nymphs and fawns, where'er ye be, / To this your Father's Jubilee, / With a tivy, tivy, tivy-tivie, ti," runs one such ditty.[32] Yet, she notes, "it is important to see that these apparently . . . natural folk rhythms are also closely connected with the more commercial aspects of the Jubilee."[33] Rumbold explains that "the songs were . . . on sale at the birthplace; and Garrick reckoned that the inclusion of 'catches, glees and ballads, all New' after dinner would make visitors feel they were getting their money's worth. These songs are deemed objects for consumption by fashionable metropolitan visitors."[34] Not only are the songs' apparent pre-modern origins a mirage, but the songs are in fact part of a profit-driven enterprise—a vital component of the very system to which they appear to provide the antidote.

Rumbold thus elucidates the contradictions embedded in Garrick's *Collection of New Songs, Ballads, Roundelays, Catches, . . . &c.* But, significantly, as Gay's use of ballads in *The What D'Ye Call It* and *The Beggar's Opera* helps us to see, it seems safe to posit (as I do in chapter 4) that there never has been a ballad—or, perhaps, a roundelay or catch—that was not already fabricating a nostalgic past from a position of "fallen" modernity. Indeed, in Gay's various allusions to Shakespeare throughout his satiric pastorals, he seems to be hinting that Shakespeare's own uses of folkish traditions, or purportedly "simple" characters, function in ways that are more complex than we initially realize.

The allusions to Shakespeare in *The What D'Ye Call It* are too numerous to count—starting, of course, with the title, which, as John Fuller points out, is "in the tradition of Shakespeare's *As You Like It* and *Twelfth Night; or, What you Will*"; Gay's subtitle, meanwhile—*A Tragi-comi-pastoral Farce*—suggests Polonius's famous line introducing the traveling players in *Hamlet*.[35] In its moments of heightened emotion, the play makes continual reference to *Othello, Julius Caesar, Macbeth, Hamlet,* and more (as the *Key* obsessively draws our attention to).[36] Most pertinent to our purposes here, however, are Gay's borrowings from Shakespeare that, via the inclusion of nontraditional characters and character types, vernacularize classical dramaturgy by infusing it—pastorally, as it were—with "low" or "unlearned" elements. Perhaps the most obvious of these borrowings consists in Gay's naming conventions: Peascod, one of Gay's male leads, is the name of Peaseblossom's father in *A Midsummer Night's Dream* (there is also a mention of Touchstone's "wooing of a peascod" in *As You Like It*); Kitty Carrot's name may allude to Mistress Squash (Peaseblossom's mother); and Peter Nettle may invoke Peter Quince (also of *Midsummer*).[37] These names seem to conjure a specifically English rural setting—not the stylized Mediterranean landscape of laurel or myrtle, but the humble kitchen garden with its root vegetables and peapods. Yet, in adopting these names Gay does not imply, exactly, that the characters bearing them are somehow "purer" for their refusal to conform to the classical canon—nor, inversely, that this divergence from the classical norm renders the characters ridiculous. Rather, Gay suggests that the supposed ingenuousness of English rustics may be as much a fiction as that of Virgil's or Theocritus's shepherds. (Indeed, Peter Quince, though a "rude mechanical," is also, of course, often seen as a stand-in for Shakespeare himself.)

Paul Alpers makes a similar point about Shakespeare's "naïve" characters: reviewing a series of seeming malapropisms riddling the speech of the rustic Costard in *As You Like It,* Alpers notes that it is impossible to determine whether his verbal perversions are "naïve or consciously witty," and that this ambiguity is precisely what makes them "pastoral."[38] Alpers goes on to link Costard to the literary type of the "clown or fool": Shakespeare's fools in particular, of course, are infamous for—in the words of Leo Salingar—combining the "simpleton" and the "jester" in ways that make "unconscious humour" essentially indistinguishable from "wry wit."[39] Alpers concludes that Empson himself might very well say that, by thus "fusing... a simple and a sophisticated awareness of an experience,"[40] all of "these figures in Shakespeare are 'versions of pastoral.'"[41] I would agree, and would suggest that Gay, too, recognizes and extends these versions.

Beyond *The What D'Ye Call It*'s allusions to Shakespeare's more patently pastoral characters, the play invokes characters who, while less picturesquely rustic, serve what we might call pastoral ends, in that they bring an apparently simple or uncultivated viewpoint to an otherwise highly serious, "high-cultural" context. *The What D'Ye Call It*'s preface and *Key* draw particular attention to Shakespeare's nurses, grandmothers, and witches—all of whom might initially seem out of place in the tragedies they inhabit. Thus, for example, *The What D'Ye Call It*'s pseudo-scholarly preface acknowledges that the play's more unconventional characters, including "a *Justice of the Peace,* a *Parish-Clark,* and an *Embryo's Ghost,*" might seem "very improper to the Dignity of Tragedy, and were never introduc'd by the Antients," but defends the play's dramatis personae by noting that "whoever will look into *Sophocles, Euripides,* or *Seneca,* will find that they greatly affected to introduce *Nurses* in all their Pieces, which every one must grant to be an inferior Character to a Justice of Peace; in imitation of which also, I have introduced a Grandmother and an Aunt."[42] Interestingly, while the preface thus justifies the play's non-traditional demographics by citing precedents in classical dramaturgy, the *Key*—which, again, may or may not have been written by Gay himself—links such crimes against tragic "Dignity" not to the ancients but to Shakespeare. Thus, the only "Nurse" mentioned in the *Key* is that of Shakespeare's Juliet: the "source" for Kitty and Filbert's joint lament in 1.2, we are told—"O rueful Day! / Rueful indeed, I trow. / O Woeful Day! / A Day indeed of Woe!"—is supposedly the Nurse's cry upon finding Juliet in her death-like trance (which the *Key* quotes as "O lamentable Day! Oh heavy Day! O Day! O Day! O Day! Oh hateful Day! Never was seen so black a Day as this: O woeful Day! Oh woeful Day!").[43] Likewise, the *Key* specifically notes that the "Grandmother" and "Aunt" serve as "a Mimickry of *Shakespear* in several of his Historical Plays, particularly of the old *Dutchess* of *York* in *Rich.* 3d."[44]

Such echoes might lead one to conclude that Gay intends to spoof Shakespeare's tragedies, and perhaps, in particular, to mock his practice of assigning heroic histrionics to household staff and elderly female relatives. Yet the *Key* adds, in its discussion of the Aunt and Grandmother—suddenly straight-faced amid what is otherwise a fairly sarcastic commentary—that these roles "are proper to raise Compassion, however ridicul'd."[45] Indeed, Gay's preface likewise explains, in what is apparently a similar shift in tone from irony to sincerity, that while critics might condemn the high-flown speeches in *The What D'Ye Call It* for being "not Tragical, because they are those of the lowest Country People," such an objection would be entirely unfounded: "I answer that the Sentiments of Princes and Clowns have not in reality that difference which they seem to have: their Thoughts are almost the same, and they only differ as the same Thought is attended with a Meanness of Pomp of Diction, or receive a different Light from the Circumstances each Character is conversant with."[46] This statement almost eerily prefigures Empson's description of the pastoral mode's central premise: that illiterate rustics experience, and might express, sentiments just as exquisite as those felt by a civilization's elite.[47] Of course, Gay implies throughout *The What D'Ye Call It* that his characters' "Sentiments" are often maudlin, overblown, or inauthentic. Yet even these satiric jabs reveal "the lowest Country People" to be deserving of a certain respect—to be savvy, worldly, and complex. Perhaps, then, Gay, via his allusions, is suggesting that Shakespeare is up to something similar—that Shakespeare, too, by lacing his works of high tragedy with figures of domesticity and folksy wisdom, is hinting at these figures' unexamined depths.

Gay's pastoral dramas—including *The What D'Ye Call It* but also his far more famous "Newgate Pastoral"—at once offer up, while also exposing as fictitious, an original (or "originary") oral form of expression that might counteract the print capitalism of an ever more mediated, imperial modernity. In this way, Gay explores a specific kind of nostalgia—a yearning for a more "natural," native poetic mode—that, by mid-century, would become identified with Shakespeare, and would, indeed, lead to Shakespeare's eventual investiture as "the Bard." Interestingly, however, as we have seen, Gay is already positing this association—channeling Shakespeare's pastoral comedies, pastoral characters, and pastoral admixture of "low" elements into "high tragedy"—in his own work. Of course, as Garrick and others quickly realized, the primal, earthy ethos that the eighteenth-century Shakespeare would increasingly come to symbolize was not at all incompatible with the commercial middle-class culture from which it supposedly provided a respite. This irony, too, is one that Gay anticipates: by specifically invoking, in *The*

What D'Ye Call It, those of Shakespeare's characters who seem the unlikeliest candidates either to write classically inspired tragedy (Peter Quince) or to populate it (nurses, grandmothers, aunts), Gay suggests that the supposedly elemental, embodied modes of being that these figures represent often turn out to be much more sophisticated than they seem.

The eighteenth-century preoccupation with Shakespeare as the poet of "Nature" owes in part to a sense of his status as a master of "human nature"—and, thus, as a master of character.[48] Jack Lynch writes that "attention to [Shakespearean] characterization" was to become an outright "obsession" in eighteenth-century criticism, while Michael Bristol calls "character" the eighteenth-century Shakespeareans' "great discovery."[49] In many ways this focus on character can be used as a gauge for the increasing interest in the role of morality in Shakespeare's plays, as Fiona Ritchie notes; it also dovetails with an increased emphasis on affective responses to literature, and on the evocation of sympathy.[50] As Marsden asserts, such emphases signaled a "radical shift away from earlier formalist theories of aesthetics," as well as from "didactic" models of art's ability to "please and instruct."[51] But in other ways, as I already began to suggest in my introduction, character criticism has its roots in Restoration-era considerations of Shakespeare.

As Brian Vickers points out, it is only during the last quarter of the eighteenth century that "essays and whole books are devoted to individual [Shakespearean] characters" for the first time.[52] However, Vickers adds that an "interest in Shakespeare's characters is as old as an interest in Shakespeare himself,"[53] and, indeed, analyses of his "skill in creating characters" comprise some of "the earliest pieces of formal literary criticism" in English—including, as we have seen, Margaret Cavendish's "Letter 123," from 1664. For, of course, the focus of Cavendish's discussion is, in fact, character—or what she calls the playwright's ability "to Express to the Life all Sorts of Persons, of what Quality, Profession, Degree, Breeding, or Birth soever."[54]

Moreover, as I contended in chapter 2, Restoration drama—and, especially, the work of Aphra Behn—served as a site for thinking through broader questions of identity, and the relationship between mind and body, that remained fundamental to discussions of character in the years to come. Indeed, it seems no coincidence that Cavendish, the first writer to analyze

Shakespeare's characterization in any real depth, was also (as we saw in the same chapter) intently engaged in trying to make sense philosophically of the way in which our thoughts and physical actions, ideas and sense perceptions, interact. In "Letter 123" we see that Cavendish, like Behn, saw drama—in its neither-nor position, halfway between page and stage—as a particularly fertile ground in which to explore these questions of how mind and body combine to make a human being.

In my reading of "Letter 123" in my introduction, I posited that much of Cavendish's admiration for Shakespeare's characterization stems from her split awareness of his dramatis personae. On the one hand, they represent, as a group, the kind of encyclopedic overview of humankind that only a monumental text such as Shakespeare's collected plays could offer up. On the other hand, they remain roles to be enacted or made flesh, so that Cavendish fancies that Shakespeare must have been "transformed" into the characters in his plays in order to conjure them so well for us; and, by the same token, she describes how his readers come to feel that we are watching these figures walk before us incarnate, that we are "present" at their tragic peripeteias. As chapter 2 showed, this same questioning of the boundary between reading and seeing, between imagining and witnessing, permeates Behn's writing, and especially her late plays. In many ways, then, Behn provides us with another crucial context for understanding why the first critical assessment of Shakespeare's characters was undertaken in the Restoration: not only did Cavendish live through a period in which access to Shakespeare underwent two major shifts in medium, but, alongside these changes—and perhaps intertwined with them—Restoration culture was grappling with the broader questions of what kinds of knowledge can be gleaned from mental insight versus empirical observation, and of how that knowledge might change who we are and what we choose to do.

Steeped, as it was, in a specific philosophical moment—in what would, with Behn, become a specific dramaturgical moment as well—Cavendish's bifurcated sense of Shakespeare's characters continued to assert itself, I contend, into the nineteenth century, even as the Romantics insisted that Shakespeare's literariness depended on jettisoning his work's associations with the playhouse.[55] Charles Lamb's famous essay on Shakespeare's tragedies, published in 1811, illustrates this paradox.

Lamb notoriously avers in his essay that acting out Shakespeare's greatest characters onstage is a pointless, even deleterious, undertaking. Yet the intensity of Lamb's imaginative identification with these figures, I argue, may actually owe to his sharp attunement to the plays' theatrical origins. Lamb's essay argues for the relative unimportance of physical "actions" to our conception of Shakespeare's characters, privileging instead their "intellectual activity": "The truth is, the Characters of Shakespeare are so much the objects of meditation rather than of interest or curiosity as to their actions, that while we are reading any of his great criminal characters,—Macbeth, Richard, even Iago,—we think not so much of the crimes which they commit, as of the ambition, the aspiring spirit, the intellectual activity which prompts them to overleap those moral fences."[56] The fact that it is these characters' "spirit" that distinguishes them, rather than their transgressions, is what ultimately renders them fitter subjects for the page than the stage. Lamb continues, several lines later,

> [There is a] state of sublime emotion into which we are elevated by those images of night and horror which Macbeth is made to utter, that solemn prelude with which he entertains the time till the bell shall strike which is to call him to murder Duncan.... [But] when we no longer read it in a book... [and instead sit in a theatre,] see[ing] a man in his bodily shape before our eyes actually preparing to commit a murder, [especially] if the acting be true and impressive, as I have witnessed it in Mr. K.[ean]'s performance of that part, [then] the painful anxiety about the act, ... the too close pressing semblance of reality, give a pain and uneasiness which totally destroy all the delight which the words in the book convey, where the deed[-]doing never presses upon us with the painful sense of presence.[57]

Because the play's effects depend so heavily on Macbeth's inner state (his "intellectual activity," to return to the earlier passage), an unfortunate irony arises: the "true[r] and [more] impressive ... the acting," the more the theatrical production actually detracts from our enjoyment of Shakespeare's play, replacing the "delight" of the dramatist's "words" with the "pain ... of ... pressing ... presence."[58] Yet the grammatical structure here suggests, surprisingly, a conception of Macbeth as himself a kind of actor: as Lamb evokes, in the passive voice, "those images of night and horror *which Macbeth is made to utter*," Macbeth emerges as a kind of diegetic version of "Mr. K.," speaking assigned lines. (The use of the word "entertains"—"that solemn prelude with which he entertains the time"—reinforces the association.)

In other words, Shakespeare's sublime poetry may be what Lamb credits most directly with the scene's emotional impact, but the lines' power also seems predicated, for Lamb, on a submerged theatrical foundation: even as Lamb attempts to forget that *Macbeth* is a script to be acted, Macbeth the character seems inescapably to remain a kind of performer, conducting himself according to external directives—whether of the weird sisters, of Lady Macbeth, of Shakespeare himself, or, perhaps, of the reader, who, in imaginatively animating him, "ma[k]e[s] him utter" the text on the page.

This subtle interdependence between page and stage in the construction of Shakespeare's characters can be seen even more clearly in Lamb's descriptions of Hamlet and Lear. He writes, for instance, that "nine parts in ten of what Hamlet does, are transactions between himself and his moral sense[;] they are the effusions of his solitary musings, which he retires to holes and corners and the most sequestered parts of the palace to pour forth.... How can [such musings] be represented by a gesticulating actor, who comes and mouths them out before an audience, making four hundred people his confidants at once?"[59] Again: "solitary" as Hamlet's "musings" may be, the urgency of these thought processes depends on their being constantly threatened with exposure. It is as if the character of Hamlet himself is aware of treading a kind of stage—aware of Elsinore's status as a thoroughly theatricalized space from which he is trying to escape ("retir[ing] to holes and corners and the most sequestered parts of the palace"). It is this "theatrical" threat—written into the play itself—that adds such poignancy to Hamlet's anguished inner drama.

Similarly, of King Lear Lamb declares (incensed, in particular, over Nahum Tate's infamous revision),

> The greatness of Lear is not in corporal dimension, but in intellectual: the explosions of his passion ... are storms turning up and disclosing to the bottom that sea, his mind, with all its vast riches.... A happy ending!—as if the living martyrdom that Lear had gone through,—the flaying of his feelings alive, did not make a fair dismissal from the stage of life the only decorous thing for him.... As if the childish pleasure of getting his gilt robes and scepter again could tempt him to act over again his misused station.[60]

Here, the essence of Lear's tragedy, as Lamb conceives of it, consists in having to submit his glorious "mind" to the tawdry indignities of "the stage of life"—in finding his soaring "intellect" weighed down by the ignobly "corporal" trappings of costumery and display, so that the "vast riches" of his spirit become embarrassingly encumbered by the flashy "gilt" of his robes. For indeed, the very "explosions of... passion" that "disclos[e]" Lear's "mind" (to readers and audience alike) are triggered in response to crises that are terribly pragmatic in nature—by the logistical complexities of dividing a kingdom, the palpable mortifications of an aging body. Lamb concludes that "Lear is essentially impossible to be represented on a stage," but the character's central struggle, as Lamb describes it, is—as for Lamb's Hamlet, too—ultimately a battle against the theatricalization of his existence: his tragedy is that he has been forced to "act ... [out] his misused station" in the first place.

In short, as much as Lamb complains that performance degrades Shakespeare's greatest characters, a haunted awareness of performativity—both the characters' own and that of human existence more broadly—is what makes these figures, for Lamb, so psychologically profound. It is the fact that Macbeth, Hamlet, or Lear—as dramatis personae—are in some sense never *not* embodied that, paradoxically, renders their powers of mind all the more transcendent, all the more tragic. ("O, that this too too solid flesh would melt!") And the articulation of this awareness—of a sense of Shakespeare's characters as hovering between imagination and somatic experience—is one that, I hope to have shown, dates back to Cavendish: in other words, it stems from a moment when, following an eighteen-year period during which Shakespeare's heroes and heroines could be encountered almost exclusively via the page, they were suddenly once again eligible for full theatrical treatment.

In the preceding pages I have tried to suggest some of the ways in which, by the late eighteenth and early nineteenth centuries, even as Restoration drama had begun to enter its long period of critical disfavor, the intellectual work of late seventeenth-century playwrights posed key questions that would continue to shape our collective sense of what a print canon is and means. Indeed, the lasting literary-theoretical impact of Restoration drama—its exploration of problems surrounding print-based inheritance and posterity, its probing of the relationship between imagination and live experience, and its struggles to understand the value of writing in a cultural landscape changed forever by an increasingly commercial book trade—is arguably still discernible. We see these same concerns reflected not just in how we construe the category of the literary but in the seemingly contradictory fact that a category so dependent on notions of reading is, nonetheless, frequently identified with the English language's most famous writer for the stage. The authors whose work I have examined here ultimately established drama, above all other modes, as the laboratory in which the literary is tested and defined—in part because of dramaturgy's inherent inability, or refusal, ever to conform itself entirely to a print canon.

NOTES

INTRODUCTION

1. Of course, the theaters' closure did not mean that performance of various kinds did not continue. Many Britons continued to experience theater in some form, whether via school productions, private theatricals, fairground drolls, or city pageants. See, for example, Randall, *Winter Fruit;* Wiseman, *Drama and Politics;* and Clare, *English Republic.*
2. See Kastan, "Humphrey Moseley," 105-24.
3. Bennett, *Theater as Problem,* 73.
4. Bennett, *Theater as Problem,* 73.
5. As Fiona Ritchie notes, although "the importance of Cavendish's ["Letter 123"] has been noted by scholars, there has been curiously little attention devoted to this essay, which is important to the history of both Shakespeare criticism and women's critical writing." *Women and Shakespeare,* 13.
6. Cavendish, *A True Relation,* 45. Cavendish does not refer directly to her own playgoing, but presumably she is including herself in her description of her family's activities.
7. See Ritchie, *Women and Shakespeare,* 15; and Britland, *Drama at the Courts,* 205. Although details about the exiled court's entertainments are difficult to pin down, Britland finds evidence of the queen's household producing a "festive masque" on New Year's Eve 1646; this would have been after Cavendish's marriage, but it suggests the kind of performance Cavendish could have witnessed. More concretely, Cavendish's "Letter 195," in her *Sociable Letters,* describes having seen a "Female Actor" in breeches on a "Mountebank's Stage" while in Antwerp after her marriage, in 1645; see *Sociable Letters,* 261-62.
8. Fitzmaurice, "Shakespeare, Cavendish, and Reading Aloud," 46. Fitzmaurice specifically cites comments by Cavendish in her work *The Worlds Olio* (published in 1655) that evince a highly developed, strongly opinionated position on how best to read her book aloud; these comments thus seem to indicate "a household where such reading and critiques of it were commonplace" (37), though families such as Cavendish's would have been unlikely to have gone so far as to have "memorized parts" (46).

9. Much scholarly debate has centered on the extent to which Britons could have encountered Shakespeare in print prior to the mid- to late eighteenth century. Don-John Dugas and Robert Hume, among others, have asserted that the cost of a Shakespeare volume would have been prohibitive for most readers until at least the 1730s. Yet Jan Fergus has shown the effect that circulating libraries may have had in disseminating Shakespeare's texts more widely; likewise, Maximillian Novak—citing the long-running and lively critical response to Shakespeare between Dryden and Pope—points out that the availability and pricing of second-hand books at this time remains unknown: the fact that the impoverished Lewis Theobald owned a First Folio suggests that there are major gaps in our understanding of how these texts landed in readers' hands. See Dugas and Hume, "The Dissemination of Shakespeare's Plays circa 1714"; Fergus, *Provincial Readers*, 98–99; Novak, "Politics of Shakespeare Criticism," 125, 139n12. See also Frank, *Novel Stage*, 32–33. For a detailed overview of literacy rates and the circulation of Shakespeare's work in the seventeenth and eighteenth centuries, see Mayer, *Shakespeare's Early Readers*, 14–43.
10. Masten, *Textual Intercourse*, 157–62. See also Miller, "'Thou art a Moniment, without a tombe.'" Miller shows how Cavendish formatted her publications so as to establish an association between herself and Shakespeare.
11. See Fitzmaurice, "William Cavendish," 63–80.
12. Ritchie, *Women and Shakespeare*, 16. The Cavendishes then left London for their seat in Nottinghamshire some time after October 1, 1660, but scholars remain unsure of the exact date. See Whitaker, *Mad Madge*, 233.
13. Coiro, "Reading," 535. See also Potter, *Secret Rites and Secret Writing*; and Sauer, '*Paper-Contestations*,' 77–99.
14. See Evans, *The Riverside Shakespeare*, 1847. See also Lynch, "Criticism of Shakespeare," 41.
15. Cavendish refers twice to his "Readers" and twice to "those that ... Read his Playes": see Cavendish, *Sociable Letters*, 177, 178.
16. Indeed, Lukas Erne contends that Shakespeare himself—contrary to longstanding scholarly orthodoxy—very much anticipated that his work would be appreciated on the page; see Erne, *Shakespeare as Literary Dramatist*; and also *Shakespeare and the Book Trade*. Certainly there is evidence that Shakespeare had joined a kind of proto-canon as early as 1647, when the writer John Denham referred to Jonson, Shakespeare, and Fletcher as the "Triumvirate of Wit." This phrase appears in Denham's prefatory poem to Humphrey Moseley's folio edition of the complete works of Beaumont and Fletcher, thus placing their work in the company of the other two playwrights' monumental folio editions. Cavendish affirms this "triumvirate" in her "General Prologue" to her 1662 *Playes*, in which she surveys the kind of drama "writ in former daies; / As Johnson, Shakespear, Beaumont, Fletcher writ" (quoted in Masten, *Textual Intercourse*, 160). This outsized print presence may have contributed to the regularity with which these same writers' works

were subsequently produced once the theaters had reopened: the dramatists whose plays were staged most often between 1660 and 1665 were (in order of frequency) Fletcher, Shakespeare, Beaumont/Fletcher, and Jonson; see Reverand, "Dryden and the Canon," 203–25, esp. 213.

17. Cavendish, *Sociable Letters*, 176.
18. Cavendish, *Sociable Letters*, 178.
19. Cavendish, *Sociable Letters*, 177.
20. Coiro points out that Milton's "On Shakespeare" (published as part of the front matter of the second folio, in 1632) likewise praises Shakespeare's "Book," celebrating it as the work of an "Admirable Dramatic Poet" ("Drama in the Epic Style," 67). Coiro looks at Milton's construal of "theater" versus "drama," and shows how he incorporated specifically dramatic elements into *Paradise Lost*.
21. Cavendish, *Sociable Letters*, 177.
22. Cavendish, *Sociable Letters*, 178. Here Cavendish participates in a growing discourse on plagiarism that is in some ways a hallmark of Restoration-era discussions of literature; I discuss this phenomenon further below.
23. Cavendish, *Sociable Letters*, 178.
24. Cavendish, *Sociable Letters*, 177–78.
25. The mind-body connections Cavendish posits here clearly relate to her more general vitalist philosophical system: see chapter 2 for a fuller discussion of these concepts in Cavendish's thought.
26. Cavendish, *Sociable Letters*, 177.
27. *Oxford English Dictionary* (hereafter *OED*), s.v. "feign." All further references to the *OED* are made parenthetically.
28. Cavendish, *Sociable Letters*, 177.
29. Cavendish, *Sociable Letters*, 177 (emphasis added). "Metamorphose" does not appear to have acquired its intransitive form (e.g., "the tadpole metamorphoses into a frog") until the nineteenth or early twentieth century (*OED, s.v.* "metamorphose," def. 2b; def. 4, quotation 2). However, the *OED* cites instances of the transitive verb being used reflexively (e.g., "He ... metamorphozed himself into an angel" [sic]) as early as 1601 (see def. 1, quotation 3).
30. Cavendish, *Sociable Letters*, 177, 178.
31. Margaret Cavendish, *Playes,* sig. A2r (quoted in Fitzmaurice, "Shakespeare, Cavendish, and Reading Aloud," 42).
32. Fitzmaurice, "Shakespeare, Cavendish, and Reading Aloud," 40–41.
33. Cavendish seems to be using "a making" intransitively here, a usage of which there are very few instances in the *OED*. One example can be seen in definition 3c, "to come to maturity" (though the editors deem this usage chiefly American, and trace it back only as far as 1714). Perhaps the most clearly relevant definition of "make" in this instance is the *OED*'s definition 4b, "to write poetry" (now obsolete), which also has an intransitive form (as in a cited example from Spenser's 1579 *Shepheardes Calendar:* "And hath he skill to make so excellent?"). Still, all of

the *OED*'s citations feature human writers doing the "making," not the written texts themselves. Cavendish's use of the prefix *a-* may help clarify her meaning: connoting movement "up," "out," or "away" (see *OED*, "*a-*" [prefix1]), the *a-*, when prefixed to "making," may evoke a composition taking shape as it moves outward or upward from Cavendish's mind.

34. David Brewer, *Afterlife of Character*.
35. Brewer is thinking in particular of Deidre Lynch (*Economy of Character*) and Catherine Gallagher (*Nobody's Story*).
36. Brewer, *Afterlife of Character*, 6.
37. Brewer, *Afterlife of Character*, 6.
38. Brewer, *Afterlife of Character*, 85–86.
39. Quoted in Brewer, *Afterlife of Character*, 86.
40. Julie Stone Peters writes, "If print did not create the notion that ideas expressed in words could be forms of property, it played a central role in the formulation and institutionalization of this idea in early modern Europe.... Printed products themselves may have reinforced the sense that the natural rights-bearer was the author: the grand author editions, with authors' names prominent on title pages, author portraits, prefaces and dedications—all ... seemed to identify the author as the one with 'title' to the poetic creation." *Theatre of the Book*, 222, 224.
41. For an excellent overview of this debate, see Terry, *Poetry*, 11–34.
42. See, for instance (and I severely limit my examples here for brevity's sake), Pask, *Emergence of the English Author;* Guillory, *Poetic Authority;* Kramnick, *Making the English Canon;* and Engell, *Creative Imagination*.
43. On the various competing definitions used by scholars, see Kastan, "Humphrey Moseley," 105–11.
44. See Helgerson, *Self-Crowned Laureates*.
45. Erne asserts that "the phrase 'literary dramatist' encapsulates at once a style of writing, an anticipated readerly reception, a claim for generic respectability, and an authorial ambition," all of which, Erne shows, seem to apply to Shakespeare; see *Shakespeare as Literary Dramatist*, 4.
46. See Gavin, *Invention of English Criticism*, 6.
47. See Wellek, "What Is Literature?," 20.
48. See Ross, "Emergence of 'Literature,'" 397–422.
49. See below for detailed citations of all of these scholars.
50. Kastan, "Humphrey Moseley," 111.
51. Kastan, "Humphrey Moseley," 114.
52. Kastan, "Humphrey Moseley," 113.
53. Kastan, "Humphrey Moseley," 114.
54. Kastan, "Humphrey Moseley," 114.
55. See Lindenbaum, "Milton's Contract," 451 (cited in Kastan, "Humphrey Moseley," 114).
56. Kastan, "Humphrey Moseley," 105.

57. Adam G. Hooks suggests that drama occupied a privileged position in the book trade more generally—partly as a result, perhaps, of Moseley's work. Hooks explains that, "beginning in 1650[,] a separate subheading" appears in booksellers' catalogues "for 'Playes,'" a distinction granted to "no other group or genre" at the time; see "Booksellers' Catalogues," 455. By 1656, "two catalogues appeared with the striking claim to list all the plays that were ever printed, rather than just the stock of a single bookseller," a development that Hooks notes is "remarkable" in that one finds no "other comparable subject or genre list" for many years to come (456).
58. See Kewes, "'Give Me the Sociable Pocket-books,'" 8. See also Wright, "Reading of Plays," 83.
59. Kewes, *Authorship and Appropriation*, 10.
60. Kewes, *Authorship and Appropriation*, 10.
61. Kewes, *Authorship and Appropriation*, 8.
62. For more on Moseley's contribution to a literary canon, see Barnard, "London Publishing," 8.
63. See Wright, "Reading of Plays," 73-108.
64. See Berek, "Defoliating Playbooks," 395-416.
65. Gavin, *Invention of English Criticism*, 25.
66. See also Straznicky, *Women's Closet Drama*, 72.
67. Coiro, "Reading," 548.
68. Hammond, "Restoration Poetic," 391.
69. See Osborn, *John Dryden*, 184-99.
70. Bernard, "Henry Herringman," 275.
71. Hammond, "Restoration Poetic," 392.
72. Hammond, "Restoration Poetic," 393.
73. Barnard, "English Literary Canon," 309, 310. See also Hammond, "Restoration Poetic," 393. For more on Tonson's contributions toward the creation of a "polite" literature, see D. F. McKenzie, "Typography and Meaning," 224. On the subscription list of Dryden's Virgil as a marker of a transition to "polite" reading audiences, see Barnard, "Dryden, Tonson, and Subscriptions," 129-51.
74. Barnard, "English Literary Canon," 307. Nicholas Hudson, surveying some of the first collections of literary biographies, finds evidence for a growing number of readers attuned to literature as an emergent field: shortly after the Restoration, we see "the first collections of . . . 'lives of poets,' aimed at an audience of aspiring literary consumers who wished to elevate their knowledge of English literary history." These include Edward Phillips's *Theatrum Poetarum* (1675), William Winstanley's *The Lives of the Most Famous Poets* (1687), and Langbaine's *An Account of the English Dramatick Poets* (1691); see Hudson, "Creating the 'Classless' Author," 1579.
75. "The theatre [of the first two decades of the seventeenth century] usually reserved no space in its play-texts for their writers; all the evidence we have

from the period suggests that the production of plays in the theatre tended to distance the performance of a play from, rather than connect it to, those who wrote it. Writers only occasionally profited directly from the performance of their work, and, as is well known, they held no proprietary rights in the scripts they sold to the acting companies." Masten, *Textual Intercourse*, 73–74.

76. Kewes, *Authorship and Appropriation*, 3.
77. Milhous and Hume, *Publication of Plays in London*, 43.
78. Milhous and Hume, *Publication of Plays in London*, 19. Milhous and Hume believe that the sixth-night benefit may have been added around 1690, and that a ninth night "became a possibility" somewhere between 1700 and 1714; see *Publication of Plays in London*, 195.
79. Milhous and Hume, *Publication of Plays in London*, 43.
80. Kewes, *Authorship and Appropriation*, 3.
81. Kewes, *Authorship and Appropriation*, 3.
82. On Restoration dramatists as key to developing concepts of proprietary authorship, see Kewes, *Authorship and Appropriation*, prologue and chapter 1; see also Hammond, *Professional Imaginative Writing*, 6, 44, and 146.
83. Milhous and Hume, after careful review of the historical archive, conclude that "Dryden, Shadwell, Behn, and a few others appear to have earned a substantial portion of their incomes from the theatre for two decades or more," though they caution against generalizing beyond these individuals: certain other playwrights might have lived by their pen for shorter periods of time; others, of course, would not have been able to support themselves this way at all; see *Publication of Plays in London*, 204.
84. Milhous and Hume, *Publication of Plays in London*, 17.
85. Milhous and Hume, *Publication of Plays in London*, 15.
86. Kewes, *Authorship and Appropriation*, 13.
87. Masten views Moseley's 1647 Beaumont/Fletcher folio as a watershed document in the move from collaborative to single authorship: "Moseley's preface isolates for us a moment in which the attempt to differentiate writers of collaborative texts written earlier in the century, to identify singular authors and organize volumes accordingly, is nascent in English culture, but that urge is neither universally prescriptive nor internally consistent. Moseley's preface begins by discussing Beaumont and Fletcher as a corporate entity, attests that it is 'not equitable to separate their ashes,' and proceeds to attempt precisely that." Masten, *Textual Intercourse*, 125.
88. Milhous and Hume, *Publication of Plays in London*, 16. Another significant shift can be seen in the percentage of post-1660 plays containing some kind of authorial apparatus (a dedication, a preface, or a note to the reader). Whereas 55 percent of plays published in the 1660s contained such material, this percentage rises to 65.5 percent by the 1670s, and 76 percent by the 1680s; see Milhous and Hume, *Publication of Plays in London*, 53. Booksellers seem to be realizing by this period

that a work's sense of authority and significance is amplified by infusing the printed text with markers of the playwright's individual voice and presence.
89. Milhous and Hume, *Publication of Plays in London,* 65.
90. Kewes, *Authorship and Appropriation,* 231. See also Milhous and Hume: "The appearance of *The Works of Mr. William Shakespear; in Six Volumes,* published by Tonson in 1709, is a sign of changing times and new views of drama. The title pages announce that the books are 'Adorn'd with Cuts' (heretofore highly unusual for plays) and that the whole has been 'Revis'd and Corrected, with an Account of the Life and Writings of the Author. By N. Rowe, Esq.'" *Publication of Plays in London,* 76. They add, "The Rowe edition seems crude and naïve by the standards of Lewis Theobald in the 1730s or Samuel Johnson of the 1760s, let alone Edmond Malone in 1790"; nonetheless, with its regularized spelling, its addition of scene divisions and location indicators, its insertion of *dramatis personae* for over thirty plays that lacked them, and its establishment of a uniform way of identifying characters within plays, "there can be no doubt that Rowe's edition was hugely important in creating Shakespeare as we now know and read him" (154).
91. Pask, "Plagiarism," 728–29.
92. Pask, "Plagiarism," 732. See also Milhous and Hume: "Demand for and pride in originality in composition is occasionally found in the first half of the seventeenth century, but it is very much on the rise after 1660 and more so by the 1690s." *Publication of Plays in London,* 17.
93. Pask, "Plagiarism," 729, 731. For more on the discourse of plagiarism in the Restoration, see Rosenthal, *Playwrights and Plagiarists.*
94. Pask, "Plagiarism," 728.
95. Pask, "Plagiarism," 735.
96. Pask, "Plagiarism," 733–34.
97. Peters's magisterial study, *Theatre of the Book,* provides the kind of historical overview that my own work does not. Tracing "the significant transformations in the relationship between print and theatre" across Europe over four centuries, Peters draws upon play-texts, engravings, actor portraits, and theatrical ephemera in order to tell the story of how text and performance interacted and shaped one another—how European theater "resist[ed] . . . and continual[ly] refashion[ed] . . . itself in the world of print" (4). Her focus, therefore, is not on producing new interpretations of plays via a handful of sustained readings but, rather, on assembling a wide spectrum of "witnesses" to a set of larger "cultural concerns," and on capturing the "expressive diversity of theatrical printing and practice" over time (3).
98. For material histories of Restoration theaters, acting, theatergoers, and performers, see, for example, Bush-Bailey, *Treading the Bawds;* Howe, *First English Actresses;* Hume, *London Theatre World;* Leacroft, *Development of the English Playhouse;* Powell, *Restoration Theatre Production;* Roach, *Player's Passion;* and Styan, *Restoration Comedy in Performance.* For a definitive account of Restoration drama and the book trade, see Milhous and Hume, *Publication of Plays in London.*

99. Kramnick, *Making the English Canon*, 3.
100. Accordingly, it is not until the 1670s and 1680s that Brean Hammond sees dramatic writing as conducting an increasingly "heated negotiation" over "the problematic nature of borrowing from earlier works," and, thus, over the question of originality; see *Professional Imaginative Writing*, 83.
101. Gavin, *Invention of English Criticism*, 30–31. See also Love, "Invention of the 'Town.'"
102. As Paul Davis explains, although "the structures of court governance were dismantled and tendencies toward broader political participation began to take hold under the Cromwellian republic," these developments "were reversed at the Restoration"; it was only after the Great Fire of 1666 that London saw "the creation of the 'Town,' which, with its coffee-houses, playhouses and prostitutes, quickly came to rival Whitehall as a site of cultural consumption and erotic adventure—not least for Charles II himself, the first English monarch to visit the public theatres." "From Script to Print," 41. Davis sees this shift epitomized in the rise of the commercial "scriptorium" in the late 1670s: whereas Rochester's poetry had circulated among his coterie, by the time of Rochester's death, in 1680, customers could purchase professionally transcribed copies of manuscript verse alongside printed books (41).
103. Love, "Crisis of Amateurism."
104. Love, "Crisis of Amateurism," 122.
105. Love, "Crisis of Amateurism," 122.
106. Significantly, Love sees the theater, or, more specifically, "the degraded tastes of theatre audiences," as prompting Rochester's sense that he must defend "aristocratic standards" in the *Allusion to Horace*; see "Crisis of Amateurism," 123.
107. It is important to note that the 1680s by no means mark the end of patronage, whether for Shadwell or any other dramatist. As Brean Hammond points out, "After *The Lancashire Witches* was caught up in controversy, Shadwell's work was suppressed and he was kept alive by the Earl of Dorset, himself a playwright, whose pension was the playwright's lifeline." *Professional Imaginative Writing*, 61. Yet Shadwell's return to the stage—notably, with *The Squire of Alsatia* (1687), the second of Shadwell's plays that I examine here—may have "brought him back to self-sufficiency": the production was said to have "set new box-office records" (61). Interestingly, Love views Shadwell's *Tenth Satyr of Juvenal* (also from 1687) as marking Shadwell's "abandon[ment]" of his earlier "pretense, if that is what it was, of amateurism," and as betokening his resolution, instead, to "meet Dryden on his own terms as a skilled and responsible professional"; see "Crisis of Amateurism," 132.
108. Hume, *Henry Fielding*, 1, 27. As Hume explains, after 1714 both Drury Lane and Lincoln's Inn Fields were loath to accept new plays, which had ceased to be lucrative. As a result, "between 1714 and 1728[,] no writer had a new play staged annually, or even close to annually" (27).
109. See also Hammond, *Professional Imaginative Writing*, 72, 74, and 191.
110. A similar case might be made for the inclusion of Henry Fielding, but Fielding—who was a generation younger than Gay, and whose very first play

premiered in the same year as Gay's magnum opus—was arguably working in a context in which print capitalism was already much more fully fledged. Perhaps for this reason, I would argue that Fielding's theatrical oeuvre is less systematically concerned with the commerce of literature than is Gay's: although *The Author's Farce* and *The Tragedy of Tragedies* are often considered inheritors to the larger Scriblerian critique of early eighteenth-century print culture, Fielding's dramaturgical career is focused more broadly on social satire, topical satire, burlesque, and farce. However, for a fascinating look at Fielding's use of written documents in his work, see Frank, *Novel Stage,* chapter 3. As Frank explains, Fielding shows letters in particular to have an "equal capacity for intimacy and anonymity, exposing the ways these can be flip sides of the same coin and providing an example of how they functioned together in the bourgeois public sphere" (80).

I. OF HEIRS AND BOLD PURLOINERS

1. Miner and Brady, eds., *Literary Transmission and Authority,* ix.
2. O'Brien, *Harlequin Britain,* xiv (emphasis original).
3. Dryden, "To My Dear Friend," line 5.
4. Frank, *Origins of Criticism,* 4.
5. See Miner and Brady, *Literary Transmission and Authority,* ix. See also Pask, "Plagiarism," 728-29. For more discussion of the rhetoric around plagiarism in the Restoration, see my introduction.
6. Ross, "The Author," 12.
7. On the Dryden-Shadwell rivalry, see Oden, *Dryden and Shadwell.* See also Slagle, "Dueling Prefaces," 17-32.
8. Kramer, *Imperial Dryden,* 23.
9. Kramer, *Imperial Dryden,* 30.
10. Dryden, *Essay of Dramatick Poesie,* 54.
11. Dryden, dedicatory epistle to *The Rival Ladies,* 99.
12. Dryden, *Essay of Dramatick Poesie,* 54.
13. Kramer, *Imperial Dryden,* 29.
14. Dryden, "Defence of the Epilogue," 204.
15. Dryden, "Defence of the Epilogue," 205.
16. Dryden, "Defence of the Epilogue," 207-10.
17. Dryden, "Defence of the Epilogue," 210.
18. Dryden, "Defence of the Epilogue," 217. See also Dryden's address to Rochester in his dedication to *Marriage A-la-Mode* (1673): "I am sure, if there be any thing in this Play, wherein I have rais'd my self beyond the ordinary lowness of my Comedies, I ought wholly to acknowledge it to the favour, of being admitted into your Lordship's Conversation" (221).
19. Love, "Crisis of Amateurism," 121.
20. Love, "Crisis of Amateurism," 123-24.

21. Love, "Crisis of Amateurism," 123-24.
22. Love, "Crisis of Amateurism," 124, 130. To be sure, Rochester and the other court wits had "at least read the conventional school Latin authors and perhaps a little Greek," and they "tenaciously maintained their right to be considered participants in the classical literary inheritance"; in comparison to Dryden, however, these aristocrats were "lightweights" when it came to classical learning (125).
23. Love, "Crisis of Amateurism," 127.
24. Alssid, *Thomas Shadwell,* 28.
25. Shadwell, preface to *The Sullen Lovers,* 11.
26. Shadwell, preface to *The Humorists,* 187.
27. Interestingly, in contrast to my contention that Dryden views his inheritance from his playwright forebears as primarily verbal or stylistic, Hoxby reads *Aureng-Zebe* as promoting theatrically based models of inheritance: "*Aureng-Zebe* asks us to admit that culture perpetuates itself only because it remembers, substitutes, and performs," he writes, averring that "succession [in the play] depends on... act[s] of surrogacy." "Dryden's Baroque Dramaturgy," 262.
28. Hoxby, "Dryden's Baroque Dramaturgy," 256, 258.
29. Dugaw, "'The ~~Rationall~~ Spirituall Part,'" 274.
30. See also Al Coppola's discussion of Dryden's "notorious deployment of spectacular politics" in his opera *Albion and Albanius* (1685): Coppola, *Theater of Experiment,* 65, 85.
31. Hoxby, "Dryden's Baroque Dramaturgy," 259.
32. Hoxby, "Dryden's Baroque Dramaturgy," 245.
33. Needless to say, there is a generic distinction at work here as well: Hoxby, Dugaw, and Coppola are describing heroic plays—tragedies, operas—whereas *The Squire of Alsatia* and *The Lancashire Witches* are, of course, comedies.
34. Kewes, *Authorship and Appropriation,* 52.
35. Kewes, *Authorship and Appropriation,* 116.
36. See Kewes, *Authorship and Appropriation,* 58-60, 127.
37. Dryden likewise weighed in on these issues in *The Spanish Fryar* (1680), in which "references to an illegitimate succession were particularly urgent," but which also seeks to defuse the issue of Catholicism by making his friar character "a nonthreatening figure of fun" (Winn, *John Dryden,* 333).
38. Berman, "Values," 380. See also Ross, "Theatricality and Revolution Politics." For a contextualization of *The Lancashire Witches* within broader political discourses of the day, see Owen, *Restoration Theatre and Crisis,* 185-94.
39. Shadwell, *Thomas Shadwell's "The Lancashire-Witches," and "Tegue o Divelly The Irish-Priest."* Text references to *The Lancashire Witches* are to act and line.
40. Alssid, *Thomas Shadwell,* 138. Inheritance is of course a common theme of comedy, with its perennial focus on intergenerational conflict. However, I believe that Shadwell focalizes problems of succession more sharply than does the typical Restoration dramatist.

41. Again, the contrast I am drawing between Dryden and Shadwell is certainly not absolute; see, for example, Dugaw, who reads Dryden's and Purcell's *King Arthur* in ways that dovetail with my reading of Shadwell here: "In *King Arthur,* a deliberately sensuous and bi-gendered sensibility counters the manly, text-based rationalism of Anglo-Protestantism." "'Rationall Spirituall Part,'" 285.
42. Munns, "'Golden Days of Queen Elizabeth,'" 202.
43. Munns, "'Golden Days of Queen Elizabeth,'" 202.
44. On the use of such caricatures in Whig propaganda, see Munns, "'Golden Days,'" 201.
45. Downes, *Roscius Anglicanus,* 38. On the Dorset Garden productions, see Milhous, "The Multimedia Spectacular on the Restoration Stage," 41–66.
46. Slagle, Introduction, 15.
47. See Borgman, *Thomas Shadwell,* 194–95.
48. For historical discussions of the 1612 and 1633–34 episodes, see the collected essays in Poole, *The Lancashire Witches.* For more on Heywood and Brome's "journalistic" take on the 1633–34 scare, see Coffin, "Theatre and/as Witchcraft."
49. For example, where Heywood and Brome have "Horse, horse, see thou be, / And where I point thee carry me," Shadwell has "A Horse, a Horse, be thou to me, / And carry me where I shall flee." (See Borgman, *Thomas Shadwell,* 194–95.)
50. For both of these parallels, see Borgman, *Thomas Shadwell,* 194–95.
51. On the complexities of Restoration concepts of plagiarism and originality, see Kewes, *Authorship and Appropriation,* esp. chapters 2 and 3.
52. As Slagle points out, another such reference occurs in Shadwell's "Notes upon the Third Act," in which he cites Jonson's *The Sad Shepherd* (see Slagle, *Dueling Prefaces,* 18–19; see also Borgman, *Thomas Shadwell,* 198). Shadwell also mentions Jonson in passing toward the beginning of his preface, where he says that he values the support of his friends in high places even more than the thought of "excelling the most admirable *Johnson,* were it possible to be done by me" (preface to *The Lancashire Witches,* lines 45–46). The suggestion, however, is that Jonson is out of Shadwell's league, and that he cannot hope to imitate him adequately, much less rewrite him.
53. Borgman, *Thomas Shadwell,* 196.
54. Borgman, *Thomas Shadwell,* 197–98.
55. Tribble, *Margins and Marginality,* 130.
56. Tribble, *Margins and Marginality,* 130.
57. Quoted in Tribble, *Margins and Marginality,* 144.
58. Tribble, *Margins and Marginality,* 144.
59. Quoted in Tribble, *Margins and Marginality,* 145.
60. Quoted in Tribble, *Margins and Marginality,* 145.
61. Meskill, "Exorcising the Gorgon of Terror," 198.
62. Meskill, "Exorcising the Gorgon of Terror," 185.
63. Meskill, "Exorcising the Gorgon of Terror," 194–95.
64. Meskill, "Exorcising the Gorgon of Terror," 195.
65. Meskill, "Exorcising the Gorgon of Terror," 185.

66. Meskill, "Exorcising the Gorgon of Terror," 188.
67. Meskill, "Exorcising the Gorgon of Terror," 195.
68. Shadwell, *Thomas Shadwell's "The Lancashire-Witches," and "Tegue o Divelly The Irish-Priest,"* 95.
69. The witches also make their own aphrodisiacs, in the form of "Love Cups" (2.483).
70. Likewise, Bellfort's "Powder" recalls the "powder" that Susan has made from hair and nails, and puts into her would-be lover's drink.
71. The book referred to here is *The Academy of Complements,* an extremely popular collection produced by Humphrey Moseley. According to Arthur Marotti, "This duodecimo volume appeared in three editions in 1640 and was also printed in 1650, 1654, 1655, 1658, 1663, 1664, 1670, 1684, 1685, 1705, 1727, 1750, 1790, and 1795" (*Manuscript, Print, and the English Renaissance Lyric,* 266n116). Marotti adds that, "Like other literary miscellanies and poetry anthologies, this text reveals a basic (but commercially exploitable) conflict between its elitist contents and the democratizing effects of print. . . . Its full title makes this quite clear: *The Academy of Complements. Wherein Ladyes, Gentlewomen, Schollers, and Strangers may accommodate their Courtly Practice with most Curious Ceremonies, Complementall, Amorous, High expression, and formes of speaking, or writing. A work perused and most exactly perfected by the Author with Additions of witty Amorous Poems, And a Table expounding the hard English words*" (266).
72. See Demos, *The Enemy Within.* According to Demos, *Malleus Maleficarum* appeared in thirteen different editions within thirty years of its first publication, and in another twenty-nine editions in the last few years of the sixteenth century, when witch hunting saw another wave of popularity.
73. See, for example, Sir William's line at 1.1.389-93: "Ah Brother, I must confess it was a kindness in you, when Heaven had blest you with a great Estate by Merchandize, to adopt my Younger Son, and take him and breed him from his Childhood: But you have been so gentle to him, he is run into all manner of Vice and Riot." Likewise, Sir Edward rebukes Sir William: "Let us calmly reason: What has your breeding made of [Belfond Senior] . . . but a Blockhead?" (2.1.353-54).
74. See Berman, "Values," 379-85.
75. Ross, "Theatricality and Revolution Politics," 223, 226-27.
76. Shadwell, *Thomas Shadwell's "The Squire of Alsatia."* Text references to *The Squire of Alsatia* are to act, scene, and, when relevant, line.
77. As Ross points out, this divergence between the two methods of defeating the Alsatians also has strong political implications: "Sir William's arbitrary . . . efforts" at channeling "absolute monarchical authority" are shown to be wholly inadequate, whereas Sir Edward and Belfond Junior's solution—namely, "mobiliz[ing] the powers of the law"—demonstrates that "the alternative to personal royal power is neither mob rule nor anarchy, but the exercise of constitutional and legal

authority by the political classes and the common lawyers." Ross, "Theatricality and Revolution Politics," 227. My own emphasis here is on how different strategies for managing and relaying power in *The Squire* translate into questions of artistic or cultural inheritance, but as Ross's reading makes clear, these questions simultaneously resonate with the central political crises of the 1680s.

78. Hume writes that, in Belfond Junior's search for a wife, "wealth is the principal factor in marital eligibility, and Lucia's attorney father does not have enough of it." *Development of English Drama*, 84. More generally, Hume points out that the end of the play sees "Belfond jun. [emerging] ... with all the odour of sanctity that money can buy" (83). Indeed, even though Belfond Junior lies about Lucia's innocence so that she'll be able to reenter the marriage market with her reputation intact, Sir Edward still decides to "pay her [off]" as well—a rather "peculiar" choice (83), implying that money is ultimately the be-all and end-all in the younger brothers' mercantile universe.

79. The *OED* dates this use of *bubble* (as in a "dupe," or "a person who is ... easily ... hoodwinked") to as early as 1668 (s.v. "bubble" [n.], def. 3). Wycherley uses the term at least three times in *The Country Wife* (1675). But Shadwell's inclusion of it in his glossary suggests that he, at least, believed it still to be in limited circulation in the 1680s.

80. "Pye Corner" would not have been found on a map; rather, it is a kind of nickname. Technically, Ross explains, it was "the corner of Giltspur St. and Cock Lane," but it earned its moniker from "the cooks' shops which stood there" (*Thomas Shadwell's "The Squire of Alsatia,"* note to 3.2.208).

81. As Cheatly declares at one point (anticipating Macheath's rhetoric), "Great Souls are above Ordinances, and never can be Slaves to Fame" (5.1.23).

82. Here I differ from J. Douglas Canfield, who, despite acknowledging the role of Sir Edward's "new" money in securing the play's denouement, sees *The Squire of Alsatia* as *not* ultimately "jettisoning patrilineal patriarchy as the system for the succession of power." In the end, he insists, the "estate in the traditional sense is reaffirmed: patrimony is passed down through the body of a woman. Hence Belfond Junior 'must' marry a virgin who is the proper conduit for his power and property." Canfield, "Late Shadwell," 108, 106.

83. For a detailed discussion of how this division works, see Ross's comments on Shadwell's use of sources: *Thomas Shadwell's "The Squire of Alsatia,"* 20–30.

84. See Ross, "Theatricality and Revolution Politics," 219. See also Hume, who notes the "rollicking vigour" of the "boisterous tavern scenes in Alsatia"; he also points out that the Alsatia setting allows for an "unusually large cast," which "makes for tremendous variety and bustle." *Development of English Drama*, 85.

85. Ross, "The Play," 31.

86. Ross, "Alsatia and the Alsatians," 230.

87. See Ross, "The Play," 31; and Borgman, *Thomas Shadwell*, 214.

88. Ross, "The Play," 22.
89. Shadwell, preface to *The Humorists*, 187.
90. To "banter" here has a less good-natured definition than it later takes on: "To make fun of (a person); to hold up to ridicule"; "To impose upon (a person)...; to delude, cheat, trick, bamboozle" (*OED*, s.v. "banter," defs. 1 and 2).
91. See Frank Kermode's commentary on the use of this same phrase in Ariel's song from *The Tempest* (1.2): Kermode believes the refrain of "Bow-wow" to be "probably derived from James Rosier's account of a ceremonial Virginan dance" (*The Tempest*, 34–35, note to 1.2.384); see also Kermode's introduction, xxxiii.
92. The reference to "Indian[s]" could also be seen as building upon the play's series of allusions to empire and mercantile capitalism: in the alternative model of inheritance represented by Belfond Junior (/Sir Edward Belfond/Cheatly), success arises not from consolidating wealth in one place but from moving throughout the globe, finding new sources of income, and becoming proficient in new languages and new ways of thinking. Of course, as we have seen, Shadwell also suggests that these new modes of wealth creation are exploitative and even criminal.
93. A more typical ratio of unfamiliar to familiar words might include this one from the 1725 *New Canting Dictionary*, which glosses *Bubble* as "an easy soft Fellow, one that is fit to be imposed on, deluded, or cheated"; by contrast, Shadwell's list glosses "*Bubble,* [or] *Caravan*" as "The Cheated." See *A New Canting Dictionary: Comprehending All the terms, Antient and Modern, Used in the Several tribes of Gypsies, Beggars, Shoplifters, Highwaymen, Foot-Pads, and all the other Clans of Cheats and Villains... Useful for all Sorts of People (especially Travellers and Foreigners) to enable them to secure their Money and preserve their Lives...* (London, 1725). *Eighteenth-Century Collections Online*, British Library copy. Gale Document Number CW0111642360.
94. Shadwell, prologue to *The Royal Shepherdess*, 101.
95. Shadwell, prologue to *The Royal Shepherdess*, 99.
96. Shadwell, prologue to *The Royal Shepherdess*, 99.
97. Shadwell, prologue to *The Royal Shepherdess*, 101.
98. See Kewes, *Authorship and Appropriation*, 44.
99. Shadwell, prologue to *The Royal Shepherdess*, 101.
100. In fact, Harold Love has characterized Shadwell as "a professional writer with the mindset of an [aristocratic] amateur." See "Crisis of Amateurism," 128.
101. Langbaine, *An Account of the English Dramatick Poets*, 450.
102. Kewes, *Authorship and Appropriation*, 40.
103. Kewes, *Authorship and Appropriation*, 57, 53–54.

2. "CAN MY IMAGINATION FEEL?"

1. Barish, *Antitheatrical Prejudice*, 139.
2. Jonson uses a similar set of metaphors in his introductory remarks to *The Masque of Blackness*, in which he refers to the masque's spectacle as its "carkasse" and its language as its "spirit" (quoted in Barish, *Antitheatrical Prejudice*, 140).
3. Straznicky, *Women's Closet Drama*, 70.
4. Berek, "Defoliating Playbooks," 398. See my introduction for a longer discussion of this development.
5. Dryden, dedication to *The Spanish Fryar*, 102 (emphasis added).
6. Dryden, dedication to *The Spanish Fryar*, 102.
7. Dryden, dedication to *The Spanish Fryar*, 101.
8. This moral objection to the sensuality of live theater—as opposed to the more rational effects of reading drama on the page—would be famously taken up later by Jeremy Collier in his *Short View of the Immorality and Profaneness of the English Stage* (1698). As Michael Dobson points out, although Collier denounces bawdry in the playhouse, he shows himself to be "deeply read" in both the classical and vernacular traditions, "excelling at a species of close reading" that suggests that "no particular shame should attach to perusing plays in the study." See *Making of the National Poet*, 114. Collier thus implicitly makes the case, in the words of John O'Brien, for turning "the English Stage" of his title into "a literary genre." O'Brien, *Harlequin Britain*, 51. Indeed, there is some sense in which the textual scrutiny of plays appears to de-"prophan[ize]" them: as Simon Shepherd and Peter Womack note, the kind of detailed analysis to which Collier subjects the plays in his tract had previously been exercised exclusively on scriptural texts; Collier's book even "appropriates the form of a biblical commentary in its ... layout and design." *English Drama: A Cultural History* (quoted in O'Brien, *Harlequin Britain*, 51).
9. Of course, Steven Shapin and Simon Schaffer's *Leviathan and the Air-Pump* remains the authoritative account of Hobbes's quarrel with Boyle and the Royal Society; on the particular debates mentioned here, see especially page 22. Lisa T. Sarasohn's *The Natural Philosophy of Margaret Cavendish* offers a comprehensive account of Cavendish's thought; chapter 7 details her objections to the work of "the Experimenters" in particular. Elizabeth Spiller asserts a direct connection between Hobbes's critique of experimentalism and Cavendish's, contending that "the tradition of speculative natural philosophy [was] defined for Cavendish by Hobbes." *Science, Reading, and Renaissance Literature*, 144. For a discussion of Hobbes's influence more generally on Cavendish, see Battigelli, *Exiles of the Mind*, 64–67.
10. Gevirtz, *Women*, 47.
11. See especially Anderson, "Novelty in Novels"; Gevirtz, *Women*, chapter 1; Starr, "Objects, Imaginings, and Facts"; and Tierney-Hynes, *Novel Minds*.
12. See McKeon, *Origins of the English Novel;* and Starr (op. cit.). See also Davis, *Factual Fictions*.

13. Marcie Frank suggests that in this regard Behn was part of a larger movement: she points to the many ways in which writers throughout the Restoration and eighteenth century insisted on the interrelationship between print and performance. See Frank, *Novel Stage,* 6 and *passim.* Frank contends that a sense of division or hierarchy between these terms did not emerge until the Romantic period (6); by contrast, as my reading of Jonson here implies, I believe there is also evidence, dating from even before the Interregnum, of a larger critical awareness of the difference between reading and spectating. In my readings, Behn and other Restoration authors who defy a firm separation between page and stage do so in dialogue with the long history of antitheatricality.

14. Of course, bed tricks are a longstanding tradition in dramatic and non-dramatic texts. However, I argue that in *The Luckey Chance,* Behn uses bed tricks in ways that many other authors do not—namely, to explore profound epistemological and ontological problems. On the history of the bed trick, and especially its implications for questions of gender and sexuality, see Desens, *The Bed-Trick.*

15. Julia suggests at one point that the marriage to Sir Cautious took place against her will—"Oh how fatal are forc'd Marriages!"—but this notion seems to be contradicted two lines later, when she expresses regret for her failure to keep her promise to Gayman: "Had I but kept my sacred Vows to *Gayman* / How happy had I been—how prosperous he!" (1.2.30, 1.2.32-33).

16. Behn, *The Luckey Chance,* ed. Aughterson and Bowditch. Text references to *The Luckey Chance* are to act, scene, and, when relevant, line.

17. Behn, *The Rover and Other Plays.* See Spencer's note to line 80 (p. 373).

18. Gallagher, *Nobody's Story,* 46-47.

19. In this context, indeed, Gayman's description of his bedfellow as an "old *Proserpine*" makes a new kind of sense: as queen of the underworld, Proserpine provides "a suitable name for a female devil," as Jane Spencer points out (note to 4.1.75); but the underworld is also, of course, the realm of the dead—a resonance that is reinforced by Proserpine's association more broadly with the changing of the seasons and the passage of time.

20. Starr, "Objects, Imaginings, and Facts," 510.

21. Starr, "Objects, Imaginings, and Facts," 506.

22. Smyth, *Women Writing Fancy,* 158.

23. Hobbes, *Leviathan,* 11.

24. Hobbes, *Leviathan,* 11.

25. Hobbes, *Leviathan,* 14.

26. Hobbes, *Leviathan,* 12.

27. Butler, *Imagination and Politics,* 160.

28. Hobbes, *Leviathan,* 16-19.

29. For a detailed treatment of the differing views on matter held by Cavendish and Hobbes, see Duncan, "Debating Materialism." The connections between the two have also been well documented, however: Hobbes had served as a tutor to

Cavendish's husband in his childhood, and William Cavendish continued to be a patron to Hobbes in later years. See Cunning, *Margaret Cavendish,* 6; and Sarasohn, *Natural Philosophy,* 3.

30. Cavendish, *Observations upon Experimental Philosophy,* 99.
31. See Sarasohn, who explains that Cavendish "adapted the ontology of the mechanistic philosophers—matter in motion—but reconfigured it to suit her own view of nature. Her natural philosophy was a form of vitalistic materialism that posited a universe composed of three kinds of matter—rational, sensitive, and inanimate." *Natural Philosophy,* 2.
32. Starr, "Anti-Platonic Line," 298.
33. Starr, "Anti-Platonic Line," 299.
34. Cavendish, *Observations upon Experimental Philosophy,* 180n111. (This quotation is taken from the 1666 edition, whereas O'Neill generally uses the 1668 version and thus reproduces the 1666 variant in a footnote to page 180.)
35. Cavendish, *Observations upon Experimental Philosophy,* 180n111.
36. Cavendish, *Observations upon Experimental Philosophy,* 180n111.
37. Cavendish, *Observations upon Experimental Philosophy,* 47.
38. Cavendish, *Observations upon Experimental Philosophy,* 175.
39. Cavendish, *Poems, and Fancies,* 8, 43.
40. It is worth noting here that Cavendish, as Starr puts it, probably "does not offer a pattern of imitation for other writers" of her time: she was never widely read, and many factors—her sex, her lack of a formal education—contributed to her marginalization as a thinker. Yet, as Starr has demonstrated, Cavendish's philosophical affinity for Lucretius, along with her more generally anti-Platonic approach to matter, imagination, and pleasure, is "mirrored by other women authors [during this] period," perhaps most notably by Aphra Behn; see Starr, "Anti-Platonic Line," 295, 301. Indeed, even if Behn was not personally familiar with Cavendish's writings, often only a single degree of separation stood between the two women: Thomas Sprat, for instance—who, in addition to writing the *History of the Royal Society,* also penned a eulogy for Cavendish—was an acquaintance of Behn's as well. If no direct lines of influence can be traced between these two figures, then, Cavendish's work piquantly articulates an imagination-based epistemology that retained its appeal—especially for female thinkers—long after experimentalism had become the more dominant paradigm.
41. Dryden, dedication to *The Spanish Fryar,* 99.
42. Jean Marsden makes the point that the trick is a "violation" in a number of respects ("Restoration Stage," 194–95), and Ann Marie Stewart argues for seeing it as "rape" (*Ravishing Restoration,* 84). For, of course, even if Julia invited Gayman to have sex with her in the earlier trick, she has not consented to it here. Moreover, there is certainly an unfair discrepancy between Julia's trick, in which Gayman willingly agrees to exchange his body for money (even if he feels he has no choice, financially), and Gayman's trick, in which Julia's body is also essentially sold, but without her knowledge.

43. *OED*, s.v. "enjoy," def. 4b.
44. Gallagher, *Nobody's Story*, 46–47.
45. Behn, "The Disappointment," lines 71–90.
46. Note that a number of critics (such as Jessica Munns) have read these lines as narrating an instance of premature ejaculation (as in Rochester's *Imperfect Enjoyment*). However, upon close inspection it appears that the lines evoke, more simply, an unsustained erection. Although the "weeping" of the "Insensible" penis might seem to allude to spilled semen, such an interpretation does not accord with the description of the lover's "Power" having being "snatch[ed]," or of his "slack'ned Nerves" having been "invade[d]" by "Faintness." It seems to me that "weeping" could simply mean "drooping" (the *OED* cites a quotation from 1606 referring to a "weeping Elme" ["weeping" (adj.), def. 6]). Alternatively, M. L. Stapleton speculates that the penile "weeping" refers to preejaculate. In either of these cases, the poem would be describing an instance not of virility defying its owner's control but, rather, of a failed virility. This distinction is obviously important in thinking about how the phrase "excess of love" works in *The Luckey Chance* as well. See Munns, "'But to the touch were soft,'" 182. And see Stapleton, *Admired and Understood*, 224.
47. Interestingly, however, the use of the word "betray'd" in both "The Disappointment" and *The Luckey Chance* may actually support such a reading. Recall Gayman's report that "my Excess of Love betray'd the Cheat"—a phrase that echoes the poem's wording not once but twice ("Excess of Love his Love betray'd"). We might at first assume that each use of the word "betray" here means something different: Gayman's cheat is "betray'd" in the sense of being revealed or disclosed (*OED* defs. 5, 6, and 7), whereas Lisander's love is "betray'd" in the sense of having fallen victim to treachery (def. 1). But it is also possible to understand Gayman's excess of love as having not just discovered but traitorously *undermined* the cheat—that is, as having both exposed the ruse as a ruse and interrupted or (to invoke another of the *OED*'s definitions) "disappoint[ed]" the ultimate "hopes or expectations" behind the trick (def. 2a). Such an interpretation would further imply that, in *The Luckey Chance*, "Excess of Love" refers not to Gayman's overwhelming physicality but, rather, to (in some form or other) his mental overwhelmedness.
48. Susan Green glosses "Excess of Love" as "a second erection." Presumably such an occurrence would not be a routine component of Julia's nights with her aged husband. Green's hypothesis, however, assumes a much longer period of ignorance prior to the bed trick's revelation: Green implicitly describes a situation in which Julia fails to identify Gayman not just during the initial phase of their lovemaking but throughout the whole, fully consummated process, from start to finish and back again. While Green does, therefore, posit a scenario in which a mental reality is ultimately shattered by a physical reality, at the same time, her reading also grants that mental reality an even greater force prior to its dissolution. See Green, "Semiotic Modalities," 129.

49. Cavendish, *Observations upon Experimental Philosophy*, 151.
50. Cavendish, *Observations upon Experimental Philosophy*, 151-52.
51. Fawcett, "Unmapping London," 164-65.
52. See Bush-Bailey, *Treading the Bawds*, 86. Bush-Bailey suggests that Barry's association with avarice in the public imagination may have derived from the fact that, in 1685, she renegotiated her contract with the United Company to include an annual benefit night—the first time that this form of compensation (originally intended for playwrights) had been extended to an individual performer (62-64). See also Hume, "Origins of the Actor Benefit."
53. Barry may also have been the mistress of George Etherege and the Earl of Dorset, as well as Sir Henry St. John Bart. See Howe, *First English Actresses*, 31.
54. Cited in Howe, op. cit., 116.
55. Markley, "Behn and the Unstable Traditions"; on Nokes, see 109-12.
56. Gallagher writes that although "Julia appears outraged at the attempted deception[,] . . . we can only see this tirade as more deceit on Julia's part, since we know she tricked the same man into bed the night before. . . . But since her deceit was not immediately discovered and his was, she is able to feign outrage and demand a separation from her husband." *Nobody's Story*, 47. Ecclesiastical courts could grant married couples the right to separate on grounds of cruelty or adultery; see Alleman, *Matrimonial Law*, 112-13.
57. See Spencer's endnote in her edition: "How long has he known this news, and has he only been pretending to be poverty-stricken?" (note to 5.7.202).
58. See Markley, "Behn and the Unstable Traditions," 113.
59. Intriguingly, Barry and Betterton had played opposite each other in Thomas Otway's 1680 tragedy *The Orphan* (written in blank verse), of which *The Luckey Chance* could in many ways be seen as a comic inversion. *The Orphan* dramatizes the story of two twins, Castalio (played by Betterton) and Polydore, both of whom are in love with Monimia (played by Barry). Castalio and Monimia marry, but secretly. Then Polydore, overhearing what he believes are plans for an unmarried assignation between Castalio and Monimia, and "enrag'd to think / [Castalio has] out-done me in successful Love," deceives his way into the bedchamber on the couple's wedding night: "I in the dark went and supply'd thy place, / Whilst all the Night, midst our Triumphant Joys, / The trembling, tender, kind, deceiv'd *Monimia*, / Embrac'd, Carest, and call'd me her *Castalio*" (5.528-33). Realizing afterward what has happened, Monimia poisons herself, Polydore runs on Castalio's sword, and Castalio stabs himself; see Otway, *The Orphan*.
60. Fawcett, "Unmapping London," 167.
61. Gallagher, *Nobody's Story*, 47-48.
62. Hume, *Development of English Drama*, 376-77.
63. Hume, *Development of English Drama*, 371.
64. Hume, *Development of English Drama*, 370.
65. Hume, *Development of English Drama*, 340.

66. Kavenik, "Playwright as 'Breeches Part,'" 189.
67. Kavenik, "Playwright as 'Breeches Part,'" 189.
68. Settle, *Farther Defence of Dramatick Poetry*, 53. Collier's *Short View of the Immorality and Profaneness of the English Stage* (1698) had appeared earlier that year.
69. Settle, *Farther Defence of Dramatick Poetry*, 54.
70. Bennett, *Theater as Problem*, 61.
71. Bennett, *Theater as Problem*, 67 (emphasis added).
72. Bennet, *Theater as Problem*, 67.
73. For discussions of Behn's often sarcastic, defiant, or tonally ambiguous prefaces, see Payne, "'Patron Princes'"; and Munns, "'Sugar-Candied Reader.'"
74. *The Luckey Chance*, ed. Aughterson and Bowditch, 231n24.
75. For additional readings of this famous passage, see Kavenik, "Playwright as 'Breeches Part'," 179. See also Munns, "'I by a double right thy bounties claim,'" 195.
76. Coppola, *Theater of Experiment*, 5.
77. Coppola, *Theater of Experiment*, 65, 76. Coppola here is citing Paula Backscheider's concept of "spectacular politics"; see Backscheider, *Spectacular Politics*.
78. Coppola, *Theater of Experiment*, 81, 64.
79. See Kenyon, *Popish Plot*, 257.
80. Coppola, *Theater of Experiment*, 82.
81. Several references are made to Titus Oates and/or St. Omers, where he had studied: 1.1.238 and 1.1.254, and 1.3.120–21. Mention of the Aldermen needing to meet at the Guildhall to discuss "some damnable Plot" in 3.2.36 may likewise allude to the conspiracy invented by Oates. When Gayman, dressed as the "dead" Belmour, scares Sir Feeble and Sir Cautious into a panic, they declare that the demon they have seen is "as tall as the Monument"—namely, the column commemorating the Great Fire of London (1666), whose inscription had been revised in 1681 (in the midst of the Popish Plot hysteria) to blame Catholics for the fire (3.5.167). For discussions of Behn's treatment of the Popish Plot more generally in her oeuvre, see Shell, "Popish Plots," and Ballaster, "Fiction Feigning Femininity."
82. Coppola, *Theater of Experiment*, 5.
83. See Ezell, "Public Spectacles: The Popish Plot and Public Mass Media," in *The Oxford English Literary History*.
84. Walker, "Remember Justice Godfrey," 121–22.
85. Walker, "Remember Justice Godfrey," 125–26.
86. Walker, "Remember Justice Godfrey," 125–26, 127.
87. See Kenyon, *Popish Plot*: hundreds of Catholics were imprisoned, and at least twenty-four were put to death.
88. Walker, "Remember Justice Godfrey," 131. See also Knights, *Representation and Misrepresentation*.
89. For details on the campaign by seventeenth-century booksellers to create and market a print canon, see my introduction. Moseley's main impact had been felt

during the Interregnum; Tonson's influential *Miscellanies,* edited by Dryden, had begun appearing in 1684.

90. Gert, "Hobbes' Psychology," 158. The quotation from Hobbes is from *Leviathan,* 11.
91. Hobbes, *Leviathan,* 13.
92. Hobbes, *Leviathan,* 13.
93. Shapin and Schaffer, *Leviathan and the Air-Pump,* 60, 61 (emphasis original).
94. Johns, "Reading and Experiment," 249.
95. Quoted in Shapin and Schaffer, *Leviathan and the Air-Pump,* 63-64.
96. Behn, *The Emperor of the Moon,* ed. Hobby and Hogarth, 1.1.84, 95. Text references to *The Emperor of the Moon* are to act, scene, and, when relevant, line.
97. Coppola posits that theatricality constitutes both the disease and the cure: "Behn's elaborate farce summons the audience's blank wonder in order to correct it." *Theater of Experiment,* 66.
98. "Gonzales" (or "Gonsales") is actually a fictional character, who relates his fantastic travels in *The Man in the Moon,* by Francis Godwin (1629). Here, Scaramouch apparently attributes another volume to him as well.
99. For an extended consideration of the meaning of *curiosity* in the early modern period, see Benedict, *Curiosity.*
100. *Rapture,* in the seventeenth century, could function essentially as a synonym for *ravish* (see *OED* defs. 2a and 2b).
101. To be "astonished" can specifically mean "to [be] stun[ned] mentally," to be "shock[ed] out of [one's] wits" (*OED,* s.v. "astonished," def. 2).
102. Cavendish, *Observations upon Experimental Philosophy,* 182.
103. Cavendish, *Philosophical and Physical Opinions,* 21.
104. See Perry, *Women, Letters, and the Novel,* 130-31. See also Ballaster, *Seductive Forms,* especially chapter 2, in which she explores a conventional late seventeenth-century analogy between "the female 'form,' or body, and female forms, or amatory fictions" (31). And see Warner: "A specter haunted early-modern Europe: that of the novel reader reading. This specter ... is understood to be mindlessly absorbed by the text ..., and compulsively addicted to its pleasures"; it is "an inverse image of the Enlightenment project of a rationally motivated reading; the latter produces the former as its own particular nightmarish phantasm." *Licensing Entertainment,* 139-42.
105. See Johns, "The Physiology of Reading." See also Schoenfeldt, "Reading Bodies."
106. Settle, *Farther Defence of Dramatick Poetry,* 54.
107. Settle, *Farther Defence of Dramatick Poetry,* 54-55.
108. Here Settle anticipates Charles Lamb's notorious objections, over a century later, to the theatrical representation of Shakespeare's characters. I discuss Lamb's arguments in my conclusion.
109. Betterton of course played Pericles in the first Restoration-era production of a Shakespeare play. See Taylor, *Reinventing Shakespeare,* 20-24.
110. Behn, prologue to *The Amorous Prince,* lines 13-28.

111. In 1671 the word *don* seemingly did not yet refer to the head of a college (for which the *OED*'s first citation dates from 1681; see def. 4); instead, it referred to a man of distinction or importance more generally (the *OED* cites the epilogue to Dryden's 1667 *Indian Emperour*: "the great Dons of Wit" [def. 3]).
112. Interestingly, *Catiline* seems to have epitomized for Samuel Pepys, too, what we would now call a "reading play" (the *OED* cites Fielding's 1730 *Author's Farce* as its earliest example of this usage), as opposed to a play that works well in performance. Pepys writes in his diary entry for December 19, 1668, "saw 'Catiline's Conspiracy,' yesterday being the first day: a play of much good sense and words to read, but that do appear the worst upon the stage, I mean, the least diverting, that ever I saw any, though most in fine clothes; and a fine scene of the Senate, and of a fight, that ever I saw in my life. But the play is only to be read." McAfee, *Pepys on the Restoration Stage*, 112.
113. Barish, *Antitheatrical Prejudice*, 139.
114. Hume, *Dryden's Criticism*, 63.
115. *Aristotle's Poetics*, 62–64.
116. Rymer, *Tragedies of the Last Age*, 18.
117. Dryden, "Heads of an Answer to Rymer," 192.
118. Hume, *Dryden's Criticism*, 60. Song and Spectacle, meanwhile, seem to fall out of the picture altogether; see Hume, *Dryden's Criticism*, 58.
119. *Aristotle's Poetics*, 62.
120. *Aristotle's Poetics*, 102–3.
121. Hume, *Dryden's Criticism*, 18, 12.
122. Hume, *Dryden's Criticism*, 12, 18–19. Edward Pechter describes this same critical shift in a slightly different light, and singles out the rise of empiricism as a key contributor: noting that "Renaissance theory tends to emphasize the metaphysical, the ability of poetic imagination to express 'the very truth,'" Pechter points out that, by contrast, the New Philosophy posited a "new split between human consciousness and reality," so that "it could no longer have made as much sense to focus on the relation between poetry and truth as on the relation between poetry and mind"; as a consequence, "literary theory" transferred its focus "from metaphysical to psychological." Pechter, *Dryden's Classical Theory*, 147.
123. Henke, *Performance and Literature*, 51.
124. Meagher, "Commedia dell'arte."

3. TEXTUAL TIMELESSNESS, PERFORMATIVE TIME

1. Dryden, "To My Dear Friend," line 67.
2. Dryden, "To My Dear Friend," line 6.
3. Dryden, "To My Dear Friend," lines 11–19.
4. Weber, "'Double Portion,'" 360.

5. Weber, "'Double Portion,'" 361.
6. Barnard, "English Literary Canon," 307-9. For more on the collaboration between Tonson and these authors, see McKenzie, who notes that Congreve was living with Tonson in 1695, and had probably begun to do so as early as 1693; McKenzie also points out that "it was Tonson who suggested that Dryden translate the *Aeneid*," and Dryden likewise worked with Tonson on the series of poetic miscellanies he published in the 1680s and 1690s; see "Typography and Meaning," 225, 227; McKenzie is also citing Treadwell, "Congreve, Tonson, and Rowe's 'Reconcilement.'"
7. McKenzie, "Typography and Meaning," 227.
8. Barnard, "English Literary Canon," 310.
9. As Humphrey Moseley had done before him (whose list of authors he had inherited), Tonson sought to create a distinct "series" of volumes, defining a specific body of works in English as "literary" (by Beaumont and Fletcher, Suckling, Cowley, etc.); these included both old standbys as well as more recent candidates for classic status, among which he counted the writings of Congreve, as well as, for example, Vanbrugh; see Barnard, "Creating an English Canon," 314. See also McKenzie, who deems Tonson's larger publishing project to be the period's "most notable development in the London [book] trade." "Typography and Meaning," 226.
10. Barnard, "English Literary Canon," 310.
11. McKenzie points out that Tonson essentially invented "subscription publishing for selling English literature" when, in 1688, he used it for *Paradise Lost*; Tonson then arranged for Dryden's *Aeneid* to be sold by subscription as well (1697), thereby using this model to support a living writer for the first time. "Typography and Meaning," 227.
12. McKenzie, "Typography and Meaning," 227.
13. McKenzie, "Typography and Meaning," 226.
14. Holland, *Ornament of Action*, 130. McKenzie likewise believes that the revisions "reduc[e]" the "vitality" of Congreve's two earlier plays in particular. "Typography and Meaning," 224.
15. Holland, *Ornament of Action*, 224.
16. McKenzie, "Typography and Meaning," 227.
17. McKenzie, "Typography and Meaning," 227.
18. McKenzie, "Typography and Meaning," 230.
19. Holland, *Ornament of Action*, 136-37.
20. Holland, *Ornament of Action*, 136.
21. Lyons, *Kingdom of Disorder*, 152.
22. Lyons, *Kingdom of Disorder*, 154, 187.
23. Lyons, *Kingdom of Disorder*, 166 (emphasis added).
24. See also Peters, who writes that "the normative aesthetic ... expressed in the Rules" of neoclassical dramaturgy was seen as imposing "a new set of literate standards ... on the natural 'license' of the popular theatre"; "the insistence on

the 'Rules'... stressed the importance for the drama of adhering [instead] to critical norms capable of validation through printed authorities." *Theatre of the Book,* 124. Peters contends that this focus on the "Rules" therefore amounted, essentially, to a new iteration of antitheatricality (122).
25. Holland, *Ornament of Action,* 238.
26. States, "Performance as Metaphor," 73. States bases his statements on Schechner's *Between Theater and Anthropology* and *Future of Ritual.*
27. States, "Performance as Metaphor," 73, citing Phelan's *Unmarked.*
28. States, "Performance as Metaphor," 74, citing Schechner.
29. Phelan, *Unmarked,* 146.
30. States, "Performance as Metaphor," 73, citing Schechner.
31. Eliade, *Patterns in Comparative Religion,* 392 (quoted in Cole, *Theatrical Event,* 7).
32. Cole, *Theatrical Event,* 6.
33. Castle, *Masquerade and Civilization,* 55.
34. For a detailed discussion of Congreve's and Locke's construals of knowledge and epistemology, see Jarvis, "Philosophical Assumptions."
35. Note that courtship *per se* is no longer at issue in *The Way of the World,* as Mirabell and Millamant in fact already tried to elope prior to the opening of act 1.
36. Congreve, *Love for Love: A Comedy,* 2.3.9-23. Text references to *Love for Love* are to act, scene, and, when relevant, line.
37. We learn early on in act 1 that Valentine has fathered more than one bastard child, in addition to running through much of his cash (1.4).
38. Valentine's faith in the relative reliability of texts over libertine pleasures turns out to be temporary: when Mr. Scandal describes him as more intent on finding ways to evade his creditors "than [he] would be to invent the honest Means of keeping [his] Word," Valentine does not deny that he has made multiple past promises that he is able to honor neither in the immediate present nor in the foreseeable future. Words, it seems, whether spoken or written, are just as fickle as the flesh. Indeed, he then links bodies and words directly when he warns his friend, "this Liberty of your Tongue, will one Day bring a Confinement on your Body" (1.3.10-14).
39. Note, too, that the quarto edition of the play prints the prophecy in blackletter—a typeface dropped in 1710, presumably for reasons of visual polish—thus suggesting its status as a written object, rather than simply a series of words that Foresight has memorized. Another function of this use of blackletter, I would contend, is to emphasize further the connection between Foresight's textual faith and Sir Sampson's: the typeface appears again in 4.8, when Sir Sampson brandishes the bond he has coerced Valentine into signing.
40. Peters, *Congreve,* 68.
41. Obviously "masquerade," in one form or another, is central to all theater. Here I am interested specifically in *Love for Love*'s engagement with the tropes and language of late seventeenth- and early eighteenth-century masquerade balls, the cultural impact of which Castle explores.

42. Congreve, preface to *Incognita*, p. 5, lines 36–40.
43. Relatedly, Castle's study of masquerade, though it mentions in passing a few theatrical iterations (such as the masquerade in Shadwell's *Virtuoso*, or in Dryden's *Marriage A-la-Mode*), focuses mainly on the use of the masked ball in eighteenth-century novels (part 2 of *Pamela*; *Amelia*; *Cecilia*; etc.). It would seem, then, that Congreve is not the only writer who saw masquerade as a very specific kind of cross-generic tool, by which one could import the "dramatic" into prose fiction. See Castle, *Masquerade and Civilization*.
44. Castle, *Masquerade and Civilization*, 58–70.
45. Castle, *Masquerade and Civilization*, 69. This scene also alludes, clearly, to other moments of "feigned madness" in drama (as in *Hamlet*). For a discussion of simulated lunacy and its relationship to metatheatricality more generally, see Smith, "Ironic Distance."
46. Castle, *Masquerade and Civilization*, 4. As Castle notes, moralistic objections to the seventeenth- and eighteenth-century masquerade phenomenon clearly echoed antitheatrical discourse, as both institutions threatened traditional delineations between fact and feigning; see *Masquerade and Civilization*, 79.
47. Castle, *Masquerade and Civilization*, 35. Although Castle's focus is on the eighteenth century, when masquerade became a widespread commercial phenomenon, these phrases seem already to have been well established as early as 1673, when Palamede and Rhodophil, in Dryden's *Marriage A-la-Mode*, engage in "Masquerading": here Palamede remarks, "What with our antique habits, and feign'd voices, do you know me? and I know you? Methinks we move and talk just like so many over-grown Puppets." Dryden, *Works*, vol. 11, 281.
48. Castle, *Masquerade and Civilization*, 35.
49. In addition to various versions of "I/We know you" (five times) and "do you/you don't know me" (eight times), characters speak of knowing their own or each other's "minds" or "sel[ves]" (three times), and of knowing the person of whom someone else is speaking (dozens of times).
50. Castle, *Masquerade and Civilization*, 7
51. Cole, *Theatrical Event*, 7.
52. Note that this inversion is also alluded to in Angelica's announcement that she has made the "utmost trial of [Valentine's] Virtue": for while "virtue" itself obviously need not be feminine, the language of testing or proving carries overtones of sexual virtue in particular. Unlike other kinds of goodness, chastity—as Milton's *Comus* insists (for example)—gains meaning only in the face of temptation or trial. (*Love for Love* contains its own glancing allusion to this principle in the song performed in act 3: "*He alone won't betray in whom none will Confide; / And the Nymph may be Chaste that has never been try'd*" [3.3.172–73].) And, of course, throughout the literary tradition, sexual virtue is valued most in women ("*Nymph[s]*"), and tested most by men. On the inversion of typical gender roles in masquerade, see Castle: "Much of the fear the masquerade generated . . . is related to the belief

that it encouraged female sexual freedom, and beyond that, female emancipation generally." *Masquerade and Civilization,* 33.
53. See Kroll, "Discourse and Power," 731.
54. Lyons, *Kingdom of Disorder,* 153.
55. Lyons, *Kingdom of Disorder,* 153.
56. Lyons, *Kingdom of Disorder,* 141, 122. Note that Lyons is primarily discussing tragedy in his study; however, Joseph Harris, in his book *Inventing the Spectator,* is considering a range of genres, including comedy and opera, when he writes, "Theorists from the Renaissance to the Enlightenment... regarded [the neoclassical] rules as a means to... wholly suspend or override... spectators' critical faculties" (4).
57. As Castle notes, masquerade "offered a *Spielraum,* an environment where repressed impulses could be acted out safely," even, perhaps, systematically: "If the masked ball was a kind of anarchy, it was paradoxically a systematic anarchy, a *discordia concors."* *Masquerade and Civilization,* 74, 5. She reminds us that masquerade crowds were always "structural[ly] enclos[ed]... within walls,... relegate[ed] to an assembly room, or a similarly bounded space like the Ranelagh amphitheater." Yet Castle finds evidence that "this attempt at enclosure, though maintained in the architectural sense, never entirely succeeded in a sociological one" (27-28).
58. Holland, *Ornament of Action,* 242.
59. Congreve, *The Way of the World,* 4.5. Text references to *The Way of the World* are to act, scene, and, when relevant, line.
60. According to the *OED,* this phrase is used to refer to horses, but also sheep and beasts more generally—hence, Fainall becomes (potentially) a ram, goat, bull, etc. (*OED, s.v.* "pasture" [n.], def. 6a).
61. Kroll, "Discourse and Power," 728, 745.
62. Congreve, dedication to *The Way of the World,* 98.
63. Hinnant, "Wit, Propriety, and Style," 380.
64. Braverman, "Capital Relations." For statements of Braverman's larger historical argument, see in particular 137-38 and 142.
65. Braverman, "Capital Relations," 141.
66. For a similar discussion of *The Way of the World* as a transitional play signaling the shift from an aristocratic to a bourgeois ethos, see Brown, *English Dramatic Form.* See also Susan McCloskey, who views the play as enacting in miniature the two-century transformation of the traditional kinship system into a society defined by the conjugal family. "Knowing One's Relations," esp. 70-72. Kevin J. Gardner likewise asserts that Mirabell, "combining his rakish wit with a new reliance upon the civilizing elements of self-restraint and legality,... represents an evolution in the Restoration comic hero.... He is the new social and sexual authority rising in the wake of the collapse of aristocratic authority at the end of the Stuart era." "Patrician Authority," 69.
67. Peters, *Congreve,* 25.

68. For more on the importance of contracts in Congreve—and the importance of the law more generally to the comedy of this period—see Caldwell, "'Drink up all the Water.'"
69. Mueschke and Mueschke, *New View*, 12.
70. Kroll, "Discourse and Power," 750. Gardner expresses a similar view: "Britain's growing status in colonial commerce creates a disruption in cultural power which Mirabell attempts to negate in the microcosmic arena of the domestic household." "Patrician Authority," 70.
71. These terms are inverted yet again a few scenes later, when Sir Wilfull Witwoud, now thoroughly drunk, defends himself—in song—against Lady Wishfort's charge of "beastly Pagan[ism]" (4.11.6): "*To Drink is a Christian Diversion,/ Unknown to the* Turk *or the* Persian:/ *Let* Mahometan *Fools/ Live by Heathenish Rules,/ And be damn'd over Tea-Cups and Coffee*" (4.11.14-18). Here tea and coffee are rendered "foreign," both in their association with Turks and Persians and in their role as ersatz liquors, usurping alcohol's rightful position. Yet the play's opening scene, set in a "Chocolate-house" rather than a tavern, suggests that this same substitution is one that the play's English characters have already effected.
72. McKenzie, in his editorial commentary on these lines, seeks to salvage the list's classificatory legitimacy by distinguishing "fortified" or "intoxicating" drinks (such as the strictly forbidden ratafia or orange brandy) from what he calls "medicinal cordial[s]" (such as the permissible poppy water); see *The Works of William Congreve*, vol. 2, 590; see also vol. 1, 532. In fact, however, many eighteenth-century cordials were made with spirits: contemporary recipe books direct anyone wishing to make the *"Cordial Poppy Water"* to do so by first assembling "a peck of poppies" and "two gallons of very good brandy." See Henderson, *The Housekeeper's Instructor*, 317. Essentially the same recipe is given in Francis Collingwood's *The Universal Cook*, 349. Other recipes call for placing poppies into white wine and then distilling the mixture; see Woolley, *The Compleat Servant-Maid*, 41. These same instructional texts likewise seem to refer interchangeably to "Ratafia," "Cordial," and "Ratafia Cordial": see Borella, *The Court and Country Confectioner: or, the House-Keeper's Guide*, 16; and Abbot, *The Housekeeper's Valuable Present: or, Lady's Closet Companion*, 98.
73. "Atlas" here refers to a "silk-satin manufactured in the East" (*OED, s.v.* "atlas" [n.], def. 2), though the reference also evokes, of course, the collection of maps in a volume that we tend to associate with the word. The term "muslin" comes from "Mosul," the city in what is now Iraq, where the fabric was originally produced (*OED, s.v.* "muslin").
74. Laura Rosenthal rereads the female characters in *The Way of the World* in a manner that complements my own reassessment of what the male characters symbolize. The value of "cosmopolitanism," she explains—reflected in part by Mirabell's lists of exotic imports here—had been closely associated, since the Restoration, not necessarily with imperial bureaucracy but, rather, with

the theater, and especially with the figure of the professional actress, herself "imported," of course, from the Continent. See *Ways of the World*, 5. Just as I posit that Mirabell is less different from Fainall than we initially think, so Rosenthal, similarly, argues that Millamant is less unlike her aunt, Lady Wishfort, than we tend to assume, and for many of the same reasons. Specifically, she writes, "With an aging diva at its vulnerable center"—Wishfort was in fact performed by Elinor Leigh, who had debuted during Charles II's reign—"*The Way of the World* plays the Restoration invention of the actress for comedy"; yet "Millamant wins the love of Mirabell ... not because she rejects Restoration cosmopolitan values, but because she masters them skillfully, especially in comparison with her theater-deprived cousin, Mrs. Fainall" (179).

75. Again, to draw this parallel between Mirabell and Millamant goes against critical consensus, which tends to see the two characters as opposites (though less so than Mirabell and Fainall). See, for example, Mueschke and Mueschke, *New View*, 32.

76. In modern terminology, an unborn child at this stage of development (i.e., with a differentiated head and other body parts) would be referred to as a "fetus," in contrast to the (earlier-stage) "embryo"; the seventeenth century did not make this distinction, however. See *OED*, s.v. "embryo."

77. Alan Roper points out the "semantic pun operative here which permits the association between hair, straight and curled, and writing, straightforward and turned," conjuring "an absurd world whose reality is determined by the curious ways in which words go together." "Language and Action," 48.

78. Fujimura adds that "if there is a flaw in Mirabell, it is his sobriety." *Restoration Comedy of Wit*, 187.

79. Of her daughter's strict upbringing, Lady Wishfort declares, "She was never suffer'd to play with a Male-Child, tho' but in Coats; Nay her very Babies were of the *Feminine Gender*" (5.5.9-11).

80. To her servant Peg, Wishfort exclaims, "Dost thou understand that, Changeling, dangling thy Hands like Bobbins before thee? Why dost thou not stir, Puppet? thou wooden Thing upon Wires" (3.1.13-16).

81. Mirabell accuses Wishfort of being willing to "marry any thing that resembl'd a Man, though 'twere no more than what a Butler could pinch out of a Napkin" (2.4.56-58).

82. Witwoud and Sir Wilfull Witwoud, being half-brothers, are each said to be half a fool (1.6.18) and half an ass (4.9.14), while Witwoud and Petulant together are said to comprise one man (1.1.51-54).

83. "Prithee don't look with that violent and inflexible wise Face," Millamant teases Mirabell, "like *Solomon* at the dividing of the Child" (2.6.36-38).

84. Sir Willful refers to "Suckling[s]" and "Stripling[s]" (4.4.16-17).

85. Aubrey Williams likewise notes the proliferation of "birth" metaphors, but believes them to be tied to what he sees as the play's "providential" moral message—namely, that time reveals all mysteries. Such a reading of Congreve is

deeply problematic, I think—as I hope my discussion here makes clear. See Williams, *Approach to Congreve*.

86. I offer a very selective sampling below: *Marwood*: "the Secret [of Mirabell and Millamant's love] is grown too big for the Pretence: 'Tis like Mrs. *Primly*'s great Belly; she may lace it down before, but it burnishes on her Hips" (3.10.33-35). *Petulant*: "'Sbud a Man had as good be a profess'd Midwife, as a profess'd Whoremaster, at this rate; to be knock'd up and rais'd at all Hours, and in all Places. Pox on 'em I won't come... Let 'em snivel and cry their Hearts out" (1.9.2-6). *Lady Wishfort*: "I'm as pale and as faint, I look like Mrs. *Qualmsick* the Curate's Wife, that's always breeding" (3.2.1-2); and (to Foible) "O thou frontless Impudence, more than a big-belly'd Actress" (5.1.35-36).
87. To name a few: mustard seed, aniseed, grey peas, apples, crab-apples, medlars, cherry brandy, orange brandy, citron waters, and poppy waters. Plans are described as "ripe for discovery," while ladies are found to be "panting ripe"; Mirabell refers to Wishfort's "affected bloom."
88. Hunt and Willis, *Genius of the Place,* 8-11.
89. Hunt and Willis, *Genius of the Place,* 48.
90. Hunt and Willis, *Genius of the Place,* 48.
91. Braverman, *Plots and Counterplots,* 289.
92. Braverman, *Plots and Counterplots,* 289. Braverman is of course alluding to Mirabell's description of Millamant at 1.3.21-37.
93. See also David Brown and Tom Williamson, who view the rise of the eighteenth-century landscape garden as specifically Whiggish in its ideology: just as a healthy nation should combine the principles of monarchy and democracy, the ideal English landscape should maintain a harmonious balance between form and freedom. *Lancelot Brown,* 15.
94. Braverman, *Plots and Counterplots,* 290.
95. *Letters of Joseph Addison,* 10-11.
96. As Braverman points out, garden history is full of references to designed landscapes as a kind of theater, or series of "decorously framed visual displays"; Addison may thus also be drawing on what Braverman calls the "time-honored metaphor" comparing horticulture to dramaturgy. See *Plots and Counterplots,* 299.
97. Congreve compares himself to a gardener in his dedication to *The Double-Dealer* (after first echoing Dryden's figuration of him as Vitruvius): "Yet I must take the Boldness to say, I have not miscarry'd in the whole; for the Mechanical part of it is regular. That I may say with as little Vanity, as a Builder may say he has built a House according to a Model laid down before him; or a Gardner that he has set his Flowers in a Knot of such or such a Figure" (127, lines 15-21).
98. *OED* def. 5. See, for example, the entry's 1683 quotation: "We are deeply apprehensive of the Confluences of Blessings, which... we enjoy."
99. Cynthia Klekar similarly complicates the standard reading of the deed's significance, insisting that Mirabell's deed "does not cement the antagonistic ideologies

of Mirabell and Fainall"—namely, of a "utilitarian ethic of mutual exchange and contractual obligation" over and against "an economy of honor and patronage." On the contrary, the deed "demonstrates the interrelatedness of conceptions of obligation in both aristocratic and capitalist [systems]." "Obligation, Coercion, and Economy," 125–41, 126, 125, 127. For, as Klekar explains, it is actually "not the legal document that secures Mirabell's ultimate triumph" but, rather, "the relations of obligation, debt, and gratitude that underwrite the interpersonal relationships in the play" (127–28). Aspasia Velissariou shares this more nuanced sense of Mirabell's character vis-à-vis Fainall's: Mirabell succeeds in the play, she avers, "*because* he incorporates the ruthlessness of Hobbesian politics into his contractual order. In this sense, he 'absorbs' rather than rejects Fainall." "Hobbesian Other," 69 (emphasis original).

100. See Loftis, "Congreve's *Way of the World.*"

4. "TAKE THIS SAD BALLAD, WHICH I BOUGHT AT FAIR"

1. O'Brien, *Harlequin Britain,* 63; and Anderson, *Imagined Communities,* 39–45.
2. Hammond, *Professional Imaginative Writing,* 32. Hammond borrows the term "commercial capitalism" from Barker-Benfield's *Culture of Sensibility,* and describes it as "compris[ing] a network of interconnecting developments and practices," including the Financial Revolution, the New Science, and improvements in "communications infrastructure" (which, of course, print helped to facilitate). *Professional Imaginative Writing,* 32n20.
3. Empson, *Some Versions of Pastoral,* 11. On the pastoral and its history, see also Alpers, *What Is Pastoral?;* and Patterson, *Pastoral and Ideology.*
4. O'Brien, *Harlequin Britain,* xiv, 44–47.
5. O'Brien, *Harlequin Britain,* 64, 32.
6. Quoted in Watt, *Rise of the Novel,* 53.
7. See Fuller's introduction to *John Gay: Dramatic Works,* vol. 1, 54. Milhous and Hume believe that, between subscriptions and "over-the-counter" sales, Gay may have ultimately earned between 1600 and 1700 pounds total. Yet they also note that such sums were anomalous: indeed, they see Gay's windfall from *Polly* as essentially unique; see *Publication of Plays in London,* 153.
8. Nokes writes that, following the success of *The Beggar's Opera* and *Polly,* Gay "was able to boast to Swift that his fortune 'amounts to at present (all debts paid) above three thousand four hundred pounds,' and his estate when he died was worth over 6,000 pounds"; as Nokes points out, this relative prosperity stands in stark contrast to the myth of Gay, perpetuated by the other Scriblerians and possibly also by Gay himself, according to which he is a kind of "feckless Peter Pan with ... no head for finance." *John Gay,* 423. Interestingly, then, the writing of Gay's biography (even while he was still alive) seems to reflect the same "pastoral" desires and contradictions that his work both indulges in and exposes.

9. Poovey, *History of the Modern Fact,* 29. For photographic reproductions of pre-printed double-entry account-book pages, see 44-53.
10. McDowell, *Invention of the Oral,* 3-4, 7.
11. McDowell, *Invention of the Oral,* 233.
12. McDowell, *Invention of the Oral,* 229-30.
13. McDowell, *Invention of the Oral,* 233.
14. McDowell, *Invention of the Oral,* 4.
15. McDowell, *Invention of the Oral,* 7.
16. McDowell, *Invention of the Oral,* 8.
17. Stewart, "Scandals of the Ballad," 135.
18. Stewart, "Scandals of the Ballad," 135.
19. Anderson, *Imagined Communities,* 37.
20. Stewart, "Scandals of the Ballad," 138.
21. Sir Philip Sidney, *Apology for Poetry,* 99 (lines 5-10).
22. Fox, *Oral and Literate Culture,* 5.
23. Only halfway through the play's run of twenty-one performances, Pope estimated that Gay would earn one hundred pounds for it, and Fuller notes that he was paid over sixteen pounds for the copyright. See *John Gay: Dramatic Works,* vol. 1, 14. See also *Letters of John Gay,* 19; and Nokes, *John Gay,* 182.
24. "The chivalric code of the word as the bond of society . . . included not only the pledge of allegiance between subject and king, but also the betrothal of lovers, the vow of friendship, and the judicial oath. These various forms of the pledged word constitute a crucial part, a 'master trope', of the 'hegemonic code' invented to establish and maintain feudal Europe's version of patriarchy." Canfield, *Word as Bond,* xi.
25. For an overview of the conflicting evidence vis-à-vis the *Key*'s authorship, see *John Gay: Dramatic Works,* vol. 1, 418-19.
26. *Letters of John Gay,* 18.
27. *Letters of John Gay,* 20
28. Gay, *The What D'Ye Call It.* Text references to *The What D'Ye Call It* are to act, scene, and, when relevant, line.
29. Erskine-Hill, "Significance of Gay's Drama," 149-50.
30. Note that an assumed stammer was apparently one of the comic trademarks of William Penkethman, the actor playing Peascod (or, rather, playing "*Jonas* Dock, alias *Thomas Peascod*"), and even in the frame play he is made to trip over his syllables: "My Name? Jo—Jo—Jonas. No—that was the Name my Godfathers gave me. My Play Name is *Timothy Pea—Pea—Peascod;* ay, *Peascod*" (introductory scene, lines 15-17). (See Fuller's commentary on act 1, line 124 of *Three Hours After Marriage,* in *John Gay: Dramatic Works,* vol. 1, 445.) However, the primary comic effect in these lines clearly derives from the combination of the absurd rhyme and emotion.
31. "Burthen" here refers either to "The low undersong or accompaniment, which was sung while the leading voice sang a melody" or to "The refrain or chorus of a song; a set of words recurring at the end of each verse" (*OED,* s.v. "burden," defs. 9

and 10). The *OED* cites *The Tempest:* "Foote it featly heere, and there, and sweete Sprights beare the burthen" (1.2.383).
32. Of course, as I will show, Gay finds other ways of linking ballad singing to print capitalism in the later play.
33. See Fuller's note on page 432 in his edition of *The What D'Ye Call It.*
34. Gardner, "George Farquhar's *The Recruiting Officer,*" 54.
35. Standing in public in a white sheet was a traditional punishment for sexual transgression. See Williams, *Dictionary of Sexual Language,* s.v. "sheet penance."
36. Interestingly, the frame play of *The Beggar's Opera* suggests a similar dynamic. As Empson points out in *Some Versions of Pastoral,* "The prologue of the *Opera* explains that it is a revival of the marriage masques" originally staged "for the beggar artists James Chanter and Moll Lay"—"aristocrats no doubt in their own world"; likewise, Empson sees "the dance of prisoners in chains" in act 3 as "a regular antimasque." In thus superimposing the beggars' scrappy play-acting onto aristocratic pageantry, Gay not only executes a particularly effective version of the high-low parallel that defines the pastoral mode but simultaneously "refers us back," as Empson notes, to "the Elizabethans" (198), for whom the feudalism invoked by pastoralism would have been less anachronistic (but also, therefore, less powerful as a nostalgic fantasy).
37. The unique effect of the pageant becomes clearer via a comparison with *Hamlet*'s play within the play (a comparison, after all, that *The What D'Ye Call It*'s subtitle asks us to draw). For *The Mouse-Trap* also seeks to redress an injustice in the outer play, yet Hamlet's pantomime merely diagnoses guilt, and it is then left to the characters in the outer play to act (or, tragically, not to act) upon the information. Here, by contrast, the pageant both exposes and corrects an iniquity in a single stroke: performance collapses representation and reality and, indeed, purges reality of the "misrepresentations" embedded within it.
38. Fuller, "Introduction," in *John Gay: Dramatic Works,* vol. 1, 20.
39. Fuller, "Introduction," in *John Gay: Dramatic Works,* vol. 1, 20.
40. McDowell, *Women of Grub Street,* 182.
41. Erskine-Hill, "Significance of Gay's Drama," 152.
42. Interestingly, the *Key* itself draws attention to a handful of moments that privilege reader over playgoer. For example, the *Key* notes, in regard to the final scene of act 1, that "there's much more *Wit* in the printed *Farce* than in the Representation. For we are informed of a *Song Sung dismally by a Ghost.* Every Body perceives the waggery of a *Ghost's singing dismally;* but it is a Pity that the Audience lost the Jest." *Complete Key,* 12. See also page 26: "Our Authors not contented with being Witty in the Lines of their *Farce,* strike upon their Readers, at the opening of their Scenes, with Prose-wit, distinguish'd (for fear the Jest should pass unperceiv'd) *by Italick* Characters." (This is in a note on Kitty's entrance at 2.8: "Kitty *with her Hair Loose.*")
43. As Sir Roger's Steward (Kitty's father) laments in the introductory scene, "My Daughter debauched! and by that Booby Squire!" (introductory scene, line 44).

44. Swift had suggested to Pope, in a 1716 letter, that Gay should write a "Newgate Pastoral," but it is not necessarily clear that *The Beggar's Opera* was a direct response to this prompt.
45. From *The Augustans* (1961), reprinted in Noble, *Twentieth-Century Interpretations*, 42.
46. Mary Poovey points to "the metaphorical persistence of bookkeeping" in British discourse dating back to at least the seventeenth century, noting that accounting and account books emerge as a symbol for the nascent "'sciences' of wealth and society" in writing throughout the seventeenth, eighteenth, and nineteenth centuries (*History of the Modern Fact*, 29). Thus, in Hobbes's *Leviathan* (1651), "'reckoning' appears as the very type of rationality," signaling a "precise adherence to rules"; more specifically, bookkeeping came to symbolize "the systematic representation of ... facts," and the way in which such representation could "produce ... general theoretical knowledge" (29).
47. Bender, *Imagining the Penitentiary*, 165.
48. Christopher Dandeker, glossing Max Weber, similarly emphasizes the dependence of modern bureaucracy on written documents: "bureaucratic decisions and calculations depend on *knowledge of the files*, that is on a mastery of the information stored centrally in the organization, rather than on tradition or charismatic inspiration." *Surveillance, Power, and Modernity*, 9-10.
49. Bender, *Imagining the Penitentiary*, 140.
50. Howson, *Thief-Taker General*, 66.
51. Howson, *Thief-Taker General*, 69.
52. Howson, *Thief-Taker General*, 68.
53. Howson, *Thief-Taker General*, 68.
54. Quoted in Howson, *Thief-Taker General*, 103.
55. Howson, *Thief-Taker General*, 254.
56. Howson, *Thief-Taker General*, 257.
57. Howson, *Thief-Taker General*, 258.
58. Quoted in Howson, *Thief-Taker General*, 258-59.
59. See also Howson, *Thief-Taker General*, esp. 116-20.
60. Few, if any, of the ballads used by Gay seem to originate any earlier than 1500, the year by which Benedict Anderson believes that print had come into its own; see Anderson, *Imagined Communities*, 37. Indeed, most of the songs Gay uses date from the seventeenth century, or even the early eighteenth (*Chevy Chase* may prove an exception).
61. Gay, *The Beggar's Opera*. Text references to *The Beggar's Opera* are to act, scene, and, when relevant, line.
62. As Andrea McKenzie notes, as a so-called gentleman of the road, Macheath takes on all of the symbolic resonance that this figure possessed in the early eighteenth century: she writes (partly quoting the historian Peter Linebaugh), "the highwayman expressed the values of the 'master artisan'—independent, 'proud, muscular, bluff and hearty', taking to the road both as a casualty of early industrial

capitalism and in resistance to the 'new discipline' it attempted to impose." McKenzie, "Real Macheath," 582; quoting Linebaugh, *London Hanged*, 189, 218.

63. Denning, "Beggars and Thieves," 34-35. See also Daniel Gustafson: "Macheath partakes in the gang's rhetoric of free circulation, [as] opposed to the hoarding tendencies of the bourgeois villains Peachum and Lockit," but predatory greed defines libertine and shopkeeper alike: "whatever liberality [Macheath] does possess is belied by his self-centric desire," as evidenced three scenes earlier, when he compares Polly to a "shilling" coveted by a "miser." *Lothario's Corpse*, 90.

64. Jenny Divers's kiss, of course, alludes to Judas's kiss.

65. Denning, "Beggars and Thieves," 44.

66. Indeed, in this sense the contrast between Macheath's type of law and Peachum's is as stark as the contrast between life and death: while the account books deal out (or deal in) hangings, the escapes, by contrast, grant life—a correlation that is further emphasized by the fact that each of the three escapes is associated, respectively, with marriage (to Polly), pregnancy (Lucy's), and a parade of children (by four additional "wives," each with "a Child a-peice! [*sic*]" [3.15.23]).

67. Denning, "Beggars and Thieves," 44.

68. I do not mean to mischaracterize Denning's nuanced argument here by focusing on his discussion of the play's ending; he does make clear elsewhere in the essay that, "though there are two types of rogues, all are rogues," and that, "though there are two types of predators, all are predators." "Beggars and Thieves," 35.

69. Interestingly, the fact that Peachum's accounts are dispersed over several books does not seem to suggest an anomaly or flaw in his own personal system; rather, it constitutes a standard aspect of double-entry bookkeeping. According to Poovey, double-entry accounting consisted of an "inventory," a "memorial," a "journal," a "ledger," and possibly additional books as well; see *History of the Modern Fact*, 42. Some of these were open for all to see, while others (including the inventory and the journal) were "secret books": access to them was limited "to the merchant and his most trusted steward" (59).

70. Gay seems implicitly, in this scene, to be making a version of the argument that Poovey would formulate two hundred years later: "*as a system of writing*," she explains, "double-entry bookkeeping" in particular (the first manual for which was published in 1494) "produced effects that exceeded transcription and calculation. One of its *social* effects was to proclaim the honesty of merchants as a group. One of its *epistemological* effects was to make the formal precision of the double-entry system, which drew on the rule-bound system of arithmetic, *seem* to guarantee the accuracy of the details it recorded." *History of the Modern Fact*, 30 (emphasis original). The result was what Poovey calls a "fiction of total disclosure" (59), or "the effect of accuracy" (63): "because all early modern merchants depended for their profits on some long-distance trade or credit transactions, the ledgers could never be temporally aligned with the company's actual money," she explains; "some of the debts owing to the merchant would only eventually be paid, for example (and some would never be), even though the books recorded these debts as if repayment could be taken for granted" (63-64). Thus, "even though

the accuracy of the initial records could not be verified, the formal precision of the books made the records function *as if* they were not only precise but accurate as well" (64 [emphasis original]).

71. Peachum, upon hearing that Tom Gagg has been found guilty, exclaims, "A lazy Dog! When I took him the time before, I told him what he would come to if he did not mend his Hand. This is Death without Reprieve. I may venture to Book him. [*writes*] For *Tom Gagg,* forty Pounds" (1.2.20).
72. Gildon, *History of the Athenian Society,* 9.
73. Culler, *Structuralist Poetics,* 172.
74. Stone, *Uncertain Unions,* 98. Stone explains that clandestine marriages, though a phenomenon that predated the Restoration, became much more widespread starting in the 1660s (Hardwick's Marriage Act of 1753 was designed to finally put a stop to the practice).
75. Verbal spousals could take two forms: a man and woman could agree to marry *per verba de presenti,* which would be considered binding "if duly attested by two credible witnesses," or they could agree to marry *per verba de futuro,* an agreement that would be considered binding if "followed by consummation"; see Stone, *Uncertain Unions,* 53–56.
76. Cited by Fuller, *John Gay: Dramatic Works,* vol. 2, in his commentary on 1.6.32 (p. 378).
77. E.g., *The Fair Penitent* or *Lady Jane Grey;* these may well be the "Play-books" Polly has been reading.
78. The *OED* cites the use of "Poll" as a "conventional proper name or pet name for a parrot" as early as 1600 ("Pretty Poll" and "Pretty Polly" are also frequent usages: see "Poll" and "Polly").
79. Stewart, "Scandals of the Ballad," 150.
80. One notable exception is Margaret Doody, who in my opinion provides what is still the most clear-eyed assessment of the function of *The Beggar's Opera*'s songs when she describes them as tools with which Gay's characters attempt either to "romanticiz[e] themselves" or to "rationaliz[e]" their behavior, or both. *Daring Muse,* 213.
81. Newman, "Value of 'Nothing,'" 279.
82. "Introduction," in Noble, *Twentieth-Century Interpretations,* 11.
83. Noble, *Twentieth-Century Interpretations,* 12.
84. McDowell, *Invention of the Oral,* 230–31, 248.
85. Thus, McDowell writes that "the earliest [theorizations of 'oral tradition'] . . . were prompted . . . by a profound discomfort with new cultures of reading, writing, and even speaking shaped by print." *Invention of the Oral,* 4. See also Stewart, "Scandals of the Ballad."
86. Stewart points out that broadside ballads date to the very "onset of printing in England." "Scandals of the Ballad," 136.
87. See Bryan Loughry and T. O. Treadwell's introduction to the Penguin Classics edition of *The Beggar's Opera:* "instead of the floridly baroque arias of Scarlatti or Handel, [Gay offers us] English and Irish folk songs"; "compared to the airy

confections of the Italian opera, the world of Gay's comedy is grittily real" (12). See also Vivien Jones and David Lindley's introduction to the New Mermaids edition: "In a telling departure from the heroic or tragic modes which dominated the Italian and the British operatic traditions, [*The Beggar's Opera*] is a 'low' comedy," steeped "in the realm of popular culture" (x).

88. See Hume, "Economics of Culture," esp. 515-17.
89. *Letters of John Gay*, 43
90. Nokes, *John Gay*, 409.
91. Hume, "Economics of Culture," 516. Indeed, the Royal Academy of Music, which produced Italian opera in London, was bankrupt by 1729 (a fate that some scholars have claimed *The Beggar's Opera* helped to bring about). See Hume, "Economics of Culture," 517; and Nokes, *John Gay*, 427.
92. Peter Lewis comes to a related conclusion: "Gay condemns not Italian opera but the completely uncritical theatregoers who had turned it into a fashionable cult." *John Gay: The Beggar's Opera*, 23.
93. Dugaw, "'Popular Marketing of Old Ballads,'" 73.
94. Fox, *Oral and Literate Culture*, 41-42.
95. Fox, *Oral and Literate Culture*, 8.
96. Dugaw, "'Popular Marketing of Old Ballads,'" 72.
97. Dugaw, "'Popular Marketing of Old Ballads,'" 75.
98. Day, "Pills to Purge Melancholy," 181.
99. Simpson, *British Broadside and Its Music*, 70.
100. For "The London Lottery," see the Samuel Pepys Collection, *University of California Santa Barbara English Broadside Ballad Archive* online, EBBA 22343.
101. Dugaw, *Deep Play*, 176-77.
102. Duffey (D'Urfey), *The Hubble Bubbles: A Ballad to the tune of O'er the Hills and far a way* (n.p.).
103. A highly detailed account of the bewildering bibliographical issues surrounding the *The Beggar's Opera*'s early editions can be found in Lewis, *John Gay: The Beggar's Opera*, 23-42.
104. This treatment of the songs as portable consumer goods is taken even further in the advertisement appearing on the verso of the title page of some copies (seemingly the second edition's third impression; see Lewis, *John Gay: The Beggar's Opera*, 32), which promotes an additional volume containing *only* the songs, this time with the music transposed for flute: "May 24, 1728. / This Day is Publish'd, / The TUNES to the SONGS in the BEGGAR's OPERA Transpos'd for the FLUTE. Containing Sixty-Nine Airs. Printed for John Watts, at the Printing Office in Wild-Court, near Lincoln's-Inn-Fields. Price I s." See, for example, the British Library's edition as reproduced by *Eighteenth-Century Collections Online* (Gale Document Number CW0111057133).
105. Gay makes mention, in a letter to Swift, of "a Mezzo-tinto Print publish'd to day of Polly." Burgess, *Letters of John Gay*, "Gay to Swift 20 March 1727/8," 72. A number

of "miscellaneous anonymous prints" can likewise be found depicting scenes from the play; see Schultz, *Gay's "Beggar's Opera,"* 17. A volume of "Memoirs concerning the Life and Manners of Captain Mackheath [*sic*]" was published on May 14 of 1728, which, according to one contemporary commentator, was to be much preferred to the countless other "senseless and insipid Pamphlets" that had been recently published "with Relation to *The Beggar's Opera*" (quoted in Schultz, *Gay's "Beggar's Opera,"* 19).

106. Schultz, *Gay's "Beggar's Opera,"* 18.
107. Schultz, *Gay's "Beggar's Opera,"* 19.
108. Playing cards actually have an interesting role in the history of printing; they are believed to have been the first objects to be created using copper-plate engraving: see Lehmann-Haupt, *Master of the Playing Cards*.

CONCLUSION

1. See, for example, Jean Marsden: "In the period between 1740 and the publication of Samuel Johnson's edition in 1765, literary critics began to establish a new iconography of Shakespeare," granting him a "symbolic post as the father of English literature." *Re-Imagined Text*, 103–4.
2. Ritchie and Sabor, *Shakespeare in the Eighteenth Century*, 6.
3. Marsden, *Re-Imagined Text*, 75.
4. Marsden, *Re-Imagined Text*, 116.
5. Marsden, *Re-Imagined Text*, 78.
6. Dobson, *Making of the National Poet*, 209.
7. Dobson, *Making of the National Poet*, 211. Gefen Bar-On Santor makes a similar argument about Garrick's surprising contribution to the enshrinement of Shakespeare's text: although Garrick "was a man of the theatre first and foremost," and "was an avid adapter of Shakespeare"—developing "many popular alterations, deletions, and additions" to the plays—he also "worked earnestly to give Shakespeare's *texts* a stronger stage presence," feeling "passionately . . . that the text was a treasure that the audience would enjoy" ("Shakespeare in the Georgian Theatre," 216–17 [emphasis added]).
8. Dobson, *Making of the National Poet*, 211.
9. Lamb, "On the Tragedies of Shakespeare," 137.
10. As Jonathan Bate notes, although "a new age of bardolatry" is frequently said to have commenced with Garrick's 1769 Stratford Jubilee, the Jubilee was in fact "the summation of a hundred years in which Shakespeare's supremacy as the poet of the English people remained unquestioned," as testified to by the ongoing "demand for editions, the prevalence of casual quotation from the plays and the assimilation of phrases into everyday speech, and the success of production after production" from the 1660s onward; see Bate, *Genius of Shakespeare*, 8.

11. Kewes explains that "the elevation of the Bard" was a process whose "decisive stages... occurred within the period covered by this study [i.e., 1660-1710]," for "if there is one era of English history during which dramatic authorship may be said to have achieved cultural respectability, it is the half-century following the Restoration of Charles II in 1660." *Authorship and Appropriation,* 231. I discuss Kewes's larger claims about authorship in my introduction.
12. See also David Kastan, who observes that Shakespeare has, perhaps more than any other writer in history, "preeminently become The Author." He adds that it is therefore "not surprising" that, as the year 2000 approached, Shakespeare was deemed "'the man of the millennium' in many polls": for, "increasingly[,]... the familiar image of a man with a receding hairline and shiny forehead, a ruff around his neck, and a quill pen in hand serves not only to identify Shakespeare 'the author' but [indeed] has become an emblem of human creativity itself." *Shakespeare and the Book,* 14.
13. The phrase is of course from Jonson's "To the Memory of... William Shakespeare," printed among the prefatory materials in the First Folio.
14. Orgel, "Renaissance Artist as Plagiarist," 494.
15. Lynch, "Criticism of Shakespeare," 55. See also Bate, who notes that Shakespeare is one of the "archetypal Original Geniuses" precisely "because the idea of original genius emerged as a way of explaining the phenomenon of Shakespeare." *Genius of Shakespeare,* 168 (quoted in Lynch, 55).
16. See Pask, "Plagiarism," 741. Pask argues that Langbaine's larger bibliographical work—and, in particular, his focus on plays—contributed signally to a discourse of artistic originality. For more on this, see my introduction.
17. Aphra Behn, preface to *The Dutch Lover,* 157.
18. De Grazia, *Shakespeare Verbatim,* 200.
19. See also Kastan: "The scholarly project that had begun with the goal of establishing a 'correct' text of Shakespeare's plays, which could be easily and confidently read in that knowledge, in fact produced a text in which arguments about its correctness were the very justification for its existence." *Shakespeare and the Book,* 107.
20. De Grazia, *Shakespeare Verbatim,* 200.
21. De Grazia, *Shakespeare Verbatim,* 195-96, 200.
22. Barnard, "English Literary Canon," 307-8.
23. Barnard, "English Literary Canon," 314.
24. Barnard, "English Literary Canon," 308-9.
25. Pope famously writes that "it must be own'd that with all [of his] great excellencies [Shakespeare] has almost as great defects; and that as he has certainly written better, so he has perhaps written worse, than any other...."; Pope accounts for these "defects" in part by pointing to the pragmatic concerns of the playhouse: "it will be but fair to allow, that most of our Author's faults are less to be ascribed to his wrong judgment as a Poet, than to his right judgment as a Player." Preface to *The Works of Shakespear,* 46, 48.
26. Pope, preface to *The Works of Shakespear,* 52.

27. Pope, preface to *The Works of Shakespear*, 44.
28. This conception largely contradicts, of course, the simultaneous critical assumption that Shakespeare's "defects" arise from the need to please his audience; but the history of Shakespeare reception is not without inconsistencies.
29. Pope, preface to *The Works of Shakespear*, 44.
30. Johnson, preface to *The Plays of Shakespear*, 106.
31. Fairer, "Shakespeare in Poetry," 106-7.
32. Rumbold, "Shakespeare and the Stratford Jubilee," 260.
33. Rumbold, "Shakespeare and the Stratford Jubilee," 260.
34. Rumbold, "Shakespeare and the Stratford Jubilee," 260, citing Garrick's correspondence.
35. See *John Gay: Dramatic Works,* vol. 1, 419. Fuller quotes Polonius's line from *Hamlet*: "The actors are come hither, my lord.... The best actors in the world, either for tragedy, comedy, history, pastoral, pastoral-comical, historical-pastoral, tragical-historical, tragical-comical, historical-pastoral, scene individable, or poem unlimited" (2.2.359, 2.2.363-66).
36. Recall that the *Key*'s authorship remains uncertain, but some scholars have concluded that it is the work of Gay's own hand. For an overview of the conflicting evidence, see *John Gay: Dramatic Works,* vol. 1, 418-19.
37. These parallels are observed by Dane Farnsworth Smith in *Plays about the Theatre in England*, 99.
38. Alpers, *What Is Pastoral?*, 196.
39. Salingar, *Shakespeare and the Tradition of Comedy,* 16 (quoted in Alpers, *What Is Pastoral?*, 196).
40. Alpers, *What Is Pastoral?*, 21.
41. Alpers, *What Is Pastoral?*, 196.
42. From the preface to *The What D'Ye Call It*, 174-75. (Italic and roman type have been reversed.)
43. *Complete Key,* 9. The *Key* slightly misquotes the Nurse's dialogue.
44. *Complete Key,* 4. *The What D'Ye Call It*'s preface further notes that the Ghost of an Embryo, however absurd or incongruous, has precedent in Aristophanes's Chorus of Frogs, but also in Shakespeare's *"speaking Wall,* and *Moonshine* [from *A Midsummer Night's Dream*] ... the latter [of which] comes in with a Lanthorn and Candle; which in my Opinion are Characters that make a good Figure in the Modern Farce" (177, italic and roman type have been reversed).
45. *Complete Key,* 4.
46. Gay, preface to *The What D'Ye Call It*, 175.
47. See my discussion of Empson in chapter 4.
48. As Fiona Ritchie explains, the idea of Shakespeare as a poet of nature "tak[es] on changing nuances" over the decades: "whereas Heminge and Condell [in the First Folio] portray Shakespeare as inspired by a natural gift"—referring to Shakespeare as "a happie imitator of Nature" and "a most gentle expresser of it"—later discussions of "Shakespeare's naturalness" are more often referring (as does Cavendish in "Letter 123") to "his ability to depict human nature." *Women and Shakespeare,* 14.

49. Bristol, "'System of Oeconomical Prudence,'" 13.
50. Ritchie, *Women and Shakespeare*, 79-80. See also Kathryn Prince, who underlines a connection between character criticism and the political/ideological orientation of a growing middle class: "eighteenth-century Shakespeare appreciation turned to character criticism ... because of [a] convergence between bourgeois and nationalistic ideals." "Shakespeare and English Nationalism," 285.
51. Marsden, "Shakespeare and Sympathy," 29, 32.
52. Vickers, "Emergence of Character Criticism," 11.
53. Vickers, "Emergence of Character Criticism," 11.
54. Cavendish, *Sociable Letters*, 177.
55. See also Julie Stone Peters, who quotes a 1815 essay by William Hazlitt: "poetry and the stage do not agree together"; thus, if "the reading of [*A Midsummer Night's Dream*] is like wandering in a grove by moonlight," by contrast, producing the play onstage causes "that which is merely an airy shape, a dream, a passing thought" to become "an unmanageable reality." Quoted in Peters, *Theatre of the Book*, 294.
56. Lamb, "On the Tragedies of Shakespeare," 135.
57. Lamb, "On the Tragedies of Shakespeare," 135-36.
58. Indeed, in discussing Lamb's playgoing habits, Joan Caldwell insists that "when [Lamb] spoke of staging being unsatisfactory," he did so not because he was dismissive of the theater's capacities but, rather, because he knew personally how intense its effects could be. "Playgoer as Critic," 195. She concludes that although Lamb's essay on the tragedies is premised on a thorough "rejection of the stage Shakespeare," in the end "almost every point in his argument reflects the fact that it was theatrical performances which had sharpened his critical faculties and shaped his views" (185).
59. Lamb, "On the Tragedies of Shakespeare," 128.
60. Lamb, "On the Tragedies of Shakespeare," 137.

BIBLIOGRAPHY

Abbot, Robert. *The Housekeeper's Valuable Present: or, Lady's Closet Companion*. London: Printed for the Author; and Sold by C. Cooke, 1790.

Addison, Joseph. *The Letters of Joseph Addison*. Edited by Walter James Graham. Oxford: Clarendon Press, 1941.

Alleman, Gellert Spencer. *Matrimonial Law and the Materials of Restoration Comedy*. Wallingford, PA: For the author, 1942.

Alpers, Paul. *What Is Pastoral?* Chicago: University of Chicago Press, 1996.

Alssid, Michael. *Thomas Shadwell*. New York: Twayne Publishers, 1967.

Anderson, Benedict. *Imagined Communities: Reflections on the Origins and Spread of Nationalism*. Revised edition. London: Verso, 2006.

Anderson, Emily Hodgson. "Novelty in Novels: A Look at What's New in Aphra Behn's Oroonoko." *Studies in the Novel* 39, no. 1 (Spring 2007): 1-16.

Anonymous. *A Complete Key to the last New Farce "The What D'Ye Call It." To Which is prefix'd a Hypercritical "Preface" on the Nature of Burlesque, and the Poets Design*. London: Printed for James Roberts at the Oxford Arms in Warwick-lane, 1715.

Aristotle. *Aristotle's Poetics*. Translated by S. H. Butcher, with an introductory essay by Francis Fergusson. New York: Hill and Wang, 1961.

Backscheider, Paula. *Spectacular Politics: Theatrical Power and Mass Culture in Early Modern England*. Baltimore: Johns Hopkins University Press, 1993.

Ballaster, Ros. "Fiction Feigning Femininity: False Counts and Pageant Kings in Aphra Behn's Popish Plot Writings." In Todd, *Aphra Behn Studies*, 50-65.

———. *Seductive Forms: Women's Amatory Fiction from 1684 to 1740*. Oxford: Clarendon Press, 1992.

Barish, Jonas. *The Antitheatrical Prejudice*. Berkeley: University of California Press, 1981.

Barker-Benfield, G. J. *Culture of Sensibility: Sex and Society in Eighteenth-Century Britain*. Chicago: University of Chicago Press, 1992.

Barnard, John. "Creating an English Literary Canon, 1679-1720: Jacob Tonson, Dryden and Congreve." In *Literary Cultures and the Material Book*, edited by Simon Eliot, Andrew Nash, and Ian Willison, 307-22. London: The British Library, 2007.

———. "Dryden, Tonson, and Subscriptions for the 1697 Virgil." *Papers of the Bibliographical Society of America* 57, no. 2 (1963): 129-51.

———. "London Publishing, 1640–1660: Crisis, Continuity, Innovation." *Book History* 4, no. 1 (2001): 1–16.

Bate, Jonathan. *The Genius of Shakespeare*. London: Picador, 1997.

Battigelli, Anna. *Margaret Cavendish and the Exiles of the Mind*. Lexington: University Press of Kentucky, 1998.

Behn, Aphra. "The Disappointment." In *The Works of Aphra Behn,* vol. 1, edited by Janet Todd, 65–69. Columbus: The Ohio State University Press, 1992.

———. *The Emperor of the Moon*. In *Aphra Behn: The Rover and Other Plays,* edited by Jane Spencer, 271–335. Oxford: Oxford World's Classics, 1995. Reissued 2008.

———. *The Emperor of the Moon: A Farce,* edited by Elaine Hobby and Alan James Hogarth. In *The Cambridge Edition of the Works of Aphra Behn*. Vol. 4: *Plays 1682–1696,* edited by Rachel Adcock, Kate Aughterson, Claire Bowditch, Elaine Hobby, Alan James Hogarth, Anita Pacheco, and Margarete Rubik, 373–530. Cambridge: Cambridge University Press, 2021.

———. *The Lucky Chance.* In *Aphra Behn: The Rover and Other Plays,* edited by Jane Spencer, 183–270. Oxford: Oxford World's Classics, 1995. Reissued 2008.

———. *The Luckey Chance,* edited by Kate Aughterson and Claire Bowditch. In *The Cambridge Edition of the Works of Aphra Behn*. Vol. 4: *Plays 1682–1696,* edited by Rachel Adcock, Kate Aughterson, Claire Bowditch, Elaine Hobby, Alan James Hogarth, Anita Pacheco, and Margarete Rubik, 191–372. Cambridge: Cambridge University Press, 2021.

———. Preface to *The Dutch Lover*. In *The Works of Aphra Behn,* vol. 5, edited by Janet Todd, 160–63. Columbus: The Ohio State University Press, 1996.

———. Prologue to *The Amorous Prince*. In *The Works of Aphra Behn,* vol. 5, edited by Janet Todd, 87. Columbus: The Ohio State University Press, 1996.

Bender, John. *Imagining the Penitentiary: Fiction and the Architecture of Mind in Eighteenth-Century England.* Chicago: University of Chicago Press, 1987.

Benedict, Barbara M. *Curiosity: A Cultural History of Early Modern Inquiry.* Chicago: University of Chicago Press, 2001.

Bennett, Benjamin. *Theater as Problem: Modern Drama and Its Place in Literature.* Ithaca, NY: Cornell University Press, 1990.

Berek, Peter. "Defoliating Playbooks and the Reading Public." *Studies in English Literature 1500–1900* 56, no. 2 (2016): 395–416.

Berman, Ronald. "The Values of Shadwell's *Squire of Alsatia*." *ELH* 39, no. 3 (Autumn 1972): 375–86.

Bernard, Stephen. "Henry Herringman, Jacob Tonson, and John Dryden: The Creation of the English Literary Publisher." *Notes and Queries* 62, no. 2 (2015): 274–77.

Borella, Señor. *The Court and Country Confectioner: or, the House-Keeper's Guide.* London: Printed for G. Riley, and A. Cooke, at their Circulating Library, 1770.

Borgman, Albert Stephens. *Thomas Shadwell: His Life and Comedies.* New York: New York University Press, 1928.

Braverman, Richard. "Capital Relations and *The Way of the World*." *ELH* 52, no. 1 (Spring 1985): 133–58.

———. *Plots and Counterplots: Sexual Politics and the Body Politic in English Literature, 1660-1730.* Cambridge: Cambridge University Press, 1993.

Brewer, David. *The Afterlife of Character, 1726-1825.* Philadelphia: University of Pennsylvania Press, 2011.

Bristol, Michael. "'A System of Oeconomical Prudence': Shakespearean Character and the Practice of Moral Inquiry." In *Shakespeare and the Eighteenth Century*, edited by Peter Sabor and Paul Yachnin, 13-28. Burlington, VT: Ashgate Publishing, 2008.

Britland, Karen. *Drama at the Courts of Queen Henrietta Maria.* Cambridge: Cambridge University Press, 2006.

Brown, David, and Tom Williamson. *Lancelot Brown and the Capability Men: Landscape Revolution in Eighteenth-Century England.* London: Reaktion Books, 2016.

Brown, Laura. *English Dramatic Form, 1660-1760: An Essay in Generic History.* New Haven, CT: Yale University Press, 1981.

Bush-Bailey, Gilli. *Treading the Bawds: Actresses and Playwrights on the Late Stuart Stage.* Manchester: Manchester University Press, 2006.

Butler, Todd. *Imagination and Politics in Seventeenth-Century England.* New York: Ashgate Publishing, 2008.

Caldwell, Joan. "The Playgoer as Critic: Charles Lamb on Shakespeare's Characters." *Shakespeare Quarterly* 26, no. 2 (Spring 1975): 184-95.

Caldwell, Lauren. "'Drink up all the Water in the Sea': Contracting Relationships in Congreve's *Love for Love* and *The Way of the World*." *ELH* 82, no. 1 (Spring 2015): 183-210.

Canfield, J. Douglas. "Late Shadwell and Early Bourgeois Comedy." *The Eighteenth Century: Theory and Interpretation* 46, no. 2 (Summer 2005): 105-28.

———. *Word as Bond in English Literature from the Middle Ages to the Restoration.* Philadelphia: University of Pennsylvania Press, 1989.

Carlson, Marvin. *Haunted Stage: The Theatre as Memory Machine.* Ann Arbor: University of Michigan Press, 2003.

Castle, Terry. *Masquerade and Civilization: The Carnivalesque in Eighteenth-Century English Culture and Fiction.* Stanford, CA: Stanford University Press, 1986.

Cavendish, Margaret. *Observations upon Experimental Philosophy.* Edited by Eileen O'Neill. Cambridge: Cambridge University Press, 2001.

———. *The Philosophical and Physical Opinions, Written by her Excellency, the Lady Marchionesse of Newcastle.* London: Printed for J. Martin and J. Allestrye at the Bell in St. Pauls Church-Yard, 1655.

———. *Poems, and Fancies* (1653). Menston: Scolar Press, 1972.

———. *Sociable Letters.* Edited by James Fitzmaurice. Peterborough, Ontario: Broadview Press, 2004.

———. *A True Relation of my Birth, Breeding and Life* (1656). In *Paper Bodies: A Margaret Cavendish Reader*, edited by Sylvia Bowerbank and Sara Mendelson. Peterborough, Ontario: Broadview Press, 2000.

Clare, Janet, ed. *Drama of the English Republic: 1649-1660.* Manchester: Manchester University Press, 2002.

Coffin, Charlotte. "Theatre and/as Witchcraft: A Reading of *The Late Lancashire Witches* (1634)." *Early Theatre* 16, no. 2 (2013): 91-119.

Coiro, Ann Baynes. "Drama in the Epic Style: Narrator, Muse, and Audience in *Paradise Lost*." *Milton Studies*, vol. 51, edited by Laura L. Knoppers, 63-100. Pittsburgh, PA: Duquesne University Press, 2010.

———. "Reading." In *Early Modern Theatricality*, edited by Henry S. Turner, 534-55. Oxford: Oxford University Press, 2013.

Cole, David. *The Theatrical Event: A Mythos, a Vocabulary, a Perspective*. Middletown, CT: Wesleyan University Press, 1975.

Collingwood, Francis. *The Universal Cook*. London: Printed by R. Noble, No. 12, Ave-Maria-Lane, 1792.

Congreve, William. Dedication to *The Double-Dealer*. In *The Works of William Congreve*, vol. 1, edited by D. F. McKenzie, 127-30. Oxford: Oxford University Press, 2011.

———. *Incognita*. In *The Works of William Congreve*, vol. 3, edited by D. F. McKenzie, 1-62. Oxford: Oxford University Press, 2011.

———. *Love for Love: A Comedy*. In *The Works of William Congreve*, vol. 1, edited by D. F. McKenzie, 247-392. Oxford: Oxford University Press, 2011.

———. *The Way of the World. A Comedy*. In *The Works of William Congreve*, vol. 2, ed. D. F. McKenzie, 95-226. Oxford: Oxford University Press, 2011.

Coppola, Al. *The Theater of Experiment: Staging Natural Philosophy in Eighteenth-Century Britain*. Oxford: Oxford University Press, 2016.

Culler, Jonathan. *Structuralist Poetics: Structuralism, Linguistics, and the Study of Literature*. Ithaca, NY: Cornell University Press, 1975.

Cunning, David. "Introduction." In *Margaret Cavendish: Essential Writings*, edited by David Cunning, 1-22. Oxford: Oxford University Press, 2019.

Dandeker, Christopher. *Surveillance, Power, and Modernity: Bureaucracy and Discipline from 1700 to the Present Day*. New York: St. Martin's Press, 1990.

Davis, Lennard J. *Factual Fictions: The Origins of the English Novel*. Philadelphia: University of Pennsylvania Press, 1997.

Davis, Paul. "From Script to Print: Marketing Rochester." In *Lord Rochester in the Restoration World*, edited by Matthew C. Augustine and Steven N. Zwicker, 40-57. Cambridge: Cambridge University Press, 2015.

Day, Cyrus. "Pills to Purge Melancholy." *Review of English Studies: A Quarterly Journal of English Literature and the English Language* 8, vol. 30 (1932): 177-84.

De Grazia, Margaret. *Shakespeare Verbatim: The Reproduction of Authenticity and the 1790 Apparatus*. Oxford: Clarendon Press, 1991.

Demos, John. *The Enemy Within: 2,000 Years of Witch-Hunting in the Western World*. New York: Viking, 2003.

Denning, Michael. "Beggars and Thieves: *The Beggar's Opera* as Crime Drama." Reprinted in *Popular Fictions: Essays in Literature and History*, edited by Peter Humm. London: Routledge, 2003.

Desens, Marliss C. *The Bed-Trick in English Renaissance Drama: Explorations in Gender, Sexuality, and Power*. Newark: University of Delaware Press, 1994.

Dobson, Michael. *The Making of the National Poet: Shakespeare, Adaptation, and Authorship.* Oxford: Clarendon Press, 1992.

Doody, Margaret. *The Daring Muse: Augustan Poetry Reconsidered.* Cambridge: Cambridge University Press, 1985.

Downes, John. *Roscius Anglicanus.* Edited by Robert D. Hume and Judith Milhous. London: Society for Theatre Research, 1987.

Dryden, John. *Dedication of the Aeneis.* In *The Works of John Dryden,* vol. 5, edited by William Frost, 267-341. Berkeley: University of California Press, 1987.

———. Dedication to *Marriage A-la-Mode.* In *The Works of John Dryden,* vol. 11, edited by Vincent A. Dearing, John Loftis, and David Stuart Rodes, 221-24. Berkeley: University of California Press, 1978.

———. Dedication to *The Spanish Fryar.* In *The Works of John Dryden,* vol. 14, edited by Vinton A. Dearing and Alan Roper, 99-104. Berkeley: University of California Press, 1992.

———. Dedicatory epistle to *The Rival Ladies.* In *The Works of John Dryden,* vol. 8, edited by John Harrington Smith, 95-102. Berkeley: University of California Press, 1962.

———. "Defence of the Epilogue [of the second part of *The Conquest of Granada*]." In *The Works of John Dryden,* vol. 11, edited by Vincent A. Dearing, John Loftis, and David Stuart Rodes, 203-18. Berkeley: University of California Press, 1978.

———. *An Essay of Dramatick Poesie.* In *The Works of John Dryden,* vol. 17, edited by Samuel Holt Monk, 8-82. Berkeley: University of California Press, 1971.

———. "Heads of an Answer to Rymer." In *The Works of John Dryden,* vol. 17, edited by Samuel Holt Monk, 185-94. Berkeley: University of California Press, 1971.

———. "To My Dear Friend Mr. Congreve." In *The Works of John Dryden,* vol. 4, edited by A. B. Chambers, William Frost, and Vinton A. Dearing, 432-34. Berkeley: University of California Press, 1974.

Duffey, Mr. (John D'Urfey). *The Hubble Bubbles: A Ballad to the tune of O'er the Hills and far a way.* 1720. Broadside in the collection of the Baker Library, Harvard Business School (featured in online exhibition on the South Sea Bubble: https://curiosity.lib.harvard.edu/south-sea-bubble/catalog/68-990092192080203941).

Dugas, Don-John, and Robert Hume. "The Dissemination of Shakespeare's Plays circa 1714." *Studies in Bibliography* 56 (2003-4): 261-75.

Dugaw, Dianne. *Deep Play: John Gay and the Invention of Modernity.* Newark: University of Delaware Press, 2001.

———. "'The Popular Marketing of Old Ballads': The Ballad Revival and Eighteenth-Century Antiquarianism Revisited." *Eighteenth-Century Studies* 21, no. 1 (1987): 71-90.

———. "'The ~~Rationall~~ Spirituall Part': Dryden and Purcell's Baroque *King Arthur.*" In Lewis and Novak, *Enchanted Ground: Reimagining John Dryden,* 271-86.

Duncan, Stewart. "Debating Materialism: Cavendish, Hobbes, and More." *History of Philosophy Quarterly* 29, no. 4 (October 2012): 391-409.

Eagleton, Terry. *Literary Theory: An Introduction.* 2nd ed. Minneapolis: University of Minnesota Press, 1996.

Eliade, Mircea. *Patterns in Comparative Religion.* Translated by Rosemary Sheed. New York: Sheed & Ward, Inc., 1958.

Empson, William. *Some Versions of Pastoral.* New York: New Directions, 1974.

Engell, James. *The Creative Imagination: Enlightenment to Romanticism.* Cambridge, MA: Harvard University Press, 1981.

Erne, Lukas. *Shakespeare and the Book Trade.* Cambridge: Cambridge University Press, 2013.

———. *Shakespeare as Literary Dramatist.* Cambridge: Cambridge University Press, 2003.

Erskine-Hill, Howard. "The Significance of Gay's Drama." In *English Drama: Forms and Development,* edited by Marie Axton and Raymond Williams, 142-63. Cambridge: Cambridge University Press, 1977.

Evans, G. Blakemore, ed. *The Riverside Shakespeare.* Boston: Houghton Mifflin, 1974.

Ezell, Margaret J. M. *The Oxford English Literary History, Volume 5, 1645-1714: The Later Seventeenth Century.* Oxford: Oxford University Press, 2017.

Fairer, David. "Shakespeare in Poetry." In Ritche and Sabor, *Shakespeare in the Eighteenth Century,* 99-117.

Fawcett, Julia. "Unmapping London: Urbanization and the Performance of Personal Space in Aphra Behn's *The Lucky Chance.*" *Eighteenth-Century Studies* 50, no. 2 (2017): 155-71.

Fergus, Jan. *Provincial Readers in Eighteenth-Century England.* New York: Oxford University Press, 2007.

Fitzmaurice, James. "Shakespeare, Cavendish, and Reading Aloud." In *Cavendish and Shakespeare, Interconnections,* edited by Katherine Romack and James Fitzmaurice, 29-46. New York: Routledge, 2016. First published 2006 by Ashgate.

———. "William Cavendish and Two Entertainments by Ben Jonson." *The Ben Jonson Journal* 5 (1999): 63-80.

Fox, Adam. *Oral and Literate Culture in England, 1500-1700.* Oxford: Clarendon Press, 2000.

Frank, Marcie. *Gender, Theatre, and the Origins of Criticism from Dryden to Manley.* Cambridge: Cambridge University Press, 2002.

———. *The Novel Stage: Narrative Form from the Restoration to Aphra Behn.* Lewisburg, PA: Bucknell University Press, 2020.

Fujimura, Thomas. *The Restoration Comedy of Wit.* Princeton, NJ: Princeton University Press, 1952.

Fuller, John. Introduction to *John Gay: Dramatic Works,* vol. 1, edited by John Fuller, 1-76. Oxford: Clarendon Press, 1983.

Gallagher, Catherine. *Nobody's Story: The Vanishing Acts of Women Writers in the Marketplace, 1670-1820.* Berkeley: University of California Press, 1994.

Gardner, Kevin J. "George Farquhar's *The Recruiting Officer:* Warfare, Conscription, and the Disarming of Anxiety." *Eighteenth-Century Life* 25, no. 3 (2001).

———. "Patrician Authority and Instability in *The Way of the World.*" *South Central Review* 19, no. 1 (Spring 2002): 53-75.

Gavin, Michael. *The Invention of English Criticism, 1650-1760.* Cambridge: Cambridge University Press, 2015.

Gay, John. *The Beggar's Opera.* In *John Gay: Dramatic Works,* vol. 2, edited by John Fuller, 1-66. Oxford: Clarendon Press, 1983.

———. *The Letters of John Gay.* Edited by C.F. Burgess. Oxford: Clarendon Press, 1966.

———. *The What D'Ye Call It.* In *John Gay: Dramatic Works,* vol. 1, edited by John Fuller, 173-206. Oxford: Clarendon Press, 1983.

Gert, Bernard. "Hobbes' Psychology." In *The Cambridge Companion to Thomas Hobbes,* edited by Tom Sorell, 157-74. Cambridge: Cambridge University Press, 2006.

Gevirtz, Karen. *Women, the Novel, and Natural Philosophy, 1660-1727.* New York: Palgrave Macmillan, 2014.

Gildon, Charles. *The History of the Athenian Society.* London: Dowley, 1692.

Green, Susan. "Semiotic Modalities of the Female Body in Aphra Behn's *The Dutch Lover.*" In *Rereading Aphra Behn: History, Theory, and Criticism,* edited by Heidi Hutner, 121-47. Charlottesville: University Press of Virginia, 1993.

Guillory, John. *Poetic Authority: Spenser, Milton, and Literary History.* New York: Columbia University Press, 1983.

Gustafson, Daniel. *Lothario's Corpse: Libertine Drama and the Long-Running Restoration, 1700-1832.* Lewisburg, PA: Bucknell University Press, 2020.

Hammond, Brean. *Professional Imaginative Writing in England, 1670-1740: "Hackney for Bread."* Oxford: Oxford University Press, 1997.

Hammond, Paul. "The Restoration Poetic and Dramatic Canon." In *The Cambridge History of the Book in Britain,* vol. 4 (1557-1695), edited by John Barnard and D. F. McKenzie, with the assistance of Maureen Bell, 388-409. Cambridge: Cambridge University Press, 2002.

Harris, Joseph. *Inventing the Spectator: Subjectivity and the Theatrical Experience in Early Modern France.* Oxford: Oxford University Press, 2014.

Helgerson, Richard. *Self-Crowned Laureates: Spenser, Jonson, Milton, and the Literary System.* Berkeley: University of California Press, 1983.

Henderson, William Augustus. *The Housekeeper's Instructor.* London: Printed and sold by W. and J. Stratford, Holborn-Hill, 1790.

Henke, Robert. *Performance and Literature in the Commedia dell'Arte.* Cambridge: Cambridge University Press, 2002.

Hinnant, Charles H. "Wit, Propriety, and Style in *The Way of the World.*" *SEL* 17, no. 3 (Summer 1977): 373-86.

Hobbes, Thomas. *Leviathan.* Edited by Richard E. Flathman and David Johnston. New York: W. W. Norton & Co., 1997.

Holland, Peter. *The Ornament of Action: Text and Performance in Restoration Comedy.* Cambridge: Cambridge University Press, 1979.

Hooks, Adam G. "Booksellers' Catalogues and the Classification of Printed Drama in Seventeenth-Century England." *The Papers of the Bibliographical Society of America* 102, no. 4 (December 2008): 445-64.

Howe, Elizabeth. *The First English Actresses: Women and Drama, 1660-1700.* Cambridge: Cambridge University Press, 1992.

Howson, Gerald. *Thief-Taker General: Jonathan Wild and the Emergence of Crime and Corruption as a Way of Life in Eighteenth-Century England.* New Brunswick, NJ: Transaction Books, 1985.

Hoxby, Blair. "Dryden's Baroque Dramaturgy: The Case of *Aureng-Zebe*." In Lewis and Novak, *Enchanted Ground: Reimagining John Dryden,* 244-70.

Hudson, Nicholas. "Creating the 'Classless' Author: Authorship and the Social Hierarchy, 1660-1800." *Textual Practice* 33, no. 9 (2019): 1577-96.

Hume, Robert D. *The Development of English Drama in the Late Seventeenth Century.* Oxford: Clarendon Press, 1976.

———. *Dryden's Criticism.* Ithaca, NY: Cornell University Press, 1970.

———. "The Economics of Culture in London, 1660-1740." *Huntington Library Quarterly* 69 no. 4 (2006): 487-533.

———. *Henry Fielding and the London Theatre, 1728-1737.* Oxford: Clarendon Press, 1988.

———. *The London Theatre World, 1660-1800.* Carbondale: Southern Illinois University Press, 1980.

———. "The Origins of the Actor Benefit in London." *Theatre Research International* 9, no. 2 (1984): 99-111.

Hunt, John Dixon, and Peter Willis, eds. *The Genius of the Place: The English Landscape Garden 1620-1820.* Cambridge, MA: The MIT Press, 1988.

Jarvis, F. P. "The Philosophical Assumptions of Congreve's *Love for Love*." *Texas Studies in Language and Literature* 14, no. 3 (Fall 1972): 423-34.

Johns, Adrian. "The Physiology of Reading in Restoration England." In *The Practice and Representation of Reading in England,* edited by James Raven, Helen Small, and Naomi Tadmor, 138-61. Cambridge: Cambridge University Press, 1996.

———. "Reading and Experiment in the Early Royal Society." In *Reading, Society, and Politics in Early Modern England,* edited by Kevin Sharpe and Steven N. Zwicker, 244-74. Cambridge: Cambridge University Press, 2003.

Johnson, Samuel. Preface to *The Plays of Shakespear.* 1765. In Smith, *Eighteenth Century Essays on Shakespeare,* 104-50.

Jones, Vivien, and David Lindley. Introduction to *The Beggar's Opera,* by John Gay, vii-xxx. London: Bloomsbury (New Mermaid Edition), 2010.

Kastan, David Scott. "Humphrey Moseley and the Invention of English Literature." In *Agent of Change: Print Culture Studies after Elizabeth L. Eisenstein,* edited by Sabrina Alcorn Baron, Eric N. Lindquist, and Eleanor F. Shevlin, 105-24. Amherst: University of Massachusetts Press, 2007.

———. *Shakespeare and the Book.* Oxford: Oxford University Press, 2001.

Kavenik, Frances. "Aphra Behn: The Playwright as 'Breeches Part.'" In Schofield and Macheski, *Curtain Calls: British and American Women and the Theater, 1660-1820,* 177-92.

Kenyon, John. *The Popish Plot.* London: Heinemann, 1972.

Kermode, Frank, ed. *The Tempest,* by William Shakespeare. Arden Edition. Cambridge, MA: Harvard University Press, 1958.

Kewes, Paulina. *Authorship and Appropriation: Writing for the Stage in England, 1660–1710.* Oxford: Clarendon Press, 1998.

———. "'Give Me the Sociable Pocket-books...': Humphrey Moseley's Serial Publication of Octavo Play Collections." *Publishing History* 38 (January 1995): 5–21.

Klekar, Cynthia. "Obligation, Coercion, and Economy: The Deed of Trust in Congreve's *The Way of the World.*" In *The Culture of the Gift in Eighteenth-Century England,* edited by Linda Zionkowski and Cynthia Klekar, 125–42. New York: Palgrave MacMillan, 2009.

Knights, Mark. *Representation and Misrepresentation in Later Stuart Britain: Partisanship and Political Culture.* Oxford: Oxford University Press, 2005.

Kramer, David Bruce. *The Imperial Dryden: The Poetics of Appropriation in Seventeenth-Century England.* Athens: University of Georgia Press, 1994.

Kramnick, Jonathan. *Actions and Objects from Hobbes to Richardson.* Stanford: Stanford University Press, 2010.

———. *Making the English Canon: Print-Capitalism and the Cultural Past, 1700–1770.* Cambridge: Cambridge University Press, 1998.

Kroll, Richard. "Discourse and Power in *The Way of the World.*" *ELH* 53, no. 4 (winter 1986), 727–58.

Lamb, Charles. "On the Tragedies of Shakespeare, Considered with Reference to Their Fitness for Stage Representation." 1811. In *The Oxford Edition of the Works in Prose and Verse of Charles and Mary Lamb,* edited by Thomas Hutchinson, 124–41. London: Oxford University Press, 1924.

Langbaine, Gerard. *An Account of the English Dramatick Poets.* Vol. 2, with an introduction by John Loftis. Los Angeles: William Andrews Clark Memorial Library, 1971.

Leacroft, Richard. *The Development of the English Playhouse.* Ithaca, NY: Cornell University Press, 1973.

Lehmann-Haupt, Helmutt. *Gutenberg and the Master of the Playing Cards.* New Haven, CT: Yale University Press, 1966.

Lesser, Zachary. *Drama and the Politics of Publication: Readings in the English Book Trade.* Cambridge: Cambridge University Press, 2004.

Lewis, Jane, and Maximillian E. Novak, eds. *Enchanted Ground: Reimagining John Dryden.* Toronto: University of Toronto Press, 2004.

Lewis, Peter. *John Gay: The Beggar's Opera.* London: Edward Arnold, 1976.

Lindenbaum, Peter. "Milton's Contract." *Cardoza Arts & Entertainment Law Journal* 10 (1992): 439–54.

Linebaugh, Peter. *The London Hanged: Crime and Civil Society in the Eighteenth Century.* Cambridge: Cambridge University Press, 1992.

Loftis, John E. "Congreve's *Way of the World* and Popular Criminal Literature." *SEL* 36, no. 3 (Summer 1996): 561–78.

Loughry, Bryan, and T. O. Treadwell. Introduction to *The Beggar's Opera.* Hammondsworth: Penguin, 1986.

Love, Harold. "Dryden, Rochester, and the Invention of the 'Town.'" In *John Dryden (1631-1700): His Politics, His Plays, and His Poets*, edited by Claude Rawson and Aaron Santesso, 36-51. Newark: University of Delaware Press, 2003.

———. "Shadwell, Rochester, and the Crisis of Amateurism." *Restoration: Studies in English Literary Culture, 1660-1700* 20, no. 2 (Fall 1996): 119-34.

Lynch, Deidre. *The Economy of Character: Novels, Market Culture, and the Business of Inner Meaning*. Chicago: University of Chicago Press, 1998.

Lynch, Jack. "Criticism of Shakespeare." In Ritche and Sabor, *Shakespeare in the Eighteenth Century*, 41-59.

Lyons, John D. *Kingdom of Disorder: The Theory of Tragedy in Classical France*. West Lafayette, IN: Purdue University Press, 1999.

Mack, Maynard. "Introduction." In *The Augustans*, 2nd ed., edited by Maynard Mack, 17-19. English Masterpieces Series 5. Englewood Cliffs, NJ: Prentice Hall, Inc., 1961. Reprinted in *Twentieth-Century Interpretations of "The Beggar's Opera": A Collection of Critical Essays*, edited by Yvonne Noble, 41-43. Englewood Cliffs, NJ: Prentice Hall, 1975.

Markley, Robert. "Behn and the Unstable Traditions of Social Comedy." In *The Cambridge Companion to Aphra Behn*, edited by Derek Hughes and Janet Todd, 98-117. Cambridge: Cambridge University Press, 2004.

Marotti, Arthur F. *Manuscript, Print, and the English Renaissance Lyric*. Ithaca: Cornell University Press, 1995.

Marsden, Jean. "Rape, Voyeurism, and the Restoration Stage." In *Broken Boundaries: Women and Feminism in Restoration Drama*, edited by Katherine M. Quinsey, 185-200. Lexington: University of Kentucky Press, 1996.

———. *The Re-Imagined Text: Shakespeare, Adaptation, and Eighteenth-Century Literary Theory*. Lexington: University of Kentucky Press, 1995.

———. "Shakespeare and Sympathy." In *Shakespeare and the Eighteenth Century*, edited by Peter Sabor and Paul Yachnin, 29-41. Burlington, VT: Ashgate Publishing, 2008.

Masten, Jeffrey. *Textual Intercourse: Collaboration, Authorship, and Sexualities in Renaissance Drama*. Cambridge: Cambridge University Press, 1997.

Mayer, Jean-Christophe. *Shakespeare's Early Readers: A Cultural History from 1590 to 1800*. Cambridge: Cambridge University Press, 2018.

McAfee, Helen, ed. *Pepys on the Restoration Stage*. New Haven, CT: Yale University Press, 1916.

McCloskey, Susan. "Knowing One's Relations in Congreve's *The Way of the World*." *Theatre Journal* 31, no. 1 (March 1981): 69-79.

McDowell, Paula. *The Invention of the Oral: Print Commerce and Fugitive Voices in Eighteenth-Century Britain*. Chicago: University of Chicago Press, 2017.

———. *The Women of Grub Street: Press, Politics, and Gender in the London Literary Marketplace, 1678-1730*. Oxford: Oxford University Press, 1998.

McKenzie, Andrea. "The Real Macheath." *Huntington Library Quarterly* 69, no. 4 (December 2006): 581-605.

McKenzie, D. F. "Typography and Meaning: The Case of William Congreve." In *Making Meaning: "Printers of the Mind" and Other Essays*, 198-236. Amherst: University of Massachusetts Press, 2000.

McKeon, Michael. *The Origins of the English Novel, 1600-1740.* Baltimore: Johns Hopkins University Press, 1987.

Meagher, Jennifer. "Commedia dell'arte" (2007). *Heilbrunn Timeline of Art History.* Metropolitan Museum of Art. https://www.metmuseum.org/toah/hd/comm/hd_comm.htm.

Meskill, Lynn Sermin. "Exorcising the Gorgon of Terror: Jonson's *Masque of Queenes.*" *ELH* 72, no. 1 (Spring 2005): 181-207.

Milhous, Judith. "Company Management." In *The London Theatre World, 1660-1800,* edited by Robert D. Hume. Carbondale: Southern Illinois University Press, 1980.

———. "The Multimedia Spectacular on the Restoration Stage." In *British Theatre and the Other Arts, 1660-1800,* edited by Shirley Strum Kenny, 41-66. Washington, D.C.: Folger Shakespeare Library, 1984.

Milhous, Judith, and Robert D. Hume. *The Publication of Plays in London, 1660-1800: Playwrights, Publishers and the Market.* London: The British Library, 2015.

Miller, Shannon. "'Thou art a Moniment, without a tombe': Affiliation and Memorialization in Margaret Cavendish's *Playes* and *Plays, Never before Printed.*" In *Cavendish and Shakespeare, Interconnections,* edited by Katherine Romack and James Fitzmaurice, 7-28. New York: Routledge, 2016. First published by Ashgate, 2006.

Miner, Earl, and Jennifer Brady. Preface to *Literary Transmission and Authority,* edited by Earl Miner and Jennifer Brady. Cambridge: Cambridge University Press, 1993.

Mueschke, Paul, and Miriam Mueschke. *A New View of Congreve's* Way of the World. Ann Arbor: University of Michigan Press, 1958.

Munns, Jessica. "'But to the touch were soft': pleasure, power, and impotence in 'The Disappointment' and 'The Golden Age.'" In Todd, *Aphra Behn Studies,* 178-96.

———. "'The Golden Days of Queen Elizabeth': Thomas Shadwell's *The Lancashire-Witches* and the Politics of Nostalgia." *Restoration: Studies in English Literary Culture, 1660-1700* 20, no. 2 (1996): 195-216.

———. "'Good, Sweet, Honey, Sugar-Candied Reader': Aphra Behn's Foreplay in Forewords." In *Rereading Aphra Behn: History, Theory, and Criticism,* edited by Heidi Hutner. Charlottesville: University of Virginia Press, 1993.

———. "'I by a double right thy bounties claim': Aphra Behn and Sexual Space." In Schofield and Macheski, *Curtain Calls: British and American Women and the Theater, 1660-1820,* 193-210.

Newman, Steve. "The Value of 'Nothing': Ballads in *The Beggar's Opera.*" *The Eighteenth Century* 45, no. 3 (2004): 265-83.

Noble, Yvonne, ed. *Twentieth-Century Interpretations of "The Beggar's Opera": A Collection of Critical Essays.* Englewood Cliffs, NJ: Prentice Hall, 1975.

Nokes, David. *John Gay: A Profession of Friendship.* Oxford: Oxford University Press, 1995.

Novak, Maximillian E. "The Politics of Shakespeare Criticism in the Restoration and Eighteenth Century." *ELH* 81, no. 1 (Spring 2014): 115-42.

O'Brien, John. *Harlequin Britain: Pantomime Entertainment, 1690-1760.* Baltimore: Johns Hopkins University Press, 2004.

Oden, Richard. *Dryden and Shadwell: The Literary Controversy and Mac Flecknoe (1668-1679)*. New York: Scholars' Facsimiles & Reprints, 1977.

Orgel, Stephen. "The Renaissance Artist as Plagiarist." *ELH* 48, no. 3 (Autumn 1981): 476-95.

Osborn, J. M. *John Dryden: Some Biographical Facts and Problems*. Gainesville: University of Florida Press, 1940.

Otway, Thomas. *The Orphan,* edited by Aline Mackenzie Taylor. Lincoln: University of Nebraska Press, 1976.

Owen, Susan J. *Restoration Theatre and Crisis*. Oxford: Clarendon Press, 1996.

Pask, Kevin. *The Emergence of the English Author: Scripting the Life of the Poet in Early Modern England*. Cambridge: Cambridge University Press, 1996.

———. "Plagiarism and the Originality of National Literature: Gerard Langbaine," *ELH* 69, no. 3 (Autumn 2002): 727-47.

Patterson, Annabel. *Pastoral and Ideology: Virgil to Valéry*. Berkeley: University of California Press, 1987.

Payne, Deborah (Deborah Payne Fisk). "'And Poets Shall by Patron Princes Live': Aphra Behn and Patronage." In Schofield and Macheski, *Curtain Calls: British and American Women and the Theater, 1660-1820*, 105-19.

Pechter, Edward. *Dryden's Classical Theory of Literature*. London: Cambridge University Press, 1975.

Perry, Ruth. *Women, Letters, and the Novel*. New York: AMS Press, 1980.

Peters, Julie Stone. *Congreve, the Drama, and the Printed Word*. Stanford: Stanford University Press, 1990.

———. *Theatre of the Book, 1480-1880: Print, Text, and Performance in Europe*. Oxford: Oxford University Press, 2000.

Phelan, Peggy. *Unmarked: The Politics of Performance*. New York: Routledge, 1993.

Poole, Robert, ed. *The Lancashire Witches: Histories and Stories*. Manchester: Manchester University Press, 2013.

Poovey, Mary. *A History of the Modern Fact: Problems of Knowledge in the Sciences of Wealth and Society*. Chicago: University of Chicago Press, 1998.

Pope, Alexander. Preface to *The Works of Shakespear* (1725). In Smith, *Eighteenth Century Essays on Shakespeare*, 44-58.

Potter, Lois. *Secret Rites and Secret Writing: Royalist Literature, 1641-1660*. Cambridge: Cambridge University Press, 1989.

Powell, Jocelyn. *Restoration Theatre Production*. London: Routledge & Kegan Paul, 1984.

Prince, Kathryn. "Shakespeare and English Nationalism." In Ritche and Sabor, *Shakespeare in the Eighteenth Century*, 277-94.

Randall, Dale B. J. *Winter Fruit: English Drama 1642-1660*. Lexington: University of Kentucky Press, 1995.

Reverand, Cedric D. "Dryden and the Canon: Absorbing and Rejecting the Burden of the Past." In Lewis and Novak, *Enchanted Ground: Reimagining John Dryden*, 203-25.

Ritchie, Fiona. *Women and Shakespeare in the Eighteenth Century.* Cambridge: Cambridge University Press, 2014.

Ritchie, Fiona, and Peter Sabor, eds. *Shakespeare in the Eighteenth Century.* Cambridge: Cambridge University Press, 2012.

Roach, Joseph R. *The Player's Passion: Studies in the Science of Acting.* Ann Arbor: University of Michigan Press, 1993.

Roper, Alan. "Language and Action in *The Way of the World, Love's Last Shift,* and *The Relapse.*" *ELH* 40, no. 1 (Spring 1973): 44–69.

Rosenthal, Laura J. *Playwrights and Plagiarists in Early Modern England: Gender, Authorship, Literary Property.* Ithaca, NY: Cornell University Press, 1996.

———. *Ways of the World: Theater and Cosmopolitanism in the Restoration and Beyond.* Ithaca, NY: Cornell University Press, 2020.

Ross, John C. "Alsatia and the Alsatians." Appendix D in *Thomas Shadwell's "The Squire of Alsatia": A Critical Edition,* edited by John C. Ross, 230–42. New York: Garland, 1987.

———. "The Author." In *Thomas Shadwell's "The Squire of Alsatia": A Critical Edition,* edited by John C. Ross, 5–13. New York: Garland, 1987.

———. "The Play." In *Thomas Shadwell's "The Squire of Alsatia": A Critical Edition,* edited by John C. Ross, 31–44. New York: Garland, 1987.

———. "Theatricality and Revolution Politics in *The Squire of Alsatia* and *Bury-Fair.*" *Restoration: Studies in English Literary Culture* 20, no. 2 (1996): 217–35.

Ross, Trevor. "The Emergence of 'Literature': Making and Reading the English Canon in the Eighteenth Century." *ELH* 63, no. 2 (Summer 1996): 397–422.

Rumbold, Kate. "Shakespeare and the Stratford Jubilee." In Ritche and Sabor, *Shakespeare in the Eighteenth Century,* 254–76.

Rymer, Thomas. *Tragedies of the Last Age.* In *The Critical Works of Thomas Rymer,* edited by Curt A. Zimansky, 17–76. New Haven, CT: Yale University Press, 1956.

Salingar, Leo. *Shakespeare and the Tradition of Comedy.* Cambridge: Cambridge University Press, 1974.

Santor, Gefen Bar-On. "Shakespeare in the Georgian Theatre." In *The Oxford Handbook of Georgian Theatre,* edited by Julia Swindells and David Francis Taylor, 213–28. Oxford: Oxford University Press, 2014.

Sarasohn, Lisa T. *The Natural Philosophy of Margaret Cavendish.* Baltimore: Johns Hopkins University Press, 2010.

Sauer, Elizabeth. *'Paper-Contestations' and Textual Communities in England, 1640–1675.* Toronto: University of Toronto Press, 2005.

Schechner, Richard. *Between Theater and Anthropology.* Philadelphia: University of Pennsylvania Press, 1985.

———. *By Means of Performance: Intercultural Studies of Theatre and Ritual.* Cambridge: Cambridge University Press, 1990.

———. *The Future of Ritual: Writings on Culture and Performance.* New York: Routledge, 1993.

Schoenfeldt, Michael. "Reading Bodies." In *Reading, Society, and Politics in Early Modern England,* edited by Kevin Sharpe and Steven N. Zwicker, 215-43. Cambridge: Cambridge University Press, 2003.

Schofield, Mary Anne, and Cecilia Macheski, eds. *Curtain Calls: British and American Women and the Theater, 1660-1820.* Athens: Ohio University Press, 1991.

Schultz, William. *Gay's "Beggar's Opera": Its Content, History, and Influence.* New York: Russell & Russell, 1923. Reissued 1967.

Settle, Elkanah. *A Farther Defence of Dramatick Poetry.* 1698. In *A Defence of Dramatick Poetry and A Farther Defence of Dramatick Poetry.* Facsimile reprint, New York: Garland, 1972.

Shadwell, Thomas. Preface to *The Humorists.* In *The Complete Works of Thomas Shadwell,* vol. 1, edited by Montague Summers, 183-89. London: Fortune Press, 1927.

———. Preface to *The Sullen Lovers.* In *The Complete Works of Thomas Shadwell,* vol. 1, edited by Montague Summers, 9-12. London: Fortune Press, 1927.

———. Preface to *The Royal Shepherdess.* In *The Complete Works of Thomas Shadwell,* vol. 1, edited by Montague Summers, 99-100. London: Fortune Press, 1927.

———. Prologue to *The Royal Shepherdess.* In *The Complete Works of Thomas Shadwell,* vol. 1, edited by Montague Summers, 101. London: Fortune Press, 1927.

———. *Thomas Shadwell's "The Lancashire-Witches," and "Tegue o Divelly The Irish-Priest": A Critical Old-Spelling Edition.* Edited by Judith Bailey Slagle. New York: Garland Publishing, 1991.

———. *Thomas Shadwell's "The Squire of Alsatia": A Critical Edition.* Edited by John C. Ross. New York: Garland, 1987.

Shapin, Steven, and Simon Schaffer. *Leviathan and the Air-Pump: Hobbes, Boyle, and the Experimental Life.* Princeton: Princeton University Press, 1985.

Shell, Alison. "Popish Plots: *The Feign'd Curtizans* in Context." In Todd, *Aphra Behn Studies,* 30-49.

Sidney, Philip. *An Apology for Poetry (Or the Defence of Poesy).* Edited by Geoffrey Shepherd, revised and expanded for the third edition by R.W. Maslen. Manchester: Manchester University Press, 2002.

Simpson, Claude M. *The British Broadside and Its Music.* New Brunswick, NJ: Rutgers University Press, 1966.

Slagle, Judith Bailey. "Dueling Prefaces, Pamphlets, and Prologues: Re-visioning the Political and Personal Wars of John Dryden and Thomas Shadwell." *Restoration and Eighteenth-Century Theatre Research* 21, no. 1 (Summer 2006): 17-32.

———. "Introduction." In *Thomas Shadwell's "The Lancashire-Witches," and "Tegue o Divelly The Irish-Priest": A Critical Old-Spelling Edition,* edited by Judith Bailey Slagle, 1-30. New York: Garland Publishing, 1991.

Smith, D. Nichol, ed. *Eighteenth Century Essays on Shakespeare.* Oxford: Clarendon Press, 1963.

———. "Introduction: Shakespearian Criticism in the Eighteenth Century." In Smith, *Eighteenth Century Essays on Shakespeare,* xi-xxxvii.

Smith, Dane Farnsworth. *Plays about the Theatre in England.* London: Oxford University Press, 1936.

Smith, Susan Harris. "Ironic Distance and the Theatre of Feigned Madness." *Theatre Journal* 39, no. 1 (March 1987): 51-64.

Smyth, Maura. *Women Writing Fancy: Authorship and Autonomy from 1611-1812.* New York: Palgrave Macmillan, 2017.

Spiller, Elizabeth. *Science, Reading, and Renaissance Literature: The Art of Making Knowledge, 1580-1670.* Cambridge: Cambridge University Press, 2004.

Stapleton, M. L. *Admired and Understood: The Poetry of Aphra Behn.* Newark: University of Delaware Press, 2004.

Starr, Gabrielle G. "Cavendish, Aesthetics, and the Anti-Platonic Line." *Eighteenth-Century Studies* 39, no. 3 (Spring 2006): 295-308.

———. "Objects, Imaginings, and Facts: Going Beyond Genre in Behn and Defoe." *Eighteenth-Century Fiction* 16, no. 4 (July 2004): 499-518.

States, Bert O. "Performance as Metaphor." *Afterall: A Journal of Art, Context and Enquiry* 3 (2001): 64-86.

Stewart, Ann Marie. *The Ravishing Restoration: Aphra Behn, Violence, and Comedy.* Selinsgrove, PA: Susquehanna University Press, 2010.

Stewart, Susan. "Scandals of the Ballad." *Representations* 32 (Autumn 1990): 134-56.

Stone, Lawrence. *Uncertain Unions: Marriage in England, 1660-1753.* Oxford: Oxford University Press, 1992.

Straznicky, Marta. *Privacy, Playreading, and Women's Closet Drama, 1550-1700.* Cambridge: Cambridge University Press, 2004.

Styan, J. L. *Restoration Comedy in Performance.* Cambridge: Cambridge University Press, 1986.

Taylor, Gary. *Reinventing Shakespeare: A Cultural History, from the Restoration to the Present.* Oxford: Oxford University Press, 1991.

Terry, Richard. *Poetry and the Making of the English Literary Past, 1660-1781.* Oxford: Oxford University Press, 2001.

Thomas, David. "The 1737 Licensing Act and its Impact." In *The Oxford Handbook of the Georgian Theatre, 1737-1832,* edited by Julia Swindells and David Francis Taylor, 90-106. Oxford: Oxford University Press, 2014.

Tierney-Hynes, Rebecca. *Novel Minds: Philosophers and Romance Readers, 1680-1740.* New York: Palgrave Macmillan, 2012.

Todd, Janet, ed. *Aphra Behn Studies.* Cambridge: Cambridge University Press, 1996.

Treadwell, J. M. "Congreve, Tonson, and Rowe's 'Reconcilement.'" *Notes and Queries* 220 (June 1975): 265-69.

Tribble, Evelyn. *Margins and Marginality: The Printed Page in Early Modern England.* Charlottesville: University of Virginia Press, 1993.

Velissariou, Aspasia. "The Hobbesian Other in Congreve's Comedies." *Restoration and Eighteenth-Century Theatre Research* 23, no. 1 (Summer 2008): 68-81.

Vickers, Brian. "The Emergence of Character Criticism, 1774-1800." In *Shakespeare Survey,* vol. 34, *Characterization in Shakespeare,* edited by Stanley Wells, 11-22. Cambridge: Cambridge University Press, 1981.

Walker, Claire. "'Remember Justice Godfrey': The Popish Plot and the Construction of Panic in Seventeenth-Century Media." In *Moral Panics, the Media, and the Law in*

Early Modern England, edited by David Lemmings and Claire Walker, 117-38. New York: Palgrave Macmillan, 2009.

Warner, William. *Licensing Entertainment: The Elevation of Novel Reading in Britain, 1684-1750.* Berkeley: University of California Press, 1988.

Watt, Ian. *The Rise of the Novel.* Chatto and Windus, 1957. Reprint, Berkeley: University of California Press, 2001.

Weber, Harold. "A 'double Portion of his Father's Art': Congreve, Dryden, Jonson and the Drama of Theatrical Succession." *Criticism* 39, no. 3 (Summer 1997): 359-82.

Wellek, René. "What Is Literature?" In *What Is Literature?,* edited by Paul Hernadi, 16-23. Bloomington: Indiana University Press, 1978.

Whitaker, Katie. *Mad Madge: The Extraordinary Life of Margaret Cavendish, Duchess of Newcastle, the First Woman to Live by Her Pen.* New York: Basic Books, 2002.

Williams, Aubrey. *An Approach to Congreve.* New Haven, CT: Yale University Press, 1979.

Williams, Gordon, ed. *A Dictionary of Sexual Language and Imagery in Shakespearean and Stuart Literature.* New York: Bloomsbury Academic, 1994.

Winn, James. *John Dryden and His World.* New Haven, CT: Yale University Press, 1987.

Wiseman, Susan. *Drama and Politics in the English Civil War.* Cambridge: Cambridge University Press, 1998.

Woolley, Hannah. *The Compleat Servant-Maid.* London: Printed for E. Tracy, at the Three Bibles on London-Bridge, 1704.

Wright, Louis B. "The Reading of Plays During the Puritan Revolution." *Huntington Library Bulletin* 6 (1934): 73-108.

INDEX

account books, 175, 195-203, 208, 215, 271n46, 272n66, 272n69
Addison, Joseph: composition-oriented criticism by, 124; Congreve and, 164-65, 267n96; Gay's borrowings from, 179; *Pleasures of the Imagination,* 164
Alpers, Paul, 230-31
Alssid, Michael, 31, 35
amateurism, 16, 20-21, 72, 246n107, 252n100
Anderson, Benedict, 172, 176, 271n60
Anne (English queen, daughter of James II), 20, 211
anonymous authorship, 17, 244n75
Applebee's Original Weekly Journal, 198
Aristophanes, 277n44
Aristotle, 122-24; *Poetics,* 204
audience. *See* textuality vs. theatricality
authenticity, 23, 25, 178, 180, 183, 187, 217, 229
authorship: anonymous authorship, 17, 244n75; collaborative authorship, 17, 244n87; proprietary authorship and remuneration of playwrights, 16-18, 21, 225, 242n40, 244nn82-83, 244n88, 246nn107-8; Shadwell reimagining, 33, 73-74; Shakespeare's understanding of, 224; Tonson's tactics to promote concepts of literary authorship, 14, 107, 133, 226-27; transcendence and permanence of, 10. *See also* borrowings

ballads and ballad form: *Chevy Chase* (ballad), 176, 177, 271n60; *Collection of Old Ballads* (anon., 1723), 211; collections of, since sixteenth century, 176, 211; Gay and, 11-12, 25, 171, 229, 271n60; in Gay's *The Beggar's Opera,* 194-95, 199, 208-14, 273n80, 274n104; in Gay's *The What D'Ye Call It,* 178, 181-83, 190, 209, 229-30, 270n32; "The Hubble Bubbles" (ballad parody), 213; immediacy of, 208-9; "The London Lottery" (ballad parody), 213; nostalgia of society for, 171, 173, 176-78, 229-30, 232; oral and print nature of, 175-76; "O the Broom" (ballad), 212; "Over the Hills and Far Away" (ballad), 213; print commerce and capitalism of, 182, 188, 199, 211-14, 216, 270n32, 271n60, 274n104; recurrent characters in, 210; revival in Romantic period, 211; for Shakespeare Jubilee (1769), 229-30; supposed distinction between vulgar and traditional, 209; *Wit and Mirth, or Pills to Purge Melancholy* (D'Urfey, ed.), 211-12
Ballaster, Ros, 116, 259n104

Barish, Jonas, 76-77, 122
Barnard, John, 12, 15, 133-35, 227
Barry, Elizabeth, 95-96, 117-18, 257nn52-53, 257n59
Bate, Jonathan, 275n10, 276n15
Bateson, F. W., 206-7
Beaumont and Fletcher volume (1647), 14, 240n16, 244n87, 261n9; borrowings from, 28-29; Dryden on, 29; frequency among plays staged in Restoration, 241n16
Beggar's Opera, The (Gay), 21, 25, 194-217; account books of tradesman characters (Peachum and Lockit), 175, 195-203, 208, 215, 272n69; artistic and narrative responses to, 215, 274-75nn104-5; ballad culture and ballads in, 175, 178, 181-82, 195, 196, 199, 207, 208-16, 229-30, 271n60, 273n80, 274n104; blurring of pastoral with corrupt capitalistic system, 203, 215-16; "book" as multivalent term, 206-7, 215, 273n71; clandestine marriage, recognition of, 205, 206, 273nn74-75; compared to *The What D'Ye Call It*, 194, 196, 208, 215; document-based system of contracts, laws, and bureaucracy governing society, 195-96, 200, 204, 271n48; emotion and passion vs. rationality and business sense, 201-2, 208; Gay's income from theatrical run, 174, 268n8; as Gay's most successful play, 178, 194, 214; Handelian opera allusion, 202; harmony between aristocracy and the people, 201, 209, 210; literary conventions used by characters, 198, 204, 206-8; Macheath compared to Peachum and Lockit, 272n63; Macheath's relationship to the law/text, 201, 204-5, 272n66; Macheath's symbolism of highwayman, 271-72n62; Macheath's three escapes (one per act), 199-204, 206, 208; Newgate Ordinary's (chaplain) "Paper," 206-7; opera's use and allusions, 209-10, 273-74n87, 274n87, 274nn91-92; parodies of older tunes by substituting alternative lyrics, 209, 212; pastoralism and, 194-96, 199, 207-9, 213-14, 216; playing cards with theme of, 215, 275n108; play within the play, 178, 199, 203; poetic justice and, 203-4; Polly as stock character, 202, 205, 207-8, 215-16; print capitalism and, 175, 199, 214-16; Rich as producer of, 173; "scripting" of Macheath's fate and that of the other characters, 203-5, 206; second edition's introduction of numbering system for songs and Table of Songs, 214-15; skepticism of Gay toward nostalgia, 178, 199, 209-10, 216; Swift's phrase "Newgate Pastoral" associated with, 194, 232, 271n44; textuality vs. theatricality and, 175, 178, 195, 208, 216-17; Wild as basis for character Peachum, 196, 198
Behn, Aphra, 2, 77-130; *The Amorous Prince, or, The Curious Husband*, 121-22; Cavendish compared to, 89, 115-16, 234, 255n40; Congreve and Gay compared to, 217, 219; "The Disappointment" (poem), 90-92; Dryden's thinking on literary vs. theatrical aspects of a play and, 89, 125; *The Dutch Lover*, 224-26; *The Feign'd Courtesans*, 98; Hobbes, 108, 110; on imagination vs. reality (mind-body problem), 24, 77-79,

84, 86–87, 91–92, 94, 101–2, 103, 107, 110, 115–17, 128–29, 233, 234; income from writing, 17, 244n83; later comedies said to emphasize morality, 98–99; on male-oriented culture, 90, 224–25; *Oroonoko,* 87; overcredulity and, 105–6; philosophical debates of, 78–79; on reading vs. spectating of plays, 11, 121–22; *The Roundheads,* 98; *The Second Part of the Rover,* 98; Settle compared to, 117–19, 128–29; Shadwell compared to, 217, 219, 225; on Shakespeare's legacy and characterization, 226, 234; textuality vs. theatricality and, 77, 225; "The Unfortunate Bride, or the Blind Lady a Beauty," 87. See also *Emperor of the Moon, The; Luckey Chance, The*

Bell, John, 1773–74 edition of Shakespeare, 221

Bender, John, 196–97

Benjamin, Walter, 176

Bennett, Benjamin, 2, 102

Berek, Peter, 78

Berman, Ronald, 34, 58

Bernard, Stephen, 15

Betterton, Thomas, 96, 117–19, 257n59

bibliographies and catalogues of literary texts, 18–19

bodies. *See* imagination vs. reality

Bodin, Jean, 54; *Demonomanie,* 41

booksellers and bookselling. *See* literature and book trade; publishers and publishing

Borgman, Albert, 44, 65

borrowings: from Addison, 179; from Beaumont and Fletcher volume, 28–29; Gay as borrower, 178–79; from Jonson, 28; Jonson as borrower, 18, 223; Restoration authors as borrowers, 18; Shadwell as borrower, 23, 31, 33, 35, 40–44, 72–75, 249n52; from Shakespeare, 18, 28, 41, 73, 179, 229–33; Shakespeare as borrower, 5, 10, 223; from Terence, 23, 28, 35, 56, 65, 66, 73

Bowdler, Thomas and Henrietta, *Family Shakespeare,* 221

Boyle, Robert, 109; *New Experiments,* 109–10

Braverman, Richard, 158, 163–64, 267n92, 267n96

Brewer, David, 8–9, 242n35

Bristol, Michael, 233

Britland, Karen, 239n7

Brome, Richard, 74; *Five New Playes,* 14. *See also* Heywood, Thomas, and Richard Brome

Brown, David, 267n93

Buckingham, 2nd Duke of (George Villiers), *The Rehearsal,* 66

Bunyan, John, *The Pilgrim's Progress,* 180–81, 183, 191

Bush-Bailey, Gilli, 257n52

Butler, Todd, 87

Caldwell, Joan, 278n58

Canfield, J. Douglas, 251n82

capitalism: live performance as supposedly subverting, 178; profiteering of mercantile capitalism vs. inheritance, 64–65, 252n92; related to theft, 71. *See also* print capitalism

Carlell, Lodowick, *Two New Playes,* 14

Castle, Terry, 138, 144–47, 262n41, 263n43, 263n47, 264n57

Catholicism and anti-Catholic sentiment, 36, 105–6, 248n37, 258n81, 258n87

Cavendish, Margaret: access to drama during closure of theaters, 3–4, 237, 239nn6–7; autobiographical memoir of, 3; Behn compared to, 89,

Cavendish, Margaret (*continued*) 115–16, 234, 255n40; on fantasy vs. reality (mind-body problem), 24, 78, 88–89, 93–94, 115–16, 241n25; Hobbes and, 87–88, 254–55n29; marginalization as writer, 255n40; natural philosophy of, 78, 87–89, 253n9, 255n31; *Observations upon Experimental Philosophy,* 115; *Philosophical and Physical Opinions,* 115–16; on plagiarism, 241n22; *Playes,* 240n16; plays by, 3, 8; on Shakespeare, 3–11, 18, 233–34, 237, 240n10, 277n48; *The Worlds Olio,* 239n8. See also *Sociable Letters*

Cavendish, William, 3

censorship, 23, 36, 55

Chapman, George, 14

characters and characterization: ability to cross over into new media and modes, 9; in Aristotle's categories of drama analysis, 123; ballads' recurrent use of, 210; in Behn's *The Emperor of the Moon,* 128–29; in Congreve's *Love for Love* verbal exchanges, 146–50, 152; in Gay's *The What D'Ye Call It,* 231–32; mimetic vs. anti-mimetic, 125–26; nontraditional characters in tragedy, 231–32; in Shakespeare, 6–7, 10, 222, 223, 226, 230–37, 278n49

Charles II (English king), 3, 29, 30, 246n102; ballads as entertainment for, 211; fictitious conspiracy to assassinate, 105

Chaucer, Geoffrey, 12

Chevy Chase (ballad), 176, 177

Christian symbolism, 47

circulating libraries, 240n9

Civil War, English, 4, 10, 27

classicism and classical models: aristocratic authors and, 248n22; Dryden acknowledging classical literature as source of authority, 30; Dryden's equating of Congreve with, 132; Gay's acknowledgment of (preface to *The What D'Ye Call It*), 230–31; oral and modern culture vs., 69–71; Shadwell borrowing from, 41; Shadwell's character Belfond Junior educated in, 66; Shakespeare and, 223–27; Tonson's publishing agenda and, 133; translations of, 15. See also neoclassicism; *specific classical authors*

closing of the theaters, 3–4, 8, 14, 27, 77, 78, 134, 237, 239n1

Coiro, Ann Baynes, 3–4, 12, 14, 241n20

Cole, David, 137, 147–48

collaborative authorship, 17, 244n87

Collection of Old Ballads (anon., 1723), 211

Collier, Jeremy, 101, 117, 253n8

Collingwood, Francis, 265n72

comedies: exemplary comedies of late 1600s, 98; as focus of study, 22; inheritance and succession as common theme in, 248n40; wit vs. humors, 28, 31, 231

Complete Key to the Last New Farce, The What D'Ye Call It. See *What D'Ye Call It, The*

Congreve, William, 2, 131–71; Addison and, 164–65, 267n96; *The Double-Dealer,* 132–33, 267n97; Dryden on, 132–33, 267n97; editing of 1710 *Works* to enhance literary dignity, 135, 142, 226, 228; era of, 10; *Incognita* (prose fiction), 143, 147; on incompetence of critics, 157; legacy of (and his interest in), 11, 131–34, 139, 142, 151–52, 226, 227; *The Mourning Bride,* 191, 193; neoclassical rules and, 135–36, 142, 151–52, 157, 227; play-text created by, 131, 137,

142, 151–53, 157, 169, 171; poetic works dedicated to, 142; posterity, concept of, 137–39, 141–42, 152, 158, 171, 226; Shadwell, Behn, and Gay compared to, 217, 219; stability vs. instability of texts, 139–40, 142, 145, 149, 167–69, 262nn38–39; textuality vs. theatricality and, 131–35, 137, 143, 145–46, 152; time, treatment of, 136, 137–38; Tonson and, 131, 133, 142, 151, 169, 171, 226–27, 261n6; *Works* (1710), 133–35, 137, 142, 151–52, 165, 169, 226–28. See also *Love for Love*; *Way of the World, The*
Coppola, Al, 105–6, 248n30, 248n33, 259n97
Cowley, Abraham, 13, 261n9
Crashaw, Richard, 13
Creech, Thomas, 79
Crowne, John, *Sir Courtly Nice*, 98
Culler, Jonathan, 204

Daily Journal (May 23, 1728), 215
Dandeker, Christopher, 271n48
Davenant, William, 72, 100
Davies, Thomas, 9
Davis, Paul, 246n102
Day, Cyrus, 212
Defoe, Daniel, 174, 211
de Grazia, Margareta, 226–27
Delrio, Martin, 54; *Disquisitiones Magicae*, 41
Demos, John, 250n72
Denham, John, 13, 240n16
Denning, Michael, 200–201, 272n68
Dennis, John, 65
Dibdin, Charles, 229
diction: in Aristotle's categories of drama analysis, 123; in Dryden's assessment of elements of drama, 124
Dobson, Michael, 221, 253n8

Don Quixote, 9, 144
Doody, Margaret, 273n80
Dorset Garden theater, 42
Downes, John, 42
drama: Aristotle's categories of analysis for, 122–24; becoming literature in late seventeenth century, 13–15, 17, 76–78, 122, 125; destabilization of author's and reader's roles, 9; Gay's hybrid of print and performance, 173–74, 175, 177–78, 191–94, 216–17; hybrid of print and performance in early eighteenth century, 178; *lazzi* (interpellated interludes) in, 125, 126; morality coming to fore in, 98–99, 159–60, 188; performance, defined, 137; print as method to preserve for posterity, 134; as public pastime under Stuarts, 173, 179; shared cultural heritage of, 4; willing suspension of disbelief for, 97. See also plays as texts; textuality vs. theatricality
Dryden, John: *All for Love*, 32; *Aureng-Zebe*, 32, 248n27; on Congreve, 132–33, 267n97; *The Conquest of Granada*, 30; "Defense of the Epilogue," 30–31; *Essay of Dramatick Poesie*, 29; as first English literary critic, 27; Herringman as publisher, 15; income from writing, 17, 244n83; on Jonson, 30, 31; *King Arthur* (with Purcell), 249n41; on language as most important element in plays, 123; on language improvements of the Restoration, 30–31, 33; literary heritage in which he places himself, 28–33, 74, 224, 227, 248n27; *Mac-Flecknoe*, 20, 28; *Marriage A-la-Mode*, 263n43, 263n47; *Miscellanies*, 15; neoclassical rules and, 227; prefaces by, 28, 30; rhyme use by, 29–30, 32;

Dryden, John (*continued*)
The Rival Ladies, 29; Rymer and, 123; scenic tableaux used by, 32; Shadwell as rival of, 24, 28, 246n107; Shadwell compared to, 36; Shakespearean criticism by, 29, 30, 123, 240n9; *The Spanish Fryar*, 78, 89, 123–24, 248n37; on style or stylistic problems in plays, 122–26, 128; textuality vs. theatricality and, 28, 30, 32–33, 34, 78–79, 89, 126; "To My Dear Friend Mr. Congreve, on his Comedy, call'd, *The Double-Dealer*" (poem), 132–33; Tonson and, 15, 227, 261n6, 261n11; *Troilus and Cressida*, 32; *Virgil* (1697), 15, 243n73, 261n6, 261n11; *Virgil* (1709), 227; writing as serious career for, 30, 79

dual awareness of Restoration writers. *See* textuality vs. theatricality

Dugas, Don-John, 240n9

Dugaw, Dianne, 32, 211, 213, 248n33, 249n41

D'Urfey, Thomas: "The Hubble Bubbles" (song), 213; *Wit and Mirth, or Pills to Purge Melancholy* (ed.), 211–12

Eliade, Mircea, 137

Elizabeth I (English queen), 36, 45

Elizabethan drama, 123, 270n36

Emperor of the Moon, The (Behn), 24, 77, 107, 110–21, 125–30; Baliardo, main character, driven mad by reading, 110, 112–13, 129; clowning scenes, use of, 125–28; compared to *The Luckey Chance*, 129; curiosity of Baliardo, 112; as farce and slapstick comedy, 107, 111, 120–21, 125, 126, 128, 259n97; Italian *commedia* in, 107, 117, 120, 125, 126–27; mimetic characters in, 125–26; mind-body problem in, 115, 128; overcredulity and, 105; pageant in, 110, 118–20, 128–29; play-acting within the play, 119–21, 129; sexual inclinations related to reading in, 113–14; telescope as phallic symbol, 113; textuality vs. theatricality and, 77, 80, 99, 107, 110–12, 121, 125, 128

empire. *See* imperialism and empire

empiricism, rise of, 260n122. *See also* experimentalism; New Science

Empson, William, 173, 193, 196, 231, 232, 270n36

English landscape garden, 163–65, 267n93, 267n96

Erne, Lukas, 12, 240n16, 242n45

Erskine-Hill, Howard, 181, 191

Etherege, George, 15, 159

Euripides, 73, 204, 231

Exclusion Crisis (1679–81), 34

experimentalism, 108–9. *See also* empiricism, rise of; New Science

Ezell, Margaret, 106

Fairer, David, 228

Falstaff, 6, 7, 9, 144

Fawcett, Julia, 95, 97

femininity, 34, 36, 39, 45–46, 53, 222

Fenton, Lavinia, 215

Fergus, Jan, 240n9

feudalism, 173, 176, 178, 187, 210, 213, 269n24, 270n36

Fielding, Henry, 246–47n110; *The Author's Farce*, 247n110, 260n112; *The Tragedy of Tragedies*, 247n110

Filmer, Robert, *Patriarcha: A Defence of the Natural Power of Kings against the Unnatural Power of the People*, 58

Fitzmaurice, James, 239n8

Fletcher, John, 30, 240–41n16. *See also* Beaumont and Fletcher volume

Fontenelle, Bernard Le Bovier de, 79
Fountain, John, *The Rewards of Virtue*, 71-73
Fox, Adam, 177; *Oral and Literate Culture in England, 1500-1700*, 210-11
Frank, Marcie, 27, 247n110, 254n13
French drama and literature, 3, 29, 73, 133, 227
Freudian elements, 52
Fujimura, Thomas, 162, 266n78
Fuller, John, 188, 206, 230, 269n23, 277n35

Gallagher, Catherine, 83-84, 90, 93, 95-97, 257n56
gardens. *See* English landscape garden
Gardner, Kevin J., 185, 264n66, 265n70
Garrick, David, 220-21, 232, 275n7; *Shakespeare's Garland. Being A Collection of New Songs, Ballads, Roundelays, Catches, Glees, Comic-Serenatas, &c. Performed at the Jubilee at Stratford Upon Avon*, 229-30
Gavin, Michael, 14, 20
Gay, John, 2, 172-217; compared to Shadwell, Behn, and Congreve, 217, 219; hybrid of print/text and performance/orality in work of, 11-12, 21, 173-74, 175, 177-78, 191-94, 216-17; income from writing, 174-75, 268n7, 269n23; *The Mohocks*, 21; oral culture and, 25, 175-77, 216; pastoral poetry and drama by, 173-75, 178, 187, 193-96, 199, 207-9, 213-14, 216, 231, 232; patronage unsuccessfully sought by, 174, 179; *Polly*, 174, 268n7; press coverage recognized as essential for success, 179; profitability of writing as threat to humanistic values, 229; *Rural Sports* (poem), 21; satire and parody in the work of, 173, 176, 179, 192-93, 199, 209, 212-13; Shakespeare and, 179, 229-33; skepticism of nostalgia, 171, 173, 178, 194, 199, 209-10, 214, 216, 229, 232; Swift and, 210, 274-75n105, 271n44; *The Wife of Bath*, 21. See also *Beggar's Opera, The*; textuality vs. theatricality; *What D'Ye Call It, The*
George I (English king), 211
Georgian era, 25
Gert, Bernard, 108
Gevirtz, Karen, 79
Gildon, Charles, 95, 204; *A Comparison between the Two Stages* (attrib.), 95
Glorious Revolution (1688), 20, 34, 58
Godwin, Francis, *The Man in the Moon*, 259n98
Green, Susan, 256n48
Griffin, Benjamin, 179
Gustafson, Daniel, 272n63

Hammond, Brean, 17, 18, 172, 246n100, 246n107, 268n2
Hammond, Paul, 12, 15
Harris, Joseph, 264n56
Haywood, Eliza, 211
Hazlitt, William, 278n55
Helgerson, Richard, 12
Henke, Robert, 125-26
Henrietta Maria (English queen, mother of Charles II), 3
Henry, Prince of Wales (son of James I), 45, 56
heroic plays, 32, 98, 248n33
Herringman, Henry, 1, 15, 27
Heywood, Thomas, and Richard Brome, 28; *The Late Lancashire Witches*, 35, 43, 249n48
Hinnant, Charles, 158

Hitchen, Charles, "A Discovery of the Conduct of Receivers and Thief-Takers," 197
Hobbes, Thomas, 24, 78, 79, 87–88, 93, 108, 110, 253n9, 254–55n29, 268n99; *Leviathan*, 271n46
Holland, Peter, 134–35, 152, 167
Holt, John, 183–84
Homer, 210
Hooks, Adam G., 243n57
Horace, 41; *Epodes*, 49; *Odes*, 66
Howson, Gerald, 197–98
Hoxby, Blair, 32, 248n27, 248n33
Hudson, Nicholas, 243n74
Hume, David, 146, 210
Hume, Robert D., 16–18, 21, 98, 122–24, 240n9, 244n78, 244n83, 245n92, 246n108, 251n78, 251n84, 268n7
Hunt, John Dixon, 163

illiteracy. *See* literacy/illiteracy
imagination vs. reality (mind-body problem): Behn on, 24, 77–79, 84, 86–87, 91–92, 94, 101–2, 103, 107, 110, 115–17, 128–29, 233, 234; Cavendish on, 24, 78, 88–89, 93–94, 241n25; Hobbes on, 108; Jonson on, 77–79, 122; play requiring equal attention to mind and body, 102; Restoration drama probing, 237; Settle on, 101, 128–29
imperialism and empire, 161, 185, 213, 265n73
inheritance (of property) and succession, 33–40, 248n40; poetic and literary inheritance linked to, 23, 58, 242n40; profiteering of mercantile capitalism vs., 64–65, 252n92; in Shadwell's *The Lancashire Witches*, 34–40, 56, 74, 224; in Shadwell's *The Squire of Alsatia*, 33–36, 51–52, 56, 57–61, 64, 74, 224, 251n82

Institor. *See* Kramer, Heinrich, and Jacob Sprenger
Interregnum: Moseley as publisher of drama throughout, 14–15; print canon of plays arising in part due to ban on live theater, 3–4, 16; reopening of theaters after, 20, 241n16. *See also* closing of the theaters
Italian *commedia* tradition, 107, 117, 120, 125–26
Italian opera craze in eighteenth-century London, 209–10, 273–74n87, 274nn91–92

James I (English king), 45
James II (English king, brother of Charles II), 34, 105
Johns, Adrian, 109, 116
Johnson, Samuel, 228, 245n90, 275n1
Jones, Vivien, 274n87
Jonson, Ben: *The Alchemist*, 44, 225; Behn and, 24, 116, 225; borrowings by, 18, 223; borrowings from, 28; *Catiline*, 29–30, 122, 260n112; distinguishing between play's literary and theatrical sides (mind-body divide), 77–79, 122; Dryden on, 29–30; Dryden vs. Shadwell in evaluation of, 28; frequency among plays staged in Restoration, 241n16; *Hymenaei*, 76, 78; imitation of classics by, 18; literary status of, 17, 28, 29, 134, 240n16; *The Masque of Blackness*, 253n2; *Masque of Queenes*, 23, 35, 44–46, 55, 56; *The Sad Shepherd*, 249n52; Shadwell's borrowing from, 23, 31, 35, 44, 74, 249n52; Shadwell's rejection of textual strategies of, 28, 56; Shakespeare contrasted with, 222, 223; succession as issue in, 45; textuality and authorial control

of, 44, 46; *Works* (1616), 14, 76, 77, 133, 134

Kastan, David Scott, 1, 12–13, 276n12, 276n19
Kavenik, Frances, 98
Kermode, Frank, 252n91
Kewes, Paulina: on authorship, 17, 225; on Moseley's standardization of play collections, 14; on playwrights as entrepreneurs, 16; on Restoration drama enabling Shakespeare's cultural position, 222, 276n11; on rise of drama in book trade of seventeenth century, 12; on Shadwell's borrowings, 33, 72; on transformation of playwright into poet, 18
Key (to *The What D'Ye Call It*). See *What D'Ye Call It, The*
Killigrew, Charles, 55, 100
Kirkman, Francis, 18–19
Klekar, Cynthia, 267–68n99
Kramer, David Bruce, 29–30
Kramer, Heinrich, and Jacob Sprenger, 47; *Malleus Maleficarum*, 41, 54, 250n72
Kramnick, Jonathan, 20
Kroll, Richard, 149, 157, 158, 160

Lamb, Charles, "On the Tragedies of Shakespeare" (essay), 223, 234–37, 259n108, 278n58
Lamb, Charles and Mary, *Tales from Shakespeare*, 221
Lancashire: witch scare (1633–34), 43, 249n48; witch trials (1612), 43, 249n48
Lancashire Witches, The (Shadwell), 23–24, 28–29, 33–56, 225; annotative apparatus of, 23, 35, 44, 46–52, 70, 71, 224; Bellfort's discounting of supernatural in strange events, 49; Bellfort's language similar to the witches', 50; black magic linked to corrupt, irreligious bids for power in, 47; borrowing from previous plays, 41–44, 73–74; classical references to spells and women's magical abilities, 49; cliché (dead metaphor) of love as bewitchment in, 53–54, 57; as comedy, 248n33; compared to *The Squire of Alsatia*, 56–57, 64, 70, 71; controversy over and suppression of, 36, 246n107; Devil vs. witches in, 40; failure of textual authority to rein in witches' theatrical impact, 51; inheritance and patriarchal lineage as topic of, 34–40, 56, 74, 224; integration of witches in, 43, 50–51; Jonson's *Masque of Queenes* and, 44–46, 55; Jonson's textual strategies rejected in, 56; literary convention rejected in, 42; as "machine farce," 42; male textual authority in, 54–55; political leanings of, 36–37, 248n38; preface, 41–42, 44, 55, 249n52; satirizing superstition in, 43; slapstick violence in, 48; textual authority anchored in the theatrical in, 55–56; theatricality of, 28, 33, 56; "witchmongers" references in, 46–52; young women's free will in marriage choices in, 49, 56–57
Langbaine, Gerard, 18–19, 73, 224, 276n16
law and legal documents: in Congreve's *Love for Love*, 138, 139, 141, 142, 145, 149–50; in Congreve's *The Way of the World*, 136, 152, 157, 158, 167–69, 265n68; in Gay's *The Beggar's Opera*, 195–96, 200, 201, 204–5, 271n48, 272n66; in Gay's

law and legal documents (*continued*) *The What D'Ye Call It,* 183-86, 188, 270n35; in Shadwell's *The Squire of Alsatia,* 58, 66-67. *See also* inheritance (of property) and succession
Leigh, Anthony, 103
Leigh, Elinor, 266n74
L'Estrange, Roger, 100
Lewis, Peter, 274n92, 274n103
Licensing of the Press Act, lapse of (1679), 106, 176
Lindenbaum, Peter, 13
Lindley, David, 274n87
Linebaugh, Peter, 271n62
literacy/illiteracy, 26, 176-78, 189-91
literary biographies, 243n74
literary canon, 15-16, 22, 27-28, 107, 133-35, 170-71, 226-27, 237, 258-59n89, 261n9, 261n11
literary criticism and scholarly editing, 226
literary succession: Congreve's interest in, 142, 151-52; Restoration dramatists' interest in, 27, 226; Shadwell and, 23-24, 28, 74. *See also* literary canon
"literature," definition of, 12-13, 217
literature and book trade: as defined in Restoration, 12-13, 222; Moseley as seminal publisher for literary market, 13-15; publisher serving also as agent, 15; reputation of authors, 17, 244-45n88; Restoration drama's role in, 16, 222; Tonson's role in, 107, 133-35, 170-71, 226-27, 259n89, 261n9, 261n11. *See also* literary canon
Locke, John, 34; *Some Thoughts Concerning Education,* 58; *Two Treatises of Government,* 18, 58
Loftis, John, 170
London Gazette (first regular English newspaper), 179
Loughry, Bryan, 273-74n87

Love, Harold, 20, 30, 246nn106-7, 252n100
Love for Love (Congreve), 24-25, 139-52; act of reading in, 140; Angelica's approach to texts, 149-50; comparison with *The Way of the World,* 153, 155, 157, 163; inversion of conventional gender roles, 149, 263n52; legal contracts, bonds, and other documents in, 138, 139, 141, 142, 145, 149-50; masquerade motif and epistemology, 142-49, 226, 262n41; posterity, conception of, 138, 141-42, 147, 171, 226; problems of knowing and being known, 138, 146-48, 263n49; prophecy in, 138, 140-42, 145, 149, 262n38; refusal to offer temporal finality, 147-48, 150; repetition in masquerade, 137-38, 143, 147-48; structural and stylistic principles of masquerade used within, 148; supposed stability of texts, 139-40, 142, 145, 149, 262nn38-39; textuality vs. theatricality and, 143, 145-46, 152; Valentine's feigned madness, 146-47, 263n45
Lucan, 41
Luckey Chance, The (Behn), 24, 77, 79-107; actor Thomas Betterton as Gayman in, 96; actress Elizabeth Barry as Julia in, 95-96; bed tricks as device to question reality vs. imagination and to question epistemology of drama, 79-80, 254n14, 255n42; Behn's poem "The Disappointment" compared with, 90-92; compared to *The Emperor of the Moon,* 129; conclusion posing psychological question, 97-98; critical objections to performance of, 100-101, 103; dedicatory epistle to Lord Hyde, Earl of Rochester,

99, 100, 101; metatheatrical humor of casting and, 95-96, 257n52; mind-body problem (imagination vs. reality) in, 77, 84, 86-87, 94, 101-2, 103, 107, 114, 116, 118; morality and, 98-99, 102-5; Otway's *The Orphan*'s relationship to, 257n59; politics and overcredulity in, 105-7; preface, 98, 99, 101-3; reading vs. spectatorship and, 94, 105; textuality vs. theatricality and, 99-100, 128; youth vs. old age in, 84-86

Lucretius, 79, 255n40

Lynch, Jack, 224, 233

Lyons, John D., 136, 151, 264n56

Mack, Maynard, 195

Markley, Robert, 95-96

Marsden, Jean, 220-21, 233, 255n42, 275n1

Marston, John, 14

Martial, 41

Mary Stuart (mother of James I), 45

masquerade motif: centrality to all theater, 262n41, 262n43; Congreve's use of, 137-38, 142-49, 226, 262n41; as systematic anarchy, 264n56. See also *Love for Love*

Massinger, Philip, *Three New Playes*, 14

Masten, Jeffrey, 3, 240n16, 244n87

McCloskey, Susan, 264n66

McDowell, Paula, *The Invention of the Oral*, 175-77, 209, 273n85

McKenzie, Andrea, 271n62

McKenzie, D. F., 133-35, 261n6, 261n11, 265n72

Meagher, Jennifer, 125

Meskill, Lynn Sermin, 45-46

middle class, 12, 15, 133, 158-59, 172, 211, 221, 232, 278n50

Middleton, Thomas, *Two New Playes*, 14

Milhous, Judith, 16-18, 244n78, 244n83, 245n92, 268n7

Miller, Shannon, 240n10

Milton, John, 13; *Comus*, 263n52; "On Shakespeare," 241n20; *Paradise Lost*, 15, 241n20, 261n11

mind-body problem. *See* imagination vs. reality

modernity, birth of, 158, 172

Molière, 73

Monmouth, James (duke), 34

Monthly Review on 1773-74 (Bell) edition of Shakespeare, 221

morality: in Behn's *The Luckey Chance*, 98-99, 102-5; Congreve's *The Way of the World* and, 159-60; Gay's *The What D'Ye Call It* and, 188; objections of seventeenth and eighteenth centuries, 98-99, 253n8, 263n46; Shakespeare as exemplar of bourgeois morality, 221

Moseley, Humphrey, 1, 12-15, 27, 107, 240n16, 244n87, 258-59n89, 261n9

Mueschke, Paul and Miriam, 159

Munns, Jessica, 36, 256n46

neoclassicism: Behn and, 126-27; Congreve and, 135-36, 151-52, 165, 226; dramaturgical rulebook of, 24, 135-36, 225, 261-62n24, 264n56; French neoclassicists, 133, 227

Newgate Ordinary's (chaplain) "Paper," 206-7

Newman, Steve, 208

New Science, 77, 268n2. *See also* empiricism, rise of; experimentalism

Noble, Yvonne, 208-9

Nokes, James, 96, 210, 268n8

North, Thomas, *Plutarch* (trans.), 223

Norton, Thomas, *Gorboduc* (with Sackville), 29

nostalgia of society for pre-modern times, 171, 173, 176-78, 214, 229-30, 232
Novak, Maximillian, 240n9
novel, development of, 79, 259n104

Oates, Titus, 105, 258n81
O'Brien, John, 27, 172, 173, 253n8
ontology and ontological problems, 2, 4, 99, 103, 146, 254n14, 255n31
opera, 209-10, 273-74n87, 274nn91-92
oral culture, 25, 70, 140, 175-77. *See also* nostalgia of society for pre-modern times; textuality vs. theatricality
Orgel, Stephen, 223
originality, 17, 18, 27, 246n100. *See also* plagiarism
Otway, Thomas, *The Orphan*, 257n59
Ovid, 41; *Metamorphoses*, 32, 49, 66
ownership. *See* inheritance (of property) and succession; patrimony and masculine authority as subject matter

pantomime, 173
Parnell, Thomas, 179
parody. *See* satire and parody
Pask, Kevin, 18-19, 276n16
pastoralism: Elizabethans invoking of feudalism through, 270n36; Empson's formulation of, 173; Gay's *The Beggar's Opera* and, 194-96, 199, 207-9, 213-14, 216; Gay's *The What D'Ye Call It* and, 178, 187, 193-94, 231, 232; "mock pastoral," 207, 209, 213; Shakespeare and, 229, 231. *See also* ballads and ballad form; nostalgia of society for pre-modern times
patriarchy: in Behn's *The Luckey Chance*, 84-85; feudal Europe's version of, 269n24; in Shadwell's plays, 35-40, 49, 51-52, 56, 58, 63-64

patrimony and masculine authority as subject matter, 28-29, 34, 35, 37-39, 52, 58, 248n27. *See also* inheritance (of property) and succession
patronage, 16, 20-21, 174, 179, 211, 246n107
Pechter, Edward, 260n122
Penkethman, William, 269n30
Pepys, Samuel, 78, 260n112
Percy, Thomas, "Essay on the Ancient Minstrels of England," 175
performance. *See* drama; textuality vs. theatricality; *specific plays by title or playwright*
Perry, Ruth, 116
Peters, Julie Stone, 142, 158, 242n40, 245n97, 261-62n24, 278n55
Phelan, Peggy, 137-38, 157
Philips, Ambrose, 179
Philomusus, *The Academy of Complements*, 250n71
Pinkerton, John, "Dissertation on the Oral Tradition of Poetry" (preface to *Scottish Tragic Ballads*), 175
plagiarism, 18, 27, 33, 73-74, 241n22. *See also* borrowings
Plautus, 133
playing cards with theme of Gay's *The Beggar's Opera*, 215, 275n108
plays as texts, 4, 11, 22, 24; Congreve's play-text, 131, 137, 142, 151, 153, 157, 169, 171; method to preserve for posterity, 134; reading during closure of theaters, 3-4, 78, 239nn6-7; Shakespeare and, 3, 7-8, 10, 240n16. *See also* textuality vs. theatricality
plays within plays: Behn's *The Emperor of the Moon*, 119-21, 129; Gay's *The Beggar's Opera*, 178, 199; Gay's *The What D'Ye Call It*, 180, 187-88; Shakespeare's *Hamlet*, 270n37

plot: in Aristotle's categories of drama analysis, 123; Dryden valuing diction over, 124
Plutarch, *Lives* (North trans.), 223
poetic justice, 203-4
politics: in Behn's *The Luckey Chance*, 105-7; in Shadwell's *The Lancashire Witches*, 36-37, 248n38; in Shadwell's *The Squire of Alsatia*, 58, 250-51n77; spectacle for political ends, 105-7. *See also* Whigs
Poovey, Mary, 175, 271n46, 272nn69-70
Pope, Alexander: *Dunciad*, 21, 25, 216; on Gay's earnings from *The What D'Ye Call It*, 269n23; *Iliad*, 142; as possible co-author of *Complete Key to the Last New Farce, The What D'Ye Call It*, 179; print capitalism and, 176, 216; on Shakespeare, 227-28, 276n25
Popish Plot (1678-81), 105-7, 258n81, 258n87
Porta, Giambattista della, 48
Potts, Thomas, *The Wonderfull Discoverie of Witches in the Countie of Lancaster*, 43
Press (Recruitment) Act, 180, 184-85, 193
Prince, Kathryn, 278n49
print and print culture: double-entry bookkeeping and, 272n70; emergence of (1642-60), 107; expansion of commercially lucrative writing in early eighteenth century, 174; in Gay's *The What D'Ye Call It*, 191; headpieces, ornamental elements, etc., use of, 14, 70, 107, 133, 151, 169, 226; lapse of Licensing Act (1679), effect of, 106, 176; popularity of criminal biographies and scandal sheets, 197, 206; prestige aligned with, 107, 109; use of term "print culture," 177. *See also* literature and book trade; Tonson, Jacob

print capitalism: ballads as part of, 182, 188, 199, 211-14, 216, 270n32, 271n60, 274n104; drama as part of, 174-75, 179; effect of, 21, 232, 237; emergence of, 19, 174-75, 176, 229; English book market as component of commercial capitalism, 172, 174, 268n2; Fielding and, 247n110; Gay's *The Beggar's Opera* and, 175, 199, 216; Gay's *The What D'Ye Call It* and, 193; laws as part of, 185; Pope and, 176, 216; profitability of writing as threat to humanistic values, 229
Propertius, 41
property inheritance. *See* inheritance (of property) and succession
publishers and publishing, 2-3, 14-18, 258n89. *See also* literature and book trade; Moseley, Humphrey; print and print culture; print capitalism; Tonson, Jacob
Purcell, Henry, *The Fairy Queen* (opera-masque), 212-13

Rapin, René, 123
Ravenscroft, Edward, *Dame Dobson*, 98
reading: during closure of theaters, 3-4, 78, 239nn6-7; in Congreve's *The Way of the World*, 153-54; corporeality of, 111-12, 116, 129; Settle finding more affective than theater-going, 101; vs. spectating, 11, 94, 105, 121-22, 254n13; as verification method for scientific advances, 110; writing overlapping with, 111-12. *See also* literacy/illiteracy; textuality vs. theatricality
Rémy, Nicholas, *Demonolatreiae*, 41
Renaissance literature and drama, 7, 12, 16; Dryden's focus compared with, 124-25; Shadwell borrowing

Renaissance literature and drama (*continued*)
from, 41. *See also* Jonson, Ben; Shakespeare, William

Restoration drama and dramatists: definition of period, 12, 20; lasting literary-theoretical impact of, 237; legacy of, 23, 25-26, 131; ownership of scripts and remuneration of playwrights, 16-18, 21; plays as reading material vs. plays as performed pieces, 4, 254n13; relationship to print and literature, 1-2, 16-18, 219, 222; as symbol of difference from past culture, 27; valuing Shakespeare's plays as literature, 222. *See also* authorship; textuality vs. theatricality; *specific authors and their works*

Rich, John, 173
Richelieu, Cardinal, 99
Ritchie, Fiona, 3, 220, 233, 239n5, 277n48
Roberts, James, 211
Rochester, 1st Earl of (Laurence Hyde), 99
Rochester, 2nd Earl of (John Wilmot), 95, 246n102, 248n22; *Allusion to Horace*, 20, 246n106; *Imperfect Enjoyment*, 91, 256n46
Romanticism and Romantic period, 12, 18, 211, 234, 254n13
Roper, Alan, 266n77
Rose, Mark, 17
Rosenthal, Laura, 265n74
Ross, John C., 28, 34, 58, 65, 66, 250-51n77, 251n80
Rowe, Nicholas, 207, 227; *Jane Shore*, 179
Royal Academy of Music, 274n91
Royal Society, 78, 109-10, 253n9
Rumbold, Kate, 229
Rymer, Thomas, *Tragedies of the Last Age*, 123

Sabor, Peter, 220
Sackville, Thomas, *Gorboduc* (with Norton), 29
Salingar, Leo, 231
Santor, Gefen Bar-On, 275n7
Sarasohn, Lisa T., 253n9, 255n31
satire and parody: ballad parodies, history of, 209, 212; Behn and, 96, 127; Congreve and, 144, 166; Fielding and, 247n110; Gay and, 25, 173, 176, 179, 192-93, 199, 209, 212-13, 229, 230, 232; of pastoralism, 213-14; Shadwell and, 43, 62
Schaffer, Simon, 109, 253n9
Schechner, Richard, 137, 138
Schoenfeldt, Michael, 116
Schultz, William, 215
Scot, Reginald, *Discoverie of Witchcraft*, 50
Scriblerians, 179, 216, 268n8
Sedley, Charles, 15
Select Trials at the Old Bailey, 198
Seneca, 231
Senesino, 210
Settle, Elkanah, *A Farther Defence of Dramatick Poetry*, 101, 117-19, 121, 128-29, 259n108
sexism. *See* women
Shadwell, Thomas, 2, 28-37; anti-authoritarian defiance of, 36, 74-75; Behn, Congreve, and Gay compared to, 217, 219; borrowing from Jonson, 23, 31, 35, 46, 74, 249n52; borrowing from previous plays, 33, 35, 40-44, 72-75; borrowing from Shakespeare, 28, 41, 73; bridging theatrical void of Interregnum, 11; dedications and prefaces by, 21, 28, 32, 33-34, 41-42, 56, 72; Dryden as rival of, 24, 28, 246n107; equating professional-playwright status with that of thief, 73, 224; era of, 10;

favoring humors over wit in comedy, 31; femininity and illegitimacy as topics of, 34; *The Humorists,* 32, 66, 73; income from writing, 17, 244n83; on inheritance and succession issues, 33–40, 51–52, 56, 57–61, 64, 74, 224, 248n40, 251n82; on literary legacy, 55–56, 59; rejecting Jonson's association of textuality with authorial control, 46; on Restoration's literary inheritance, 28, 224; *The Rewards of Virtue,* 71; *The Royal Shepherdess,* 71–73; selective acknowledgment of sources, 224; *The Sullen Lovers,* 28; *The Tenth Satyr of Juvenal,* 246n107; theatricality vs. textuality of, 11, 31–34, 74–75, 79; *Virtuoso,* 263n43. See also *Lancashire Witches, The; Squire of Alsatia, The*

Shakespeare, William: *As You Like It,* 230; authorship and, 224–25; availability to general reading public, 240n9; Behn on, 226, 234; borrowings by, 5, 10, 223; borrowings from, 18, 28, 230–33; canonical status of, 5, 220, 227, 240n16; Cavendish on, 3–11, 18, 233–34, 237, 240n10, 277n48; characters and characterization by, 6–7, 10, 222, 223, 230–37, 278n49; Davenant's adaptations of, 72; Dryden on, 29, 30, 123, 240n9; 1807 (Bowdlers) edition of *Family Shakespeare,* 221; 1807 (Lambs) edition of *Tales from Shakespeare,* 221; eighteenth-century obsession with characters in, 233; eliminating line between reality and representation, 6, 7; Falstaff character in, 7, 9, 144, 225; "fools" in, 230–31; frequency among plays staged in Restoration, 241n16; Gay borrowing from, 179, 229–33; hallmarks of Shakespeare criticism, 222; *Hamlet,* 230, 236, 237, 263n45, 270n37, 277n36; *Henry IV,* 225; history of Shakespearean scholarship, 222–23; humor and wit in, 231; irregularities and "defects" addressed by editors, 226–27, 277n28; Jonson contrasted with, 222; *Julius Caesar,* 6, 7, 10, 11, 230; *King Lear,* 236–37; lack of classical learning by, 223, 228; legacy of, 5, 10, 220, 226; in literary history, 29, 222, 227; *Macbeth,* 35, 230, 235–36; *A Midsummer Night's Dream,* 230, 277n44, 278n55; as National Poet/the Bard/Original Genius, 11, 17, 25–26, 220–21, 224, 229, 232, 240n16, 275n1, 276n12; nostalgia for pre-print world and, 229, 232; *Othello,* 230, 235; pastoralism and, 229, 231; as poet of "Nature," 222, 228, 233, 277n48; Pope on, 227–28, 276n25; publishing and marketing of works by, 14, 220–21, 226–27, 240n9; *Richard III,* 235; *Romeo and Juliet,* 231; 1709 (Rowe) edition of, 227, 245n90; 1725 (Pope) edition of, 228; 1765 (Johnson) edition of, 245n90, 275n1; 1773–74 (Bell) edition of, 221; Shadwell borrowing from, 28, 41, 73; Shakespeare Jubilee (1769) staged by Garrick, 229–30, 275n10; 1623 edition of, 14; textuality vs. theatricality and, 3, 5, 7–8, 10, 220–21, 227–28, 236–37, 240n16; tourism industry created around, 229; *Twelfth Night; or, What you Will,* 66, 230

Shapin, Steven, 109, 253n9
Shepherd, Simon, 253n8
Shirley, James, *Six New Playes,* 14
Sidney, Philip, *Apologie,* 176–77

Slagle, Judith Bailey, 249n52
slang, removal from Congreve's 1710 *Works*, 135. See also *Squire of Alsatia, The*
Smyth, Maura, 87
Sociable Letters (Cavendish): "Letter 123," 3-8, 10-11, 18, 233-34, 239n5, 277n48; "Letter 195," 239n7
Socrates, 129-30
Sophocles, 73, 204, 231
South Sea Bubble (1720), 210, 213
spectatorship. *See* textuality vs. theatricality
Spencer, Jane, 83, 254n19
Spiller, Elizabeth, 253n9
Sprat, Thomas, 79, 255n40
Sprenger, Jacob. *See* Kramer, Heinrich, and Jacob Sprenger
Squire of Alsatia, The (Shadwell), 23-24, 28-29, 56-75, 225; Alsatia (or Whitefriars) as depicted in, 61-62, 64, 65, 70-71, 251n84; artistic inheritance as concern of, 58; Cheatly's ability to speak in both "cant" and "University" slang, 68-69; as comedy, 248n33; commercial success of, 246n107; compared to *The Lancashire Witches*, 56-57, 64, 70, 71; on consolidation vs. expansion of power, 59; dual fluency of Shadwell in classical and modern trends in, 69-70; education of Belfond Junior and his bookish knowledge, 66; "Explanation of the Cant," 23, 36, 56, 65, 67, 68, 69-71, 252n93; extending theatrical genealogical paradigm in, 28, 65, 66; inheritance and succession as topic of, 33-36, 51-52, 56, 57-61, 62, 64, 65, 74, 224, 251n82; legal texts (will and marriage-related documents) in, 58, 66-67; on literary legacy, 59, 225; male textual authority in, 52-53, 58-59; near marriage between Belfond Senior and Mrs. Termagant, 60, 62-63; political orientation of, 58, 250-51n77; popularity of, 65; profiteering of mercantile capitalism vs. inheritance, 64-65, 252n92; similarities between Belfond Junior and Cheatly (the chief villain), 61, 63-64; similarities between Belfond Junior and Shadwell, 61, 65; temporality in, 59-60; Terence's *Adelphi*, borrowing from, 23, 35, 56, 65, 66, 73; women's powers of theatricality in, 53
Stapleton, M. L., 256n46
Starr, G. Gabrielle, 86-88, 255n40
States, Bert O., 137
stationers' register, plays entered by Moseley in, 13
Steele, Richard, *Poetical Miscellanies*, 142
Stewart, Susan, 176-77, 208, 273n86
Stone, Lawrence, 205, 273n74
Stratford Jubilee (1769), 229-30, 275n10
Straznicky, Marta, 78
Stuart monarchy, 34, 36, 173
succession. *See* inheritance (of property) and succession
Suckling, John, 13, 261n9
Swift, Jonathan: Gay and, 210, 264-75n105; phrase "Newgate Pastoral" associated with, 194, 232, 271n44; on print as unregulated trade, 176

Tacitus, 223
Tate, Nahum, 236
Terence: *Adelphi*, Shadwell's borrowing from, 23, 35, 56, 65, 66, 73; borrowings from, 28; typographical treatment of editions of, 133

textual authority: Congreve's skepticism toward, 171; Gay's critique of, 171; in Shadwell's *The Lancashire Witches*, 51, 54–56. *See also* reading

textuality vs. theatricality, 2, 23, 254n13; in Behn's *The Emperor of the Moon*, 77, 80, 99, 107, 110–12, 121, 125, 128; in Behn's *The Luckey Chance*, 99–100, 128; Congreve and play-text design, 131–35, 137, 143, 145–46, 151–53, 157; Congreve on stability vs. instability of texts, 139–40, 142, 145, 149, 167–69, 262nn38–39; in Congreve's *The Way of the World,* 169–70; Dryden on, 28, 30, 32–33, 34, 78–79, 89, 126; in Gay's *The Beggar's Opera,* 175, 178, 195, 208, 216–17; in Gay's *The What D'Ye Call It,* 180, 191–94; Jonson on, 44, 77; nostalgia of society for pre-print means of communication, 171; reading vs. spectatorship, 11, 94, 105, 121–22, 254n13; Shadwell and, 11, 31–34, 46, 74–75, 79; Shakespeare and, 3, 5, 7–8, 10, 220–21, 227–28, 236–37, 240n16

theaters, closure of. *See* closing of the theaters

theatricality. *See* drama; textuality vs. theatricality

Theobald, Lewis, 179, 240n9

Theocritus, 47, 230

Theophrastus, 47

Tibullus, 47

time, concepts of: Congreve's attempt to forge "time out of time" (textual temporality), 136, 147–48, 151, 158; Congreve's concept of posterity, 137–39, 147, 152, 158, 171, 226; in Shadwell's *The Squire of Alsatia,* 59–60; theatricality and, 137–39, 153; unity of time in neoclassical dramatic rules, 136

Tonson, Jacob: Congreve and, 131, 133, 142, 151, 169, 171, 226–27, 261n6; Dryden and, 15, 227, 261n6, 261n11; frontispiece portraits used to highlight concepts of literary authorship, 14, 107, 133, 226–27; as pioneering publisher, 1, 15, 243n73; in price war over Shakespeare's works, 220; publishing and marketing strategies of forming English canon, 107, 133–35, 170–71, 226–27, 259n89, 261n9, 261n11; Shakespeare editions of, 226–27, 245n90

Tories, 58

tragedies: in Aristotle's categories of drama analysis, 123; nontraditional characters in, 231–32; Restoration tragedy vs. comedy, 23

Treadwell, T. O., 273–74n87

Tribble, Evelyn B., 44–45

True, Perfect, and Exact Catalogue of All the Comedies, Tragedies, Tragi-Comedies, Pastorals, Masques, and Interludes, that Were Ever Yet Printed and Published, till this Present Year, A (1661), 18

Vaughan, Henry, 13

Velissariou, Aspasia, 268n99

Vickers, Brian, 233

Virgil, 173, 210, 230; *Aeneid,* 49; Dryden's translation, 15, 227, 243n73, 261n6, 261n11; *Eclogues,* 49; *Georgics,* 49

Vitruvius, 132, 267n97

Walker, Claire, 106–7

Walker, Robert, 220

Waller, Edmund, 13, 30

Warner, William, 116, 259n104

Way of the World, The (Congreve), 24–25, 138–39, 152–71; comparison with *Love for Love*, 153, 155, 157, 163; contracts and legal documents in, 136, 152, 157, 158, 165–69, 265n68; cosmopolitanism of exotic imports, meaning of, 159–61, 265–66nn72–74; cuckolding and possibility of tainted genetic posterity, 154–56; dedication, 157–58; empire allusions, 161, 265n73; English landscape garden metaphor, 163–64; fertility allusions, 156, 161–63, 165–67, 226, 266n76, 266–67nn85–86; Mirabell's vs. Fainall's use of language, 152–65, 265nn71–73, 266n74; modern society heralded in, 158; orality of lower class mixed with texts of the educated, 169–70; play-text and, 153, 157, 169, 171; plot outcome shaped by texts, 152–53; posterity, shaping of, 138–39, 152, 158; "presencing" in, 137, 138, 153, 155–57; as sequel to *Love for Love*, 138; texts' instability revealed, 167–69; textuality vs. theatricality and, 169–70; theatrical temporality in, 153, 155, 157; as transitional play depicting shift from aristocratic to bourgeois ethos, 264n66; verbal theatricality, 157–58; *Works* (1710) version, 165, 169

Weber, Harold, 133

Weber, Max, 271n48

What D'Ye Call It, The (Gay), 25, 177–94; ballads and ballad form, 178, 181–83, 209, 229–30, 270n32; ballads purchased as textual commodities, 190; borrowings from other dramatists, 178–79; comic effect of print's failure to engage in dramatic situation, 180–81; compared to *The Beggar's Opera*, 194, 196, 208, 215; *Complete Key to the Last New Farce, The What D'Ye Call It*, 179, 191, 193, 230–32, 270n42, 277n36; desire to liberate performance from print culture, 179; Gay's concern over press coverage, 179; Holt reference to printed collection of legal judgments, 183–84; humor that is solely text-based, 192–93, 270n42; hybrid of print and performance in, 193; illiteracy/literacy in rural life, 189–91; inseparability of performance from print, 180, 193; juxtaposing print and orality, 175, 177–78, 185–86; law as antithetical to natural desires, 186, 270n35; law's association with mechanical (nonhuman) reproduction of language, 184–85; nostalgic aspect of ballads, 178; originally afterpiece to Rowe's *Jane Shore*, 179; pastoralism and, 178, 187, 193–94, 231, 232; performance as alternative to writing and print, 178, 186–91; "perform" taking on multiple connotations, 187, 189; *The Pilgrim's Progress* in, 180–81, 183, 191; play within the play (yuletide theatrical), 180, 187–88; preface's explanation of nontraditional characters, 231–32, 277n44; "press," use in varying contexts in, 184–85; print associated with technology, capitalism, and unnatural outcomes, 184–86, 188; reader privileged at times over playgoer, 192–93, 270n42; rhyme, use of, 193; Rich as producer of, 173; Shakespearean allusions in, 229–33; stage conventions, spoof of, 191, 192, 194; subtitle (*A Tragi-comi-pastoral Farce*), 230; textuality vs. theatricality and, 180, 191–94

Whigs, 34, 36, 58, 267n93
Wier, Johannes, *De Lamiis*, 49
Wild, Jonathan, 196–98
William and Mary (William of Orange, English king, and Mary, Protestant daughter of James II), 34, 58, 211
Williams, Aubrey, 266n85
Williamson, Tom, 267n93
Willis, Peter, 163
Wilmot, John. *See* Rochester, 2nd Earl of
witches. *See* Lancashire
wit vs. humors comedy, 28, 31, 231
Womack, Peter, 253n8
women: Behn's critique of male-centric society, 90; Behn's defense against gender-based attacks on her work, 224–25; Cavendish marginalized as writer due to her sex, 255n40; control of, in Shadwell's *The Lancashire Witches*, 224; as playwrights, different standard than applied to male playwrights, 103–4; powers of theatricality in Shadwell's *The Squire of Alsatia*, 53; sexuality, cultural denial of, 83–84. *See also* femininity
Wycherley, William, *The Country Wife*, 98

www.ingramcontent.com/pod-product-compliance
Lightning Source LLC
Chambersburg PA
CBHW030607230426
43661CB00053B/1882